Oxford AQA History

A LEVEL AND AS
Component 2

Revolution and Dictatorship: Russia 1917–1953

D1368288

Chris Rowe

Sally Waller

SERIES EDITOR
Sally Waller

OXFORD

UNIVERSITY PRESS

Great Clarendon Street, Oxford, OX2 6DP, United Kingdom

Oxford University Press is a department of the University of Oxford. It furthers the University's objective of excellence in research, scholarship, and education by publishing worldwide. Oxford is a registered trade mark of Oxford University Press in the UK and in certain other countries.

British Library Cataloguing in Publication Data
Data available

Print: 978-0-19-835458-1

Kindle: 978-0-19-836382-8

10 9 8 7 6 5 4

Printed and bound by CPI Group (UK) Ltd, Croydon, CR0 4YY

The publisher would like to thank the following people for offering their contribution in the development of this book: Roy Whittle, Sally Waller and Indexing Specialists (UK) Ltd.

Links to third party websites are provided by Oxford in good faith and for information only. Oxford disclaims any responsibility for the materials contained in any third party website referenced in this work.

Approval message from AQA

This textbook has been approved by AQA for use with our qualification. This means that we have checked that it broadly covers the specification and we are satisfied with the overall quality. Full details of our approval process can be found on our website.

We approve textbooks because we know how important it is for teachers and students to have the right resources to support their teaching and learning. However, the publisher is ultimately responsible for the editorial control and quality of this book.

Please note that when teaching the AQA A Level History course, you must refer to AQA's specification as your definitive source of information. While this book has been written to match the specification, it does not provide complete coverage of every aspect of the course.

A wide range of other useful resources can be found on the relevant subject pages of our website: www.aqa.org.uk.

Please note that the Practice Questions in this book allow students a genuine attempt at practising exam skills, but they are not intended to replicate examination papers.

Contents

Contents (continued)

Introduction to features

The *Oxford AQA History* series has been developed by a team of expert history teachers and authors with examining experience. Written to match the new AQA specification, these new editions cover AS and A Level content together in each book.

How to use this book

The features in this book include:

TIMELINE

Key events are outlined at the beginning of the book to give you an overview of the chronology of this topic. Events are colour-coded so you can clearly see the categories of change.

LEARNING OBJECTIVES

At the beginning of each chapter, you will find a list of learning objectives linked to the requirements of the specification.

SOURCE   EXTRACT

Sources introduce you to material that is primary or contemporary to the period, and **Extracts** provide you with historical interpretations and the debate among historians on particular issues and developments. The accompanying activity questions support you in evaluating sources and extracts, analysing and assessing their value, and making judgements.

PRACTICE QUESTION

Focused questions to help you practise your history skills for both AS and A Level, including evaluating sources and extracts, and essay writing.

STUDY TIP

Hints to highlight key parts of **Practice Questions** or **Activities**.

ACTIVITY

Various activity types to provide you with opportunities to demonstrate both the content and skills you are learning. Some activities are designed to aid revision or to prompt further discussion; others are to stretch and challenge both your AS and A Level studies.

CROSS-REFERENCE

Links to related content within the book to offer you more detail on the subject in question.

A CLOSER LOOK

An in-depth look at a theme, event or development to deepen your understanding, or information to put further context around the subject under discussion.

KEY CHRONOLOGY

A short list of dates identifying key events to help you understand underlying developments.

KEY PROFILE

Details of a key person to extend your understanding and awareness of the individuals that have helped shape the period in question.

KEY TERM

A term that you will need to understand. The terms appear in bold, and they are also defined in the glossary.

AQA History specification overview

Part One content

The Russian Revolution and the rise of Stalin, 1917–1929

1 Dissent and revolution, 1917
2 Bolshevik consolidation, 1918–1924
3 Stalin's rise to power, 1924–1929

Part Two content

Stalin's rule, 1929–1953

4 Economy and society, 1929–1941
5 Stalinism, politics and control, 1929–1943
6 The Great Patriotic War and Stalin's dictatorship, 1941–1953

AS examination papers will cover content from Part One only (you will only need to know the content in the blue box). A Level examination papers will cover content from both Part One and Part Two.

The examination papers

The grade you receive at the end of your AQA AS History course is based entirely on your performance in two examination papers, covering Breadth (Paper 1) and Depth (Paper 2). For your AQA A Level History course, you will also have to complete an Historical Investigation (Non-examined assessment).

Paper 2 Depth study

This book covers the content of a Depth study (Paper 2). You are assessed on the study in depth of a period of major historical change or development, and associated primary sources or sources contemporary to the period.

Exam paper	Questions and marks	Assessment Objective (AO)*	Timing	Marks
AS Paper 2: Depth Study	**Section A: Evaluating primary sources** One compulsory question linked to two primary sources or sources contemporary to the period (25 marks) • The compulsory question will ask you: *'with reference to these sources and your understanding of the historical context, which of these sources is more valuable in explaining why…'* **Section B: Essay writing** One from a choice of two essay questions (25 marks) • The essay questions will contain a quotation advancing a judgement and will be followed by: *'explain why you agree or disagree with this view'.*	AO2 AO1	Written exam: 1 hour 30 minutes	50 marks (50% of AS)
A Level Paper 2: Depth Study	**Section A: Evaluating primary sources** One compulsory question linked to three primary sources or sources contemporary to the period. The sources will be of different types and views (30 marks) • The compulsory question will ask you: *'with reference to these sources and your understanding of the historical context, assess the value of these three sources to an historian studying…'* **Section B: Essay writing** Two from a choice of three essay questions (2 x 25 marks) • The essay questions require analysis and judgement, and <u>could</u> include: *'How successful…'* or *'To what extent…'* or *'How far…'* or a quotation offering a judgement followed by *'Assess the validity of this view'.*	AO2 AO1	Written exam: 2 hours 30 minutes	80 marks (40% of A Level)

*AQA History examinations will test your ability to:

A01: Demonstrate, organise and communicate **knowledge and understanding** to analyse and evaluate the key features related to the periods studied, **making substantiated judgements and exploring concepts**, as relevant, of cause, consequence, change, continuity, similarity, difference and significance.

A02: **Analyse and evaluate** appropriate source material, primary and/or contemporary to the period, within the historical context.

A03: **Analyse and evaluate**, in relation to the historical context, different ways in which aspects of the past have been interpreted.

Visit **www.aqa.org.uk** to help you prepare for your examinations. The website includes specimen examination papers and mark schemes.

Introduction to the *Oxford AQA History* series

Depth studies

The exploration of a short but significant historical period provides an opportunity to develop an 'in-depth' historical awareness. This book will help you to acquire a detailed knowledge of an exciting period of historical change, enabling you to become familiar with the personalities and ideas which shaped and dominated the time. In-depth study, as presented here, allows you to develop the enthusiasm that comes from knowing something really well.

However, 'depth' is not just about knowledge. Understanding history requires the piecing together of many different strands or themes, and depth studies demand an awareness of the interrelationship of a variety of perspectives, such as the political, economic, social and religious – as well as the influence of individuals and

ideas within a relatively short period of time. Through an 'in-depth' study, a strong awareness of complex historical processes is developed, permitting deeper analysis, greater perception and well-informed judgement.

Whilst this book is therefore designed to impart a full and lively awareness of a significant period in history, far more is on offer from the pages that follow. With the help of the text and activities in this book, you will be encouraged to think historically, question developments in the past and undertake 'in-depth' analysis. You will develop your conceptual understanding and build up key historical skills that will increase your curiosity and prepare you, not only for A Level History examinations, but for any future studies.

> **Key Term**, **Key Chronology** and **Key Profile** help you to consolidate historical knowledge about dates, events, people and places

▲ Revolution and Dictatorship: Russia 1917–1953

> **Source** features support you with assessing the value of primary materials

This book also incorporates primary source material in the **Source** features. Primary sources are the building blocks of history, and you will be encouraged to reflect on their value to historians in trying to recreate the past. The accompanying questions are designed to develop your own historical skills, whilst suggestions for **Activities** will help you to engage with the past in a lively and stimulating manner. Throughout the book, you are encouraged to think about the material you are studying and to research further, in order to appreciate the ways in which historians seek to understand and interpret past events.

The chapters which follow are laid out according to the content of the AQA specification in six sections. Obviously, a secure chronological awareness and understanding of each section of content will be the first step in appreciating the historical period covered in this book. However, you are also encouraged to make links and comparisons between aspects of the period studied, and the activities will help you to relate to the key focus of your study and the key concepts that apply to it. Through intelligent use of this book, a deep and rewarding appreciation of an important period of history and the many influences within it will emerge.

Developing your study skills

You will need to be equipped with a paper file or electronic means of storing notes. Organised notes help to produce organised essays and sensible filing provides for efficient use of time. This book uses **Cross-References** to indicate where material in one chapter has relevance to that in another. By employing the same technique, you should find it easier to make the final leap towards piecing together your material to produce a holistic historical picture. The individual, group and research activities in this book are intended to guide you towards making selective and relevant notes with a specific purpose. Copying out sections of the book is to be discouraged, but recording material with a particular theme or question in mind will considerably aid your understanding.

There are plenty of examples of examination-style 'depth' **Practice Questions** for both AS Level, in Part One, and A Level in Parts One and Two of this book. There are also **Study Tips** to encourage you to think about historical perspectives, individuals, groups, ideas and ideology. You should also create your own timelines, charts and diagrams, for example to illustrate causation and consequence, analyse the interrelationship of the differing perspectives, consider concepts and identify historical processes.

It is particularly important for you to have your own opinions and to be able to make informed judgements about the material you have studied. Some of the activities in this book encourage pair discussion or class debate, and you should make the most of such opportunities to voice and refine your own ideas. The beauty of history is that there is rarely a right or wrong answer, so this supplementary oral work should enable you to share your own opinions.

Writing and planning your essays

At both AS and A Level, you will be required to write essays and, although A Level questions are likely to be more complex, the basic qualities of good essay writing remain the same:

- **read the question carefully** to identify the key words and dates
- **plan out a logical and organised answer** with a clear judgement or view (several views if there are a number of issues to consider). Your essay should advance this judgement in the introduction, while also acknowledging alternative views and clarifying terms of reference, including the time span
- use the opening sentences of your paragraphs as stepping stones to take an argument forward, which allows you to **develop an evolving and balanced argument** throughout the essay and also makes for good style
- **support your comment or analysis** with precise detail; using dates, where appropriate, helps logical organisation
- **write a conclusion** which matches the view of the introduction and flows naturally from what has gone before.

Whilst these suggestions will help you develop a good style, essays should never be too rigid or mechanical.

This book will have fulfilled its purposes if it produces, as intended, students who think for themselves!

Sally Waller

Series Editor

Timeline

The colours represent different types of events, legislation and changes as follows:

Blue: economic **Red: Political**

Black: foreign policy/international **Green: social**

1917
- Strikes in Petrograd
- Formation of the Petrograd Soviet and Provisional Government
- Abdication of Tsar Nicholas II (2 March)
- Return of Lenin, and April Theses
- 'July Days' riots
- Attempted coup by Kornilov
- Bolshevik seizure of power (25 October)
- Decrees on Peace and Land
- Establishment of Sovnarkom
- Formation of the Cheka

1918
- The Constituent Assembly forcibly dissolved
- Start of Civil War
- First Soviet constitution

1919
- Comintern established

1920
- Russo-Polish war

1926
- United Opposition formed
- Zinoviev, Kamenev and Trotsky removed from Politburo
- Treaty of Berlin

1927
- Defeat of Left Opposition

1928
- Shakhty Trial
- First Five Year Plan

1929
- Defeat of Right Opposition
- Celebration of Stalin's 50th birthday
- Call for mass collectivisation and liquidation of kulaks

1936
- Family Law to restrict abortion and divorce
- Show Trial of Zinoviev, Kamenev and others, Yezhov appointed head of NKVD
- Stalin constitution
- Soviet intervention in Spanish Civil War

1937
- Show Trial of Radek and others
- Execution of Marshal Tukhachevsky and Red Army officers
- Height of Great Terror (to late 1938)

1938
- Third Five Year Plan
- Show Trial of Bukharin, Rykov and others
- 'Labour Book' for workers introduced
- Yezhov replaced by Beria

1939
- Nazi-Soviet Pact
- Soviet invasion of Eastern Poland and Finland

1944
- Siege of Leningrad broken
- Soviet armies advance into eastern Europe

1945
- Soviet Invasion of Germany
- Yalta Conference
- German and Japanese surrender
- Potsdam Conference

1946
- Beginning of Zhdanovschina

1947
- Post-war famine
- Cominform established

1921

- Kronstadt revolt
- Tenth Party conference
- Launch of New Economic Policy
- Ban on factions

1921–22

- Widespread famine

1922

- Stalin elected General-Secretary
- Treaty of Rapallo
- 'Testament' dictated by Lenin

1924

- Zinoviev Letter
- Lenin's death

1932–3

- The Great Famine in Ukraine and elsewhere

1933

- Second Five Year Plan

1934

- Assassination of Kirov
- Soviet entry into League of Nations

1935

- Beginning of Stakhanovite movement
- Pacts signed between USSR and France, and Czechoslovakia

1940

- Soviet annexation of Baltic States

1941

- Nazi invasion of USSR
- Emergency legislation
- Beginning of siege of Leningrad
- Battle for Moscow
- US Lend-Lease agreed
- December-Soviet counter-offensive

1942

- Battle of Stalingrad

1943

- German surrender at Stalingrad
- Battle of Kursk
- Deportations from North Caucasus

1948

- Communist coup in Czechoslovakia
- Berlin blockade

1949

- Leningrad Affair
- Soviet atomic bomb

1952

- Doctors Plot and new political purges

1953

- Death of Stalin

Introduction

Fig. 1 *Russia was considered backwards in the early twentieth century*

The nineteenth and early twentieth centuries had seen huge industrial and political advances in Western Europe. The development of new forms of energy, the spread of railways and the expansion of trade together with advances in medicine and improvements in public health had helped raise living standards for an increasing proportion of the population. Alongside such change, social and political advances had occurred. Standards of literacy had increased, the old social hierarchies had broken down and an increasing number of people had gained the right to vote for a law-making assembly.

Russia, although considered a 'great' power because of its size and structured society, had trailed behind in every one of these developments. Serfdom, whereby the peasants at the bottom of the social hierarchy were 'owned' by their landlords, had disappeared from Western and Central Europe after a spate of revolutions in 1848; but it was not until 1861 that serfs finally acquired their freedom in Russia. Even after this their civil rights and status in society were very much determined by their position as 'former serfs', and this continued right up until 1917.

There are good reasons for Russia's backwardness. Russia was a vast empire of roughly 8 million square miles, twice the size of Europe and a sixth of the globe's surface. It had been acquired through military conquest and colonisation, much of it in the nineteenth century. However, large swathes of this Russian territory were inhospitable (over two thirds lay to the north of the 50th parallel), comprising tundra, forests and vast barren areas especially to the north and east. Consequently, both size and climate placed severe strains on economic development. Furthermore, within this vast land mass lived many different ethnic groups, each with its own culture, customs, language and, in some cases, religion. Of the total population of just under 185 million people, less than half was Russian by 1917, and around three quarters of the total population lived within European Russia – to the west of the Urals.

Nevertheless, although it was still a predominantly agricultural country, the rate of industrialisation in Russia since the 1890s had been rapid, with an annual industrial growth rate of more than 8 per cent a year between 1894 and

1904, and again, after a European trade recession, between 1908 and 1913. By 1917, Russia was the world's fifth largest industrial power (after Britain, USA, Germany and France) with c25,000 factories employing c3 million workers. There was strong growth in coal, pig iron and oil and some cities, particularly around Moscow and St Petersburg and in the 'Baku' area by the Caspian Sea, grew phenomenally. The Empire's urban population quadrupled from 7 to 28 million between 1867 and 1917. St Petersburg, which already comprised just over a million inhabitants in 1900, grew to 2.4 million by 1916. Communications, including the roads and railways, were also much improved, although the outbreak of the First World War in 1914 revealed continuing transport deficiencies.

The countryside also saw changes, particularly after 1905 when the peasants were given more opportunities to leave the *mirs* (or communes) in which they farmed and schemes were launched to encourage them to buy their own land and develop larger farming units. This was an ambitious project which was cut short by the coming of war in 1914. By 1915, hereditary peasant ownership of land had increased from 20 per cent in 1905 to nearly 50 per cent, while 3.5 million peasants had been encouraged to move away from the overpopulated rural districts of the south and west to Siberia, which consequently grew as a major agricultural region. Nevertheless, the changes to land tenure arrangements were slow and by 1914 there were still only around 10 per cent of peasant holdings that had moved beyond the traditional and inefficient strip-farming.

Such industrial and agricultural change also came at a social cost. It brought a growing and frustrated middle class, whose economic gains were not matched by equal political advancement, and an urban working class which suffered harsh conditions – with long hours, low pay and limited machinery to lighten their physical labour. Factories and mines were all too often unsafe, while living quarters were cramped and dirty, with factory barracks and lodgings shared between families. Although some efforts were made in the years before the war to improve conditions by introducing insurance schemes for those who fell ill or who were injured by machinery, the workers' lot was grim. While trade unions were allowed after 1905, strikes were theoretically forbidden, although they occurred nonetheless. When the goldminers working on the Lena River in Siberia went on strike in 1912, the government used troops to fire on the workers, killing 200 of them. There were over 2000 strikes in 1913 and although they fell back with the outbreak of war, by 1917 their number had increased again.

There was also unease in the countryside as the reforms there produced a growing class of alienated, poor and landless peasants. While some peasants rose in rank and became 'kulaks' (small peasant proprietors with sufficient wealth to employ others to help work their farms), for every family that improved its status, another 'sold out', descended into deeper hardship and joined the wandering bands of those who drifted to the towns in search of work. Until 1916, Russia had no form of income tax, so the burden of taxation had fallen on the peasantry producing periodic riots.

Politically, any change had been slow in coming. Until 1905, Russia had remained the only country in Europe (except Turkey and Montenegro) without a parliament. Even in 1917, the Empire was, in essence, an **autocracy** headed by a tsar who still regarded himself as possessing **divine right** to rule. The Tsar was also the titular head of the Russian **Orthodox Church**. The land of Russia was his private property and the Russian people his children. The structures of Church and State were thus entwined, as archbishops and bishops at the head of the church hierarchy were subject to tsarist control over appointments, religious education, most of the Church's finances and issues of administration.

KEY TERM

autocracy: rule by one person who had no limits to his power (as opposed to democracy, which means 'rule by the people')

divine right: this refers to a monarch appointed by God and answerable to God alone for actions

Orthodox Church: the Eastern Orthodox Church, with Moscow as its spiritual capital; it had its own beliefs and rituals, following a split in the Christian Church in the eleventh century

bureaucracy: the state's administrative officials

Okhrana: the secret police force of the Russian Empire; its name comes from the initial letters (in Russian) of its full title – the Department for Protecting Public Security and Order

A CLOSER LOOK

The 1905 revolution

In 1904 Russia went to war with Japan as the result of imperial rivalry in the Far East. Russia's catastrophic defeat sparked the 1905 revolution. The revolution was not a coordinated attack on the regime but a series of dramatic events that took place over several months. They included 'Bloody Sunday' in January, which saw the massacre of workers peacefully marching to the Tsar's Winter Palace in the capital, plus innumerable strikes and mutinies. In several cities, including the capital, workers set up elected 'soviets' (the Russian word for council) and tried to assume control.

KEY TERM

zemstva: elected councils responsible for the local administration of provincial districts

socialist: supporting a political and economic theory of social organisation which believes that the means of production (e.g. factories), distribution (e.g. railways), and exchange (e.g. what buys what), should be controlled by the whole community

constitutional monarchy: a form of democratic government in which a monarch acts as the head of state within the boundaries of a constitution giving real power to a representative assembly

The Tsar ruled through imperial edicts, or *ukase*, and was advised by ministers, who were chosen by the Tsar himself and unable to act without his approval. He also depended on the provincial nobility and imperial **bureaucracy** (a highly stratified and conservative group, riddled with internal corruption and incompetence) and the world's largest army (which consisted of 6 million in 1914 and rose to a force of 12 million during the First World War). To maintain the autocracy, Russia had developed into a police state with curbs on freedom of speech, of the press and of travel. Censorship existed at every level of government and was carried out by the State and the Church as well as by the police. A strict surveillance was maintained over the population, ensuring that any subversive activites were exposed. Political meetings were forbidden and the **Okhrana** had unlimited powers to carry out raids, arrest and ensure the imprisonment or exile of anyone suspected of anti-tsarist behaviour, sometimes merely on the word of an informer.

This autocratic system of government had not been without critics. These ranged from the moderate 'liberals' (many drawn from the professional middle classes) who had gained some influence over local government since 1864 when the *zemstva* were created (as were elected town councils or dumas from 1870), to more extreme **socialists**, many influenced by Marxism. In **1905**, the disparate **opposition groups** had combined to pressurise the tsarist autocracy in the wake of defeat in war with Japan. Riots and strikes caused an almost total breakdown of control, forcing the Tsar to concede his 'October Manifesto'. This promised an elected representative assembly or State Duma, appeasing the more moderate Kadets (in favour of a **constitutional monarchy**) and Octobrists (who saw the manifesto as the first step towards responsible government). However, in April 1906, before the First Duma met in May, the Tsar issued the 'Fundamental Laws', reaffirming his autocracy. He made it clear that the State Duma had no control over state ministers or parts of the state budget. Furthermore, the Tsar's power to dissolve the Duma and rule by decree when it was not sitting undermined what had at first appeared a significant change.

A CLOSER LOOK

Opposition groups

- **The Liberals** This is a loose name for those groups who favoured moderate reform and constitutional monarchy. Included among these were the Constitutional Democrats (Kadets), the Octobrists and the Progressives – a loose grouping of businessmen. The Trudoviks were a non-revolutionary breakaway from the Social Revolutionary Party of moderate liberal views.
- **The Social Revolutionaries (SRs)** The Social Revolutionary Party was formed in 1901, and evolved from groups that had tried to organise and improve the position of the peasantry from the 1860s. The movement had also tried to attract workers as industrialisation grew in the 1890s. However, it suffered from internal divisions. There were extreme terrorist elements who believed in political assassination but, from 1905, the moderate elements within the Party became more influential and gained support from some trade unions and members of the middle class. The Party always suffered from a lack of discipline and coordination; this limited its chance of realising its ambitions, which included land reform.
- **The Social Democrats (SDs)** The All-Russian Social Democrat Labour Party was founded in 1898. Its programme was based on the theories of **Karl Marx**. Led mainly by educated intellectuals, the Party based its support on the rapidly expanding industrial working

class, the proletariat. However, in 1903 the Party split, when **Vladimir Ilyich Ulyanov (Lenin)** won a vote in favour of a strong disciplined organisation of professional revolutionaries against **Julius Martov**, who wanted a broad party with mass working class membership and favoured working through the trade unions to destroy the tsarist government. Lenin's 'Bolsheviks' and Martov's 'Mensheviks' spent much of their time before 1917 arguing with one another.

Marxist stage theory

Marx believed that history was composed of a series of class struggles, driven by economic conditions:

- In stage 1 (the time of the hunter-gatherers) there were no classes or private property.
- In stage 2 (imperialism) a strong man rose to the top and a new land-owning aristocracy was created.
- In stage 3 (feudalism) land was owned by the aristocracy who exploited the peasantry.
- In stage 4 (capitalism) merchants and the 'bourgeoisie' obtained political control and exploited the workers (proletariat).
- In stage 5 (socialism) the workers took control in a 'dictatorship of the proletariat', sharing food, goods and services according to need.
- In stage 6 (communism) all would join together for the common good and money and states would no longer be needed. Wars and competition would cease.

Vladimir Ilyich Ulyanov (Lenin) (1870–1924) came from a well-to-do professional family and trained as a lawyer. He was attracted by Marxism and his activities brought him to the attention of the secret police. He was in exile in Siberia when the new Social Democrat Party was launched in 1898, but he wrote a programme for it. After his release, he went into exile in Switzerland. In 1902, he produced the pamphlet, 'What is to be done?', in which he argued that the Party needed to re-direct the workers away from trade unionism towards a revolution that would destroy the tsarist autocracy. He founded a new revolutionary newspaper *Iskra* (Spark) and helped develop a strong underground Party network. His harsh and uncompromising attitude led the

Fig. 3   *Ulyanov was known as Lenin from 1901 after his exile by the River Lena in Siberia*

Social Democrats to split in 1903 into Bolsheviks and Mensheviks. Lenin remained in exile until 1917, except for a brief return to St Petersburg in October 1905.

Fig. 2   *Marx was a revolutionary socialist*

Karl Marx (1818–83) was a German Jew who wrote *The Communist Manifesto* with his friend Friedrich Engels in 1848. The first volume of his mammoth work, *Das Kapital*, was published 1867 and subsequent ones in 1885 and 1894. (*The Communist Manifesto* was translated into Russian in 1869, and the first volume of *Das Kapital* was published in Russia in 1872.) At the time of his writing, he believed that Britain and Western Europe had reached stage 4 of his **'stage theory'** of history. He suggested that stages 5 and 6 must inevitably follow.

Julius Martov (1873–1920) came from a Jewish middle class background. He helped found the Emancipation of Labour and the Social Democrat movement. He contributed to the Party journal *Iskra* and was editor from 1903 to 1905, after breaking with Lenin when he led the 'Mensheviks'. He favoured working through trade unions, cooperatives and soviets (workers' councils) to destroy the government. He was not invited to join the Bolshevik government after October 1917 and the Mensheviks were banned in 1918. Martov was exiled in 1920.

The Russian Calendar

The Russians used the Julian calendar until 31 January 1918, rather than the Gregorian calendar adopted by the rest of Europe in the seventeenth and eighteenth centuries. Consequently, by 1918, Russia was 13 days behind Western Europe. Some books (including this one) use the old-style calendar, so that the two revolutions of 1917 are given as 23 February and 25 October. However, others use the 'modern' dating so that the first revolution took place on 8 March and the second on 7 November. Russia finally adopted the Gregorian calendar in February 1918. Dates after this are therefore the same as Western dates.

The four State Dumas that met between 1906 and 1917 offered a forum for debate about politics and legislation but were constantly muzzled by tsarist interference. Furthermore, they became the preserve of the liberal moderates and well-to-do, driving the more radical opposition to acts of terrorism, including frequent political assassinations and subversion. Although the most prominent radical leaders were forced into exile, there was an underlying restlessness and discontent among peasants and industrial workers. This was easily exploited by the radical groups and would rise to the surface with the disruptions caused by the coming of the First World War in 1914.

In the 50 years up to 1917 there was constant struggle between progress and control. The gains of industrialisation were offset by an escalation of workers' discontent created by over-rapid urbanisation, and the transition to a modern society brought into prominence revolutionary movements which went even further than the moderate liberals in their criticisms of autocracy. Successive governments were forced to choose between modernisation and maintaining political control over society in order to protect themselves, and the greater the concessions, the louder became the voices demanding more. This conundrum would remain a constant force in the development of Russia even after 1917.

KEY CHRONOLOGY

1905	Jan	'Bloody Sunday' massacre leads to revolutionary upheavals
	Oct	The St Petersburg Soviet is formed; the Tsar's October Manifesto authorises elections to a State Duma
1906	Apr	The Fundamental Laws reaffirm the autocracy
1906–11		A programme of agrarian reform is attempted
1906–15		Four State Dumas meet but their influence is controlled
1912		Lena Gold Fields Massacre – renewed industrial unrest
1914		First World War begins

1 Dissent and revolution, 1917

1 The condition of Russia before the revolution of February/March 1917

Fig. 1 *The royal family is greeted by the crowd at the tercentenary celebrations at the Kremlin, Moscow, in 1913*

The Tsar and political authority

The autocratic Emperor of Russia in 1917 was **Tsar Nicholas II**, a member of the Romanov dynasty that had ruled Russia since 1613. Tsar Nicholas II had inherited the throne in 1894, at the age of 26. He had been just 12 years old when his **reformist** grandfather, Tsar Alexander II, had been blown up by a revolutionary bomb. Both this incident, and the behaviour of his **reactionary** father, Alexander III, who was determined to uphold tsarist power without concessions, had profoundly influenced him. Brought up in a sheltered environment, Nicholas had been tutored by the arch-conservative Konstantin Pobedonostsev, who had ensured that he had the moral correctness of autocracy instilled in him from a very young age.

KEY TERM

reformist: a supporter of gradual reform; Alexander II was known as the 'Tsar reformer' for measures such as the 1861 Emancipation of the Serfs, but he never intended to weaken tsarist autocracy

reactionary: backward-looking and opposed to change, particularly political and social reform; a reactionary could also be described as an **arch-conservative** – averse to innovation and upholding traditional values

Fig. 2 *Nicholas II – a devout and dutiful ruler*

Tsar Nicholas II (1868–1918)

Nikolai Aleksandrovich Romanov had never wanted to be Tsar and, although determined to fulfil his divine calling and uphold autocracy, he found escape in family life with his wife, Alexandra, and his four daughters and son. Defeat in a war against Japan in 1904 to 1905 brought strikes. This led to a 'revolution' as events spiralled out of Nicholas' control after the Tsarist army shot at a crowd demanding reforms in St Petersburg on 'Bloody Sunday' in January 1905. Nicholas was forced to establish a State **Duma**, but he restricted its powers and continued to use his Okhrana to crush opposition. Nicholas' handling of the First World War led to popular demonstrations in February 1917, which forced the Tsar to abdicate. He was executed by Bolsheviks in January 1918.

CROSS-REFERENCE

To recap on the *zemstva* and the establishment of the **State Duma**, look back to the Introduction, page xiv.

KEY PROFILE

Aleksandr Kerensky (1881–1970) was a lawyer who became involved in radical politics. In 1905 he served four months in gaol for publishing a socialist newspaper. In 1912, he was elected to the State Duma and in February 1917 he joined the Social Revolutionaries. He became an SR representative in the Petrograd Soviet and Minister of Justice in the Provisional Government after the February Revolution. He became Minister of War in May and Prime Minister in July 1917. He was deposed by the Bolsheviks in October and fled to France. He finally moved to the USA where he wrote extensively on the Russian Revolution.

ACTIVITY

Evaluating primary sources

With reference to Source 1 and what you have read so far, write a brief character profile of Nicholas II.

Although he was convinced of his divine right to rule, Nicholas' personality ill-suited him for his position as Tsar. He was naturally rather shy and awkward in public; he found the intricate details of political affairs boring and tended to be over-cautious, struggling to make clear political decisions. Nevertheless, he could also be extremely stubborn, resenting any uncalled-for advice, which he saw as criticism. Shortly after coming to power, he dismissed a *zemstvo* petition for an elected National Assembly as a 'senseless dream' and whilst he did, under duress, agree to a State Duma from 1906, he did all in his power to minimise its influence.

Nicholas felt he needed to keep his ministers weak, so as to preserve his own authority. He constantly pitted them against each other, becoming suspicious of those who grew powerful, and since he hated confrontations, dismissed ministers by note behind their backs rather than speaking to them personally. He was not ill-meaning; indeed, he liked to think of himself as ruling in the tradition of the earlier Muscovite rulers of Russia, with a strong bond between himself and the masses. However, his reluctance to innovate combined with perpetual problems of state finance and the disorganisation brought by the many overlapping institutions of Tsarist government, all helped weaken political authority in Russia by early 1917.

SOURCE 1

Adapted from Aleksandr Kerensky's memoirs, *Crucifixion of Liberty*, 1934

Aleksandr Kerensky was a socialist member of the third and fourth State Dumas and Prime Minister between August and October 1917, after the Tsar's abdication. In this extract he describes Nicholas II:

He merely believed what his father and Pobedonostsev had instilled into him; there would be no Russia without autocracy; Russia and the autocracy were one; he himself was the impersonation of the autocracy. So the magic circle closed. There was no way out, unless it was into disaster and void. Living in the twentieth century, he had the mentality of the Muscovite Kings. The daily work of a monarch he found intolerably boring. He could not stand listening long or seriously to ministers' reports, or reading them. He liked such ministers as could tell an amusing story and did not weary the monarch's attention with too much business. When it came to defending his divine right his usual indifference left him, he became cunning, obstinate and cruel, merciless at times.

Nicholas' wife Alexandra (the Russian name for **Princess Alix** of Hesse-Darmstadt), was a German princess, whom he had married two weeks after his father's death in 1894. She proved a devoted wife and mother but was a strong-willed woman and her advice to Nicholas to 'stand firm', for example in 1905, had often proven misguided. She had also introduced her husband to the self-styled 'holy man' and faith-healer, Grigorii Rasputin (literally 'the ill-behaved one'). Rasputin had been able to ease the pain of their only son, Aleksei, who suffered from haemophilia, an inherited disease that prevented his blood from clotting. However, Rasputin's influence over the Tsar had extended to interfering in government appointments, particularly after war broke out in 1914. He was known for womanising and drunkenness, and the favours heaped on him did much to damage Nicholas' reputation with the very people the Tsar relied upon to prop up the autocracy: politicians inside and outside the court, civil servants, Orthodox bishops and army officers.

In 1913, the last year of peace, Nicholas seemed barely aware of the discontent that was fomenting around him. The year was marked by a violent wave of strikes, yet, far more important to Nicholas and Alexandra were a series of jubilee rituals organised to celebrate the **tercentenary** of Romanov rule. They indulged in a round of joyous festivities across Russia and when Nicholas returned to the capital he declared his conviction that 'my people love me'. Alexandra retorted, 'Now you can see for yourself what cowards those state ministers are. They are constantly frightening us with threats of revolution and here – you see it for yourself – we need merely to show ourselves and at once their hearts are ours.'

Tsarina Alexandra (1872–1918)

Princess Alix had a German father but her mother was the youngest child of Queen Victoria of England. She abandoned her Protestant faith and converted to the Russian Orthodox Church when she married Nicholas, taking the Russian name, Grand Duchess Alexandra Feodorovna. She proved a great comfort to Nicholas but her lack of political understanding and her devotion to Rasputin weakened his position. She was distraught by Rasputin's murder in 1916 but continued to urge Nicholas to stand up to the revolutionaries in February 1917. She was shot, along with her family, in March 1918.

A CLOSER LOOK

The Romanov tercentenary, 1913

The Tsar and his family left their Winter Palace in St Petersburg to drive through the streets in open carriages for the first time since the troubles of 1905. Crowds flocked to cheer, wave banners, wonder at the decorated streets and thank God for their Tsar. At Kazan Cathedral, where an elaborate thanksgiving service took place, a pair of doves briefly flew from the rafters and hovered over the heads of the Tsar and his son, which the former interpreted as a sign of God's blessing on his dynasty. After a round of balls and dinners in the capital, the royal family embarked on a three-month tour of 'old Muscovy', the original heartland of Russia where they enjoyed a triumphal entry into Moscow. Nicholas led the way on a white horse, to the adulation of confetti-throwing crowds who had gathered beneath the Romanov flags that filled the streets.

The Russian war effort

Fig. 3 *In 1914, Russia mobilised for war*

KEY TERM

pan-Slavism: a belief that Slav races should be united – and look to Russia as the supreme Slav country for leadership

KEY TERM

war credits: the raising of taxes and loans to finance war

In 1914, Russia found itself embroiled in war. In June 1914, the Austrian Archduke Franz Ferdinand was assassinated by a young Slav in the town of Sarajevo, part of the Austro-Hungarian Empire. The assassination was a protest against Austria's rule over many Slav peoples and the Austro-Hungarian Emperor held the Serb government responsible. Russia, which had long held ambitions to dominate the Balkan area, identified with Balkan state of Serbia, a fellow Slav nation. **Pan-Slavism** was strong in European Russia and in July 1914 the Tsar mobilised his armies in support of Serbia. Since Germany immediately went to the aid of its ally, Austria, Russia was rapidly drawn into war with Germany. Russia's allies, Britain and France, also declared war, but they fought largely on the Western Front, leaving Russia to struggle alone against Germans and Austro-Hungarians on the Eastern Front.

The Tsar's decision to go to war in 1914 was popular initially, and supported by a wave of anti-German sentiment. The social and political disorder that had dominated Nicholas' reign ceased and, having voted for **war credits**, the State Duma dissolved itself, declaring that it did not want to burden the country with 'unnecessary politics' in war time. The capital, with its Germanic name 'St Petersburg', became the new Slavonic 'Petrograd' and a vast army was rapidly assembled, amazing the Germans with the speed at which this Russian 'steam-roller' was able to get to the Front.

However, the spirit of national solidarity was dampened when initial victories gave way to defeat at the hands of the Germans in the disastrous Battle of Tannenburg in East Prussia in August 1914, which left 300,000 dead or wounded. Thousands were taken prisoner. A subsequent defeat at the Masurian Lakes in September forced the Russian army into a temporary retreat from East Prussia. Despite greater success for the Russian troops in the south against Austria-Hungary, it was soon clear that the war would not end in a quick victory, as had been hoped, and reports of military incompetence inflamed the simmering discontent in the Russian capital.

Although the Russian government managed to mobilise around 12 million men between 1914 and 1917, mainly conscript peasants, it proved unable to provide for them. The problems of the early years grew steadily worse so that soldiers were sent to fight not only without suitable weaponry, but also lacking basic warm clothing and properly fitting, waterproof footwear. In 1914, the infantry had only two rifles for every three soldiers and, in 1915, it was not unusual for Russian artillery to be limited to two to three shells per day. In these early years, the soldiers had to rely on the weapons of fallen comrades in order to fight at all.

By the time of the Brusilov offensive (a Russian attempt to push westwards from the Ukraine and break through the Austro-Hungarian lines in June 1916), some of the deficiencies in equipment and arms had been rectified. However, the loss of experienced officers, killed in the early stages of war, continuing heavy casualties and a deteriorating economic and political situation within Russia itself led to a fall in morale and 1.5 million desertions by the end of that year.

A CLOSER LOOK

The Russian Army

Despite the problems, Russia's military capacity should not be underestimated. Russia managed to tie down the German armies on the Eastern Front for three years and, in 1916, Russia was able to manufacture more shells than Germany. Russian military breakdown should not therefore be over-emphasised as the reason for the revolution in February 1917.

SOURCE 2

Adapted from official government reports into the state of the war in October 1916

The atmosphere in the army is very tense, and the relations between the common soldiers and the officers are much strained, the result being that several unpleasant incidents leading even to bloodshed have taken place. The behaviour of the soldiers, expecially in the units located in the rear is most provocative. They openly accuse military authorities of cowardice, drunkenness and even treason.

Everyone who has approached the army cannot but carry away the belief that complete demoralisation is in progress. The soldiers began to demand peace a long time ago, but never was this done so openly and with such force as now. The officers, not infrequently, even refuse to lead their units against the enemy because they are afraid of being killed by their own men.

ACTIVITY

Make a list of reasons why the ordinary soldiers had become disillusioned with the war by the end of 1916. Try to provide some precise evidence to support your reasons.

The years between 1914 and 1917 were also marked by disputes over the organisation of the war effort. In July 1914, the Tsarist government had set up 'military zones' within which all civilian authority was suspended and the military assumed command. This, however, had been opposed by the liberal *zemstva* who regarded the government as insensitive to the needs of the people and believed that civilians needed to play a major part in running the war. The *zemstva* had established a 'Union of Zemstva' to provide the medical facilities which the state seemed to neglect, while factory owners and businessmen had set up a Congress of Representatives of Industry and Business (which included representatives from the dumas and of workers) to help coordinate production.

In June 1915, *zemstva* and municipal dumas had joined to form Zemgor – the All Russian Union of Zemstva and Cities. This was chaired by **Prince Lvov** and claimed the right to help the Tsar's government in the war effort. However, Nicholas shunned it and it turned into a focus for liberal discontent.

Nicholas was given a chance to institute political reform and save his own position by transferring responsibility for the war effort to a civilian government, in August 1915. Over half the Fourth Duma deputies (Kadets, Octobrists and Progressives) organised themselves into a 'Progressive bloc' and demanded that the Tsar change his ministers and establish a 'government of public confidence'. They were effectively asking for a constitutional monarchy, in which they would have a dominant voice. Had Nicholas II been a more astute man, he might well have seized this chance but he refused to contemplate such a move.

KEY PROFILE

Prince Lvov (1861–1925)

Prince Georgi Yevgenyevich Lvov was a wealthy aristocratic landowner who began his career as a lawyer and in 1905 joined the Constitutional Democratic Party (Kadets) and won election to the first Duma. He became chairman of the Union of Zemstva in 1914 and leader of Zemgor in 1915. He became the head of the Provisional Government of Russia, after the Tsar's abdication, from March to July 1917. Although later arrested by the Bolsheviks, he escaped and lived out his days in Paris.

Fig. 4 *Nicholas II encouraging his army officers*

In September 1915, defeats in Galicia (on the Austro-Hungarian front) led the Tsar to make the disastrous decision to take the role of Commander-in-Chief of the Russian Army and Navy and, 'with firm trust in Divine mercy and unshakeable confidence in ultimate victory' to travel to the front line. The move did nothing to help his cause. Although it had overtones of bravery and heroism, Nicholas had already lost the confidence and support of the Russian General Staff and did not possess the military experience to turn the war effort around. Instead, his new position simply made him appear yet more responsible for the varying disasters which befell his troops and state.

Nicholas had also distanced himself from developments in Petrograd, where Rasputin meddled in political appointments and policy decisions.

Mikhail Rodzianko (1859–1924)
was a wealthy landowner who had
joined the Octobrist party. He was
elected chairman of the Fourth
Duma, where he supported Russia's
entry into the First World War
and tried to serve the Tsar loyally.
He was chosen as the head of the
Duma's Provisional Committee,
which set up the Provisional
Government in 1917. He went into
exile in November 1917.

Fig. 5 *What is this cartoonist's view of
Rasputin?*

Work in pairs to construct a diagram
that shows the ways in which the
war undermined Tsar Nicholas II's
authority.

inflation: an increase in prices and
fall in the purchasing value of
money brought about by having
more money in circulation than
there are goods to buy

Rumours abounded that Rasputin was having an affair with Alexandra, who,
as a German, was accused of sabotaging the Russian war effort. There were so
many changes of ministers in 1915–16, including four Prime Ministers, three
Foreign Secretaries, three Ministers of Defence and six Interior Ministers, that
opponents spoke of Rasputin's game of ministerial leapfrog.

The President of the Fourth Duma, **Mikhail Rodzianko**, warned Nicholas
in vain of Rasputin's unpopularity and the damage he was doing the Tsarist
cause, but to no avail. It was in an attempt to save the reputation of the
monarchy that Prince Yusupov (a nephew by marriage to the Tsar) murdered
Rasputin in December 1916.

Nicholas' letters to Alexandra, whom he addressed with such terms of
endearment as 'my own lovebird', showed more anxiety about the children's
measles than (as Alexandra wrote in a message on 25 February 1917) 'young
boys and girls running about and screaming that they have no bread'. Nicholas
reassured his wife that, 'this will all pass and quieten down'.

The economic and social state of Russia

Mobilising the Russian economy for war proved as difficult as mobilising the
munitions. To pay for the war, the government increased taxes and raised
huge loans at home and from abroad. Given the damage done to industrial
and grain exports by the war, this produced massive **inflation**. Money was
virtually worthless by 1917, and prices rose much more steeply than wages.
The millions conscripted into the Russian armies left a shortage of men in the
countryside. Supplies of food to the towns fell due to a shortage of workers in
the fields, the fact that peasants began to hoard food instead of selling it, and
the inadequacy of the transport and distribution systems. Poland and other
parts of western Russia were overrun by the Germans, removing important
industrial capacity, while naval blockades of the Baltic and Black Sea ports,
together with the loss of overland routes to Europe, brought Russian trade to a
virtual standstill. Rationing scarcely helped and, for many, the war years were
years of acute hunger, if not famine.

The railway system virtually collapsed under the strain of war. Railways
were taken over to transport men and goods to the front, while railway
locomotive production halved between 1913 and 1916 and there were severe
fuel shortages. Some foodstuffs that should have found their way to the
cities were left to rot beside railway sidings for lack of transport, while some
huge cargoes of grain were sent to the front line at the expense of desperate
townsfolk. The discontent caused by long queues to buy bread in Petrograd
was an important factor in the 1905 Revolution.

Adapted from a 1916 Bolshevik report into the food crisis in Bryansk, a city
near the front line, south-west of Moscow. The report was made by Alexander
Shliapnikov, a Russian communist revolutionary, metalworker, and trade
union leader who published it in, On the Eve of 1917, in 1923.

In Bryansk there is no rye flour, salt, paraffin or sugar. Discontent is rife and
more than once there have been strikes in the factories with the demand for
'flour and sugar'. There is, in Bryansk country, a village called Star, where there
is a factory making glass products and is engaged in war contracts. Workers
there went on strike on 8 October 1916 because they had not eaten bread for
two weeks, having only potatoes. They selected two spokesmen and sent them
to the factory manager with a demand for flour and sugar (for the company
had undertaken to procure the items at pre-war prices as it had kept wages
at peacetime levels). The manager could not give an answer but just made

promises. The following day the two spokesmen were arrested as unreliable elements and held under emergency regulations. Two days later the workers went back but still did not get bread. I travelled round the villages: grumbling, discontent and a vague apprehension all around.

In many urban centres, particularly in Petrograd and Moscow, unemployment soared as non-military factories, deprived of vital supplies, were forced to close. Lock-outs and strikes (some directly encouraged by the German government in a deliberate attempt to foster industrial unrest and undermine the Russian war effort) financially crippled what little industry survived. A 300 per cent rise in the cost of living, rising death rates because of the workers' insanitary lodgings and the inadequacies of their diets left thousands living on the brink of starvation. In such circumstances, in January 1917 30,000 workers went on strike in Moscow and 145,000 in Petrograd.

Discontent in Russia

By February 1917, loss of confidence in the Tsarist regime was clear in all levels of society. At the lowest level there was the everyday grumbling, at times despair and despondency, at others demonstrations and outbursts. Most ordinary men and women were still patriotic at heart and many would have claimed their love for the Tsar, but their struggle to survive and meet their everyday needs increased their indifference to the fate of their rulers. Their anger was mostly directed at those immediately above them and came in the form of strikes, riots or violence against employers or landlords.

There were also outbursts of anger, sometimes leading to desertion, within the army. The rank and file soldiers faced hardship and horrendous casualties on the front line. Operating conditions were appalling and in the winter of 1916 to 1917 temperatures fell to 35 degrees below zero. It is little wonder that there was near mutiny in some regiments as peasant conscripts lost any heart they had to fight on.

Political discontent was also strong. **Aleksandr Guchkov**, one of the founders of the Progressive bloc, engaged in talks with senior army officers in 1916 about a possible coup to force the abdication of the Tsar. His colleague, **Pavel Milyukov**, openly accused the Tsar's ministers of seeking peace with Germany behind the Duma's back in November 1916. In January 1917, Prince Lvov indirectly asked the Tsar's uncle, Grand Duke Nicholas, whether he would be prepared to take over the throne.

On the left, there was less direct challenge, since most leaders were in exile and there were, in any case, differences of opinion among socialists as to whether or not they should support the war effort. Lenin, living in Switzerland, rejected the majority view and claimed that 'the war must be turned into a civil war of the proletarian soldiers against their own governments'. So, while the radical socialist agitators within Russia no doubt helped to stir up discontent, it must be remembered that Lenin had no more than 10,000 followers there.

The situation in January 1917 is summed up in the following government-commissioned Okhrana report, January 1917:

Adapted from a government-commissioned Okhrana report, January 1917

There is a marked increase in hostile feelings among the peasants, not only against the government but against all other social groups. The proletariat of the capital is on the verge of despair. The mass of industrial workers are

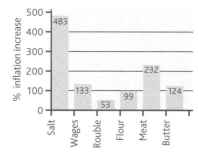

Fig. 6 *Inflation: percentage increase from pre-war figures by the beginning of 1917*

Make a wall poster to illustrate the impact of the First World War on the Russian people. You will need to include economic and social factors. Find some illustrations to accompany your ideas.

Aleksandr Ivanovich Guchkov (1862–1936) was a wealthy Moscow businessman who became the leader of the Octobrist party. He became Minister of War and of the Navy in the Provisional Government of 1917 but resigned when his policy of continuing war until victory was rejected by the Soviet in May. He supported the **Whites in the Civil War** and emigrated to Berlin in 1921.

For more detail on the **Whites in the Civil War**, see Chapter 6, page 45.

Pavel Nikolayevich Milyukov (1859–1943) was an academic historian who founded the Constitutional Democrat (Kadet) Party in 1905. He became Foreign Minister in the **1917 Provisional Government** but, along with Guchkov, was forced out in May over his support for 'war to victory'. He also supported the Whites in the Civil War, and emigrated to Paris when they were defeated.

quite ready to let themselves go to the wildest excesses of a hunger riot. The prohibition of all labour meetings, the closing of trade unions, the suspension of labour newspapers and so on, make the labour masses, led by the more advanced and already revolutionary-minded elements, assume an openly hostile attitude towards the Government and protest with all means at their disposal against the continuation of the war.

CROSS-REFERENCE

The **1917 Provisional Government** will be covered in Chapter 3, page 22.

Summary

- The vast Russian Empire already faced major economic and social problems before the outbreak of war in 1914, with growing discontent of various types from moderate to revolutionary.
- Although the Tsarist regime had survived a revolution in 1905 and promised reforms, nothing of substance had changed.
- Nicholas II's character and personality exacerbated an already difficult situation.
- The First World War proved a disaster for Russia, bringing humiliating military defeats, mounting economic problems, growing disillusionment, and increased opposition to the regime.

ACTIVITY

Summary

Consider the state of the Russian Empire at the beginning of 1917 and list at least five reasons why the tsarist regime was facing a crisis. Then put them into an order of importance. This can be used as a basis for discussion about why the regime was under threat.

STUDY TIP

In order to assess the value of the sources it is important that you examine the provenance as well as the content, tone and emphasis. For the AS question you should evaluate both sources and then make a supported judgement on which is the more valuable as a piece of historical evidence. For the A Level question you do not need to compare the sources but you should provide a thorough analysis of each in turn, together with an overall conclusion to show how the three work together to help the historian understand conditions on the eve of revolution.

 PRACTICE QUESTION

Evaluating primary sources

With reference to Sources 1 and 2 and your understanding of the historical context, which of these two sources is more valuable in explaining why there was discontent in Russia by the beginning of 1917?

 PRACTICE QUESTION

Evaluating primary sources

With reference to Sources 2, 3 and 4, and your understanding of the historical context, assess the value of these three sources to an historian studying the condition of Russia on the eve of revolution in 1917.

2 The February/March Revolution of 1917

SOURCE 1

On 26 February 1917, Mikhail Rodzianko, the conservative Russian politician who was President of the Fourth State Duma, sent the following telegram to the Tsar:

The situation is serious. The capital is already in a state of anarchy. The Government is paralysed. Transport service and the supply of food and fuel have become completely disrupted. General discontent is growing. There is wild shooting in the streets. In places troops are firing at each other. It is necessary that some person who enjoys the confidence of the country be entrusted at once with the formation of a new government. There must be no delay. Any procrastination is tantamount to death. I pray to God that at this hour the responsibility may not fall upon the monarch.

SOURCE 2

Adapted from Leon Trotsky's *History of the Russian Revolution*, written in 1930. Trotsky was a Social Democrat living in the USA in February 1917, but returned to become a leader in the Bolshevik Revolution of October 1917:

On the morning of 27 February, Rodzianko sent the Tsar a new telegram, which ended with the words: 'The last hour has come when the fate of the fatherland and the dynasty is being decided.' The Tsar said to his Minister of the Court, Vladimir Frederiks: 'Again that fat-bellied Rodzianko has written me a lot of nonsense, which I won't even bother to answer.' But no. It was not nonsense. He will have to answer.

KEY PROFILE

Leon Trotsky (1879–1940)

Lev Davodovich Bronstein (Leon Trotsky) was exiled to Siberia in 1898, for his involvement in radical groups and studied the work of Marx and Lenin there. In 1902, he escaped (using a passport in the name of a prison guard – Trotsky). He went to London, met Lenin and returned to found the St Petersburg Soviet in 1905. After 15 months in prison, he escaped in 1907, travelled, and was in the USA in 1917 at the time of the first revolution. He returned to Russia in May, became a Bolshevik, chaired the Petrograd Soviet and organised the Military Revolutionary Committee which he used to plan the Bolshevik takeover in October. He became Commissar for Foreign Affairs. In 1929, he was expelled from the party by Stalin and murdered by a Stalinist agent in Mexico in 1940.

Fig. 1 *Trotsky was a Marxist revolutionary and theorist*

LEARNING OBJECTIVES

In this chapter you will learn about:

- the causes and course of the revolution
- issues of leadership and the Tsar's abdication
- the establishment of the Provisional Government and the Petrograd Soviet
- the workings of the Dual authority.

CROSS-REFERENCE

Rodzianko is profiled in Chapter 1, page 6.

ACTIVITY

Evaluating primary sources

1. Discuss with a partner why, after receiving the telegram in Source 1, Nicholas reacted as is claimed by Source 2?
2. Analyse the value of each of these sources for an historian studying the February/March Revolution of 1917.

International Women's Day

The first National Woman's Day took place in USA in 1909. Russian women, demanding peace, not war, observed their first International Women's Day on the last Sunday in February 1913. They were led by **Aleksandra Kollontai,** who also helped organise the women's march of February 1917.

La Marseillaise: the French National Anthem, derived from the singing of the soldiers from Marseilles as they went to war on behalf of revolutionary France; to sing it is to show support for the ideals of the French Revolution – 'Liberty, Equality and Fraternity'

Cossacks: people of Ukraine and southern Russia, noted for their horsemanship and military skill, who formed military units and were fiercely loyal to the Tsar

The causes and course of the February/March revolution

By the winter of 1917, the streets of Petrograd were tense with the pent-up frustrations of the unemployed, the starving and the desperate. A demonstration by 150,000 Petrograd workers on the anniversary of Bloody Sunday in January 1917 was a hint of things to come. Nevertheless, the revolution that was to topple the Tsar was actually quite a haphazard affair, catalysed by the shortage of bread. The key events of the revolutionary days of February 1917 are given in the chart below.

Monday 14 February	c100,000 workers from 58 different factories were on strike in Petrograd. News that bread would be rationed from 1 March brought long round-the-clock queues and violent exchanges. The police were attacked as they struggled to keep order.
Wednesday 22 February	20,000 workers were locked out of the Putilov Steel Works by the management after pay talks collapsed. Workers in other factories went on strike in support.
Thursday 23 February **International Women's Day**	90,000 workers were on strike and 50 factories closed. The striking workers joined the traditional march of women from the Petrograd suburbs to the city centre for International Women's Day. Militant students and women from the bread queues also joined the lines. The city fell into chaos with c240,000 out on the streets. Order was only restored by a desperate police force in the early evening, although the day saw no loss of life.
Friday 24 February	200,000 workers were on strike and the crowds overturned Tsarist statues, waved red flags, wore red rosettes, shouted revolutionary slogans calling for an end to Tsardom and sang **'La Marseillaise'**. There was no obvious organisation from any of the radical political parties, although some radicals distributed emblems and banners bearing political demands.
Saturday 25 February	250,000 people (over half the capital's workforce) were on strike and Petrograd was at a virtual standstill. Almost all the major factories and most shops were closed. There were no newspapers and no public transport. Violence escalated as Shalfeev, in charge of the mounted police, tried to control the masses. He was set upon, dragged from his horse, beaten and shot. A band of civilians was killed by soldiers on the Nevskii Prospekt but later the same day, some **Cossacks** refused to attack a procession of strikers when ordered to do so.
Sunday 26 February	Rodzianko, the Duma President, sent the Tsar a telegram warning him of the serious situation in Petrograd (see Source 1, page 9). Nicholas ignored the warning and ordered the Duma to dissolve the next day.

Monday 27 February	The Tsar ordered Major-General Khabalov, Commander of the Petrograd Military District, to restore order by military force. Soldiers were ordered onto the streets and around 40 demonstrators in the city centre were killed. A **mutiny** began in the Volynskii regiment, where a sergeant shot his commanding officer dead. 66,000 soldiers mutinied and joined the protestors, arming them with 40,000 rifles. Police headquarters were attacked and prisons were opened. Later in the day the Duma held a meeting, despite the Tsar's orders (See Sources 3 and 4, page 13) and set up a 12-man Provisional Committee to take over the government. The army's High Command, which had already ordered troops to march to the capital to restore stability, changed their minds and ordered them to halt and give support to the Duma Committee. The same evening, revolutionaries set up a Soviet which also intended to take over the government. It began to organise food supplies for the city.
Tuesday 28 February	Nicholas II left his military headquarters at the Volynskii regiment and started to make his way back to Petrograd. He sent a telegram to Rodzianko, offering to share power with the Duma. The leader replied: 'the measures you propose are too late. The time for them has gone. There is no return.'

Aleksandra Kollontai (1872–1952) came from an aristocratic background. She studied Marx, took part in the Bloody Sunday march in 1905 and joined the Bolsheviks in 1914. She was exiled but returned from USA in March 1917, only to be arrested after the **July Days**. In government, Kollontai fought for the simplification of marriage and divorce, losing some favour with Lenin, but she later became a prominent political figure under Stalin.

CROSS-REFERENCE

For information on the **July Days**, see Chapter 3, page 21.

A CLOSER LOOK

The mutineers

Many of those ordered to shoot the demonstrators were themselves of peasant or worker background. They were the young and newly enlisted, and had joined the Petrograd garrison to await the dreaded call to proceed to the front line. Furthermore their junior officers included men from the middle-ranking 'intellectual' class, rather than from the traditional 'noble' background. These were men who had joined the army from a sense of patriotism inspired by war. Their sympathies, like the sympathies of those they commanded, lay with the masses.

Issues of leadership and the Tsar's abdication

The disturbances in Petrograd appeared spontaneous and leaderless. All the major Bolshevik leaders who had long campaigned for just this type of popular rising were absent at the time; the Social Democrats, **Vladimir Lenin** and **Julius Martov** were in Zurich and **Leon Trotsky** was in New York, while **Viktor Chernov** of the Social Revolutionary Party was in Paris. Nevertheless, research by James White, Professor of Russian History at Glasgow University in 1997, found that a liberal group, including **Pavel Milyukov**, **Aleksandr Guchkov**, Aleksandr Konovalov and Mikhail Tereshchenko, was already planning a coup to topple the Tsar and were considerably alarmed by the turn of events in February which they feared might get out of hand. White also identified a revolutionary workers' group based in the working-class Vyborg district of Petrograd. Consequently, recent thinking suggests that there were small bands of revolutionary activists at work in February 1917, although whether they instigated the troubles or merely tried to influence the progression of events is still not clear.

Fig. 2 *Aleksandra Kollontai*

CROSS-REFERENCE

Lenin and **Martov** are profiled in the Introduction, on page xv and **Trotsky** in Chapter 1, page 9.

Milyukov and **Guchkov** are profiled on page 7.

Viktor Chernov (1873–1952)
had been attracted to the Populist
cause and became engaged in
revolutionary activity as a teenager.
In 1894 he joined People's Will and
was arrested, spending some time
in exile. He travelled to Switzerland
in 1899 and was to provide
much of the intellectual input
into the founding of the Socialist
Revolutionary Party in 1901. He
went on to become the leader of
the Socialist Revolutionaries in
the Second Duma of 1907 and
was Minister of Agriculture in the
Provisional Government of 1917.
After the Bolsheviks came to power,
he settled in the USA.

ACTIVITY

Pair work

Discuss the Soviet view with a
partner. How far was the rising of
February 1917 spontaneous?

CROSS-REFERENCE

Kerensky is profiled in Chapter 1,
page 2.

ACTIVITY

Evaluating primary sources

With reference to Sources 3 and
4, and other information in this
section, make notes on the dilemma
facing the Duma on 27 February
1917. You could recreate the scene
in the Duma with members of your
group, putting forward different
views about how to react to the
circumstances of that day.

A CLOSER LOOK

The revolutionary opposition

Soviet historians (writing after the Bolsheviks came to power), interpreted
the events of February 1917 as the result of the inevitable class struggle
between the bourgeoisie-proletarian forces on one side and traditional
aristocratic forces on the urban workers in St Petersburg. Since they could
not point to direct Bolshevik leadership (as the leaders were either in
prison or exile), they preferred to accept the idea of a spontaneous rising
driven by the oppressed working class.

Certainly, the speed of events in February took both liberals and socialists by
surprise, as described in the following sources:

SOURCE 3

Adapted from Vasily Vitalyevich Shulgin, *Days of the Russian Revolution:
Memoirs from the Right, 1905–1917*, 1927. Shulgin was a Russian conservative
who had supported the Progressive Bloc and Nicholas' abdication but favoured a
constitutional monarchy under the Grand Duke Mikhail. He refers in this extract
to a meeting of Duma representatives on 27 February 1917:

The Liberals were dazed by the passing events. They wrung their hands and
repeated 'I told you so.' When they came to, they found the Socialists busily at
work. In the days of the Duma, its members regarded themselves as statesmen
and socialists like **Kerensky** as street-corner agitators. After the disappearance
of the monarchy, the tables were turned. Kerensky spoke up: 'We must not
delay! May I tell the troops that the State Duma is with them?' He spoke
with positivity as one having authority. 'He is their dictator,' I heard a fellow
Duma-member whisper near me. Kerensky stood determined, uttering sharp,
almost contemptuous words. He grew on the mud of the revolution. From that
time on, the Duma practically ceased to exist. Kerensky had revolutionary
contacts which explains why, during the first period of the revolution, (without
taking into consideration his personal qualities, for he was a first-class actor)
Kerensky played such a prominent part.

SOURCE 4

Adapted from Alexander Kerensky, *Crucifixion of Liberty*, 1934. Kerensky was
a socialist member of the third and fourth State Dumas and was to become
Minister of Justice, Minister of War and finally Prime Minister of the 1917
Provisional Government in August. Here, he is writing about the meeting of
Duma representatives on 27 February:

I was awakened by a voice saying, 'Get up! The Volynskii Regiment has
mutinied. You are wanted at the Duma at once.' I hurried to the Duma. My first
thought was to keep the Duma in session and to establish close contact with
the army and the people. How could I have guessed as I rushed out of my
apartment in what a different position I would be when I returned to it? How
could I have imagined that I would never return to my home again but for two
or three hours? I arrived at the Tauride Palace, seat of the Duma, and here I was
swept up by the whirlwind in which I was to live for eight months. It was an
extraordinary time, an inspired time. I learned that Rodzianko had received an
order from Nicholas II dissolving the Duma. I rushed to the telephone and urged
some friends to go to the barracks of the insurgent regiments. I addressed the
troops myself and asked them to follow me.

The emergence of **soviets**, both in Petrograd and in other cities and towns, suggests some sort of organisation by socialist leaders and the Petrograd Soviet set up by revolutionary leaders in the capital on 27 February was to play a major role in events.

The Petrograd Soviet agreed, under pressure from the soldiers, and from mutineers at the **Kronstadt naval base**, that each regiment should elect committees and send representatives to the Soviet. The 'Order No. 1' – a charter of soldiers' rights – was produced on 1 March. It promised:

- All units to elect a deputy to the Soviet and agree to the political control of the Petrograd Soviet.
- The Military Commission of the Duma to be obeyed, only if it agreed with the Soviet's orders.
- All weapons to be controlled by elected soldiers' committees – not officers.
- All soldiers to enjoy full citizens' rights when off duty – for example, no requirement to salute or stand to attention.
- No honorific titles to be used for officers – only Mr General, Mr Colonel, etc.
- Officers were not to address soldiers in the 'ty' form. (Like 'tu' in French, this second person singular form was used to address children and peasants.)

The Petrograd Soviet took the official title of 'Soviet of Workers' and Soldiers' Deputies' and by 10 March it had 3000 members. Because it was so large, most of its work was done by the executive committee which was dominated by socialist intellectuals including **Aleksandr Kerensky**.

Nicholas never returned to Petrograd. His train was diverted by rebellious railway workers and forced to stop at Pskov, 200 miles south of his destination. The Tsar was under pressure from the Chief of General Staff, General Alexeev, to resign. Alexeev had been reassured by an agreement on 1 March that the Petrograd Soviet would recognise a provisional government formed by members of the Duma, and suggested that the Tsar should resign in favour of his son, Aleksei, with Nicholas' younger brother, Mikhail, acting as regent. On 2 March, Nicholas agreed to their demand. However, fearing that Aleksei's health was too delicate he named Grand Duke Mikhail as the new Tsar (even though he had not been consulted). He added that Mikhail should lead the country 'in complete union with the representatives of the people in the legislative bodies on principles to be established by them and to take an inviolable oath to this effect'.

By the time the members of the Duma Committee reached Pskov on 2 March, the terms of Nicholas' abdication had already been agreed, although in the event Mikhail refused the offer of the throne.

The Tsar and his family were placed under house arrest, as were most of the members of the Tsar's Council of Ministers. Thus 304 years of the Romanov dynasty came to an end.

 PRACTICE QUESTION

'It was economic distress in Petrograd that brought about Nicholas II's abdication in March 1917.' Explain why you agree or disagree with this view.

A CLOSER LOOK

Beyond Petrograd

Revolutionary disturbances spread beyond Petrograd to the Kronstadt naval base just outside the city, Moscow and other industrial cities and rural areas. In cities, workers seized control of their factories, set up their own soviets and deposed their former bosses, sometimes dumping them in a nearby river! Everywhere, rebellious peoples set up their own elected regional assemblies and soviets. In the provinces such as Finland,

A CLOSER LOOK

Soviets

Soviets had appeared in Russia during the revolution of 1905 and were literally 'councils'. They were not necessarily supportive of any one particular party and it was not originally a political term. Following the revolution of February/March 1917, soviets sprang up in many cities and towns, but that in Petrograd, often known simply as 'The Soviet', was the most important.

KEY TERM

Kronstadt naval base: the headquarters of the Russian Baltic Fleet (19 miles west of Petrograd at the head of the Gulf of Finland)

CROSS-REFERENCE

You can find a Key Profile of **Kerensky** in Chapter 1, page 2.

STUDY TIP

It is important that you provide a balanced answer and you should bear in mind that the economic distress was more a catalyst for the abdication than its sole cause. Reflect on the situation before February 1917 and, before writing, you could make a spider diagram of long- and short-term reasons why Tsar Nicholas was forced or chose to abdicate.

Poland, Ukraine and the Caucasus, national minorities declared their independence. The army, technically under the command of the Petrograd Soviet, disintegrated into semi-independent bodies and soldiers' soviets without clear leadership and coordination. In the countryside, peasants formed peasant soviets, attacked landlords' properties and felled trees illegally. An 'All-Russian Congress of Soviets' met in Petrograd in June 1917, with representatives from 350 towns, villages and military bases throughout Russia.

The establishment of the Dual authority: the Provisional Government and the Petrograd Soviet

The Provisional Government

Grand Duke Mikhail relinquished political authority to a hastily convened 'Provisional Government', under Prince Lvov, a wealthy aristocrat and *zemstvo* leader. Its members represented a cross-section of the influential elites and comprised those who had formerly favoured constitutional monarchy – liberals, moderate socialists and Kadets.

It was the original intention that the Provisional Government would, as its name suggests, be temporary and that elections would be held as soon as possible for a new Constituent Assembly which would draw up a new **constitution** for Russia. Nevertheless, the Provisional Government was accepted as legitimate (thanks to Mikhail's blessing) by the old tsarist civil service, army officers and the police. It set itself up in the Duma chamber in the right wing of the Tauride Palace in Petrograd and so perpetuated its rule, although never rejecting the idea of elections at a later date.

The Petrograd Soviet

The mass of workers, soldiers and peasants regarded the Provisional Government as a self-appointed committee of the wealthy, tainted by their previous associations with tsardom. For them, the Petrograd Soviet was the more democratic organisation. It established its headquarters in the left wing of the Tauride Palace and was primarily composed of radical socialist intellectuals, Mensheviks and Social Revolutionaries, but also a small number of Bolsheviks. Of its executive committee, only seven of the first 42 committee members were workers themselves, although it claimed direct democratic authority since its members were elected by various lesser St Petersburg soviets. However, it seemed to lack the confidence needed to assume direct control and, thanks to some delicate negotiations by Kerensky, the only member of both the Provisional Government and the Soviet, an agreement to work together was reached. This laid the foundations for the period of 'Dual authority' or *dvoevlastie*, whereby Russia was governed by an alliance of the Provisional Government and Soviet.

The Soviet made no attempt to demand land redistribution or the nationalisation of industry but accepted the Provisional Government's promises of:

- a general amnesty for political prisoners
- civil liberties
- the abolition of legal disabilities based on class, religion and nationality
- freedom to organise trade unions and to strike
- the election of a Constituent Assembly to determine Russia's future.

In April, the Provisional Government made a further statement that 'the power of the state should be based, not on violence and coercion, but on the consent of free citizens to the power they themselves created.' The new government gave freedom of religion and the press, abolished the death penalty at the front, replaced the tsarist police force with a 'people's militia' and dismissed Provincial Governors, giving their work to the elected *zemstva*.

The workings of the Dual authority

Rule by a mixture of liberals and radicals was never going to be easy. The Soviet's 'Order No. 1' had said that soldiers and workers should obey the Provisional Government, but only when the Soviet agreed with the Provisional Government's decisions, and there were many points of disagreement.

While the Provisional Government tried to discipline army deserters and restore order in towns and countryside, the Soviet encouraged peasants and workers to defy authority and assert their 'rights'. In addition, while the Provisional Government believed that the change of regime should lead to an all-out effort to 'win' the war, the Soviet view was that the war should be ended as quickly as possible 'without annexation' of territory by the Germans as the price of peace.

Milyukov's announcement, in April 1917, that the government would continue fighting until a 'just peace' had been won, unleashed a storm of protest forcing Milyukov and **Guchkov** to resign under popular pressure led by the Petrograd Soviet in May. They were replaced by socialists from the Soviet. Viktor Chernov became Minister of Agriculture, Aleksandr Kerensky became Minister of War and two further Mensheviks were added to the cabinet. In July 1917, **Lvov** was replaced as Chairman (effectively Prime Minister) by Kerensky.

The members of the Provisional Government found themselves in a near impossible situation. The war was deeply unpopular, yet they felt bound by their alliance with Britain and France and relied on French loans for survival. Whilst committed to elections for a Constitutent Assembly, they dared not proceed since it was clear that the SRs would win the support of the peasants and, by June 1917, that the Bolsheviks would attract the workers' votes in the cities. Elections were constantly postponed and since the Provisional Government had said that key policy changes, such as land redistribution to the peasants, should await a Constituent Assembly, little got done. The Soviet offered no alternative leadership, with its largely SR and Menshevik leadership believing that their main task was to protect the rights of workers and peasants as the **'bourgeois revolution' forecast by Marx** proceeded. The result was complete paralysis.

Summary

In February 1917, as a result of a largely spontaneous breakdown of order in Petrograd and a mutiny in the Tsar's garrisons in the capital, the autocracy collapsed. The Tsar was forced to abdicate and authority passed to two bodies which, between them, claimed to represent both traditional elites and the workers and peasants: the Provisional Government and the Petrograd Soviet. The former dominated and so the traditional ruling group survived. However, this uneasy conjunction with left-wing forces made it virtually impossible for anything to get done.

 PRACTICE QUESTION

Evaluating primary sources

With reference to Sources 3 and 4 and your understanding of the historical context, which of these two sources is more valuable in explaining the role of Kerensky in establishing the Dual authority in Russia in 1917?

CROSS-REFERENCE

Marx's theory about the stages of revolution is outlined in the Introduction, page xv.

Milyukov is profiled in Chapter 1, page 7.

Guchkov is profiled in Chapter 1, page 7.

STUDY TIP

Whilst these sources share some important detail, they convey rather different views of Kerensky's actions in February 1917. You will need to evaluate the provenance of each source and comment on the tone adopted. You must also assess the value of the content and argument, applying your own contextual knowledge of the different types of opposition groups that existed at the time to explain what is written and establish which source is the more valuable.

STUDY TIP

The value of the sources should be determined by a thorough examination of their provenance, as well as comment on their content, tone and emphasis. Do not forget to use your own contextual knowledge to support the points you make.

 PRACTICE QUESTION

Evaluating primary sources

With reference to Sources 1, 2 and 3 and your understanding of the historical context, assess the value of these three sources to an historian studying how far Nicholas II was responsible for the revolution of February 1917.

STUDY TIP

An essay should be an argument and you will need to balance the impact of economic distress against other factors that produced revolution to reach a substantiated conclusion. However, it is important to look at the words of the questions in depth. You might break down 'economic distress' to look at, for example: distress in the cities and countryside; distress in Petrograd and elsewhere; distress affecting soldiers, workers and peasants.

 PRACTICE QUESTION

How significant was economic distress in the revolution of February/March 1917?

3 Developments between the revolutions of 1917

Fig. 1 *An idealised picture of the storming of the Winter Palace, Petrograd. Soldiers, sailors and workers are shown to exemplify the 'workers' revolution' in this piece of Soviet propaganda*

KEY CHRONOLOGY

1917	
3 Apr	Lenin returns and the April Theses are compiled over the next few weeks
3 Jun	The first All-Russian Congress Soviet meets
2 Jul	Trotsky joins the Bolsheviks
3–5 Jul	The 'July Days' of anti-government demonstrations in Petrograd
3–7 Jul	Bolshevik leaders (including Trotsky) are arrested; Lenin flees to Finland
18 Jul	Kerensky (Socialist) becomes Prime Minister
26–30 Aug	Kornilov's coup fails and the Bolshevik Red Guards are given arms
Sept	Trotsky becomes chairman of the Petrograd Soviet; the Bolsheviks command majorites in both the Petrograd and Moscow Soviets
10 Oct	Lenin attends a meeting of the Bolshevik Central Committee and his call for a Bolshevik-led revolution is agreed
16 Oct	Military Revolutionary Committee set up under Trotsky and Dzerzhinsky

The return of Lenin

At the time of the revolution in February/March 1917, the Bolsheviks were still only a small party of 23,000 members. They only had 40 representatives in the Soviet of 1500 and all their major leaders were in exile. The first to reach Petrograd were **Lev Kamenev** and **Josef Vissarionovich Djugashvily** (Stalin) who arrived in mid-March and took over control of the party newspaper,

Lev Borisovich Kamenev (1883–1936) was the son of a Jewish railway engineer, who joined the Social Democrats in 1901. Arrested many times, he was deported to Siberia, where he met Stalin in 1915. He returned in April 1917 and edited *Pravda*, opposing Lenin's April Theses. With Zinoviev, he voted against an armed uprising in October 1917, preferring a coalition with the Socialists. Nevertheless he was made a Commissar in Lenin's government and joined Trotsky at the Brest-Litovsk negotiations, making peace terms with the Germans in 1918. He was forced from power by Stalin, expelled from the party in 1932 and executed in 1936.

Josef Vissarionovich Djugashvily (Stalin) (1879–1953), the son of a Georgian cobbler, was one of the few leading Bolsheviks who could claim peasant roots. He had trained as a priest but was attracted by Social Democracy. He was repeatedly arrested and exiled to Siberia, but he escaped several times, taking the name 'Stalin' (man of steel). He became a Bolshevik and helped raise money by robbing banks. He was in Siberia from 1912 to 1917 but returned in 1917. He played only a minor role in the October Revolution but was made Commissar for Nationalities because of his background. He eventually took the leadership of Russia after Lenin's death and established himself as a dictator until his death.

Pravda (The Truth). They accepted the policy adopted by other left-wing socialists, to support the Provisional Government, the continuation of the war and the Soviet leadership. It was only after Lenin returned to Russia from Switzerland on 3 April 1917, that the Bolsheviks began to forge their own path.

The turn of events in February had caught the exiled Lenin by surprise and he had to enlist the help of the Germans (whom the Russians were fighting) to enable his return. The Germans saw the advantage of allowing Bolsheviks (who were opposed to the war) to enter Russia and stir up trouble. To enable his return, they allowed Lenin to travel from exile in Switzerland, through Germany to neutral Sweden and thence to Finland and Petrograd.

The sealed train

Lenin travelled with 31 comrades on a German train from Gottmadingen on the Swiss boarder via Frankfurt, Berlin and Stockholm to Petrograd. The train had only one carriage and was sealed – insofar as there were no passport or luggage inspections carried out. Lenin had his own compartment, where he worked on his own. His fellow travellers used the corridor and the other compartments, and passed their time (to his annoyance), drinking and singing. Smokers were issued with a 'first class pass' which gave them priority in the use of the lavatory – the only place where smoking was allowed.

Fig. 2 *Lenin's journey from Switzerland to Petrograd*

Apart from six months in 1905 to 1906, Lenin had been in exile for the previous 17 years and he was not quite sure what would await him in Russia. In fact, he was greeted by cheering crowds at the Finland station in Petrograd, where he gave a rousing speech, prepared during his long journey.

Lenin's ideology and the April Theses

Lenin returned with a ready-made political programme which went beyond anything that other left-wing leaders had been saying. He had mapped this programme in 'Letters from Afar', written between 7 and 26 March; in these, he made it clear that the Party's job was to lead the people forward to a second **revolution**. At the time, the Petrograd Soviet, all Mensheviks and most Bolsheviks believed in the need for a 'bourgeois stage' of revolution. Lenin (like Trotsky, who independently came to the same conclusion) did not accept this. He believed that the Russian middle class was too weak to carry through a full 'bourgeois revolution' and that to allow the middle classes to continue in power was to hold the inevitable proletarian revolution back. Since he believed that the whole of Europe was on the brink of socialist revolution anyway, he felt the Russian revolution had no need to confine itself to bourgeois democratic objectives. This belief is sometimes referred to as the theory of **'permanent revolution'**.

Lenin's political programme was reissued as his 'April Theses':

It has been suggested by Orlando Figes that many of the workers who turned out to cheer Lenin were more attracted by the prospect of free beer than by sympathies for Bolshevism. There had been a number of 'welcoming receptions' since the revolution and as Lenin's return coincided with the Easter holiday, it is perhaps not surprising that he attracted a large crowd set on 'partying'.

CROSS-REFERENCE

To recap on **Marx's theory of revolution**, look back to the Introduction, page xv.

KEY TERM

permanent revolution: the concept that continuing revolutionary progress within the USSR was dependent on a continuing process of revolution in other countries

> ### SOURCE 1
>
> Adapted from parts of Lenin's 'April Theses' (originally entitled 'The Tasks of the Proletariat in the Present Revolution') published in *Pravda* (the Bolshevik newspaper) 7 April 1917:
>
> - The specific feature of the present situation in Russia is that the country is passing from the first stage of the revolution – which, owing to the insufficient class-consciousness and organisation of the proletariat, placed power in the hands of the bourgeoisie – to its second stage, which must place power in the hands of the proletariat and the poorest sections of the peasants.
> - No support for the Provisional Government; the utter falsity of all its promises should be made clear.
> - Recognition of the fact that in most of the soviets our Party is in a minority, as against a bloc of all the petty-bourgeois opportunist elements, including Popular Socialists and Socialist-Revolutionaries who have yielded to the influence of the bourgeoisie. As long as we are in the minority we carry on the work of criticising and exposing errors and at the same time we preach the necessity of transferring the entire state power to the Soviets of Workers' Deputies.

ACTIVITY

Evaluating primary sources

With reference to Source 1 and the following text, make a list of Lenin's aims in April 1917.

As well as explaining Lenin's ideology, his April Theses also made demands that:
- the war should be brought to an immediate end
- power should be transferred to the soviets
- all land should be taken over by the state and re-allocated to peasants by local soviets.

These demands have often been summed up as 'peace, bread and land', supported by the motto, 'All power to the Soviets'.

The Bolshevik Party in April 1917 was not, however, under Lenin's tight control (that was a myth spread by later Soviet historians). When his proposals were first put to a meeting of the Social Democrats (convened in an attempt to bring about the reconciliation of the Bolsheviks and Mensheviks) they caused uproar among the delegates.

- Some Bolsheviks feared that Lenin had grown out of touch during his years of exile and that his radical proposals would do more harm than good.
- There were allegations that Lenin was in the pay of the Germans (which were to some extent true).
- The Mensheviks feared Lenin would undermine what they had been doing, and, by stirring up discontent, would provoke a right-wing reaction.
- Some thought Lenin's call to oppose the Provisional Government was unrealistic since the Bolsheviks were still in a minority among the Socialists.

SOURCE 2

Adapted from an article in the left-wing liberal British newspaper, the *Daily Chronicle* on 22 April 1917, written by journalist Harold Williams, who was a linguist living in Russia as an unofficial adviser to the British Ambassador:

Lenin, leader of the extreme **faction** of the Social Democrats, arrived here on Monday night by way of Germany. His action in accepting from the German government a passage from Switzerland through Germany arouses intense indignation here. He has come back breathing fire, and demanding the immediate and unconditional conclusions of peace, civil war against the army and government, and vengeance on Kerensky and **Chkheidze**, whom he describes as traitors to the cause of International Socialism. At the meeting of Social Democrats yesterday his wild rant was received in dead silence, and he was vigorously attacked, not only by the more moderate Social Democrats, but by members of his own faction.

Lenin was left absolutely without supporters. The sharp repulse given to this firebrand was a healthy sign of the growth of the practical sense of the Socialist wing, and the generally moderate and sensible tone of the conference of provincial workers' and soldiers' deputies was another hopeful indication of the passing of the revolutionary fever.

(AS LEVEL) PRACTICE QUESTION

Evaluating primary sources

With reference to Sources 1 and 2 and your understanding of the historical context, which of these two sources is more valuable in explaining the significance of Lenin's return in April 1917?

Fig. 3 *Lenin addressing crowds of workers in 1917*

Lenin eventually got his way due to his skills of persuasion, tactful retreat and compromise, threats of resignation and appeals to the rank and file. He sought converts at party and factory meetings (wearing a worker's cap in an attempt to look more proletarian) and abandoned his call for an immediate overthrow of the Provisional Government, thus winning over those who had feared civil war. In his speeches, he claimed personal credit for much that was already happening in Russia, not least the peasants' seizure of land in the countryside (which actually occurred in the absence of any authority to control their actions). Lenin similarly claimed credit for the massive anti-war demonstration in Petrograd in April (following Milyukov's announcement that the government would continue fighting 'until victory'), which led to Milyukov and Guchkov's resignations from the Provisional Government in May and **a move to the left** with the inclusion of four socialists in the cabinet. By the end of April, Lenin had won over the majority of the **Central Committee of the Bolshevik Party** by sheer force of personality.

However, winning wider support required persistence. When the first 'All-Russian Congress of Soviets' met in Petrograd on 3 June, it passed a vote of confidence in the Provisional Government by 543 votes to 126, although the Bolsheviks did well in the city Duma elections the same month. In massive June demonstrations, called by the leaders of the Petrograd Soviet in an attempt to outmanoeuvre the Bolsheviks, Bolshevik banners dominated the march.

The July Days

Maintaining control over the working classes who flocked to the Bolsheviks in increasing numbers as the weeks progressed was not always easy. At the **Kronstadt naval base**, the sailors organised their own armed demonstration in July, using Bolshevik slogans. The demonstrations spread to the centre of Petrograd, placing Lenin in a difficult position. He could neither condemn the action, nor give full support since he knew a premature revolution risked defeat. Although the Bolsheviks tried to turn the protests into a peaceful procession, when shots were fired at the demonstrators, there was chaos and uncontrolled rioting which threatened to undermine Lenin's credibility.

The Provisional Government, supported by Mensheviks and SRs in the Soviet, brought in reinforcements to crush the demonstrations. Although the Bolsheviks helped force the demonstrators out of the Peter and Paul Fortress, which they had seized, and played a part in negotiating the disarming and arrest of the sailors, they were blamed for the bloodshed. The offices of the Bolshevik newspaper *Pravda* were closed and warrants were issued for the arrest of their leaders. Lenin and Stalin fled but Trotsky and Kamenev were imprisoned. Even the Bolshevik newspaper *Izvestia* (News) denounced the role of their leaders, suggesting that Lenin was working in the pay of the Germans and against Russia's best interests. Bolshevik propaganda was burned and Lenin's reputation fell, for fleeing rather than leading, whilst other leaders languished in gaol. On 8 July, Kerensky replaced Prince Lvov as Prime Minister and it appeared that the Bolsheviks' moment had passed.

A CLOSER LOOK

Lenin, Trotsky and the demonstrations of the July Days

It is unclear whether the rebellion was actually fomented by the Bolsheviks. Lenin had been on holiday when the rioting broke out and always claimed that the demonstrations were spontaneous. He immediately returned, but just as quickly fled in disguise, eventually moving to Finland where he remained until October. Trotsky, who had arrived back in Russia in May, had not immediately committed himself to the Bolshevik cause.

CROSS-REFERENCE

The **move to the left** with the change in membership of the Provisional Government is discussed in Chapter 3, page 21.

KEY TERM

Central Committee of the Bolshevik Party: from 1912, this leading group determined the Bolsheviks' broad policy objectives; it comprised 21 members in 1917

CROSS-REFERENCE

The **Kronstadt naval base** and its role in the revolution are introduced in Chapter 2, page 13.

A CLOSER LOOK

The July Days (3–5 July)

Between February and June, grain prices had doubled in Petrograd, while shortages of fuel and raw materials had forced the closure of 586 factories, with the loss of 100,000 jobs. The workers were demanding price controls but the Provisional Government was frightened to act against the industrialists. Consequently, when 20,000 armed sailors from Kronstadt appeared on the streets, workers and soldiers joined them. They chanted Bolshevik slogans, attacked property, looted shops and seized the railway stations and other key buildings. Some even invaded the Tauride Palace demanding that the Soviet take power.

Nevertheless, he was elected to the Executive Committee of the All-Russian Congress of Soviets in June and was accused of stirring up the July Days demonstrations and imprisoned. It was while in prison that he became a committed Bolshevik.

The Kornilov coup and the role of the Provisional Government and Trotsky

In June 1917, a major offensive in Galicia was led by Brusilov in the hope of rallying the nation. However, the Russian advance was beaten back with heavy losses. Desertions escalated and the anti-war sentiment grew so strong that, in July, Kerensky appointed General Lavr Kornilov as Commander-in-Chief of the army in an effort to restore discipline. Among other measures, the death penalty was reinstated, as the only way of controlling the troops.

Kerensky's Moscow State Conference, called to demonstrate political unity, was boycotted by the Bolsheviks, who organised a general strike, and even the Mensheviks and SRs spoke out against Kornilov's measures. Those on the right, however, particularly landowners and businessmen who felt the Provisional Government had done little to protect their land, property and interests, saw Kornilov as their saviour. Even the moderate **Milyukov** and the **Kadets**, whose influence on the Provisional Government was waning, believed that a military takeover by Kornilov would be preferable to a Socialist regime.

CROSS-REFERENCE

Milyukov is profiled in Chapter 1, page 7.

A CLOSER LOOK

The situation in summer 1917

By the summer of 1917, the Provisional Government had little support. Food supplies were chaotic in the towns and although the government granted an eight-hour day, real wages fell rapidly as prices rose. By October prices were c755 per cent above pre-war levels. Workers' hopes that factory soviets would help them were dashed in August when the right of factory owners to dismiss workers who went on strike was confirmed and meetings of factory soviets during working hours were forbidden. The continuation of war and the government's failure to redistribute land also lost it support in the countryside. The peasants simply seized land anyway. Although an electoral commission was established in May, to arrange elections for November, suspicion that the 'bourgeois' government was deliberately delaying a move to greater democracy in order to preserve its own power was rife. The group that benefited most from this widespread disillusionment was the Bolsheviks.

STUDY TIP

It could help to make a two-column plan. On one side, list examples that would suggest an absence of support, considering the hostility of the soldiers, peasants, workers and socialists and even the right-wing; on the other, list ways in which the Provisional Government still commanded support, considering the views of the moderates as well as the government's ability to launch the Brusilov offensive and maintain control. Decide whether you would, on balance, agree or disagree with the quotation and provide an argued, but balanced response.

AS LEVEL PRACTICE QUESTION

'By the summer of 1917 there was no support for the Provisional Government in Russia.' Explain why you agree or disagree with this view.

ACTIVITY

Although it is difficult to be precise about the Kornilov coup because it was a secret plot and few written records exist, try to discover what you can about Kornilov and his plans and discuss your findings with the rest of your group.

At the end of August, Kornilov ordered six regiments of troops to march on Petrograd – presumably intending to crush the Soviet and establish a military dictatorship. However, this attempted coup failed when Kerensky, who, it would seem, had at first supported Kornilov, panicked. Kerensky ordered Kornilov to call a halt. When he failed to do so, Kerensky released imprisoned Bolsheviks (who had the confidence of the working class) and provided workers with weapons from the government's armouries to halt Kornilov's advance. Kornilov's supply lines were cut and the coup leaders arrested.

Fig. 4   *Red Guards in Petrograd*

The Bolsheviks were the main beneficiaries of the 'Kornilov coup'. Although still a minority in the Soviet, they took the lead in organising the Petrograd **Red Guards**, creating a more efficient paramilitary unit out of the various militia groups attached to factories that had been set up to defend workers' interests in March and April. They milked the propaganda opportunities the affair presented and poured scorn on the Kerensky government, basking in the reputation of being the only group to have opposed Kornilov consistently. Lenin sent orders from Finland urging his followers to keep up the pressure and 'Committees to save the Revolution' were set up throughout the country.

The Bolsheviks were elected in increased numbers to soviets throughout urban Russia. Bolshevik membership, which had stood at 23,000 in February, reached 200,000 by the beginning of October, by which time the party was producing 41 newspapers and commanded a force of 10,000 Red Guards. The Bolsheviks won a majority in both the Petrograd and Moscow Soviets in September, and on 26 September Trotsky even became chairman of the executive committee of the Petrograd Soviet.

On 5 October, Kerensky sent some of the more radical army units out of Petrograd, to prepare for front-line service. This was no doubt done out of fear of a Bolshevik uprising, but it proved a political miscalculation in the inflamed political atmosphere of the time. Claiming that Kerensky was abandoning the capital to allow it to fall to the Germans, on 9 October, the Soviet adopted a resolution, written by Trotsky, to create a 'military revolutionary centre' to protect Petrograd from the attacks being prepared by 'civil Kornilovites'. In other words, it played on the fear that government ministers might support a right-wing coup.

Lenin and the Central Committee of the Bolshevik Party

From mid-September, Lenin (still in hiding in Finland) had begun bombarding the 12-man Central Committee of the Bolshevik Party with letters demanding that they prepare for revolution and the seizure of power. On 12 September, he suggested that 'History will not forgive us if we do not assume power now,' but three days later the Committee voted against a coup. Even Lenin's threat of resignation from the Central Committee failed to move them. The Committee's two most prominent members, **Lev Kamenev** and **Grigorii Zinoviev**, in particular, urged restraint, fearing that Russia was not yet economically ready for revolution. They even burnt some of Lenin's letters.

KEY TERM

Red Guards: loyal, volunteer soldiers mostly recruited from the factory workers; they were given a basic training and comprised young and old alike

CROSS-REFERENCE

Revisit the Key Profile of **Lev Kamenev** earlier in this chapter, on page 18.

KEY PROFILE

Grigorii Zinoviev (1883–1936) was of Jewish origin. He joined the Social Democratic party in 1901 and was a member of the Central Committee from 1907 to 1927. He was close to Lenin in exile and returned with him in 1917 in the sealed train. However, he supported Kamenev against the October Revolution, favouring cooperation with other socialist groups. He became the head of the party's Petrograd organisation but was expelled from the party by Stalin and executed in 1936.

ACTIVITY

Evaluating primary sources

With reference to Source 3, discuss with a partner:
1. Why did Lenin believe that the Bolsheviks were ready for revolution in mid-October?
2. Why did he believe it was 'senseless' to wait for the Constituent Assembly?

ACTIVITY

Why do you think the members of the Central Committee were so reluctant to act in October 1917? One half of your group could give a speech, perhaps following on from Source 3, such as Lenin might have given to persuade the Committee. The other half should listen, question and point out the issues and problems.

KEY PROFILE

Felix Dzerzhinsky (1877–1926) had joined the Social Democrats in 1895 and had spent much time in exile before 1917. His loyalty to Lenin and reputation for toughness led to his involvement with the Revolutionary Military Committee. In December 1917 he was made the head of the **Cheka** – a new secret police force set up by Lenin. In this position he was to be responsible for the 'Red Terror' of the 1920s.

Kamenev and Zinoviev believed that they should not act before the Constituent Assembly elections (the date of which was still undecided). However, Trotsky suggested they should work through the Petrograd Soviet and wait for the Congress of Soviets which was due to be convened on 26 October. He believed that, at this Congress, they could win the support of all socialist parties for a soviet government without having to resort to violence.

An increasingly frustrated Lenin slipped back into Russia in disguise and on 10 October harangued the Central Committee of the Bolshevik party all night.

SOURCE 3

Adapted from a speech by Lenin to the Central Committee of the Russian Social Democrat Party, 10 October 1917, recorded in the minutes of the meeting:

The decisive moment is near. The international situation is such that we must take the initiative. On 3–5 July, positive action on our part would have failed because the majority was not behind us. Since then we have gone up in leaps and bounds. Absenteeism and indifference among the masses can be explained by the fact that the masses are fed up with words and resolutions. The majority is now behind us. Politically the situation is completely ripe for a transfer of power. The agrarian movement is going in the same direction. The slogan for the land to be transferred has become the general slogan for all peasants. So the political circumstances are ripe. We have to talk about the technical side. That is the crux of the matter. Yet we are inclined to regard the systematic preparation of an insurrection as something akin to a political sin. It is senseless to wait for the Constituent Assembly, for this means complicating our task.

Lenin finally succeeded (with a vote of ten to two) in persuading the committee that 'an armed rising is the order of the day'. Trotsky took Lenin's side but Zinoviev and Kamenev refused to agree and published their own views in the newspaper *Novaia zhin* (New Life), declaring that, 'If we take power now and we are forced into a revolutionary war, the mass of soldiers will not support us.'

Trotsky and the final preparations for revolution

Once the vote for action had been carried, it was largely left to Trotsky to organise the revolution. He sent Bolshevik speakers around the factories, whipping up support, and in accordance with the Soviet resolution of 5 October, a 'Military Revolutionary Committee' was set up under Trotsky and **Dzerzhinsky** on 16 October. This comprised 66 members – 48 of them Bolsheviks. Trotsky massed troops at the Bolshevik headquarters in the Smolny Institute and, since the Mensheviks and SRs refused to cooperate, these became a Bolshevik force made up of militias from the Bolshevik Red Guards, former soldiers and policemen.

Commissars were sent to all Petrograd's garrison units and 15 of the 18 declared their allegiance to the Soviet, rather than the Provisional Government. These Commissars ensured loyalty and issued orders and organised weapon supplies. In total, the Committee came to control 200,000 Red Guards, 60,000 Baltic sailors and 150,000 soldiers of the remaining Petrograd Garrison units. A state of mutiny and armed revolution was thus established even before the 'Bolshevik Revolution' officially began on 25 October.

Extension

John Reed, an American journalist who was in Russia in 1917 has provided a valuable account of the momentous days surrounding the Bolshevik takeover of power in his book, *Ten Days that Shook the World*. He describes, for example, how in October the Smolny Institute, a former Convent School for the daughters of the Russian nobility, was used by the Bolshevik Central Committee and the Military Revolutionary Committee as their headquarters, with throngs of workers and soldiers swarming through its hundred or so huge rooms, linked by vaulted corridors and lit by rare electric lights. Try to get hold of a copy and read about events for yourself.

Summary

Summary

1. Create a timeline table for the months between the revolutions of 1917 (February/March–October/November) with three columns. Use the first column for dates, the second for the key events and developments, and the third for a summary of the significance of each event or development. Record political developments in one colour and economic and social changes in another.
2. Divide into three groups. Each should find evidence of responsibility for the collapse of the Provisional Government with reference to one of the following: a) The role of Lenin, b) the role of Trosky and c) the role of the Provisional Government. Share your findings and debate which was the most responsible.

 PRACTICE QUESTION

Evaluating primary sources

With reference to Sources 1, 2 and 3 and your understanding of the historical context, assess the value of these three sources to an historian studying the role of Lenin in developments between the revolutions of 1917.

 PRACTICE QUESTION

To what extent can the Dual authority arrangement be held responsible for the failure of the Provisional Government to consolidate and maintain its power in Russia between March and October 1917?

You should examine the provenance, content, tone and emphasis of each source, identifying the value of each for a greater understanding of Lenin. Do not merely look at the literal meaning of the words (particularly in Sources 1 and 3) but reflect on what the choice of language and way of delivery tells us about Lenin – as a leader, theorist and personality.

It might be helpful to look back to Chapter 2 to remind yourself of the workings of the Dual authority arrangement, though it is most important to draw on the developments between the revolutions. Your chart, compiled for the Summary Activity above, could be useful for this. You could begin your planning by considering which events and developments were provoked by or made more difficult by the Dual authority arrangement. You should also consider other factors affecting the Provisional Government's consolidation and maintenance of power.

4 The October/November 1917 Revolution

A CLOSER LOOK

The storming of the Winter Palace

In 1927, Sergei Eisenstein made a famous film entitled *October*, which perpetuated the myth that the storming of the Winter Palace was a heroic popular rising. The dramatic pictures of the masses breaking down the gates and storming in were entirely fictitious. In reality, when the shot fired from the battleship *Aurora*, the women's battalion guarding the palace panicked and left, while the army cadets offered little resistance. The Red Guards walked rather than 'stormed' in and wandered around until they found the remaining members of the Provisional Government. Furthermore, the discovery of the Tsar's wine cellar fuelled a frenzy of drunkenness.

ACTIVITY

Extension

View some clips of Eisenstein's film, *October* and compare the film portrayal with what you read in this chapter.

Fig. 1 *A Soviet painting of the **storming of the Winter Palace**. In what ways is this picture an effective piece of Bolshevik propaganda?*

The causes, course and extent of the October 1917 Revolution

KEY CHRONOLOGY

1917

23 Oct	Kerensky tries to take action against the Bolsheviks
24–25 Oct	Armed workers and soldiers, led by the Bolsheviks and organised by the Military Revolutionary Committee, take over key buildings and communication centres in Petrograd
25–27 Oct	The remaining members of the Provisional Government are arrested by the Bolsheviks; the 'revolution' is announced at the Second Congress of Soviets; the Congress adopts Lenin's decree on peace and decree on land and appoints the first Soviet government, the Soviet of People's Commissars (Sovnarkom), with Lenin as Chairman
Dec	A secret police force – the Cheka – is established

Causes of the October/November Revolution

The events of the Bolshevik revolution that began on 25 October 1917 were the culmination of developments since the abdication of the Tsar in March. The weaknesses of the Provisional Government and defeat in the First World War, combined with the political manoeuvres of the Bolsheviks under Lenin and Trotsky, the deteriorating economic situation and the resentments of soldiers, peasants and workers, created an explosive mix.

Kerensky was well aware of the dangers posed by the Bolsheviks, yet he seemed powerless to do anything to stop their assault. When he did finally act on 23 October, it was to order the printers of two Bolshevik newspapers (*Pravda* and *Izvestia*) to cease activities, to attempt to restrict the power of the Military Revolutionary Committee and to send troops to raise the bridges linking the working class area of Petrograd (the Vyborg district, which was a Bolshevik stronghold) to the city centre. However, he was prevented from doing this by troops loyal to the Bolsheviks who claimed that his actions were a betrayal of the Soviet and an abandonment of the principles of the February/March revolution. Kerensky's move thus gave the Bolsheviks an excuse to act.

Fig. 2   *One of the surviving photos of the October Revolution*

The course of the October/November Revolution

The key events and developments between 24 and 27 October 1917 are given in the chart below:

Table 1

24 October	Following Trotsky's plan, through the night of 24–25 October, 5000 soldiers and sailors from Kronstadt moved into the city and Bolshevik Red Guards began to take over key government buildings and positions in Petrograd. These included the telephone exchange, post office, railway stations, news agency, state bank, bridges and power stations. Although they encountered some resistance at the main telegraph office, the troops on duty generally gave in without resistance.
	Lenin remained in hiding until the evening when he travelled to Smolny (by tram) to take charge of the insurrection.

25 October	Kerensky left Petrograd in an attempt to rally military support (borrowing a car from the American Embassy and disguising himself as a nurse).
	Red Guard soldiers and sailors surrounded the Winter Palace which was threatened by artillery from the St Peter and Paul fortress across the river and by the guns of the battleship *Aurora*, moored nearby on the River Neva and whose crew had declared their support for the revolution.
	At 9:40pm a blank shot was fired from the *Aurora*. This was the signal for the beginning of the Bolshevik attack, during which the Red Guard was easily able to penetrate the building while some members of the government left by a back entrance.
	Although further shots followed, only one hit the Palace and most went into the river.
	At 10:40pm the Second Congress of Soviets convened, although without Lenin or the Bolsheviks present as they were still out fighting on the streets. It was nearly midnight when the first Bolshevik deputies arrived with news of the day's events. Some Mensheviks and right-wing Social Revolutionaries made public a declaration of protest 'against the military conspiracy and seizure of power'.
26 October	In the early hours of the morning, the Congress greeted the announcement of the capture of the Winter Palace and the arrest of the remaining members of the Provisional Government.
	At 5:00am the Congress adopted a resolution to take power into its own hands.
	The day was spent in 'mopping up operations' on the streets.
	At 9:00pm the second session of the Congress opened and Lenin's **Decree on Peace**, to end the war, was adopted unanimously.
27 October	At 2:00am Lenin's **Decree on Land**, acknowledging the peasant seizures, was agreed and the Bolshevik faction put forward their proposals for the reorganisation of the government. These were opposed by the Mensheviks and left-wing Social Revolutionaries. However, the Congress adopted the proposals by an overwhelming majority and elected a new 'All-Russian Central Executive Committee' of 101 members, of whom 62 were Bolsheviks and 29 left-wing Social Revolutionaries.
	A 'Soviet of People's Commissars' (known as **Sovnarkom**) was created to run the government, which included only Bolsheviks because the left-wing Social Revolutionaries refused to join. Lenin was elected chairman of the Soviet of People's Commissars.
	Other resolutions were adopted, including the transfer of power in the provinces to the local soviets, the freeing of those arrested for political action by the Provisional Government, the abolition of the death penalty at the front and the immediate arrest of Kerensky. The Congress issued an appeal to the Cossacks (who had remained loyal to the Provisional Government), to switch sides, and to the railway workers, to maintain order on the railways. The Congress concluded its work at 5:15am.

CROSS-REFERENCE

Lenin's **Decree on Peace** and **Decree on Land** are outlined on page 33.

The establishment of **Sovnarkom** is covered in more detail on page 30.

SOURCE 1

Adapted from an account by Semen Leonťevich Maslov, who had recently been appointed the Minister of Agriculture in the Provisional Government, and was present within the Winter Palace on 25 October 1917. The account was published some years later:

At 7:00 pm Kishkin (appointed that day to control Defence) was handed a note signed by Antonov (Bolshevik) demanding the surrender of the Provisional

Government and the disarming of its guard. The guard of the Winter Palace was made up of some cadets, part of the Engineering School, two companies of Cossacks and a small number of the Women's battalion. At around 10:00pm, a shot was fired in the Palace, followed by cries and shots from the cadets. About 50 hostile sailors and soldiers were arrested and disarmed. In the meantime more and more sailors and soldiers arrived, until the guard seemed helpless.

At about 2:00am, there was a loud noise at the entrance to the Palace. The armed mob of soldiers, sailors and civilians, led by Antonov, broke in. They shouted threats and made jokes. Antonov arrested everyone in the name of the Revolutionary Committee and proceeded to take the names of all present. We were placed under arrest.

ACTIVITY

Evaluating primary sources

How valuable is this source for an historian studying the Bolsheviks' seizure of power?

The extent of the October/November revolution

The October/November revolution in Petrograd was actually a relatively small-scale affair. Trotsky claimed that 25,000 to 30,000 'at the most' were actively involved (this would mean around 5 per cent of all the workers and soldiers in the city) and this broadly tallies with other calculations based on the mobilisation of the Red Guards and others. There may have been 10,000 to 15,000 in the square in front of the **Winter Palace** on the evening of 25 October, but many would have been bystanders and not actually involved in the so-called 'storming'. The few surviving original photos suggest that forces were quite small, but it did, of course, suit the Bolsheviks to claim they were larger, as the legitimacy of their regime was based upon the fact that it emerged from a 'popular' revolution.

In the three days it took for the Bolsheviks to assume control of the city (25–27 October), there was actually very little fighting – and records suggest there were no more than five deaths – largely because the Provisional Government had hardly any military resources left with which to combat the assault. Indeed, much of Petrograd remained unaffected by the disturbances – trams and taxis ran as normal and restaurants, theatres and cinemas remained open. Even Trotsky had to admit that the revolution was essentially a series of 'small operations, calculated and prepared in advance'.

ACTIVITY

Evaluating primary sources

1. Using Source 1 and the Closer Look information on page 29, list the ways in which the Bolshevik seizure of the Winter Palace was more shambolic than heroic. How far did the revolution of October/November 1917 differ from that of February/March 1917?

2. Complete the following table:

	February/March 1917	October/November 1917
Participants		
Spontaneity		
Leadership		
Programme		
Actions		
Results		

ACTIVITY

Extension

Try to dip into the works and articles of different historians of the Russian Revolution (for example: Orlando Figes, Sheila Fitzpatrick, Richard Pipes, Robert Service, Adam Ulam and Dmitri Volkogonov) and decide for yourself which interpretations you consider the most convincing.

A CLOSER LOOK

Historiography of the revolution

In the aftermath of the Communist seizure of power, it suited Soviet historians to idealise Lenin's role and treat him as the heroic leader of the Bolshevik rising. British historians such as E. H. Carr writing in the 1960s also accepted the view that Lenin was the central directing force whose preparations and drive forced the action in October. However, it was Trotsky who organised the Red Guard and directed the actual seizure of power on 25 October. The British historian Robert Service writing c2000 argued that Russia was heading for a socialist takeover anyway and that Lenin merely ensured that this was a Bolshevik takeover. Critics of the 'heroic Lenin' school argue that since he was absent for most of 1917, he simply reacted to events and was not the driver of revolution. They also point out that, when in Russia, he stayed in Petrograd rather than trying to create a truly 'Russian' revolution. If this interpretation is accepted, it might be felt that the Provisional Government's failures were more important than Lenin's leadership in bringing the Bolsheviks to power.

Another difficult issue concerns whether the October/November revolution was, as Soviet historians suggested, a popular rising or whether, as the US historian Richard Pipes writing in the 1990s has claimed, it was, 'a classic coup d'état, the capture of governmental power by a small minority.' During the years of Cold War, Westerners tended to favour the latter interpretation but some historians such as the Australian-American Sheila Fitzpatrick have adopted a more liberal view, accepting that there was, at least some radicalism and spontaneous rebellion which the Bolsheviks were able to exploit.

STUDY TIP

As with all essays, you will need to provide a balanced answer, so you could begin by making a list of the ways in which Lenin could be given credit and a list of other reasons why the October/November revolution succeeded. It would probably be helpful to think of both long- and short-term reasons. When you have decided which way you will argue, offer a judgement in the introduction and try to uphold it through your answer. Your conclusion should confirm your view.

AS LEVEL **PRACTICE QUESTION**

'Lenin should be given the credit for the success of the October/November revolution.' Explain why you agree or disagree with this view.

Leadership and the establishment of Bolshevik authority under Sovnarkom

The first session of the second 'All-Russian Congress of Soviets' which met in the evening of the first day of the revolution, 25 October, was far from united in its approval of the insurrection. Even the Bolsheviks, Zinoviev and Kamenev, spoke out against the 'coup'. Tsereteli, the Menshevik leader, predicted that Bolshevik power would last no longer than three weeks, while the Social Revolutionary faction was split. Those on the left congratulated Lenin, whilst those on the right accused him of using violence to seize power illegally. Although 500 of the original 670 delegates voted in favour of a socialist government, the Mensheviks and right-wing Social Revolutionaries were dismayed to find that the majority of seats for the new executive committee to carry this out (the Soviet of People's Commissars) went to Bolsheviks and more extreme left-wing Social Revolutionaries.

In protest, these 'moderates' walked out of the Congress, leaving a Bolshevik and left-wing Social Revolutionary coalition in control. Their action simply played into the Bolsheviks' hands and Trotsky was able to shout at the retiring delegates the famous words, 'You're finished, you pitiful bunch of bankrupts. Get out of here to where you belong – in the dustbin of History.'

KEY TERM

Sovnarkom: the cabinet, made up of key government ministers who, between them, would run the country

A CLOSER LOOK

Sovnarkom

The Soviet of People's Commissars, known as Sovnarkom, comprised exclusively Bolsheviks, with Lenin as Chairman and Trotsky as Commissar for Foreign Affairs. It also included one female Commissar, **Aleksandra Kollontai**. Despite coming to power with the slogan 'All power to the Soviets'. Lenin clearly had no intention of sharing power with other socialists – particularly the Mensheviks and Social Revolutionaries. Thus he deliberately sidelined the Petrograd Soviet, which had shared power with the Provisional Government and in whose name the Bolsheviks had claimed to act.

Sovnarkom ruled by decree without seeking the Soviet's approval and Lenin immediately initiated peace talks with the Germans without reference to the Soviet. Consequently, whilst Sovnarkom met once or twice a day, the Soviet met increasingly less frequently. Its power was thus undermined – even though it continued to meet until the 1930s. The local soviets retained their importance, but they were brought into a new Bolshevik-dominated **power structure**.

CROSS-REFERENCE

Aleksandra Kollontai is profiled in Chapter 2, page 11.

CROSS-REFERENCE

The new **power structure** is discussed in Chapter 5.

A CLOSER LOOK

The First Sovnarkom

The word 'commissar' was chosen to distinguish the new officials from the old bourgeois 'ministers', although they fulfilled the same function. Their full title became 'People's Commissar.'

People's Commissar	Original incumbent
Chairman	Vladimir Lenin
Secretary	Nikolai Gorbunov
Commissar for Agriculture	Vladimir Milyutin
Commissar for War and Naval Affairs	Nikolai Krylenko (War)
	Pavel Dybenko (Navy)
Commissar for Trade and Industry	Viktor Nogin
Commissar for Education	Anatoly Lunacharsky
Commissar for Food	Ivan Teodorovich
Commissar for Foreign Affairs	Leon Trotsky
Commissar for Interior Affairs	Alexei Rykov
Commissar for Justice	Georgy Oppokov
Commissar for Labour	Alexander Shliapnikov
Commissar for Nationalities	Joseph Stalin
Commissar for Post and Telegraph	Nikolai Glebov-Avilov
Commissar for Finance	Ivan Skvortsov-Stepanov
Commissar for Social Welfare	Aleksandra Kollontai

ACTIVITY

Take one commissar each around your class and find out more about his or her career and contribution to the Bolshevik Revolution.

The consolidation of Bolshevik authority

The Bolshevik position at the end of October was far from secure. Initially, civil servants refused to serve and bankers refused to provide finance. It took them ten days to persuade the State Bank to hand over its reserves, and then only under threat of armed intervention. Furthermore, the Bolsheviks had to establish their authority outside the capital and combat the forces of Kerensky who had set up a new headquarters at Gatchina and rallied an army comprising 18 Cossack regiments and a small force of Socialist Revolutionary cadets and officers. Since many soldiers from the Petrograd garrison returned to their homes in the countryside immediately after the revolution, and Lenin had no direct contact with troops at the front, his forces were smaller in number than those of his opponents, and the Bolshevik position appeared weak.

Fig. 3 *Lenin addressing the Second Congress of Soviets*

CROSS-REFERENCE

You will find Key Profiles as follows:
Kamenev: Chapter 3, page 18.
Zinoviev: Chapter 3, page 23.
Rykov: Chapter 9, page 85.

KEY PROFILE

Yakov Mikhailovich Sverdlov (1885–1919) had joined the Social Democrats as a young man and spent long periods in prison under the Tsarist regime. He returned from exile in 1917, was elected to the Central Committee, and became a close associate of Lenin, who recognised his excellent organisational skills. He held the position of Chairman of the All-Russian Central Executive Committee until his early death, effectively acting as a 'Head of State'.

CROSS-REFERENCE

The **Civil War** that followed the Revolution is the subject of Chapter 6.

It took time for the Bolsheviks to establish their control:

October 29	An army cadet rising against the Bolsheviks, within Petrograd, was quickly defeated by the Red Guard. The Executive Committee of Railwaymen (composed of Mensheviks, SRs, and Bolsheviks) demanded a 'united socialist government' and refused to transport food. Lenin ignored the demand and the protest gradually fizzled out.
31	The Bolsheviks took control in Baku and in 17 provincial capitals.
November 2	Kerensky's opposition forces were defeated. The Soviet Government proclaimed, 'The Declaration of Rights of the Peoples of Russia' permitting the nationalities of Russia to break away and have full independence if they chose to do so. (By the end of 1917 both the Ukraine and Finland declared their right to control their own affairs.)
3	The Kremlin in Moscow was taken, ending a ten-day battle for Moscow. Lenin issued an ultimatum to end division within the Bolshevik party. Those who were unhappy with the new government were given the choice of accepting it or leaving. **Kamenev**, **Zinoviev**, **Rykov** and others left and **Sverdlov** was elected Chairman of the All-Russian Central Executive Committee to replace Kamenev.
5	Lenin proclaimed the victory of the revolution, assuring people: 'Remember that now you yourselves are at the helm of state. No one will help you if you yourselves do not unite and take into your hands all affairs of the state. Your Soviets are from now on the organs of state authority, legislative bodies with full powers'.

By the end of 1917, the Bolsheviks dominated the major towns and railways, although large areas of countryside were still outside their control and it would take four more years of bitter **Civil War** before the Communists could claim full victory and military control of the country.

Lenin reluctantly agreed to allow seven left-wing Social Revolutionaries to join Sovnarkom in November, in the wake of protests about the establishment of a purely 'Bolshevik' state, but he was hostile to any further suggestions of '**power-sharing**', and it was made clear to the delegates that they had to follow the Bolshevik lead.

Lenin's hostility to power-sharing

Lenin's determination to avoid a socialist coalition government appears strange, given both his ideological belief and the practical situation in 1917. Petitions from factory workers and soldiers demanded a broad socialist government and the railwaymen's strike demonstrated the strength of feeling for 'democratic government'. Even members of his own party favoured this, yet Lenin probably resisted because he feared other socialist leaders might challenge him and dilute his own vision for the future.

Lenin's decrees and actions to December

Between the Bolshevik seizure of power and the end of 1917, Lenin issued a large number of decrees. Optimism was high and this period is sometimes known as the '**utopian** phase' of Bolshevik rule. Lenin needed to fulfil his promises of change and win support, but, more than this, Lenin seems to have been genuinely convinced of the capacity of the masses to instigate a new social order. He gave practical expression to such beliefs in decrees such as that on workers' control in the factories in November.

The main decrees were:

1917	Decrees
October	**Workers' decree**: established a maximum 8 hour day. **Social insurance decree**: provided old age, health and unemployment benefits. **Press decree**: banned the opposition press. **Decree on Peace**: promised an end to war 'without annexation and indemnities' (an armistice followed in November, accompanied by an official demobilisation process in December). **Decree on Land**: abolished private ownership of land and legitimised peasant seizures without compensation to landlords (this reduced peasant support for the SRs and provided a breathing space for the consolidation of Bolshevik rule).
November	**Rights of the people of Russia decree**: abolished titles and class ranks. **Nationality decree**: promised self-determination to the peoples of the former Russian Empire; in December, Finland became an independent state, and an elected *rada* (parliament) was set up in the Ukraine. **Decree on Workers' Control of Factories**: gave workers the right to 'supervise management'. **Judicial Decree**: established a new legal system of elected people's courts. **Decree to outlaw sex discrimination**: gave women equality with men and right to own property.
December	**Decree to establish the 'All-Russian Commission for the Suppression of Counter-Revolution, Sabotage and Speculation'**: created a secret police force, known as the Cheka, after its initial letters, to root out opposition. **Bank decree**: nationalised banks and ended the private flow of capital. **Military decree**: removed class ranks, saluting and military decorations from the army and placed the army under the control of soldiers' soviets, which would elect officers. **Decrees on the Church**: nationalised Church land, removed marriage and divorce from Church control and gave women the right to initiate divorce.

utopian: means 'idealised perfection' and comes from Sir Thomas More's *Utopia* (1516), which describes an imaginary island that is almost too perfect to exist

Regroup these decrees into political, economic, social, military and 'other' categories. Beside each, comment on who the decree would appeal to and why.

Veshenka: the council responsible for state industry 1917–1932 (see under NEP for its rival, Gosplan)

nationalisation: taking businesses out of private hands and placing them under state control

While the new Bolshevik government was driven by a strong desire to create a new-style state, Lenin spoke out against the danger of moving towards 'socialism' too quickly. He seemed to envisage a long transition during which the first stage would be a form of 'state capitalism', throughout which there would be a degree of state control over economic affairs but private markets would remain as an important feature of economic life. In December 1917, **Veshenka** (the Council of the National Economy) was established to supervise and control economic development, but Lenin remained cautious in the face of the demands of some in his party that he should set about the complete **nationalisation** of industry.

These early months also saw steps to combat opposition:

- A propaganda campaign mounted against political and 'class' enemies – particularly the *burzhui* (bourgeois). From November, it was decreed that everyone had to be addressed as a 'Citizen' or '*Grazhdanin*' and party members as *Tovarishch* (Comrade).
- Anti-Bolshevik newspapers were closed down.
- There was a purge of the civil service.
- The Cheka was established as a secret police body in December.
- Leading Kadets, right-wing Social Revolutionaries and Mensheviks were rounded up and imprisoned in December.

Fig. 4 *The Bolshevik army marches through Red Square*

Lenin tried to emphasise that the Bolshevik policies were not simply intended to intimidate enemies but to transform society.

Adapted from a speech given by Lenin at a Joint Meeting of the Petrograd Soviet of Workers' and Soldiers' Deputies and Delegates From the Fronts, 4 November 1917:

We are accused of making arrests. Indeed, we have made arrests; today we arrested the director of the State Bank. We are accused of resorting to terrorism, but we have not resorted, and I hope will not resort, to the terrorism of the French revolutionaries who guillotined unarmed men. I hope we shall not resort to it because we have strength on our side. When we arrested anyone we told him we would let him go if he gave us a written promise not to engage in sabotage. Such written promises have been given.

SOURCE 3

Adapted from a speech by Trotsky to the Petrograd Soviet on 29 October 1917, following an army cadet uprising against Bolshevik rule. This was published in the Bolshevik newspaper *Izvestia* the following day:

In Petrograd we won easily. We must bear in mind, however, that the dominant classes never relinquish their power without a bitter struggle. They have already begun to gather their forces and are assuming the offensive. We had to take decisive steps. The Pavlovsky Cadet School is destroyed. We hold the cadets as prisoners and hostages. If our men fall into the hands of the enemy, let him know that for every worker and for every soldier, we shall demand five cadets. We have demonstrated today that we are not joking. They thought that we would be passive but we showed them that we can be merciless when it is a question of holding onto the conquests of the revolution.

 PRACTICE QUESTION

Evaluating primary sources

With reference to Sources 2 and 3 and your understanding of the historical context, which of these two sources is more valuable in explaining the Bolshevik attitude to dealing with opposition after seizing control in 1917?

STUDY TIP

These two sources offer an insight into the attitude of the Bolshevik leadership to opposition. However, their tone, and to some extent the views expressed in their content, differs. You must decide which you believe to be more valuable as a piece of historical evidence, based on your own contextual knowledge and the provenance of each. You may, of course, suggest that neither conveys a truthful picture, but you must ensure you back your criticisms from your knowledge.

Summary

The Bolsheviks launched their revolution on 25 October and easily removed the weak Provisional Government. However, it took time to establish their hold over Russia to consolidate their power. Lenin issued decrees and established Sovnarkom, so establishing Bolshevik, rather than Soviet rule. By the end of 1917, Lenin had made it clear that he had no wish to share power (allowing only the left-wing Social Revolutionaries to participate in government, and those only as a lesser partner). The establishment of a secret police force, the Cheka, in December 1917 demonstrated Lenin's conviction that the 'dictatorship of the proletariat' would require the active repression of 'counter-revolutionary' enemies.

 PRACTICE QUESTION

'By the end of 1917, it was already clear that the Bolshevik state would be oppressive and authoritarian.' Assess the validity of this view.

STUDY TIP

It will be important to define 'authoritarian' to answer this question. Try making a list of the key features of a repressive and authoritarian state and see to what extent the measures taken by Lenin to secure his new regime match these. You could consider how the new state introduced reform and listened to the people's wishes.

5 The consolidation of the Communist dictatorship

CROSS-REFERENCE

John Reed's book *Ten Days that Shook the World* is discussed in Chapter 3, page 25.

ACTIVITY

Evaluating primary sources

With reference to Source 1 and your own knowledge, explain the ways in which Karakhan anticipated that the new Bolshevik government would be more 'democratic' than the Provisional Government.

KEY CHRONOLOGY

1918	Jan	Constituent Assembly meets and is dispersed; Decree on workers' control of railways; Creation of Red Army; Separation of Church and State
	Feb	Decree on nationalisation of industry
	March	Treaty of Brest-Litovsk
	March	Bolsheviks become the Communist Party with capital in Moscow
	July	Constitution of Russian Soviet Federal Socialist Republic adopted

SOURCE 1

Adapted from the words of Lev Karakhan, a member of the Bolshevik Central Committee as told to John Reed, a communist American journalist, in the corridor of the Smolny Institute on 21 October 1917. The conversation was reported in Reed's book, *Ten Days that Shook the World*, written in 1919:

The new government will be a loose organisation, sensitive to the popular will, as expressed through the soviets, allowing local forces full play. At present, the Provisional Government obstructs the action of the local democratic will, just as the Tsar's government did. The initiative of the new society shall come from below. The form of the government shall be modelled on the constitution of the Social Democrat Party. The new ruling committee, responsible to frequent meetings of the All-Russian Congress of Soviets, will be the parliament. The various Ministries will be headed by committees instead of by Ministers, and will be directly responsible to the peoples' soviets.

Fig. 1 *Propaganda poster from the Bolshevik era, showing Lenin*

The establishment of one-party control

The Bolsheviks came to power with the claim that they were acting in the interests of the proletariat – the ordinary working people of Russia. Indeed, they encouraged people to think that the October/November revolution was a popular rising and, according to John Reed, 'the only reason for Bolshevik success lay in their accomplishing the vast and simple desires of the most profound strata of the people'. However, 'democracy' in the way the term is usually defined in Western 'liberal democracies' such as Britain, was an alien concept to Lenin. For Lenin and his colleagues, the idea of trying to compete for the votes of ordinary citizens, allowing different views to exist and for policy to emerge through discussion and argument, belonged to an old, class-ridden world.

Lenin was convinced that the establishment of a 'dictatorship of the proletariat' (the first step to true socialism) would require the active repression of 'counter-revolutionary' elements. Driven by Marxist ideology, in *State and Revolution* (produced August–September 1917) he had argued that 'revolutionary morality' justified strong action. Lenin had always been ruthless against opponents. He believed that the Bolsheviks were acting in the interests of the working class and this was all the authority he needed.

The removal of the Constituent Assembly

Having previously attacked Kerensky for postponing **elections for a Constituent Assembly**, Lenin permitted these to go ahead in November 1917. Over 41 million votes were cast in the election, which appeared to have been conducted fairly. The results were as follows:

Table 1   Votes for a Constituent Assembly

	Votes (in millions)	Number of seats	% vote
Socialist Revolutionaries	21.8	410 (including 40 left-wing)	53
Bolsheviks	10.0	175	24
Kadets	2.1	17	5
Mensheviks	1.4	18	3
Others	6.3	62	15

A CLOSER LOOK

Elections for the Constituent Assembly

The elections for the assembly had been held in a crisis atmosphere soon after the revolution and it is likely that many of those who voted in areas away from Moscow and Petrograd had little idea of what was really happening in the capital. They may have known little about the Bolsheviks. This has sometimes been suggested almost as a justification for Lenin's action in dissolving the Assembly. A more convincing argument might be that Lenin could not afford to risk being shackled by arguments in an elected assembly.

Fig. 2 *Painting of the only meeting of the Constituent Assembly, 5 January 1918*

Lenin promptly declared, 'we must not be deceived by the election figures. Elections prove nothing.' by the time the Assembly met on 5 January 1918, the Kadets had already been outlawed, for expressing approval for Alexei Kaledin, a Cossack general who had begun a counter-revolutionary rebellion in the Don region. The Bolsheviks proposed that the meeting be chaired by a left-wing Social Revolutionary, Maria Spiridovna, but were overruled by the right-wing Social Revolutionary majority who chose **Viktor Chernov**.

CROSS-REFERENCE

Viktor Chernov is profiled in Chapter 1, page 12.

SOURCE 2

Adapted from an account by Viktor Chernov, SR leader, former Minister of Agriculture under the Provisional Government and the elected Chairman of the Constituent Assembly. Chernov fled to the USA in 1918 and published this account in the socialist magazine, *New Leader*, in January 1948:

When we entered the Tauride Palace at Petrograd, we found that the corridors were full of armed guards. I delivered my inauguration address, amidst a cross-fire of interruptions and cries. The Bolshevik speeches were, as usual, shrill, provocative and rude. Lenin demonstrated his contempt for the Assembly by lounging in his chair and putting on the air of a man who was bored to death. I proceeded amidst incessant shouts of, 'that's enough', 'stop it now', 'clear the hall'. I declared recess until noon. At noon, several members reported that the door of the Tauride Palace was sealed and guarded by a patrol with machine guns. Thus ended Russia's first and last democratic parliament.

ACTIVITY

Evaluating primary sources

Discuss with a partner: How does Chernov make his account vivid ? Does his style and use of language make this source more or less valuable to historians?

ACTIVITY

Write a newspaper commentary on the closure of the Constituent Assembly, for either a Bolshevik or an opposition newspaper, perhaps published abroad.

The Constituent Assembly was forcibly closed and never met again. When civilians demonstrated against this action, they were fired on and 12 killed. Although such action appears to contradict the Marxist ideological principle of 'power to the people', in *State and Revolution* Lenin had written of the need for a strong party to provide for 'the dictatorship of the proletariat' and crush any bourgeois attitudes or values that remained after the revolution. Thus, in 1919, he was able to say with satisfaction that, 'The dissolution of the Constituent Assembly means the complete and open repudiation of democracy in favour of dictatorship. This will be a valuable lesson.'

PRACTICE QUESTION

Evaluating primary sources

With reference to Sources 1 and 2 and your understanding of the historical context, which of these two sources is more valuable in explaining the Bolshevik attitude to government in October 1917 to January 1918?

While Lenin claimed that his government represented the 'people' and a higher form of 'democracy', some Bolsheviks and some foreign socialists expressed concern at Lenin's actions.

SOURCE 3

Adapted from an account by the German Socialist, Rosa Luxemburg, in *The Russian Revolution*, 1918:

Trotsky has written of 'the cumbersome mechanism of democratic institutions' but this represents the living movement of the masses, their unending pressure. And the more democratic the institutions, the livelier and stronger the pulse-beat of the political life of the masses, the more direct and complete is their influence – despite rigid party banners. To be sure, every democratic institution has its limits and shortcomings. But the remedy which Trotsky and Lenin have found, the elimination of democracy as such, is worse than the disease it is supposed to cure; for it stops up the very living source from which alone can come correction of all the innate shortcomings of social institutions. That source is the active, untrammelled, energetic political life of the broadest masses of the people.

The contempt shown for other political parties in the dissolution of the Constituent Assembly was only one of the ways the Bolsheviks showed how they understood what a government based on 'the dictatorship of the proletariat' would mean. It was made increasingly difficult for groups such as the Mensheviks and the Social Revolutionaries to exist at all. For example, the decree on the press of October 1917 curbed their ability to publish their own newspapers. The ' bourgeoisie' (which included employers, priests, anyone who was regarded as 'middle class' and in practice anyone the Bolsheviks decided was untrustworthy) lost their right to vote in the new soviet government structure in July 1918. Eventually, in 1921 all other political parties were banned.

 PRACTICE QUESTION

Evaluating primary sources

With reference to Sources 1, 2 and 3 and your understanding of the historical context, assess the value of these three sources to an historian studying Bolshevik attitudes to democracy in 1917–1918.

Lenin and Germany

A more controversial explanation for Lenin's willingness to sign a peace treaty with Germany is that he was dependent financially on the Germans. Research has shown that the German government continued to finance the Bolsheviks even after the October/November revolution.

Bukharin was a close associate of Lenin, who joined the Central Committee but opposed the Treaty of Brest-Litovsk. His Key Profile appears in Chapter 9, page 84.

The ending of involvement in the First World War

The Bolsheviks had come to power promising peace. However, this was never going to be easy to accomplish, given that the Russians had been driven back by the Germans and that **Germany** was already occupying large swathes of Russian territory and would undoubtedly demand major concessions as the price of a cease-fire. The problem was further complicated by differences of opinion between Lenin and Trotsky. Trotsky baulked at the idea of making a peace that would involve harsh terms for Russia. Lenin was apparently less concerned, on both ideological and practical grounds:

- Ideologically, Lenin was convinced that revolution would soon engulf Germany, and that German workers would join their comrades in Russia in creating a new world, rather than continue fighting them. Therefore, any peace agreement would only be 'temporary'.
- Lenin knew that the Russian army could not stop the Germans. On practical grounds, a compromise with the enemy seemed the only way forward and a price worth paying to preserve what the Bolsheviks had already accomplished.

Trotsky had negotiated an armistice with the Germans at the beginning of December 1917, but once the actual peace talks began, the Bolsheviks found themselves divided. **Bukharin** led the 'revolutionary war group' of those who believed the Russians should fight on, in order to defend both socialism and Russia itself, but others saw this as a betrayal of the promises the Bolsheviks had made on seizing power.

Trotsky dragged proceedings out. He was probably hoping that the Germans would experience their own revolution before a peace was signed, particularly if the German war effort in France and Belgium failed. Trotsky called his approach 'Neither peace nor war'. This angered the German negotiators, particularly since they knew that the Bolsheviks were using propaganda to try to stir up mutiny in the German army. Field Marshal Hindenburg complained that Trotsky behaved as if the Russians were the victors rather than the defeated party seeking peace.

Fig. 3 *Trotsky in negotiations with the Germans, December 1917*

The Treaty of Brest-Litovsk

Fig. 4 *Territory lost to Russia under the Treaty of Brest-Litovsk in 1918*

Eventually an agreement had to be made, because the Germans, exasperated by Trotsky's behaviour, began to renew their advance into Russia. The Treaty of Brest-Litovsk was signed on 3 March 1918 and ratified by an emergency Party Congress.

The terms were harsh. Russia lost Finland, Estonia, Latvia, Lithuania, Poland, Bessarabia, Georgia, Belarus and the Ukraine. Germany and Austria-Hungary were to 'determine the future fate of these territories in agreement with their populations' and Germany intended to make them economic and political dependencies.

The losses amounted to a sixth of Russia's population (62 million people) and 2 million square kilometres of land, including the area that produced almost a third of Russia's agricultural produce. Also lost were 26 per cent of Russia's railways lines and 74 per cent of its iron ore and coal supplies, and Russia had to pay 3 billion roubles in war reparations to Germany.

Lenin agreed that it was a 'robber peace', but argued that Russia had to accept the 'naked truth'. However, he struggled to persuade other Bolsheviks of this viewpoint and the left-wing Social Revolutionaries argued strongly against the acceptance of the treaty.

Extract from a speech by Lenin in March 1918, arguing in favour of signing the treaty demanded by Germany:

Russia can offer no physical resistance. There may be people who are willing to fight and die in a great cause. But they are romanticists, who would sacrifice themselves without prospects of real advantage. Wars are won today not by enthusiasm alone, but by technical skill, railways and abundant supplies. Has the Russian Revolution any of these in the face of an enemy equipped with all the techniques of bourgeois 'civilisation'? The Russian Revolution must sign the peace to obtain a breathing space to recuperate for the struggle.'

CROSS-REFERENCE

Kamenev and **Dzerzhinsky** are profiled in Chapter 3, pages 18 and 24 respectively.

Only after Lenin had twice threatened to resign, did he get his way. Trotsky, Stalin and Zinoviev, on the Party's Central Committee, supported Lenin although Trotsky spoke of sacrificing his deepest convictions in the interests of Bolshevik unity. Bukharin, **Kamenev** and **Dzerzhinsky** voted against the peace, and the terms were only agreed by a majority of one.

This decision was important for the future direction of the Soviet state. It set a precedent for future action by establishing that 'socialism at home' would take priority over the spread of international revolution. It also confirmed that Russia would be a one-party state, since the left-wing Social Revolutionaries walked out of Sovnarkom in protest at the treaty. The Bolsheviks, who in March 1918 formally adopted the title of the 'Communist Party', governed alone. All other groupings, whether former opponents or allies, were treated as 'enemies'.

ACTIVITY

Write and deliver a short speech that might have been made by Lenin when he offered to resign. Make it clear why peace with Germany was so important to him and why he regarded it as necessary for the preservation of the Bolshevik state. Try to think how Lenin might try to use his ideological beliefs to justify his support for the peace treaty.

The consolidation of the one-party state

Sovnarkom continued its spate of decrees in the first months of 1918 and these helped to define the new one-party state. In January 1918 workers were put in charge of the railways. The old **Red Guards** were demobilised and a new **Red Army** of workers and peasants was formed to protect the regime. Trotsky was placed at the head of this army in March 1918, in the same month as the capital was transferred to Moscow, to be more central.

CROSS-REFERENCE

The formation of the **Red Guards** is outlined in Chapter 3, page 23.

A CLOSER LOOK

The Red Guards and the Red Army

The Red Guards were the base of the Red Army created in January 1918, and these terms are sometimes used interchangeably. The volunteer Red Guards had helped to carry out the October/November revolution. The Red Army was a new professional force. Both were led by Trotsky.

The Church and State were also separated and although religion was not banned, Russia became a secular state, with the government giving no further support to the Orthodox Church. The separation decree removed the Church's judicial powers and its right to own property, and many of its assets were seized. Religious printing presses were closed down and the clergy disenfranchised, left without civil rights and subject to persecution. Some priests were drafted into the Red Army, others, including prominent bishops, imprisoned. Russia's move to the **Gregorian calendar**, in February 1918, was partly made to bring Russia into line with most of the rest of Europe, but was also a statement against traditional religious practice.

Decrees nationalised industry and abolished land ownership. Land was given 'to those who wish to cultivate it not for personal profit but for the benefit of the community'. This policy of the 'socialisation of land' was essentially the programme long advocated by the Social Revolutionaries and it helped to remove that group's appeal.

The 1918 Constitution

To oversee the transition to a socialist society, the first Soviet Constitution for the 'Russian Soviet Federal Socialist Republic' (RSFSR) was proclaimed in July 1918. This stated that supreme power rested with the All-Russian Congress of Soviets, which was made up of deputies from elected local soviets across Russia. The central executive committee of that Congress was to be the 'supreme organ of power' – acting like a President. The congress was also made responsible for electing Sovnarkom for the purposes of the 'general administration of the affairs of the state'.

On the surface, the new constitution looked eminently democratic. However, there were limitations:

- The vote was reserved for the 'toiling masses'. Members of the former 'exploiting classes' (which included businessmen, clergy and tsarist officials) were excluded from voting or holding public office.
- The workers' vote was weighted in the proportion of five to one against that of the peasants in the election to the All-Russian Congress of Soviets.
- While Sovnarkom was officially appointed by the Congress, in practice it was chosen by the Bolshevik/Communist Party's Central Committee.
- The Congress was only to meet at intervals – so executive authority remained in the hands of Sovnarkom.
- The structure was centralised and the real focus of power was the Party.

CROSS-REFERENCE

For an explanation of the **Gregorian calendar**, look back to the introduction, page xvi.

ACTIVITY

Look back at the chart you made in Chapter 4 which grouped the Bolshevik decrees into political, economic, social, military and 'other' categories. Add the decrees of January–February 1918 to your chart. Use this chart to make notes on the extent to which the early decrees:

a. dealt with the problems Lenin inherited on taking power
b. put into practice Bolshevik communist beliefs.

As a group, reflect on which of these two factors was the more important to the Bolsheviks at this time.

Fig. 5   *The first state emblem of Soviet Russia showing the hammer and sickle*

Furthermore, the principle was established that, 'he who does not work shall not eat'. This was a serious threat given the difficult situation in Russia at the time, when the population largely depended on ration cards for food.

Despite the term 'Russian', the constitution welcomed the non-Russian nationalities that had been part of the old Russian Empire into the new Soviet state. This was a sensitive issue because there were many people amongst these national groups who did not want to be part of a Russian-controlled State. The extent to which they should be forced to join this new organisation, or not, was to become a source of friction amongst the leading Bolsheviks themselves.

Summary

- Having seized power in a coup, Lenin was determined to hang on to it by dealing ruthlessly with any real or potential opposition. This was seen in the immediate closure of the Constituent Assembly when the Bolsheviks found themselves without a majority.
- The Bolsheviks made a costly peace with Germany, because they had little choice. Lenin felt that the spread of revolution across Europe would soon make the peace treaty worthless, so it was irrelevant.
- The Bolsheviks made the direction of their new one-party state clear in the early months.

6 The civil war

Fig. 1   *Red Army during the Civil War, 1918–1920*

KEY CHRONOLOGY

1918

Apr/ May   Civil War begins; Czechs seize towns on the Trans-Siberian railway

Jul   Murder of the Tsar and his family at Yekaterinburg in Urals

Aug   High point of first White advance westwards

Nov   Kolchak declares himself 'Supreme Ruler' of Russia

1919

Oct   High point of Denikin's advance, 200 miles from Moscow; highpoint of Yudenich's advance to outskirts of Petrograd

1920

Feb   Kolchak is shot after being handed over to the Bolsheviks

Mar   Denikin's army is evacuated to the Crimea

May   Beginning of the Russo-Polish War

Oct   Wrangel's army is evacuated from Crimea; the Whites are defeated

1921

Mar   Russo-Polish War ends with Treaty of Riga

1922

Dec   Constitution of Union of Soviet Socialist Republics adopted

The causes of the Civil War

There was no declaration of Civil War in Russia, but fighting broke out in the summer of 1918. This was after peace had been made between Russia and Germany, but before the First World War had ended on the Western Front. The Civil War was complicated by the involvement of several other countries, whose governments had their own agendas for fighting the Bolsheviks. These included opposition to Russia's withdrawal from the war against Germany, a fear that the Bolsheviks were a threat to their own governments because of the Bolsheviks' avowed aim of spreading international revolution, and opposition to the Bolsheviks' **repudiation** of tsarist debts together with their nationalisation of foreign-owned industries.

The formation of the Whites

The main reason for this war was that a substantial section of the Russian population, on both the right and the left, had turned against the Bolsheviks by the early months of 1918. Their reasons vary:

- The Bolsheviks had seized power by force in Moscow and Petrograd in October/November 1917. Opponents on the right could claim the Bolsheviks had no right to rule Russia; those in the centre said that they had not submitted to popular elections; and those on the left, that they had largely ignored the soviet which had helped to place them in power.
- Bolshevik ideology alienated some groups. This was particularly true of the aristocrats and bourgeoisie who stood to lose the most but was also true of some on the left, such as the Mensheviks.
- On the right, some still yearned for the old tsarist regime, although they did not necessarily want Nicholas II himself back on the throne. This group included army officers, some of whom objected to the peace treaty with Germany. It also included Russians with land, money or businesses, who stood to lose everything from Bolshevik economic and social policies.
- On the left, both the moderates and the Social Revolutionaries resented the Bolsheviks. Lenin had forced the Kadets and right-wing Social Revolutionaries out of his government; he had ignored the electorate's

CROSS-REFERENCE

Foreign involvement in the Civil War is covered in detail in Chapter 8, pages 66–67.

KEY TERM

repudiation: the rejection of a proposal or idea

Whites: the forces ranged against the Bolshevik 'reds', consisting of both right- and left-wing political groupings, such as ex-tsarists, conservatives, some ethnic minorities, moderates and liberals, Social Revolutionaries, Mensheviks and other moderate socialists

A CLOSER LOOK

Attempts to assassinate Lenin, 1918

The first attempt on Lenin's life came on 14 January 1918, when he was ambushed by two assassins who had climbed into the back seat of his car in Petrograd. The second was on 30 August 1918, when the Socialist Revolutionary Fanya Kaplan called to Lenin as he was about to get into his car and shot him three times. The first bullet struck his arm, the second bullet his jaw and neck, and the third missed.

CROSS-REFERENCE

The **Treaty of Brest-Litovsk** is discussed in Chapter 5, page 41.

Fig. 2 *The 'White' Generals*

wishes in the Constituent Assembly and he had expelled the left-wing Social Revolutionaries from the government after they opposed his peace with Germany. It is little wonder there were two separate **assassination attempts** on Lenin by the left.

- There were national minorities, such as the Georgians, who had been part of the old Russian Empire, who were uncertain that Bolshevik promises to give self-determination were to be believed. These groups saw an opportunity in the prevailing chaos and uncertainty to fight for their independence.
- There were those of limited allegiance to any political group who simply saw the fluid political situation, brought by the Bolshevik revolution and the economic chaos of war, as an opportunity to win old battles and play out local rivalries.
- Some Russians were alienated by the Bolsheviks' seeming inability to solve Russia's economic problems. The loss of the Ukraine in the **Treaty of Brest-Litovsk** of March 1918 threatened to add to the food shortages in Russia, which were already exacerbated by distribution problems. There was severe rationing of essentials and while the 'bourgeois' disenfranchised fared worst of all, the initial euphoria at the collapse of tsardom had been replaced by a sense of disillusionment.

Many of these individuals and groups had very little in common with each other except for their hatred and fear of the Bolsheviks. Nevertheless, anger at the concessions of the Treaty of Brest-Litovsk merged with factors to create a force of 'Whites' in the course of 1918. Numbers of Bolshevik opponents organised themselves into armies or armed groups with the semblance of being an organised force. Their leadership was taken over by former tsarist officers. Chief among these were General Denikin in the South, Admiral Kolchak in Siberia, General Yudenich in Estonia and Baron Wrangel, who replaced Denikin, in the Crimea. Their forces became known as the Whites, to distinguish them from the Reds (the Bolsheviks).

ACTIVITY

This section has provided a good deal of detail on the Whites. Now create a chart that records this information and offers similar detail on the Reds. Use the map in Figure 3 to help.

The two sides in the Russian Civil War

	Reds	Whites
Aims		
Leaders		
Location		
Supporters		
Other		

The outbreak of war

By the spring of 1918, an anti-Bolshevik Volunteer Army had been created in the south of the country, partly financed by Germany. In anticipation of the growing threat, the Bolsheviks moved their capital from Petrograd to Moscow in March 1918. However, the spark to war came when members of the **Czech legion** began attacking Bolsheviks in Western Siberia in May.

The course of the Civil War

First stage, 1918–1920

The Civil War was characterised by very fluid campaigns, battles and skirmishes, fought over large areas in mostly European Russia. Sometimes various actions were fought simultaneously, but not in any coordinated way. Even if the intention had been there, a coordinated war by the Whites would have been difficult given the disparate forces involved, the lack of a single command and the vast geographical distances.

Broadly speaking, the Bolsheviks held the central area of European Russia. This included Petrograd and Moscow, although Petrograd was threatened by Yudenich's forces in October 1919. The White forces appeared to threaten the Reds from all directions, as can be seen on the map below.

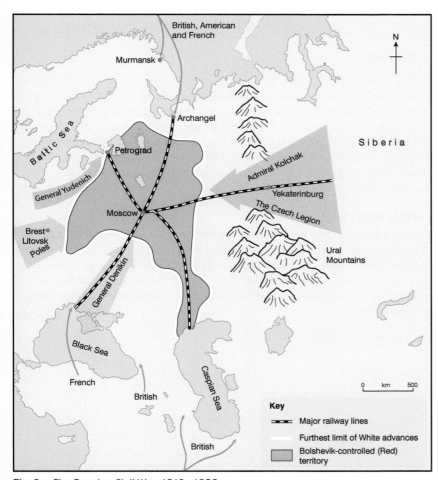

Fig. 3 *The Russian Civil War, 1918–1920*

A CLOSER LOOK

The part of the Czech Legion in provoking war

In March 1918, the Bolsheviks gave permission for the Czechoslovak 'Army of Liberation' (the Czech Legion) to travel eastwards, through Siberia, to continue the fight against their enemies on the Western Front. Formed from Czech nationalists who had arrived in Russia during the war against Germany and Austria-Hungary, by 1918 it comprised 45,000 soldiers. As this force travelled along the Trans-Siberian railway, in May, some Bolshevik officials tried to arrest some of the Czech soldiers and fighting broke out, as a result of which the Czech Legion seized the railway line through much of Western Siberia and parts of eastern European Russia. With this, they abandoned their original plans, joined forces with anti-Bolsheviks and began to advance westwards towards Moscow.

The war was fought mainly in the east and south of Russia:

- In the summer of 1918, Denikin, whose army included many Cossacks, attacked in the Don region, threatening Tsaritsyn, a city later renamed Stalingrad. Successful Red resistance here prevented Denikin from linking up with White armies in the east.
- At the same time, Kolchak's army captured the cities of Kazan and Samara, but was halted by Red counter-attacks.
- In the summer of 1919, Denikin began another offensive which got dangerously close to Moscow by October, but Trotsky forced Denikin's army south towards the Crimea.

Mikhail Nikolaevich Tukhachevsky (1893–1937) had served in the Imperial Army in the First World War and was an officer in the Red Army from 1918. He led the defence of Moscow, commanded forces that recaptured Siberia from Kolchak, and led Cossack troops against Denikin in 1920. He also took part in the Russian war with **Poland** (1920–1921) and in the suppression of the Kronstadt Rebellion (1921). He led the modernisation of the Red Army prior to the Second World War and served as Chief of Staff (1925–1928) and Deputy Commissar for Defence from 1931. He was convicted and executed by Stalin in the purges of June 1937.

CROSS-REFERENCE

The conflict with **Poland**, known as the Russo-Polish War, is covered in Chapter 8, pages 72–73.

ACTIVITY

Evaluating primary sources

Write one sentence in modern English that conveys Trotsky's message in Source 1. What evidence could you cite to illustrate the way in which the Bolsheviks had implemented Trotsky's ideas in their first year in power?

CROSS-REFERENCE

To recap on **Trotsky's** role in the October/November revolution, look back to Chapter 5, page 26.

Trotsky is profiled in Chapter 2, page 9.

- Yudenich's army in the north was relatively small, with only about 15,000 men, but he got close to Petrograd in October 1919 before being forced back by Red troops.
- By the autumn of 1919, Kolchak was in retreat. In 1920 he was captured and shot.
- In 1920, Wrangel replaced Denikin in the Crimea. His White army held out for several months, but the **Green peasant army** under Nestor Makhno fought as an irregular division for the Reds, and in November 1920 British and French ships evacuated the remnants of the White army from the Crimea.

By the end of 1920, due primarily to the Bolsheviks' geographical advantages and superior organisation in the face of White division, most of the former Russian Empire was in Communist hands. However, this came at the cost of perhaps as many as 10 million lives, lost from hunger and epidemic disease as well as military action.

A CLOSER LOOK

The Greens

The Greens were Russian fighters who had no affiliation to either the Reds or the Whites. They included Ukrainians and Georgians who wanted independence from Russia and peasants, who fought to keep both Reds and Whites out of their own area. Greens fought a guerrilla campaign in the Ukraine, under Nestor Makhno, an anarchist and skilled fighter. Makhno fought Reds, Whites and Germans at different times, supporting the Reds in the later stages. The struggle in the Ukraine lingered on into 1921.

Second stage, 1920–1921

The war continued as a more nationalist struggle against Polish armies into 1921. The Poles invaded western Ukraine but were driven back under **General Tukhachevsky**. After a second rising was crushed, the Treaty of Riga was signed (March 1921), which granted Poland self-rule along with Galicia and parts of Byelorussia. The independence of Estonia, Latvia and Lithuania was also confirmed.

The role of Trotsky

SOURCE 1

In 1920, Leon Trotsky said:

Who aims at the end cannot reject the means. The struggle must be carried on with such intensity as actually to guarantee the supremacy of the proletariat. It follows that the dictatorship must be guaranteed at all costs. The man who repudiates measures of suppression and intimidation towards determined counter-revolution, must reject all idea of the political supremacy of the working class and its revolutionary dictatorship. The man who repudiates the dictatorship of the proletariat repudiates the socialist revolution, and digs the grave of socialism.

Trotsky had already proved his value to the Bolshevik cause through his crucial role in organising the Bolshevik operations during the October/November revolution in Petrograd and his role as a speaker and theorist was unquestioned. His role in the Civil War was also important. Although he did not have a military background, he proved himself a skilful organiser and propagandist and Lenin gave Trotsky a free hand to mould the Red Army into an effective army of over three million men.

Trotsky directed the war, often from a special train, which covered over 65,000 miles during the war. He travelled with his own elite force (kitted out in black leather uniforms), visiting the various fronts and meeting commanders and their troops. He ensured that the Red Army was fed and well armed. Some critics, including the Russian historian Dmitri Volkogonov, who was a Red Army general himself, claimed that Trotsky was not a great general and made few important strategic decisions. But the reality was that Trotsky could inspire and helped to boost the morale not only of the troops but of other Bolshevik leaders who were not as convinced as he was that the Reds could win. There was certainly no leader amongst the Whites to match his effectiveness.

Fig. 4 *Trotsky visiting the Red Army during the Civil War*

Trotsky was prepared to use whatever methods were necessary. For example he recruited 50,000 former tsarist army officers for their experience and used them to train new recruits. He also appointed political commissars to army units. These were committed Party loyalists who could be relied upon to obey their political masters. The commissars had to countersign all army officers' orders as well as instilling ideological principles into the troops. Discipline was harsh: any sign of disloyalty or desertion was punishable by death. Summary executions were carried out in order to 'discourage' any waverers in the ranks, and members of the **Cheka** were used behind the lines to shoot deserters.

Trotsky made the **Red Army** a professional force, reintroducing traditional ranks and practices. When it was necessary to build up its numbers, conscription was introduced in some areas, either into fighting units or labour battalions (which were sometimes made up of bourgeoisie) and were used on the front line to clear debris and remove bodies and the wounded. For all Trotsky's professionalism, the Red Army, just like the Whites, indulged in brutal atrocities during the Civil War, including torture and massacres. Civilians in occupied areas were often badly treated in order to encourage the rest of the population to keep in line.

CROSS-REFERENCE

For the establishment of the **Cheka**, or secret police, by Lenin in 1917, look back to Chapter 4, page 34.

CROSS-REFERENCE

To recap on the **Red Guards** and the **Red Army**, look back to Chapter 5, page 42.

The **Civil War** brought about the murder of the Tsar and his family at Yekaterinburg in the Urals in July 1918. In theory, this was carried out by over-zealous local soviet officials who were afraid that the Tsar would be rescued by the White armies and used as a figurehead. In practice, it is extremely unlikely that Lenin did not authorise the assassination.

SOURCE 2

Adapted from Trotsky's order to Red Army troops on the Southern front, 24 November 1918:

Krasnov and the foreign capitalists which stand behind his back have thrown on to the Voronezh front hundreds of hired agents who have penetrated, under various guises, Red Army units and are carrying on their base work, corrupting and inciting men to desert. An end must be put to this by using merciless means. (i) Every scoundrel who incites anyone to retreat, to desert, or not to fulfil a military order, will be shot. (ii) Every soldier of the Red Army who voluntarily deserts his military post, will be shot.
Death to self-seekers and to traitors!
Long live the honest soldiers of the Workers' Red Army!

The murder of the Tsar

Tsar Nicholas II had become almost a forgotten figure after his abdication in March 1917. He had few supporters, and most of the Whites fighting in the **Civil War** were not doing so to restore the Tsar to the throne, even if they wanted the return of many other aspects of the old regime.

The Tsar and his family had been kept prisoners after the abdication and many Bolsheviks were fearful that the ex-Tsar might become the focus for resistance against the Bolsheviks, particularly as the Civil War got underway in the summer of 1918. In July 1918 the local Bolshevik police unit, part of the Cheka, which was guarding the royal family in Yekaterinburg in the Urals, shot the whole royal family without even the formality of a trial. Their bodies were drenched in acid and thrown into a disused mine shaft.

While the death of the ex-Tsar and his family was a personal tragedy, it made little real difference to subsequent events. The most that can be said is that it removed a potential figurehead for the White armies. However, since so few wanted the Tsar back in power, his loss cannot really be considered of importance in the Whites' failure to win the war.

Fig. 5 *The Russian Royal Family in exile*

Reasons for the Red Army victory

There are many reasons for the Bolshevik success, but the main ones are summarised below:

Table 1

Geography	Unity and organisation	Leadership	Support	Other
The Reds commanded the hub of communications, the armaments factories and the most densely populated regions of central Russia (including Petrograd and Moscow). Whites were widely dispersed in less-developed parts.	Reds were united in their aim to survive; they were ideologically committed in a way the Whites were not – the 'do or die' mentality. White generals operated independently and fought for different objectives, whereas the Reds had a unified command structure.	The Red Army became a well-disciplined fighting force under Trotsky's leadership. Whites had few competent commanders and ill-discipline and corruption were rife.	Although peasant support varied, generally Red land policies were more popular than the Whites' association with traditional Tsarist policies.	Hostility to foreign involvement gave the Reds a propaganda platform. It did not greatly aid the Whites as help was insufficient, sporadic and withdrawn after peace in the west. The national minorities were suspicious of the Whites, whose slogan was 'Russia One and Indivisible'.

Government and control in wartime

The Civil War increased the centralisation of power and greater party control of government. According to the modern historian, Orlando Figes, 'The totalitarian state had its origins in the Civil War, when it was necessary to control every aspect of the economy and society.' The Bolsheviks had originally formed as a group of 'disciplined revolutionaries' spearheading revolution, and Lenin and Trotsky continued to maintain this approach. Lenin's natural inclination was to control, discipline and lead from the centre and the Civil War confirmed and hardened this trend.

The centralisation of power was established early in the Civil War when Moscow replaced Petrograd as Russia's capital. This was partly due to the fact that Petrograd was closer to Russia's western frontier and more vulnerable to attack than Moscow. It was also a symbolic change from a city that had been built to open Russia up to the western world to a regime which believed itself superior to that world. From Moscow a military style of government evolved with constant 'battles' and 'campaigns' on 'fronts'.

Over half a million Party members fought for the Red Army in the Civil War. They became used to obeying orders and acting with whatever force was deemed necessary. Furthermore, in order for government to function efficiently, the Soviet bureaucracy grew enormously during these years, to the point where officials outnumbered workers by two to one. It is sometimes suggested that this extension of government control created a 'dictatorship of the bureaucracy'.

However, the real driving force behind the government was the Bolshevik/Communist Party. The Party structure appeared quite democratic. It was based on annual congresses – elected by the mass membership (these met every year during Lenin's life) but actual policies and decisions were shaped by the Party's Central Committee. **In 1919**, another body (theoretically a sub-committee of the Central Committee) was created and this became the real centre for party policy. Known as the Politburo, its first elected members included Lenin, Trotsky and Stalin. Since the Politburo members were also key government officials, this Politburo assumed increasing control of state affairs. Sovnarkom gradually met less frequently during the 1920s.

Although Lenin spoke of '**democratic centralism**', the hold of the one-party state was therefore tightened.

A CLOSER LOOK

An organisational bureau, the **Orgburo**, was also created in 1919 to supervise the work of local Party committees and the permanent secretariat which carried out the day-to-day running of the party.

A CLOSER LOOK

Democratic centralism

In theory, the Soviet Union was a democracy because the workers and peasants elected members of their local soviets who, in turn, chose those who sat on higher-level soviets and the All-Russian Congress of Soviets; they thus exerted an influence on policy decisions; this was combined with centralism because the central authorities passed decisions down to the masses.

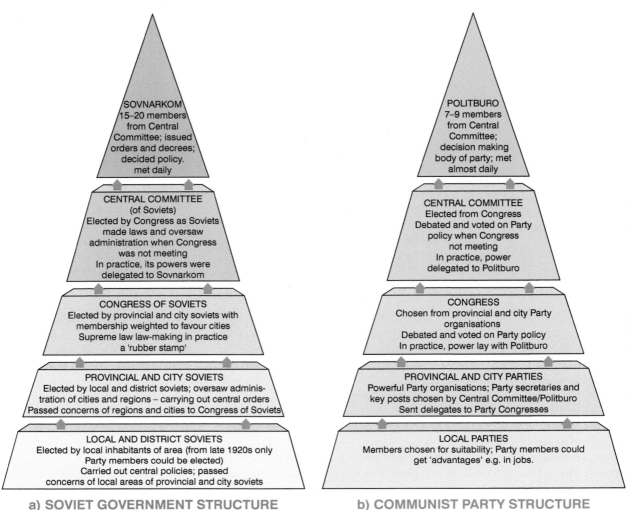

a) SOVIET GOVERNMENT STRUCTURE   b) COMMUNIST PARTY STRUCTURE

Fig. 6 *The structure of the Party and Government in the 1920s*

ACTIVITY

Draw a diagram to illustrate the ways in which the Civil War helped make the Communist State more centralised.

A CLOSER LOOK

Centralisation and the one-party state

While fighting a brutal war for survival, it is perhaps not surprising that the Bolsheviks had no regard for democratic niceties. However, there was very little soul-searching about the dangers of centralised power, since it was a concept already embedded in the Bolshevik way of thinking. The Party had never been democratic in structure, and there was no real experience of democracy in Russia. The Bolsheviks quickly adopted the practices of a one-party state.

CROSS-REFERENCE

The **central controls** brought in to manage the economy and deal with food shortages were known as 'war communism'. They are discussed in Chapter 7, page 62.

Between 1918 and 1921, the impact of fighting a Civil War associated the new Communist State more firmly with repression and 'terror'. The demand for obedience to the Party tightened, new **central controls** were brought in to manage the economy and deal with food shortages, and terror was used systematically to enforce the stringent new measures and eradicate opposition. The Bolsheviks/Communists adopted a 'siege mentality' as they faced internal and external enemies bent on their destruction. This mentality never left the Party, even when the war was over, and future Communist governments always reflected it.

From a decree by Sverdlov, Chairman of the Party Central Committee, April 1918:

The Government deems it its immediate task to enlist all citizens in universal labour conscription and military service. This work is meeting with stubborn resistance on the part of the bourgeoisie, which refuses to part with its economic privileges and is trying, through conspiracies, uprisings and traitorous deals with foreign imperialists, to regain state power. Female citizens are trained, with their consent, on an equal footing with males. Military training is compulsory for workers and peasants who do not exploit the labour of others. Persons who avoid compulsory training or neglect their duties stemming therefrom shall be called to account.

 PRACTICE QUESTION

Evaluating primary sources

With reference to Sources 2 and 3 and your understanding of the historical context, which of these two sources is more valuable in explaining the Bolshevik response to the difficulties faced during the Civil War?

STUDY TIP

You will need to think about the provenance of both sources and in particular should reflect on who the sources were intended for. You should also evaluate their content using your own knowledge of the Bolshevik struggle for survival at this time.

As a result of the Civil War, areas conquered by the Red Army were either absorbed into the 'Russian Soviet Federal Socialist Republic' (the name given to the Bolshevik State in January 1918) or allowed to remain as separate republics, as in the case of Ukraine, Belorussia and Georgia. Stalin, the Commissar for Nationalities, disagreed with Lenin about the status of these independent republics. Stalin wanted them directly controlled by Moscow, but Lenin favoured a federation of soviet republics, and he won the dispute. At the end of 1922, the Union of the Soviet Socialist Republics (USSR) was formally established. Henceforth 'Russia' was known as the USSR or Soviet Union.

Summary

- The Civil War broke out because the Bolsheviks had seized power in a coup and faced opposition both within Russia and from foreign powers.
- The Civil War was fought on several fronts. The White forces comprised various separate groups, whereas the Bolsheviks were more united and held the central ground. The Bolsheviks also had Trotsky, a ruthless and inspiring commander.
- The Civil War was a brutal affair, symbolised by the murder of the royal family.
- The Civil War led to greater governmental centralisation and increased Party control. These changes lasted beyond the war, and the experience of this time influenced communist attitudes for years to come.

 PRACTICE QUESTION

To what extent was the communist victory in the Civil War dependent on the skilful leadership of Trotsky?

STUDY TIP

This question may appear deceptively simple. You should be aware of a range of factors that produced the communist victory and you could offer one paragraph on the part of Trotsky followed by paragraphs on other factors. While this would not be entirely unreasonable, a good essay should spend some time analysing Trotsky's contribution in depth. Was he a skilful leader? In what ways did he show leadership? You might want to separate his skills as a politician from those he showed as a military leader. Think carefully just how important leadership was to communist success.

7 Economic and social developments

LEARNING OBJECTIVES

In this chapter you will learn about:

- state capitalism and social change
- conditions in cities and countryside during the Civil War
- war communism and the Red Terror
- revolts of 1920–21, including the Tambov revolt and Kronstadt rising
- the NEP and its political and economic impact.

KEY TERM

socialist economy: one in which there is no private ownership and in which all members of society have a share in the State's resources

state capitalism: a 'compromise' economy, which embraced some elements of socialism by imposing a degree of state control but retained elements of capitalism such as private markets and the profit incentive

KEY CHRONOLOGY

1917–18	State capitalism
1918–21	War communism
1921+	New Economic Policy

CROSS-REFERENCE

The **Decree on Land** and the **Decree on Workers' Control of Factories** are outlined in Chapter 4, page 33.

Fig. 1 *The Russian people suffered horrendously during the Civil War of 1918–1921*

State capitalism

Lenin came to power with the promise of building a '**socialist economy**' but, like all Marxists, he knew that socialism could only develop properly in an industrialised society, and that Russia was far from attaining that ideal. Therefore, he made it clear that, for the foreseeable future, the new Bolshevik government would have to manage the existing economic structure, with some important modifications in the workers' interests, until the conditions were ripe for socialism. This phase was to be known as '**state capitalism**': a halfway house between unfettered capitalism, based on private wealth and free market competition, and socialism.

There were many Bolsheviks who disapproved of any compromise with the old capitalist system. They demanded radical measures such as the nationalisation of all businesses and the abolition of money, and wanted trade to be determined by people's needs rather than the desire to make profit. However, Lenin seemed to envisage a long transition to socialism and spoke of the danger of moving too quickly. He felt that these ideals would simply not work in the Russia of 1918.

Unless peasants had an incentive to produce grain, Russians in the cities would starve. That is why the **Decree on Land** of October 1917 acknowledged that although 'Private ownership of land shall be abolished for ever', land was not actually nationalised but allowed to 'pass into the use of all those who cultivate it'. Similarly, the **Decree on Workers' Control of Factories**, of November 1917, was simply acknowledging the fact that many factories had already been taken over by workers and the decree was cautious, adding that those in control 'are responsible to the state for the maintenance of the strictest order and discipline and for the protection of property.'

In order to develop greater state control over the economy the Bolsheviks established:

- the **nationalisation** of the banks (December 1917), of external trade (June 1918) and of the railways (June and September 1918)
- Veshenka (The Supreme Council of the National Economy) in December 1917. This took responsibility for 'all existing institutions for the regulation of economic life.'

- GOELRO (a special State Commission) in 1920, which was to organise the production and distribution of electricity throughout Russia. This was to become one of the Bolsheviks' most significant achievements. Lenin understood its importance with his much-quoted assertion that 'Communism equals Soviet power plus electrification'.

These measures provided only partial state control of the economy and represented a compromise with previous economic practice, but they were a significant stage on the way to a more rigorous and total state control of the economy.

Problems of state capitalism

The early months of Bolshevik rule were not easy and the shortcomings of the early Bolshevik decrees on land and industry rapidly became apparent. Workers failed to organise their factories efficiently and output shrank at the time it was most needed. Some workers awarded themselves unsustainable pay rises, others helped themselves to stock and equipment. There were even cases (reported by **Viktor Serge**) of workers spending time making penknives out of bits of machinery or shoe soles out of the leather conveyor belts, to barter on the black market. However, the real problem was that they simply lacked the skills needed for successful management. The Civil War brought further disruption and a shortage of raw materials caused industrial output in the Bolshevik-held areas to plummet.

Conditions in cities and countryside during the Civil War

Life during the years of the Civil War was grim. Industrial production fell back drastically as disrupted communications meant raw materials were in short supply, workers were taken off to serve in the army, and non-essential businesses were forced to close. This brought rampant inflation and those peasants who had surplus produce were not prepared to sell it in the city. Since money was worthless to them as there were no goods to buy, some reverted back to subsistence farming, catering just for themselves. While some Bolsheviks argued that Russia was moving towards socialism and breaking away from a capitalist economy based on money, the reality was that Russia was facing an acute economic breakdown.

Some peasants did quite well in the early years of the war, selling their horses for military use and maintaining a reasonable diet by killing their livestock, but as the fighting dragged on, they found conditions more difficult. However, they could at least scavenge for food, and find wood to warm their huts. Urban dwellers, on the other hand, suffered a severe shortage of food, fuel and basic necessities. Some were even reduced to stripping their own houses of wood in order to keep warm in winter. The **blockade of trade** maintained by hostile foreign powers and the loss of the Ukraine, formerly Russia's main provider of grain, markedly reduced supplies to the cities and by early 1918, the bread ration in Petrograd was only 50 grammes per person per day.

Those living in the towns resorted to the **'black market'** for food. Up to two thirds of what was consumed in the cities came from this source. Urban inhabitants sometimes travelled into the nearby countryside to **barter** goods for produce. At other times peasant **'sackmen'** found their way into the towns to try to make a little from undercover trading. Both sellers and purchasers were hounded by the 'cordon detachments' of special army units which were established in 1918 to prevent such illegal activities. However, the authorities failed to stamp out the black market (which they often used themselves) because there was really no alternative if people were to survive.

CROSS-REFERENCE

Viktor Serge is profiled on page 58; an extract from his book *Memoirs of a Revolutionary* is supplied in Source 2.

ACTIVITY

Divide a large A3 or poster-sized sheet into three sections. You are going to make a diagram of economic policies under Lenin. In the first section draw a diagram to illustrate the main features of state capitalism. When you have read further, you should add a diagram in the second section to illustrate war communism. Use the third section for a diagram of Lenin's New Economic Policy, which is described later in this chapter.

CROSS-REFERENCE

The **blockade of trade** by foreign powers is outlined in Chapter 8, page 70.

A CLOSER LOOK

The black market and barter

The black market refers to the illegal trading of goods. Under the system of barter, goods were exchanged without using money. Petty 'black market' traders exploited the system by exchanging goods on behalf of others, making a profit for themselves.

KEY TERM

'sackmen': peasants with sacks of goods to sell

Adapted from an eyewitness account of activities at Petrograd Station during the Civil War by Paul Dukes. Dukes was sent into Russia in 1918, to spy for the British. His memoirs of his time in Russia were published in 1922 as *Red Dusk and the Morow:*

At the end of each platform stood a string of armed guards, waiting for the onslaught of passengers, who flew in all directions as they surged from the train. How shall I describe the scene of unutterable pandemonium that ensued! The soldiers dashed at the fleeing crowds, brutally seized single individuals, generally women, and tore the sacks off their backs and out of their arms. Shrill cries, shrieks and howls rent the air. Between the coaches and on the outskirts of the station you could see the lucky ones who had escaped, gesticulating frantically to the unlucky ones who were still dodging guards. I found myself carried along with the running stream of sackmen towards the Suvorov Prospect. Only here, a mile from the station, did they settle into a hurried walk, gradually dispersing down side streets to dispose of their precious goods to eager clients. I wondered if people in England had any idea at what cost the population of Petrograd secured the first necessities of life in the teeth of the 'communist' rulers.

ACTIVITY

Evaluating primary sources

With reference to provenance, how trustworthy do you think the account in Source 1 is?

KEY TERM

pogrom: an organised massacre – in this case, of Jews

Desperate for food, a good number of workers left the cities. They went to villages or joined the Red Army, where rations were higher. According to the historian Beryl Williams, 60 per cent of the Petrograd workforce had left the city by April 1918. Between January 1917 and January 1919 Russia's urban proletariat declined from 3.6 million to 1.4 million.

Food and fuel were in such short supply that many succumbed to disease. It is probable that nearly 5 million people died during the Civil War – from starvation and diseases such as typhus, typhoid, cholera and dysentery. (This was far more than the number of deaths in action, which has been calculated at around 350,000.) A typhus epidemic swept through the cities and caused the death of more than 3 million in 1920. There was a scarcity of soap, and medicines were also difficult to obtain. There were also few doctors left to tend the ill after the assault on the bourgeoisie and those remaining found themselves conscripted to practise on the front lines, supporting the troops.

Former members of the nobility and bourgeoisie probably fared the worst. With no ration cards, they were reduced to begging or to selling what few possessions they had left. Some were given manual tasks such as sweeping the streets or clearing snow and ice; others were sent to help out in the labour battalions on the war fronts. Large houses and palaces were divided up by Bolshevik building committees and their former occupants were reduced to occupying one small area, as flats were created in proportion to family size.

In both town and countryside, the Russian people were subject to the atrocities carried out by the competing armies and marauding, ill-disciplined groups of fighters. Whole villages in the Ukraine were wiped out during this Civil War period, mostly in Cossack attacks. Kiev changed hands 16 times – and each brought further hardship to its citizens. Rape and murder were all too common while Jews suffered abominably from White **pogroms**.

War Communism

The regime's response was to introduce the radical policy of '**war communism**'. There is no evidence that Lenin had originally planned to radicalise the economy so quickly, and Trotsky initially opposed war communism, putting forward his own mixed socialist/capitalist scheme in 1920. However, when this was rejected, he accepted the measures and spoke of building communism by force. War communism primarily existed to ensure that the Red Army was supplied with munitions and food by the towns but whether it was intended to be more than this and lead the country towards a more socialist economy (as some Bolsheviks tried to argue) is an issue that has vexed contemporaries and historians alike.

The Bolsheviks decided to treat the Russian economy as if it were a single enterprise. That 'enterprise' would be geared to making the best use of Russia's productive capacity without worrying about the individual concerns of managers, workers or consumers, whose interests constantly changed and often conflicted in economies driven by **market forces**. This approach does, of course, reflect Bolshevik ideology; the good of all was more important than the self-interest of individuals. Concepts such as freedom or personal choice had no part in the equation.

Bolshevik theorists worked on the principle that the right political decisions could solve economic problems. If the whole country were treated as one giant factory or unit of production, problems of supply, demand and distribution could be disregarded. The development of war communism with its emphasis on centralised planning was nevertheless developed with economic needs in mind.

ACTIVITY

Extension

Read or watch the David Lean film of *Doctor Zhivago* by Boris Pasternak. It is set in the period of the Civil War and gives a good idea of how the revolution and war impinged upon the lives of 'ordinary people'.

KEY TERM

war communism: the political and economic system adopted by the Bolsheviks during the Civil War in order to keep the towns and the Red Army provided with food and weapons

market forces: influences such as demand and availability that determine prices in an economy which is not regulated by the government; the action of market forces makes the cost of goods go up if demand rises but the number of goods remains constant

Fig. 2 *Propaganda poster for war communism*

A CLOSER LOOK

The ideology behind war communism

The philosophy underpinning war communism proved difficult to put into practice in 1918. However, the same ideas were to re-emerge in the late 1920s when they strongly influenced the actions of those charged with drawing up Stalin's Five Year Plans, which were to be the cornerstone of Soviet economic planning for the next 50 years.

heavy industries: industries making products such as iron, coal, oil and railways, which help to support other industries, such as armaments manufacture

CROSS-REFERENCE

For the **Socialisation of Land decree**, look back to Chapter 4, page 33.

KEY TERM

collective farming: farming in a 'collective' – a single unit, usually consisting of a number of farms, which would be worked by a community under the supervision of the State

kulaks: Russian peasants who were wealthy enough to own a farm and hire labour; the Bolsheviks used the description 'kulak class' to refer to the wealthier (capitalist) peasants

KEY PROFILE

Fig. 3   *Serge was a revolutionary socialist, born in Brussels*

Viktor Serge (1890–1947) went to Petrograd in 1919 to join the Bolsheviks and later worked for the Comintern (see Chapter 8, page 70), living in Berlin and Vienna. He returned to the USSR in 1925 and supported the **Left Opposition**. He was expelled from the Party in 1928. In 1933 he was imprisoned in a gulag.

CROSS-REFERENCE

For details of the **Left Opposition**, look ahead to Chapter 9, page 82.

Measures of war communism

Under the direction of Veshenka, areas of Bolshevik control were geared for the war effort. The main emphasis was on those industries that were essential to Bolshevik survival – mainly the **heavy industries**. This, in turn meant that other sections of the economy were even more starved of labour and resources.

The key features of war communism between 1918 and 1921 were as follows.

Prodrazvyorstka – requisitioning

Peasants' grain (beyond a minimum for their own survival) was vigorously requisitioned in order to distribute it to the cities to feed the workers. This built on the **'Socialisation of Land' decree** of February 1918 and a Food Supplies Dictatorship was set up in May 1918 to organise it. Encouragement was also given to the establishment of **collective** or **cooperative farming** in the hope that if peasants pooled their resources they would farm more efficiently, but only a tiny minority of households complied.

Officially, the peasants were paid a fixed price for their grain, but the detachments of soldiers, Cheka and workers who arrived from the large towns to take the requisitioned produce, often seized more and offered inadequate vouchers (to be exchanged at a later date), rather than money. Livestock, carts and firewood disappeared, leaving the peasants with scarcely enough to live on, as the requisitioning detachments sought their own booty as a reward for their efforts.

The worst hit were the so-called 'grasping fists' – the **kulaks**, who had made personal wealth from their farming. They were labelled 'enemies of the people' and sometimes their entire stocks were seized. The poor and moderately poor were slightly better treated and generally regarded as allies of the urban proletariat but the requisition measures brought misery to rural areas and many peasants resisted. They hid supplies, although soldiers often searched these out and any who informed against those that were hiding grain were given half of any grain discovered. Peasants also reacted by growing less and murdering members of the requisition squads. The Cheka had to be used extensively to make the policy work at all.

SOURCE 2

Adapted from Viktor Serge's *Memoirs of a Revolutionary*. He left Russia and wrote his memoirs in exile. They were published posthumously in 1951:

The co-operative provisioning system had to be maintained, since it catered primarily for the starved and battered proletariat, the army, the fleet and the Party activists. And so requisitioning detachments were sent out into the outlying countryside, only to be driven away, as likely as not, or sometimes even massacred by peasants wielding pitchforks. Savage peasants would slit open a Commissar's belly, pack it with grain, and leave him by the roadside as a lesson for all. This was how one of my own comrades died. It took place not far from Dno and I was sent there afterwards to explain to the desperate villagers that it was all the fault of the imperialist blockade. This was true, but all the same, the peasants continued, not unreasonably, to demand the abolition of requisitioning.

Nationalisation

Under strict centralised management, the nationalisation of foreign trade and all industries was carried out, building on the decree of February 1918. The demands of the Civil War meant that the number of nationalisations multiplied. The first entire industry to be nationalised was sugar in May 1918, followed by oil in June. By November 1920 nationalisation was extended to nearly all factories and businesses. Private trade and manufacture were banned and there was a military-style control of the railways. The workers lost the freedom they had formerly enjoyed under the **decree of November 1917** and the workers' soviets which had run the factories were abolished. Professional 'managers' (often the very same 'specialists' who had recently been displaced from factory ownership) were employed by the State to reimpose discipline and increase output.

Some workers welcomed the changes because it meant that their factories were more likely to stay open and provide employment, but those working in non-essential industries or small workshops suffered.

Labour discipline and rationing

There was strict discipline for workers. Strikes were forbidden, working hours were extended and ration-card workbooks were issued, replacing wages. Fines were imposed for slackness, lateness and absenteeism, while hard work could be rewarded by bonuses and more rations. Food, clothing and lodging were controlled through centralised distribution and regulations. There were also strict checks on freedom of movement and internal passports were introduced to stop employees drifting back to the countryside. Obligatory labour duty was demanded of the non-working classes.

Rationing was reorganised on a class basis. This was an extension of the class warfare to destroy 'bourgeois attitudes' already seen in the early months of Bolshevik rule. Red Army soldiers and factory workers got the highest rations. Smaller rations were allocated to white collar professionals such as administrators and doctors, while very limited or no rations were given to what the regime called 'the former people', the nobility, bourgeoisie and clergy.

The effects of war communism

War communism created more problems than it solved. As transport systems were disrupted by the fighting and management struggled to get factories working efficiently, production declined. By 1921, total industrial output had fallen to c20 per cent of its pre-war levels and rations had to be cut. Disease was rife and some workers went on strike, which only made matters worse. Some called for better rations, new elections and a recall of the Constituent Assembly; others ignored the passport system and braved the armed guards stationed on the city boundaries to flee to the country in the hope of finding food. By the end of 1920, the population of Petrograd had fallen by 57.5 per cent and Moscow by 44.5 per cent from the level of 1917.

The combination of harsh requisitioning and the attack on the kulaks in the countryside had reduced grain supplies to dangerous levels. There was an acute food shortage by 1920, as insufficient grain was planted. A third of land had been abandoned to grass, and cattle and horses had been slaughtered in their thousands by hungry peasants. When the harvest of 1921 produced only 48 per cent of that of 1913 there was widespread famine. Millions died from malnourishment and disease and Russia's population, which had stood at 170.9 million in 1913, had fallen to 130.9 million by 1921. Conditions were so bad that there were even reports of cannibalism and trade in dead bodies.

ACTIVITY

With reference to Source 2 and the context of the Civil War, explain the meaning of:
a. the cooperative provisioning system
b. the battered proletariat
c. requisitioning detachments
d. imperialist blockade.

CROSS-REFERENCE

For detail on the **decree of November 1917**, look back to the start of this chapter.

ACTIVITY

Extension

Look at Viktor Serge's *Memoirs of a Revolutionary* online and find an interesting extract to share with your class. You may want to look again as you learn more about Russian history. The book provides reminiscences on the years 1906 to 1941.

ACTIVITY

Design your own propaganda poster for war communism, either for a town or the countryside. Try to inspire the workers or peasants to support the policy in the interests of the State and Bolshevik (Communist) government.

ACTIVITY

Complete the second section of your diagram on economic policies under Lenin. When you have done so, identify the differences and similarities between state capitalism and war communism.

coercion: persuading someone to do something by using force or threats

Stalin's regime of terror in the 1930s is the subject of Chapter 17.

Find out more about the activities of the Cheka during the Red Terror. You could use this information to create an illustrated poster.

The Red Terror

War communism was designed by a regime, which was fighting for survival against the White armies and, at the same time, trying to carry out a class war against many of its own people. Lenin really needed a much broader base of support to enable his economic and social system to work properly, and, without that, they had to rely on **coercion**. Lenin and many other Bolsheviks, although not all, were unapologetic about the use of extreme force or terror to enforce their policies since they believed they knew best what the country needed.

Lenin himself was wounded in an assassination attempt in August 1918. This was used as an excuse for the Cheka to launch what became known as the Red Terror, which was really an intensification of what had already been happening.

The Red Terror was partly aimed at political enemies. The Cheka rounded up remaining SRs, Mensheviks, anarchists and anybody else considered a possible threat. Rather than simply imprisoning them, it more often shot them. Estimates of the numbers executed between 1918 and 1920 are usually put at about half a million, although the official records showed a fraction of this number.

The Cheka was also given the mission of carrying out class warfare. The excuse given was that the bourgeoisie was guilty of plotting counter-revolution. An intense campaign brought arrests, imprisonments and executions. However, the victims came from all levels of society, including workers and peasants, and from all ages, including many children. Sometimes the authorities had specific reasons for targeting individuals, but there seems to have been an overall policy of using arbitrary terror simply as a means of frightening all sections of society into compliance with the regime.

The Bolsheviks set up a system of concentration and labour camps. These were not as orderly as those that operated in the 1930s during **Stalin's regime**, and there are no accurate records of the numbers of prisoners or deaths in these camps during the Leninist period. Nevertheless, their existence shows that 'Terror' was certainly employed as an instrument of policy by Lenin. To him, 'Terror' was not just born out of economic or military necessity but was an integral part of class warfare. Most Bolsheviks agreed.

The Tambov revolt, 1920–1921

Fig. 4 *Starving peasants in the countryside during 1921 famine*

The famine of 1921 brought a new outbreak of peasant revolts and the Cheka reported 155 risings across Russia in February 1921. The most serious was in the rural area of Tambov province, 300 miles south-east of Moscow. It began in August 1920 and lasted until June 1921. A 70,000-man peasant army led by Alexander Antonov rose up against government forces when the grain requisitioning squads arrived in the province demanding requisitions at a time when there were almost no grain reserves left. The peasants were joined by some members of Green forces and 100,000 Red Army troops had to be deployed to deal with the uprising, which spread across large swathes of south-eastern Russia. There were brutal reprisals, particularly against those accused of being kulaks. In 1922 Red Army troops poured into Tambov province and brutally destroyed whole villages. Even poison gas was used to deal with those who hid in the forests.

The Kronstadt rising, 1921

Lenin claimed that the Kronstadt revolt was 'the flash which lit up reality better than anything else', but it was probably the coincidence of the many troubles of 1921 that persuaded him that a change of economic direction was necessary.

The food crisis of 1921 and a reduction of a third in the bread ration in several cities, including Moscow and Petrograd, brought further strikes and riots. Workers protested against a lack of union representation in factories and expressed their support for other socialist parties. Martial law was declared in January 1921, but even some regular soldiers refused to take action and the Cheka had to be used to crush the demonstrations.

It was in this situation, that 30,000 sailors stationed in the Kronstadt naval base rebelled. The **Kronstadt sailors** had been the most loyal supporters of the October/November revolution and yet, in March 1921 they sent a manifesto to Lenin demanding an end to one-party communist rule. They demanded genuine democracy and civil rights, using the slogan 'Soviets without Bolsheviks'.

The Red Army under **Marshal Tukhachevsky** was sent by Trotsky five miles across the ice (supported by an artillery force on land and Cheka men to the rear in case any soldier tried to desert) to crush the rebels. The ringleaders of the revolt were shot, while 15,000 rebels were taken prisoner and most sent to a labour camp on the White Sea. Lenin denounced the sailors as 'White Traitors', but the incident had shaken him, particularly coming at the point when the Tambov peasant rising was reaching its peak.

These troubles also caused divisions within the Bolshevik party itself. The 'Workers' Opposition' group was set up under Alexander Shlyapnikov and **Aleksandra Kollontai** and argued for greater worker control and the removal of managers and military discipline in factories. It objected to the fact that the State appointed trade union leaders, which made the unions effectively tools of the regime. It also strongly opposed those in the Party who wanted to continue and intensify war communism; from 1920, this included Trotsky.

A CLOSER LOOK

The Kronstadt sailors

In 1917 sailors had supported the Bolsheviks, the SRs and other political groups. They had their own multi-party radical soviet. In the 'July Days' disturbances, 20,000 armed sailors had taken part. Some had also taken part in the October/November revolution and had fought for the Reds during the Civil War.

CROSS-REFERENCE

Marshal Tukhachevsky is profiled in Chapter 6, page 48.

CROSS-REFERENCE

Aleksandra Kollontai is profiled in Chapter 2, page 11.

Fig. 5 *A battleship moored at the Kronstadt naval base in 1921*

ACTIVITY

Evaluating primary sources

Working with a partner or in a small group:

1. List the complaints of the Kronstadt rebels as given in Source 3. Discuss whether you think these complaints were legitimate.
2. Identify the solutions that the Kronstadt rebels sought.

SOURCE 3

Adapted from an article entitled, 'What are we fighting for', published by the Kronstadt rebels, 8 March 1921. It became known as the manifesto of the mutineers:

The glorious emblem of the workers' state – the sickle and hammer – has been replaced by the Communist authorities with the bayonet and barred window, for the sake of maintaining the calm and carefree life of the new bureaucracy of Communist Commissars and functionaries. Labour has become not a joy but a new form of slavery. To the protests of peasants and workers, they answer with mass executions and bloodthirstiness. There can be no middle ground. Victory or death! Here is raised the banner of rebellion against the three-year-old violence and repression of Communist rule. The workers and peasants steadfastly march forward, leaving behind them the bourgeois Constituent Assembly, with its Cheka, whose hangman's noose encircles the necks of the labouring masses and threatens to strangle them to death. The present uprising at last provides the toilers with the opportunity to have their freely elected soviets, operating without the slightest force of party pressure.

KEY TERM

Gosplan: the State General Planning Commission from 1921, with its headquarters in Moscow and branches in each Soviet republic; it helped coordinate economic development and, from 1925, drafted economic plans; it co-existed with Veshenka which led to conflicts of interest

CROSS-REFERENCE

Bukharin is profiled in Chapter 9, page 84.

Zinoviev is profiled in Chapter 3, page 23.

The New Economic Policy

Gosplan was formally established by a Sovnarkom decree in February 1921 to advise on a 'New Economic Policy' (NEP) which Lenin formally announced at the Tenth Party Congress in March 1921. Lenin was supported by **Bukharin**, **Zinoviev** and most of the leadership, but since he knew many rank and file Bolsheviks would see this 'NEP' as an ideological betrayal, he did not permit a vote on the measures, for fear of rejection. He relied on the force of his personality and status as leader to force them through.

The NEP consisted of a series of measures which relaxed some of the harsh economic controls imposed under war communism.

- Requisitioning of grain was ended and the ban on private trading was removed. The peasants were still required to give a quota to the State (and from 1923 this became a tax), but were allowed to sell any remaining food on the open market for their own profit. The regime also promised that it would not try to carry through forcible collectivisation of land. It was a clear signal that the peasants would be allowed to work for their own benefit and the expectation was that increased production would be encouraged and the towns would be fed again.
- The State would continue to keep control of large-scale heavy industry, such as coal, steel and oil, which were referred to as 'the commanding heights of the economy'. Small-scale industry, mainly workshops with a few employees, would return to private hands (usually operating through cooperatives and trusts). Private trade would again be allowed although transport and the banks would remain under the control of the State.
- Rationing was ended and industries were required to pay their workers out of their profits. Managers could also 'pay by the piece' (namely for the job done), rather than having central controls on wages.

The economic impact of the NEP

The NEP got the economy moving again, although the ending of the Civil War, which left the regime more firmly in control and provided more order and security, must also have helped. Private businesses quickly re-opened and small manufacturing establishments and service industries, such as shops and restaurants, began to thrive in the cities. Money started to flow more freely and industrial production recovered, although the larger state-owned industries grew more slowly than the smaller businesses.

Agricultural production recovered still faster as the peasants were anxious to take advantage of the opportunity to trade their surplus grain. A kulak class re-emerged and villages that cooperated with the NEP were rewarded with goods. However, by 1923, an imbalance began to appear in the economy as the large quantities of food that entered the cities caused food prices to drop. Before the spring of 1923 agricultural prices had been above those of industrial goods; by the summer, food prices had fallen below those of industrial goods because the factories and workshops were taking longer to rebuild and expand their output.

The gap continued to widen rapidly and produced a 'scissors crisis', as Trotsky called it. The lack of industrial goods for the peasants to buy in exchange, threatened to make peasants hold back supplies. Consequently, the government capped industrial prices and replaced the peasants' quotas with money taxes in 1923, so forcing them to sell. The crisis was short-lived and, by 1926, the production levels of 1913 had been reached again.

Private traders were active in getting the economy moving again. By 1925 there were 25,000 private traders in Moscow alone. These '**Nepmen**' were responsible for possibly 75 per cent of trade but were hated by many Bolsheviks as representatives of capitalism. Hostility towards them was heightened by the way many Nepmen flaunted their new wealth openly. They were not always averse to bribery and corruption, and indulged in prostitution and gambling. They were generally tolerated as long as taxes were paid, but Bolsheviks were prone to moralise about the evils of speculation, for example in referring to the NEP as the 'New Exploitation of the Proletariat', without considering the economic reasons that encouraged it.

KEY TERM

Nepmen: speculative traders who bought up produce from the peasants to sell in the towns, and consumer articles in the towns to sell in the peasant markets – making a profit on both transactions; it has been estimated that they controlled 75 per cent of retail trade by 1923; others became involved in bigger projects, such as building, where bribery and corruption could mean big profits

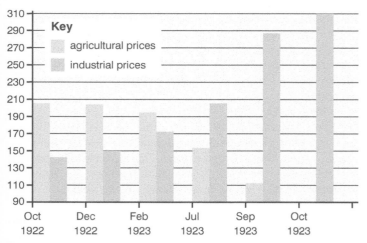

Fig. 6 *The 'scissors crisis' – what does this diagram show about the effects of the NEP?*

The NEP did not solve the fundamental problems of the Soviet economy, which still had many backward features compared with other advanced countries. However, by the time of Lenin's death in 1924, the economy was on a much more secure footing than it had been in the days of war communism.

The political impact of the NEP

To many Bolsheviks, the introduction of the NEP was regarded as a retreat back into capitalism, which put the transition to socialism much further away on the agenda. Lenin used the argument 'One step backwards, two steps forwards' and Zinoviev, one of the Politburo members who worked

ACTIVITY

You should now be able to complete the third section of your diagram of economic policies under Lenin. When you have done so, identify the similarities and differences between war communism and the NEP.

out the policy, tried to appease the discontented by suggesting that the NEP was ' only a temporary deviation, a tactical retreat'. Lenin compared it to the decision to sign the Treaty of Brest-Litovsk. It had to be done to enable the Party to stay in power.

To avoid a repetition of movements like the Workers' Opposition, Lenin also got a 'ban on factions' introduced at the 1921 10th Party Congress. This allowed senior Party figures to discuss policy, but once the Central Committee had agreed on a policy every Party member had to obey the decision. To disagree and form a 'faction' would mean expulsion from the Party. The ban on factions made it difficult to express views about policies in public, without appearing to be disloyal.

Conscious of the unease caused by the introduction of the NEP, Lenin made sure that there was no corresponding relaxation of political control. Indeed, the regime stepped up its suppression of rival views. The Mensheviks and Socialist Revolutionary organisations were banned and in 1921 several thousand Mensheviks were arrested. Some Social Revolutionaries were given a **show trial**, accused of counter-revolutionary activities, including attempts to assassinate Lenin, and found guilty. Eleven were executed.

In the country at large, Lenin also retained the repression and vigilance of the days of Civil War. The Cheka, renamed the GPU (Main Political Administration) in 1922, became even more powerful and vigilant. It had the power to arrest people at will for any reason and carry out the death penalty. It would often arrest those accused of speculation to persuade people that the regime was determined to suppress any capitalist tendencies.

There was more rigorous censorship. In 1922 it was made clear that criticism of the government was forbidden. Many writers and intellectuals, however prominent, were deported to other parts of the country. All writings had to be submitted for approval by GLAVIT (the Main Administration for Affairs of Literature and Publishing Houses) before publication. There was also a renewed attack on religion. In 1921 the **Union of the Militant Godless** was set up and from 1922 churches were stripped of valuable possessions and thousands of priests were imprisoned and some executed.

In 1923, the *nomenklatura* system was introduced. A list of over 5000 Party and government posts was drawn up. When any of these posts needed filling, only the Central Party bodies could nominate the new post-holder, whom they chose from a list of approved Party members. This placed loyalty to the Party above everything else, even the skills needed for positions. Anybody who wanted to progress in the Party or government had to be seen to be loyal and not challenge official policy in any way. In return for their loyalty, the nomenklatura could expect material rewards. This often meant access to goods and services denied to the great majority of the population and even those in the lower ranks of the Party.

Summary

- The Bolshevik regime initially established a system of state capitalism, whereby the Bolsheviks controlled the economy.
- Economic and social conditions in Russia were very harsh after 1917 and were worsened by the policy of war communism, as the regime requisitioned food from the countryside in a desperate attempt to feed the starving towns.
- The Bolsheviks introduced the Red Terror, carried out by the Cheka to eliminate real potential enemies of the regime.

---

show trial: a propagandist trial, held in public with the intention of influencing popular opinion more than securing justice for the accused

---

The Union of the Militant Godless was a group that challenged the existence of God, gave talks and published anti-religious propaganda. It expounded atheism and scientific principles, and believed the 'struggle against religion is a struggle for socialism'.

---

nomenklatura: a system whereby influential posts in government and industry were filled by Party appointees; the people who occupied these positions are sometimes also referred to as 'the nomenklatura'

- Conditions were so bad that there was dissatisfaction and revolts against the Bolshevik regime, particularly in Tambov province and Kronstadt.
- Rebellions were crushed, but Lenin realised that policy had to change to survive. The New Economic Policy was introduced. This introduced a measure of capitalism that gave the peasants and smaller businesses some economic freedom.
- The economy revived, but there was a crackdown on any form of political dissent. By Lenin's death in 1924, it was clear that the one-party state was going to remain.

 PRACTICE QUESTION

Evaluating primary sources

With reference to Sources 1 and 2 and your understanding of the historical context, which of these two sources is more valuable in explaining the Bolshevik response to the difficulties faced during the Civil War?

 PRACTICE QUESTION

With reference to Sources 1, 2 and 3 and your understanding of the historical context, assess the value of these three sources to an historian studying Bolshevik attitudes to democracy in 1917 to 1918.

STUDY TIP

As always you will need to examine both the provenance and content of these sources and comment on their value in relation to the topic of the question. For the AS question you must decide which of the two sources is the more valuable and explain why, while the A Level question requires only comment on how each contributes to the wider issue raised here. In both cases, you should show your own knowledge of context.

 PRACTICE QUESTION

'The introduction of the New Economic Policy was a betrayal of all the Bolsheviks had fought for since October 1917.' Assess the validity of this view.

STUDY TIP

As always with this type of question, you must provide a balanced answer. You will need to identify what the Bolsheviks had 'fought for' with reference to their ideological principles — and you could use examples of their policies under state capitalism and war communism to illustrate how some of those principles had been put into action. However, it is also important to consider the extent to which the NEP betrayed earlier principles. Did the compromise with capitalism represented by NEP mean that all they had done to that point been cast aside?

8 Foreign relations and the attitudes of foreign powers

LEARNING OBJECTIVES

In this chapter you will learn about:

- foreign intervention in the Civil War
- the role of the Comintern from 1919
- the Russo-Polish War
- discussions leading to the Treaty of Rapallo
- international recognition and the repercussions of the 'Zinoviev Letter'
- Lenin's rule by 1924.

CROSS-REFERENCE

The **Treaty of Brest-Litovsk** is outlined in Chapter 5, page 41.

A CLOSER LOOK

Divisions and muddled thinking in the foreign interventions

US troops provided the largest intervention forces, 11,000 at Vladivostok and 4500 in North Russia; but President Wilson was not convinced about their purpose; US forces pulled out of North Russia in June 1919 (though US troops remained at Vladivostok until 1920). France was eager to support White armies in South Russia, but had policy differences with Britain. Governments were also undecided about which, if any, **anti-Bolshevik leaders** to support: should it be Kolchak, or Denikin, or neither? There was little or no coordination between foreign forces.

CROSS-REFERENCE

The **anti-Bolshevik leaders** in the Civil War are introduced in Chapter 7.

Fig. 1 *'Lenin clears the world of filth!' A Bolshevik propaganda poster, 1920. Lenin is using the new broom of pure socialism to sweep the world clean of the evils of capitalism*

'Normal' foreign relations were not possible for Lenin and the Bolsheviks in 1918. The new regime had gained a breathing space by the **Treaty of Brest-Litovsk**, but negotiating peace with Germany and deserting its wartime alliance exposed the Bolshevik leadership to isolation and international hostility.

Foreign intervention in the Civil War

In addition to the Civil War against the anti-Bolshevik forces within Russia, the Bolshevik regime had to contend with the problem of foreign interventions. From 1918 to 1920, foreign troops were stationed in widespread areas of conflict: from the Baltic Sea, to the Black Sea to the Far East. Though the **geographical scope** of these interventions was vast, as shown in Figure 2, the number of troops engaged was small, and they did little direct fighting. However, at the time, foreign intervention seemed like an existential threat to the survival of Bolshevik Russia.

Reasons for foreign intervention

The motives behind foreign intervention were confused and shifting:

- In 1918, the main motive was to keep Russia fighting in the First World War, to prevent or delay the mass transfer of German forces from the Eastern Front to the West.
- A lesser motive was to protect the vast dumps of armaments and war materials that had been shipped to Russia by the Allies.
- After the German armistice in November 1918, the first motive no longer applied but intervention continued because of the wish to support anti-Bolshevik forces.
- Intervention also continued because of **divisions and muddled thinking** within Allied governments.

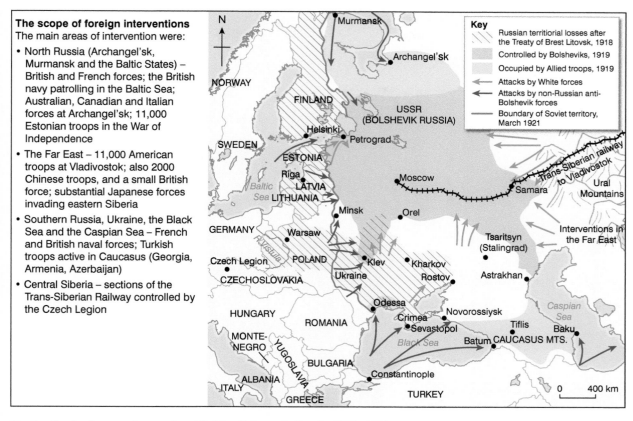

The scope of foreign interventions
The main areas of intervention were:

- North Russia (Archangel'sk, Murmansk and the Baltic States) – British and French forces; the British navy patrolling in the Baltic Sea; Australian, Canadian and Italian forces at Archangel'sk; 11,000 Estonian troops in the War of Independence
- The Far East – 11,000 American troops at Vladivostok; also 2000 Chinese troops, and a small British force; substantial Japanese forces invading eastern Siberia
- Southern Russia, Ukraine, the Black Sea and the Caspian Sea – French and British naval forces; Turkish troops active in Caucasus (Georgia, Armenia, Azerbaijan)
- Central Siberia – sections of the Trans-Siberian Railway controlled by the Czech Legion

Key
- Russian territorial losses after the Treaty of Brest Litovsk, 1918
- Controlled by Bolsheviks, 1919
- Occupied by Allied troops, 1919
- Attacks by White forces
- Attacks by non-Russian anti-Bolshevik forces
- Boundary of Soviet territory, March 1921

Fig. 2 *Foreign interventions and anti-Bolshevik forces in Russia, 1918–1921*

Foreign interventions

KEY CHRONOLOGY

1918	Jan	Arrival of Japanese warship at Vladivostok
	Mar	Treaty of Brest-Litovsk; first **British forces** sent to Murmansk; start of naval **blockade** of trade and shipping going to Soviet Russia
	Aug	9000 US troops landed at Vladivostok
	Nov	Three-day battle on the Archangel'sk front; Baku occupied by British force; Allied forces landed in the Black Sea
1919	Feb	Arrival of German forces in Latvia to oppose the Red Army
	Mar	The Bullitt peace mission gets Lenin to agree to peace terms; peace settlement rejected by Allies
	Jun	Evacuation of US troops from Archangel'sk
	Aug	British naval assault on Soviet battle fleet at Petrograd
1920	Jan	Allied governments call off blockade
	Mar	Defeated White armies evacuated by British warships
	Jun	Polish armies in Ukraine defeated by Red Army
	Aug	Red Army invasion of Poland halted
	Nov	Trade agreement with Russia authorised by British government; recognition of Bolshevik state

A CLOSER LOOK

British divisions over intervention in Russia

Britain deployed naval forces in the Baltic and in the Black Sea but only very small detachments of troops. Some British politicians wanted a maximum effort to 'smash Bolshevism'; but socialists and trade unionists in Britain strongly opposed intervention; a vocal 'Hands Off Russia' movement influenced opinion in 1919 and 1920. In the end, the British government settled on a futile, contradictory policy of 'no interference in Russia but aiding White armies when possible'.

ACTIVITY

Draw a spider diagram to show reasons for Allied intervention in the Russian Civil War.

KEY TERM

blockade: preventing goods from entering a country

Fig. 3 *A memorial to British intervention forces at Murmansk*

Foreign 'spies' in Russia

Among the individuals reporting on what was happening inside Russia were three American journalists: John Reed (author of *Ten Days That Shook The World)*, Louise Bryant and Bessie Beatty. Three British 'spies' were Arthur Ransome, who had left-wing sympathies (he fell in love with Trotsky's secretary Yevgenia), Sidney Reilly, an intelligence agent who strongly supported anti-Bolshevism, and Robert Bruce Lockhart, a young diplomat who was twice arrested as a 'British spy' before being thrown out of Russia. To find out more about these individuals, see *Spies and Commissars: Bolshevik Russia and the West* by Robert Service.

A problem for Allied governments was that they had little accurate or up-to-date knowledge of what was happening. They were often out of touch with the speed of events. In the absence of normal diplomatic activity, governments depended on a handful of individuals who sent snippets of information. These reports were sometimes misleading, encouraging a degree of wishful thinking; sometimes they were reliable but were not listened to. Sometimes they were seen by the Bolsheviks as sympathisers; sometimes they were seen as **enemy spies**.

Records of those involved in the Allied action help provide a picture of the times:

SOURCE 1

Adapted from a letter sent by the American Consul at Archangel'sk in northern Russia to the US State Department, June 1918:

Intervention will begin on a small scale, but with each step forward it will grow in scope and in its demands for ships, men, money and materials. Intervention cannot reckon on active support from Russians. All the fight has gone out of Russia. The Social Revolutionists, Mensheviks and Kadets who now advocate intervention are discredited. Their invitation to enter Russia is not an invitation from the Russian people. On the other hand, the men who do rule Russia, however badly it is done, are the Bolshevik leaders. Intervention will turn thousands of anti-German Bolsheviks against us. Every foreign invasion that has gone deep into Russia has failed. If we intervene, going farther into Russia, we, too, will be swallowed up.

From *Memoirs of a British Agent* by Robert Bruce Lockhart, a young diplomat, who had been British Vice Consul in Russia until 1917. He returned to Russia in January 1918 as Britain's envoy to the Bolshevik regime (but worked for the British Intelligence). His memoirs were published in 1932:

I was in Moscow when I heard of the British intervention in North Russia in June 1918. For forty-eight hours I deluded myself with the thought that the intervention might prove a brilliant success. I was not quite sure what we should be able to do when we reached Moscow. I could not believe that a bourgeois Russian government could be sustained in Moscow without our aid. Still less did I believe that we could persuade any number of Russians to renew the war with Germany. In the circumstances the intervention was bound to assume an anti-Bolshevik rather than an anti-German character. It was, therefore, likely that our occupation of Moscow would last indefinitely. But, with the adequate forces which I assumed we had at our disposal, I had no doubt of our being able to reach the Russian capital.

From a report to the British Cabinet by the Foreign Secretary, Arthur Balfour, November 1918:

The defeat of Germany had changed the principal motive which prompted our expeditions to Murmansk, Archangel, Vladivostok, and the Caspian. So long as a life-and-death struggle was proceeding on the Western Front between us and the Central Powers, it was of the first importance to prevent, as far as possible, the withdrawal of German forces from Russia to France; but with the conclusion of a German armistice this motive has no further force. For what then are we still maintaining troops in various parts of what was once the Russian Empire? To judge by the character of the appeals made to us from many quarters, it seems commonly supposed that these military expeditions are partial and imperfect efforts to carry out a campaign against Bolshevism, and to secure, by foreign intervention, the restoration of decent order and a stable government. This view, however, indicates a complete misunderstanding of what His Majesty's Government is able to do.

 PRACTICE QUESTION

Evaluating primary sources

With reference to Sources 1, 2 and 3 and your understanding of the historical context, assess the value of these three sources to an historian studying foreign intervention in the Russian Civil War.

You should reflect on the provenance of each source and identify its value in relation to the author, date, context and purpose. Don't forget to comment on the tone and emphasis shown in the source also. By applying your own knowledge you should be able to comment on how valuable the content would be to an historian. Focus on what is said — not what is omitted!

The confusion and uncertainty of Allied governments as to how to respond to Bolshevik Russia involved attempts at peace-making as well as military intervention. In 1919 a secret American diplomatic mission to Moscow briefly raised hopes for a **possible compromise peace.**

Lenin's peace offer

In March 1919, President Wilson sent a US diplomat, William C Bullitt, on a secret mission to discuss peace. Lenin, at that time worried about anti-Bolshevik victories in the Civil War, and the impact of an Allied blockade of trade and shipping to Russia, offered big concessions. In return for a ceasefire and an end to the blockade, Lenin was prepared to tolerate the continuation of temporary (anti-Bolshevik) governments in parts of Russia. But Britain and France were hostile to Bullitt's deal, and Wilson did not back Bullitt. The peace plan lapsed; the Civil War continued until the Bolsheviks achieved total victory.

Impact of foreign intervention

Foreign interventions did not bring down the Bolshevik regime; they were on such a small scale, with so little coordination between them, and such limited direct military action that there was little chance of their doing so. Most Allied troops remained in their bases and fought only minor skirmishes (though the Japanese did mount serious offensive operations in Siberia, including a major attack on Khabarovsk). Bolshevik survival was secured by the **military successes of the Red Army** under Trotsky and **General Tukhachevsky**; and by the disorganisation and internal feuds among the anti-Bolsheviks. Britain and France briefly considered a renewed attempt at intervention but decided against it. In November 1920, the British cabinet agreed to negotiate a trade agreement with Bolshevik Russia, thus accepting *de facto* recognition of the Soviet state.

The military successes of the **Red Army** and General **Tukhachevsky** are covered in Chapter 6, page 51.

Battle deaths in the Russian Civil War

Russia	500 000
Britain	345
United States	275
France	48
Japan	1550

The impact of foreign interventions – different views

At the time and for long afterwards, there was debate about the significance for Russia of the foreign interventions. The Bolsheviks were convinced they had fought off a major capitalist, imperialist assault. Many Western commentators, such as George Kennan, author of *Lenin and the West Under Lenin and Stalin,* claimed that the interventions, though small, poisoned relations between Soviet Russia and the West in the longer term. Other historians, however, suggest that relations between Russia and the West would have stayed the same anyway.

You need to consider the importance of allied intervention in the Civil War and, while you may want to argue that the Allies played little part in prolonging the war, you should consider how their intervention affected certain areas. To provide balance, it could be useful to look back to Chapter 6 and consider other factors that prolonged the war.

'Allied intervention was responsible for prolonging the Civil War between 1918 and 1921.'
Explain why you agree or disagree with this view.

The Comintern

The success of the Bolshevik Revolution made Russia the obvious base for the founding of the **Third Communist International (Comintern)** as an international socialist organisation promoting Marxism and spreading 'proletarian revolution' from Russia to the world. The first Founding Congress of the Comintern was held in Moscow in March 1919. Not all those invited were willing or able to attend, but there were more than 50 delegates, from all over Europe and also the United States, Australia and Japan. The chairman of all the early Comintern Congresses was Grigorii Zinoviev, but the dominating influence was always Lenin.

Even though the Congress took place at a time when the Bolshevik regime was fighting for its life against White Russian armies, national independence movements and foreign intervention, there was great optimism about the prospects for the **spread of revolution** from Russia to the wider world. Germany was believed to be ripe for revolution, even though the **Spartacist uprising** in Berlin had been brutally suppressed in January 1919. Hopes were raised by the establishment of soviet-style republics in Hungary and in Bavaria. Lenin, Trotsky and other prominent Bolshevik activists like **Karl Radek** were committed believers in the inevitability (and the necessity for Bolshevik Russia's survival) of world revolution.

The Spartacist uprising

Communist revolutionaries in Germany (calling themselves the 'Spartacus' movement after the leader of a slave rebellion against Ancient Rome) launched an uprising in Berlin in December 1918. The revolt was brutally crushed by armed German militias in January 1919. The leaders of the Spartacists, **Rosa Luxemburg** and Karl Liebknecht, were murdered.

The Second Comintern Congress took place in Petrograd in July to August 1920, at the height of the **Russo-Polish War**. The congress was dominated by debates over Lenin's '21 Conditions' defining the relationships between communist parties and 'bourgeois-democratic' socialist parties. Some European delegations broke away from the Comintern as a result. When the Congress opened, the Red Army was on the verge of capturing Warsaw; the last-gasp Polish victory over Tukhachevsky's army was a nasty shock to the delegates in Petrograd. Hopes that victory in Poland would be a springboard for communism to sweep across Western Europe were dashed. But 1920 was still a time of optimism. Ultimate victory in the Civil War was certain, the last foreign intervention forces were leaving. Bolshevik rule in Russia was secure.

By the time of the Third Comintern Congress in the summer of 1921, there was a dawning realisation that the world revolution was not as close as had been hoped. Communist regimes and uprisings had all been crushed. Moderate socialist parties who renounced revolution were becoming established; instead of communist revolution, Germany was ruled by the **'bourgeois-democratic' Weimar Republic**. Against all expectations, Bolshevik Russia was alone in a capitalist world. This led to a situation where the Comintern became totally Russian-dominated.

The 'bourgeois–democratic' Weimar Republic

During the First World War there was a bitter split within German Socialism. Left-wing extremists were outnumbered by moderate socialists within the SPD (Socialist Party of Germany). After the collapse of Imperial Germany in 1918, the leader of the SPD, Friedrich Ebert, became head of government in the Weimar Republic. Ebert's willingness to compromise with middle-class ('bourgeois') liberals was regarded by the Left as a betrayal of the revolution.

There was now a changed outlook from many in the Bolshevik leadership, who were ready to play down international revolution in order to concentrate

The Third Communist International

The Third Communist International was a revival of an international socialist organisation promoting Marxist ideology that had begun in 1849, when Marx and Engels issued *The Communist Manifesto*. The First International (the International Workingmen's Association) operated from 1864 to 1876. The Second International existed from 1889 until it was dissolved in 1916. The Third Communist International (Comintern, for short) existed from 1919 to 1943.

The **spread of revolution** was a Stage in the Marxist theory of revolution. To recap on this, look back to the Introduction.

For an extract by **Rosa Luxemburg** see Source 3, in Chapter 5, page 39.

The **Russo-Polish War**, which formed the background to the Second Comintern Congress, including the Polish victory which influenced its outcome, is discussed in the next section, page 72.

Karl Radek (1885–1939) was a revolutionary socialist active in Poland and Germany before 1914. He joined the Bolsheviks and rose to become Vice-Commissar for Foreign Affairs under Trotsky. He firmly believed in the world revolution and became secretary to the Comintern. He joined the Left Opposition in support of Trotsky in 1923; but was removed from the Central Committee in 1924, expelled from the Party in 1927, and deported to Siberia in 1928.

KEY CHRONOLOGY

Russo-Polish War

1919	Feb	First conflicts between Polish and Bolshevik forces
	Jun	End of Polish-Ukrainian War
1920	Apr	Polish-Ukrainian alliance between Pilsudski and Symon Petliura
	May	Kiev occupied by Polish-Ukrainian forces
	Jun	Evacuation of Polish forces from Kiev
	Jul	Rapid westward advances by Red Army
	Aug	Red Army driven back from Warsaw after 'Miracle on the Vistula'
	Oct	Provisional Polish-Russian peace agreement
1921	Mar	War formally ended by Treaty of Riga

CROSS-REFERENCE

Internal matters within Russia that required the Bolsheviks' attention are covered in Chapter 7, page 54.

A CLOSER LOOK

The peace conferences

The post-war peace settlement of 1919–1920 comprised numerous separate treaties designed to punish the 'losers' in the First World War – Germany, Austria-Hungary, Turkey and Bulgaria – and provide for future stability in Europe. There were six treaties in all:

- Treaty of Versailles, 1919, dealing with Germany
- Treaty of St Germain, 1920, dealing with Austria
- Treaty of Neuilly, 1920, dealing with Bulgaria
- Treaty of Trianon, 1920, dealing with Hungary
- Treaty of Sèvres, 1920, dealing with Turkey
- (The Treaty of Lausanne, 1923, renegotiated the terms of the Sèvres treaty)

on pressing **internal matters within Russia**. The Comintern remained an important symbol, and all Bolshevik leaders were at least outwardly committed to its aims, but the revolutionary force behind the Comintern slackened.

ACTIVITY

Create a three-column chart as below and complete it with bullet point notes.

	First Comintern Conference	Second Comintern Conference	Third Comintern Conference
Context in which conference met			
Attitude of delegates			
Evaluation of conference			

Fig. 4 *Contemporary painting of the Comintern Congress in Moscow, 1919*

The Russo-Polish War

The White Armies were essentially defeated by early 1920, and the last Allied Intervention forces were pulled out of the port of Novorossisk on the Black Sea in May, but Bolshevik Russia's wars of survival were not yet over. The Red Army was still fighting a war with the newly-independent Poland.

The re-creation of an independent **Poland** was one of the major commitments of the Allied Powers in the post-war peace settlement. The new Poland contained extensive territories lost by the former Tsarist Empire; and defining the borders of the new Poland was very difficult because Russia was not represented at any of the **Paris peace conferences**. For the Bolshevik regime, fighting against separatism and new national states was a key aspect of the Civil War: there were conflicts in the north-west against Estonia, Latvia and Lithuania (the Baltic States), and in the south-east against Ukraine, Georgia and Azerbaijan.

A CLOSER LOOK

Poland pre/post 1920

In the nineteenth century, Poland had been split between Austria-Hungary, Prussia and Russia. At the Treaty of Brest-Litovsk in 1918, Russia had renounced its claims to Poland. Following the German defeat, Poland became an independent republic, as confirmed by the Treaty of Versailles in June 1919. After the Russo-Polish war, Poland's frontiers were settled in 1922 and internationally recognised in 1923.

The rival ambitions of Poland and Bolshevik Russia made armed conflict very likely. The Polish Head of State, General Josef Pilsudski, dreamed of expanding the borders of Poland far to the east, into Belarus and Western Ukraine. In 1918 and 1919, Poland fought a complicated war against Ukrainian nationalists; this led to skirmishes with the Red Army. In the opposite direction, Lenin and the Bolsheviks saw Poland as a geographical bridge to the West – the essential route for exporting revolution to Germany and Western Europe. The Bolsheviks were also fighting wars to suppress independence movements in the Baltic states.

In April 1920, Pilsudski made an alliance with a new Ukrainian military leader, Symon Petliura. The former enemies made common cause against the Bolsheviks and launched an eastern offensive, towards Kiev. This offensive had rapid success; Kiev was occupied in May 1920. Had this happened in 1919, when the Bolsheviks were on the defensive on many fronts in the Civil War, it might have had a major impact. But by 1920, the Bolsheviks had achieved a string of victories against White Russian armies. Lenin (who in 1919 had been willing to accept a **compromise peace**, giving up much of Russia to his opponents) was much more confident about Bolshevik strength in 1920; hopes of spreading revolution westward had been re-awakened.

The Red Army launched a powerful counter-attack. Overstretched Polish forces crumbled and abandoned Kiev. They then began a rapid and humiliating retreat back towards Warsaw. By August 1920, the Polish army seemed on the point of catastrophic defeat; until Pilsudski mounted a desperate defence of Warsaw in the battle known to Polish nationalists as the '**Miracle on the Vistula**'. Warsaw was saved and the war settled into stalemate. Peace terms were agreed in October, and formalised by the Treaty of Riga in March 1921.

ACTIVITY

Create a flow chart to map the course of the Russo-Polish War. Use a colour to indicate the most dangerous moments for the Bolshevik government.

CROSS-REFERENCE

Lenin's proposed **compromise peace** is outlined earlier, on page 69.

A CLOSER LOOK

Poland's borders with the USSR

The borders fixed at the Treaty of Riga in 1921 did not last long. In 1940, Poland was carved up between Soviet Russia and Nazi Germany under the terms of the 1939 Molotov–Ribbentrop Pact. In 1945, after the 'liberation' of Poland by the Red Army, Stalin enforced new borders on Poland, incorporating parts of eastern Poland into the Soviet Union; in the west, Poland gained extensive territories from Germany.

A CLOSER LOOK

The 'Miracle on the Vistula'

Poland's capital city, Warsaw, stands on the banks of the River Vistula. In August 1920, after the rapid westward advance of the Red Army under General Tukhachevsky, it seemed certain that the Polish army would be defeated and Warsaw would be lost. But a last-gasp counter-offensive led by General Josef Pilsudski, won a decisive victory. This 'Miracle of the Vistula' became a heroic episode in Polish history, commemorated in 1930 by a great painting by Jerzy Kossak.

Fig. 5 *Soviet anti-Polish poster*

KEY TERM

collective security: a key principle of the post-war peace settlement, aiming to replace the dependence on military alliances between the great powers by joint measures by all members of the League to prevent acts of aggression; this principle was especially important for the many new small states that emerged after the First World War

A CLOSER LOOK

Trade with the Soviet Union

In 1921, Armand Hammer, a young American doctor-turned-businessman, made a deal with Lenin to supply large consignments of pens and pencils for the Soviet drive to eradicate illiteracy. Armand Hammer's deal with Lenin started him on a business career that made him a multimillionaire. Hammer's millions were behind the film production company Hammer Films, famous for its series of horror movies starring Peter Cushing and Christopher Lee.

KEY PROFILE

Georgy Chicherin (1872–1936) came from a noble background but joined the Bolsheviks in 1918. He specialised in foreign affairs and was Trotsky's deputy in negotiating the Treaty of Brest-Litovsk. Chicherin played a leading role in the first Comintern congress 1919; and was a key figure in the Soviet delegation at the Genoa conference and at the signing of the Treaty of Rapallo in 1922. He was chief Soviet negotiator at the Treaty of Berlin in 1926. He suffered from ill health and was replaced by his deputy, Maxim Litvinov, in 1930.

Ending isolation: discussions leading to the Treaty of Rapallo

Bolshevik Russia was diplomatically isolated in 1921. Along with Germany, it had been excluded from the **League of Nations**, the international organisation set up by the Paris Peace Conferences, which aimed to prevent war and achieve **collective security** by settling international disputes by negotiation. There was a gulf of ideology, ignorance and fear dividing Russia from the European mainstream. Lenin's regime had to come to terms with the fact that world revolution had been indefinitely postponed; the rest of the world had to face the reality that 'Bolshevism' was not suddenly going to disappear. The mutual suspicions remained strong but both sides recognised that the isolation of Russia could not be absolute. Some sort of coexistence had to be established, especially in terms of trade agreements.

A CLOSER LOOK

The Soviet Union and the League of Nations

In 1919, Bolshevik Russia was excluded from the League of Nations and the post-war arrangements for collective security. For its part, the Soviet Union had no wish to join. In 1927 Stalin explained why: 'we are fighting with all our energy against all preparations for imperialist war. The Soviet Union is not prepared to become a part of that camouflage for imperialist machinations represented by the League of Nations.'

Trade contacts began early. When finally calling off intervention in Russia in 1920, the British government authorised making trade agreements; this was effectively the point at which Britain recognised the existence of the Soviet state. Lenin was especially interested in opening trade with Germany. So was **Georgy Chicherin**, the deputy commissar for foreign affairs, who became the chief representative of the new constructive approach to Soviet foreign policy. In 1921, there were several discussions between Chicherin and Germany. In 1922, Chicherin was invited to the important international economic conference held in Genoa. This was a major step towards re-integrating Soviet Russia into international affairs; it also led to closer cooperation between Chicherin and the representatives of Weimar Germany. These contacts paved the way for the Treaty of **Rapallo** in April 1922.

A CLOSER LOOK

Rapallo, a seaside town near Genoa, was a convenient place for Walther Rathenau and Chicherin, the chief German and Russian negotiators, to slip away to during the Genoa conference.

The Treaty of Rapallo contained various 'articles':
- Articles 1 and 2 of the treaty agreed to waive claims for compensation arising from the First World War
- Article 3 concerned the reopening of formal diplomatic relations
- Articles 4 and 5 dealt with 'mutual goodwill' in commercial and economic relations.

A secret additional agreement, signed in July 1922, authorised the German Army to carry out training and military exercises inside the USSR.

Both Germany and Russia were 'outlaw' states in 1922. For both sides, the treaty agreed at Rapallo was a way out of unwelcome diplomatic isolation. In later years, great attention was focused on the secret clauses of the Rapallo treaty relating to military cooperation; but the most important factors bringing Germany and Russia together at Rapallo were trade and diplomatic recognition.

International recognition and the repercussions of the Zinoviev Letter

The Zinoviev Letter was a forgery. It was concocted by a group of conspirators led by the 'Ace of Spies', **Sidney Reilly**, a British intelligence agent of very right-wing views who had been active in Russia during the revolution and the Civil War. It was produced for a very obvious purpose: to influence public opinion against the Labour Party in the run-up to the 1924 British general election. Although a forgery, it was not entirely untrue; many of the arguments put forward in the fake letter were consistent with what Zinoviev believed, and had previously said in public.

The repercussions of the Zinoviev Letter affected Britain much more than the Soviet Union, and even in Britain the impact of the letter was actually small. In the 1924 general election, the Labour vote was not undermined by the fall-out from the Zinoviev affair but held up well. The most significant repercussions affected diplomatic relations between Britain and the Soviet Union, which were soured precisely at the time when the emphasis on exporting revolution was being downplayed by the Bolshevik leadership and Soviet foreign policy under Chicherin was ready to look outwards – instead, the diplomatic isolation of Russia was strengthened.

ACTIVITY

Divide your group in two. One half should write a newspaper article praising the Rapallo treaty from a Russian perspective and the other half from a German one. Both articles should make clear what the country hopes to gain from the agreement.

CROSS-REFERENCE

The role of **Sidney Reilly** in the Civil War is mentioned earlier in this chapter, on page 68.

ON THE LOAN TRAIL.

[In a document just disclosed by the British Foreign Office (apparently after considerable delay), M. ZINOVIEFF, a member of the Bolshevist Dictatorship, urges the British Communist Party to use "the greatest possible energy " in securing the ratification of Mr. MACDONALD's Anglo-Russian Treaty, in order to facilitate a scheme for "an armed insurrection " of the British proletariat.]

Fig. 6 Punch *cartoon, October 1924, following the* Daily Mail *scoop on the 'Zinoviev Letter' (the man carrying the sandwich board is Grigorii Zinoviev)*

ACTIVITY

What is the message of this cartoon? Use the details of the cartoon to explain your answer.

Lenin's rule by 1924

When Lenin died in 1924, he left behind him a highly centralised one-party state – but a state that faced a number of problems. Although the economy had recovered after his 'about-turn' in 1921, there were those in the Party who felt Lenin had betrayed the principles of the revolution and believed the NEP was, at best, temporary. Society had not progressed as far down the route to socialism as many supporters had hoped, while the state had a growing bureaucracy and had developed a worrying dependency on its leader. Conflicts between policies and personalities dogged Lenin's last years and look set to create problems for the future.

In order to assess Lenin's rule by 1924, complete the next activity.

Summary

Foreign troops intervened in Russia in a muddled attempt to keep Russia in the First World War and this spilled over into attempts to assist anti-Bolshevik forces in Russia's Civil War. Russia was excluded from the post-war peace settlement and from the League of Nations. The hostility was mutual. Lenin and the Bolsheviks both despised and feared the capitalist powers. The new regime saw itself as the spearhead of a revolution that would sweep the world and cleanse it of capitalist 'filth'. It was only by 1921, after the desperate struggle to survive Civil War and foreign invasions, that both sides belatedly recognised that the new Soviet state *did* exist alongside the capitalist powers, and that some sort of working relationship had to be worked out. By the time Lenin died in 1924, this process of adjusting to unwelcome realities was only just beginning.

ACTIVITY

Summary

Copy and complete the following chart by looking back at Chapters 5 to 8.

	Political control	Economic	Social	International Relations
What Lenin hoped to achieve				
What Lenin and the Bolsheviks did				
An assessment of their success in fulfilling their aims				

You might like to follow this with a class debate – with groups speaking for and against the motion 'Vladimir Lenin was a great Russian leader'.

 PRACTICE QUESTION

To what extent had Lenin achieved his aims both at home and abroad by 1924?

9 The power vacuum and power struggle

Fig. 1 *Brodsky's painting of Lenin's funeral, 1924*

Ideology and the nature of leadership

Lenin's death in January 1924 created a **power vacuum** and opened the way for a lengthy power struggle among the Party leadership. The succession to Lenin's leadership was complicated. In Marxist-Leninist ideology, power was supposed to be shared by a **collective leadership**, not held by any single, dominating leader; there was, therefore, no mechanism for any such leader to be chosen or appointed. However, Lenin had proved a very forceful leader and it was difficult to imagine a future without a single figure of authority directing policy.

KEY TERM

power vacuum: this occurs when there is no identifiable central power or authority

A CLOSER LOOK

Collective leadership

Marxist theory never envisaged a single leader as necessary in a socialist state; many in the Party felt that, after Lenin, it was time to abandon the strong central leadership principle. They argued that this might have been justified in order to safeguard Bolshevik rule through the Civil War, but was no longer required after 1924. They now wanted collective leadership by a committee of equals. This was a genuinely ideological view, but was mainly advanced by those who feared Trotsky.

Lenin's role as leader had been shaped by his Marxist ideological beliefs (which had, for example, made him refuse any 'power-sharing' with 'bourgeois elements') and also by the events and pressures of the revolution. These had resulted in many apparent changes of direction in the implementation of 'Marxism-Leninism', and led to ideological debates after Lenin's death.

CROSS-REFERENCE

The 1921 **ban on factions** is outlined in Chapter 7, page 64.

KEY TERM

'party democracy': this did not mean democracy in the normal sense – all leading Bolsheviks believed firmly in the dictatorship of the proletariat and the suppression of rival parties; party democracy meant allowing dissent and debates *within* the inner circle of the party elite

CROSS-REFERENCE

It would be useful to recap on the concept of **'democratic centralism'** in Chapter 6, page 51.

A CLOSER LOOK

Trotsky and his supporters believed that there should be **party democracy**. Stalin and his supporters stressed the importance of avoiding 'factionalism' and maintaining Party unity.

ACTIVITY

Look back at earlier chapters and identify some 'changes of direction' in Lenin's leadership. To what extent do you feel Lenin guided by his ideology and how far was he a 'pragmatic leader', that is, one who reacted to circumstances?

CROSS-REFERENCE

You will find Key Profiles for these contenders for power as follows:
Trotsky: Chapter 2, page 9
Stalin, Zinoviev and **Kamenev:** Chapter 3, pages 18 and 23 respectively
Bukharin, Rykov and **Tomsky:** this chapter, pages 84 and 85 respectively
Radek: Chapter 8, page 71.

Lenin's dictatorial style and his refusal to admit any errors had strengthened his authority as leader, and established the concept that the Party could never be wrong. The 1921 **ban on factions** had cemented the idea of a leader who commanded loyalty and obedience to the 'party line'. This clashed with elements in the Party who believed in **'party democracy'**.

By 1924 Lenin's actions and his force of personality had made him a dominant, seemingly irreplaceable leader. Yet major issues concerning the future direction of policy were still unresolved: issues concerning the extent to which party democracy should replace the **centralised control** and large, state bureaucracy that he developed under Lenin; the organisation of the economy; and the future relations of Soviet Russia with the outside world. Political ambitions and intense ideological differences were thus intertwined in the transition to an uncertain future.

The power vacuum after Lenin

The power vacuum did not appear suddenly after Lenin's death. It had begun to take shape in 1922, at the time that Lenin became seriously **incapacitated** following his first stroke. In 1922–23, a 'Triumvirate' (or Troika) of **Zinoviev**, **Kamenev** and **Stalin**, had formed to block the ambitions of **Trotsky**. Stalin, the General Secretary at that time, was unpopular and underrated by his colleagues, but he was central in these alliances. He joined forces with Kamenev and Zinoviev to prevent Trotsky's ascendancy. **Bukharin** was also influential in countering the Left. Other key personalities, such as **Rykov**, **Tomsky** and **Radek**, circled round the edges of this unacknowledged power struggle.

A CLOSER LOOK

Lenin's incapacity

In May 1922, Lenin had suffered the first of three strokes. The second stroke in December 1922 left him unable to speak and partially paralysed; the third stroke, in December 1922, left him bed-ridden and unable to speak. Lenin was sidelined from politics until his death in January 1924, although he was still a powerful presence. He had 'minders' to look after him and to transmit his wishes to the Party leadership: his wife, Nadezhda Krupskaya; his sister, Mariya Ulyanova; and Stalin, who tried hard to remain in personal contact with Lenin as much as possible.

Fig. 2 *The Triumvirate (Troika): Stalin, Kamenev and Zinoviev; the photograph also shows Alexei Rykov, who is standing behind Stalin)*

Lenin's Testament

The ambitions and rivalries of those around him alarmed Lenin, who attempted to guide the transition to a new leadership 'from beyond the grave'. In the last year of his life he put together his Testament – a 'political will' setting out his view of future dangers.

Lenin's Testament was a letter that was meant to be read out at the Party Congress after his death. Lenin dictated it over several days in late December 1922 (it took time because speaking was difficult for him, due to his first stroke); he added a postscript in January 1923. Much of the Testament was an assessment of his colleagues in the inner circle of the Party leadership. Lenin cast shadows of doubt over all of the men who might hope to succeed him, such as Trotsky, Zinoviev, Kamenev and Bukharin. Lenin was particularly harsh in his **criticisms of Stalin**, the Party's General Secretary since April 1922, partly because of Stalin's brutal actions in crushing opposition and dissent in **Georgia**, and partly because Stalin had recently **insulted Lenin's wife**, Krupskaya.

A CLOSER LOOK

Lenin's criticisms of Stalin's 'lies and rudeness'

Georgia: During the Civil War, Lenin had appointed Stalin as Commissar of Nationalities. When the Red Army moved in to seize control of Georgia, Stalin told his Party colleagues that Georgia had been won back from the Mensheviks (who had previously been in control there) by a mass uprising in favour of the Bolsheviks, supported by the Georgian people. Lenin and Trotsky fiercely criticised Stalin when it turned out that he had crushed Georgian independence by brute force, not by a popular uprising.

Stalin's insult to Krupskaya: When Stalin discovered, through Lenin's wife Nadezhda (who worked as Lenin's secretary during his illness), that he was in correspondence with Trotsky about the future of the Party, Stalin tried to see Lenin. However, Krupskaya prevented Stalin from doing so; it was in the angry telephone conversation after this rebuff that Stalin made a number of brutishly rude comments about her.

CROSS-REFERENCE

For the **disagreements between Lenin and Stalin**, as Commissar of Nationalities, over the status of areas conquered by the Red Army (including Georgia), look back to Chapter 6.

Lenin did not only attack Stalin. Nothing in his Testament could be considered to endorse anyone as his successor. Perhaps Lenin believed in a collective leadership combining the best features of these individuals; if so, he did not make this clear.

SOURCE 1

Adapted from Lenin's Testament, dictated to Krupskaya in 1923, given to the Central Committee in 1924 and intended to be read to the Party Congress on Lenin's death:

Stalin is too coarse and this defect, although quite tolerable among us Communists, becomes intolerable in a Secretary-General. That is why I suggest that the comrades think about a way of removing Stalin from that post and appointing another man in his stead who is more tolerant, more loyal, more polite and more considerate to the comrades.

Comrade Trotsky is distinguished not only by his exceptional abilities – he is, to be sure, the most able man in the present Central Committee – but also by his too far-reaching self-confidence. I will not characterise the other members of the Central Committee as to their personal qualities. I will only remind you that the October episode of Zinoviev and Kamenev was not, of course, accidental – though it ought as little to be used against them personally as the non-Bolshevism of Trotsky. Bukharin is the most valuable and greatest theoretician of the Party, but his views can only with the very greatest doubt be regarded as fully Marxist.

ACTIVITY

Evaluating primary sources

1. In Source 1, what is meant by
   a. the 'October episode' of Zinoviev and Kamenev
   b. the 'non-Bolshevism of Trotsky'?
2. Using the evidence in this chapter and in Source 1, consider Lenin's intentions in dictating his Testament; how might this Testament affect the power struggle?

Lenin's verdicts on the leading Bolsheviks were potentially explosive. If Lenin's Testament had been made public at the 1924 Party Congress, as Lenin intended, it would have had a dramatic impact on the power struggle that followed. But this did not happen. Stalin, Zinoviev and Kamenev, who had all been heavily criticised in the Testament, managed to persuade their colleagues not to publish the Testament. They thus contained the political damage that might have been inflicted on their position in the Party. However, the Testament could not be blotted out of existence; it remained in the political undergrowth as a dangerous secret that could be used (and frequently was used) as ammunition when the power struggle developed after 1924.

CROSS-REFERENCE

Stalin is profiled in Chapter 3, page 18.

Fig. 3 *Brodsky painting of Stalin from the 1920s*

A CLOSER LOOK

Stalin's position in the Bolshevik Party

Stalin was elected to the Central Committee of the Party in 1917. When the Politburo was set up by Lenin in 1918, Stalin was one of its five members. From 1918, Stalin was People's Commissar for Nationalities, asserting Bolshevik control in Georgia, Ukraine and elsewhere; this position also gave him power and influence over military affairs and the Red Army. In April 1922, Stalin became General Secretary, able to control the growing party bureaucracy.

Divisions and contenders for power: Stalin

Stalin

At the time of Lenin's death in January 1924, Stalin already held a **strong position in the Party**, as part of the 'Triumvirate' that dominated the Central Committee. Although underrated by many of his colleagues, Stalin was already one of the major contenders for power.

Character

By 1924, Stalin had gained the reputation of being a man of violence and an immensely hard worker who was expert in dealing with the details of bureaucratic organisation. His more experienced colleagues, who had been more prominent in the seizure of power in 1917, regarded Stalin (the son of a cobbler, with only a basic education) as intellectually inferior. But Stalin had a vast knowledge of the expanding party machinery, and had placed loyal supporters in key positions. Though often rude, he could be amiable and friendly; many of his allies, including Bukharin, used his pet nickname, Koba, and regarded him as **reasonable and reliable**. Stalin was jealous of others but also patient, able to keep his long-term aims hidden; and to wait a long time for revenge against people he perceived as enemies.

SOURCE 2

From recollections of Nadezhda Ioffe, from a televised interview broadcast in 1992; Nadezhda was the daughter of an 'Old Bolshevik', Adolf Abramovich Ioffe, who died in 1927:

Nobody of my father's generation, the Old Bolsheviks, thought Stalin represented any danger. For example: Kamenev would not have liked to see Bukharin having the role of General Secretary, and Bukharin would not have liked seeing Zinoviev have that post, and all of them were agreed they were afraid of Trotsky. But nobody seemed particularly opposed to the ideas of Stalin having the position of General Secretary. That is how it happened in the end; and Stalin got his hands on such a huge amount of power.

Strengths

- Stalin held a crucial position as General Secretary when the Party bureaucracy was expanding rapidly; he was good at gaining the loyalty of trusted subordinates.
- Stalin had worked hard to master the theories of Marxism-Leninism.
- Stalin was underrated by his opponents; and was very good at concealing his intentions.
- Stalin deliberately placed himself close to Lenin during his period of illness in 1922–3, thus enabling Stalin to claim that he knew and understood what Lenin wanted.

- Fear of Trotsky aided Stalin to make an alliance with Zinoviev and Kamenev in the Triumvirate.

Weaknesses

- Most of his colleagues saw him as crude and violent; this image was accentuated by Lenin's criticism of Stalin's actions as People's Commissar for Nationalities.
- He had played only a minor role in the 1917 Revolution and was overshadowed by others of greater prominence, like Trotsky, or greater popularity, like Bukharin.
- Although Lenin's Testament was not revealed to the wider Party in 1924, Stalin's colleagues knew Lenin had turned against him.

Stalin was fortunate that many leading Bolsheviks had their own reasons for keeping Lenin's views out of public knowledge in 1924; but Stalin remained on the defensive about Lenin's Testament for a long time afterwards. In 1926, Lenin's sister, Mariya, was enlisted to defend 'comrade Stalin' against criticisms from his opponents in the Politburo.

SOURCE 3

Adapted from a declaration to the Presidium of the Central Committee of the CPSU, 26 July 1926, by Lenin's sister, Mariya Il'ich Ulyanova:

The oppositionist minority in the Central Committee has recently been making systematic attacks on comrade Stalin, even going so far as to suggest a complete break between Lenin and Stalin in the last few months of Lenin' life. I consider it my duty to inform comrades about relations between Lenin and Stalin during the period when Lenin was ill. (I won't mention here the time preceding his illness, concerning which I have evidence of the most touching relationship between Lenin and Stalin, which CC members know as well as I do).

Vladimir Il'ich had a very high opinion of Stalin. During his illness it was Stalin who Lenin called in most, and asked to undertake the most intimate tasks, tasks that you would entrust only to someone you particularly trusted, who you knew to be a close comrade. I can therefore affirm that all the opposition's talk about relations between Lenin and Stalin does not correspond to reality at all. These relations remained very close and comradely.

 AS LEVEL PRACTICE QUESTION

Evaluating primary sources

With reference to Sources 1 and 3 and your understanding of the historical context, which of these two sources is more valuable in explaining Lenin's attitude to Stalin towards the end of Lenin's life?

A LEVEL PRACTICE QUESTION

Evaluating primary sources

With reference to Sources 1, 2 and 3 and your understanding of the historical context, assess the value of these three sources to an historian studying Stalin's position in the years immediately after Lenin's death.

CROSS-REFERENCE

Trotsky is profiled in Chapter 2, page 9.

Viktor Serge is profiled in Chapter 7, page 58.

Karl Radek is profiled in Chapter 8, page 71.

Divisions and contenders for power: Trotsky and the Left

In 1924, **Trotsky** was widely regarded as the most important man in the Party apart from Lenin himself. It was precisely because Trotsky was so able and so powerful that rivals were already moving to restrict his influence before Lenin died. Thus, Trotsky had many admirers, such as **Viktor Serge** and **Karl Radek**, who backed Trotsky on revolutionary ideology and Party democracy; but there were many who feared him, or disagreed with his philosophy, or both.

Later, Trotsky's position weakened in 1924–5 and Stalin's growing power became evident, Trotsky gained new allies. Grigorii Zinoviev and Lev Kamenev broke with Stalin and joined Trotsky in the Left Opposition.

Trotsky

Character

Trotsky was an extraordinary organiser and man of action. He was also an exceptional ideologist and theoretician. He held power and prestige, both from his past achievements in the **revolution and the Civil War**, and as a theorist and speechmaker. Few people were more impressed with Trotsky's brilliant abilities than Trotsky himself. He was arrogant and dismissive of people he saw as having lesser abilities; and he was often unwilling to get involved in the boring detail of party administration. Trotsky was also prone to sudden bouts of illness and inaction, seemingly 'freezing' at times of crisis.

- Trotsky was a brilliant intellectual and theorist, and an inspiring speechmaker.
- He was an energetic man of action during the revolution and the Civil War, second in power and influence only to Lenin.
- He had formidable political skills, ruthlessness, authority, and organisational ability.

Weaknesses

- Many Bolsheviks feared Trotsky: they thought he might use his hold over the Red Army to seize power after Lenin's death.
- Because Trotsky had been a Menshevik and was a late convert to Bolshevism, some 'Old Bolsheviks' were suspicious of him.
- Colleagues disliked his arrogance and disdain for those he thought less clever than himself; he badly underrated Stalin.
- Trotsky made no serious attempt to build a base of support within the Party.
- Trotsky was seen as inconsistent and an opportunist. He opposed the Triumvirate of Stalin, Zinoviev and Kamenev, but later allied with Zinoviev and Kamenev against Stalin.
- He could be indecisive and tended to fall ill at critical moments.
- He made serious errors of judgement, such as attacking the Party bureaucracy in 1924 when he needed its support.

Fig. 4   *Leon Trotsky (1879–1940)*

CROSS-REFERENCE

To recap on his role in the **revolution**, look back to Chapter 5.

Trotsky's part in the **Civil War** is covered in Chapter 6.

CROSS-REFERENCE

Kamenev is profiled in Chapter 3, page 18.

A CLOSER LOOK

Kamenev's position in the Party

Kamenev played an important role in the events of 1917 leading to Bolshevik seizure of power (although he clashed with Lenin in November 1917 and briefly resigned from the Party). In 1918, he became Chairman of the Moscow Soviet. He was one of the first members of the Politburo from 1919, and was Lenin's Deputy Chairman of the Council of People's Commissars. Although he was Leon Trotsky's brother-in-law, he opposed Trotsky's political ambitions; he joined with Grigorii Zinoviev and Josef Stalin in the anti-Trotsky 'Triumvirate' from 1923.

Lev Kamenev

Character

Kamenev was capable and intelligent; a skilful politician good at managing people and situations. He was closely associated with Grigorii Zinoviev – the two colleagues often acted together as a partnership. Like Zinoviev, Kamenev saw himself as an important player in a collective leadership but perhaps lacked the ambition or ruthlessness to seek power for himself. He also gained a reputation for 'flip-flopping' – being too ready to change sides.

Strengths

- As one of the 'Old Bolsheviks' a man who had helped form Party policy and was close to Lenin, he had great influence. In 1922, after his stroke, Lenin entrusted many of his personal papers to Kamenev.
- Kamenev had a strong **power base** in Moscow, where he ran the local Party.
- He was regarded as thoughtful and intelligent, good at smoothing out difficulties amongst colleagues, with the ability to get things done.

Weaknesses

- Like Zinoviev, Kamenev gained a reputation for inconsistency and opportunism by opposing Lenin in 1917 and later switching alliances between Stalin and Trotsky.
- He was too closely linked to Zinoviev, who was more popular than he was.
- Many regarded him as being too 'soft' and lacking the drive to be a sole leader.
- Kamenev seriously underestimated his rivals, especially Stalin.

Grigorii Zinoviev

Character

Zinoviev was intelligent and educated, with a wide knowledge of European culture. He was one of the Party's best speechmakers, with a commanding presence; for example as Chairman of the **Comintern** Congresses. But he had a reputation for being vain; he was also inconsistent, prone to unpredictable mood swings. Like his close associate Lev Kamenev, Zinoviev was seen as a compromiser without any consistent philosophy, and who tended to buckle under pressure.

Fig. 5 *Lev Kamenev (1883–1936)*

A CLOSER LOOK

Zinoviev's position in the Party

Zinoviev held important and influential positions in the highest ranks of the Party: he was a member of the **Politburo** and was the spokesman for the Central Committee at the annual Party Congresses. He was head of the **Comintern** and chairman of the Comintern Congresses. From 1923, with Stalin and Kamenev, Zinoviev had great political authority as part of the 'Triumvirate'.

Strengths

- As an 'Old Bolshevik', he commanded respect from some colleagues for his contribution to the revolution.
- He had been high in Lenin's favour before 1924; Lenin called Zinoviev 'closest and most trusted assistant'.
- His role as party boss in Leningrad (as Petrograd was now renamed) gave him a strong political power base, second in importance only to Moscow.

Fig. 6 *Grigorii Zinoviev (1883–1936)*

CROSS-REFERENCE

Grigorii Zinoviev is profiled in Chapter 3, page 23.

CROSS-REFERENCE

The **Comintern** is explained in Chapter 8, page 70.

The **Politburo** is explained in Chapter 6, page 51.

KEY PROFILE

Fig. 7   *Bukharin was a prominent revolutionary Bolshevik theorist*

Nikolai Bukharin (1888–1938) opposed making peace with Germany in 1918. During the Civil War, Bukharin backed war communism, but later supported the NEP. In the mid 1920s, Bukharin and Stalin were virtually joint rulers of the USSR. Bukharin opposed Trotsky and supported Socialism in One Country, but later split with Stalin and became part of the Right opposition, with Tomsky and Rykov. From 1928 Bukharin was outmanoeuvred by Stalin and his influence declined. In 1937, Bukharin was expelled from the Central Committee; in 1938 he was executed after a show trial.

CROSS-REFERENCE

War communism is discussed in Chapter 7, page 57.

The **NEP** is discussed in Chapter 7, page 62.

Weaknesses

- His opposition to Lenin over the timing of the Bolshevik coup (and his joint resignation with Kamenev and Rykov in November 1917) was held against him.
- He seriously underestimated his rivals and opponents, especially Stalin.
- He and Kamenev left it too late before switching their support to Trotsky.

Divisions and contenders for power: Bukharin and the Right

Bukharin was mostly associated with the Right of the Bolshevik Party, and was often supported by Rykov and Tomsky. Bukharin supported Stalin against the Left Opposition and, for a time, the two men developed a close working partnership, often known as the 'Duumvirate'; but Bukharin's popularity aroused Stalin's jealousy and hostility.

Nikolai Bukharin

Character

Rank-and-file Bolsheviks regarded Bukharin as both impressive and likeable. He was a brilliant intellectual and theoretician, and highly popular with his Politburo colleagues and with party members. Lenin called him 'the darling of the Party'. He was open and cooperative and had friendly relations with people on the Left as well as the Right. But he could be naive and lacked the capacity for intrigue, which made him unsuited to Party infighting.

Strengths

- Bukharin was popular within the Party, close to Lenin and for a long time friendly with Trotsky; in the 1920s, he was a close associate of Stalin and much respected by him.
- He was widely regarded as the best theoretician in the Party.
- He was a particular expert on economics and agriculture, at a time when debates about the peasantry were of major concern to the Bolshevik government.

Weaknesses

- Because Bukharin tried to remain on good terms with everyone and to avoid factional in-fighting, he had no power base.
- He seriously underestimated Stalin; he was also much more popular in the Party than Stalin, which made him a target for Stalin's enmity.
- He made tactical mistakes, such as leaving it much too late to make an alliance with Zinoviev and Kamenev.

Alexei Rykov

Character

Rykov was on the moderate wing of the Party. Although always loyal to Lenin, he had frequently disagreed with Lenin and the radicals. In his moderate and conciliatory temperament, and in questions of policy, he was more aligned to the views of Bukharin and Tomsky. As Chairman of the government he wanted to play a unifying role.

Strengths

- Rykov was widely respected in the Party for his experience as an 'Old Bolshevik', active since the early days of the revolution.

- He had shown administrative ability in the implementation of **war communism** during the Civil War; and in managing the switch of policy to **NEP**.
- He had extensive support from **Sovnarkom**, who chose him as Deputy Chairman in 1923 and then Chairman in 1924.

Weaknesses

- Rykov was a conciliator more than a plotter; and among the moderates, he was overshadowed by Bukharin's ability and popularity.
- He held a largely ceremonial position in the collective leadership and lacked a power base.
- His policy of putting heavy taxes on vodka was socially correct but politically unwise and aroused intense opposition from sections of the Party.
- As with Kamenev and Zinoviev, the fact that he had argued against Lenin over revolutionary tactics in 1917 was held against him.
- Like many others, he underrated Stalin until it was too late.

Mikhail Tomsky

Character

Tomsky was the son of a factory worker and had a long association with the trade unions. He was one of the few 'Old Bolsheviks' from a genuine working-class background, with a reputation for plain speaking. Despite his class origins, his political views were moderate.

Strengths

- Tomsky was respected for his long record as an 'Old Bolshevik', and his working-class origins made him popular in the Party.
- His role as chief spokesman for the trade unions gave him a strong position within the Party; he was General Secretary of **Red International of the Trade Unions** from 1920 and was elected to the Central Committee and the Politburo in 1922.
- He was a natural ally of moderate leaders, such as Rykov and Bukharin.

Weaknesses

- Tomsky's intense hostility to Trotsky blinded him to the danger of Stalin; his alliance with Stalin, Rykov and Bukharin in purging left-wingers from the Party in 1926 handed massive potential power to Stalin.
- His power base in the trade unions made him an obvious target for Stalin's jealousy.
- His support for the NEP was going to be used against him when the grain crisis of 1927 hit the economy.

KEY PROFILE

Fig. 8   *Rykov wanted to play a unifying role*

Alexei Rykov (1881–1938) was a moderate Bolshevik who supported the idea of a coalition with other Socialists in 1917. He was Commissar of the Interior in 1917–8 and a member of the Politburo. Rykov was Lenin's successor as Head of Government (the Council of People's Commissars) between 1924 and 1930. He was briefly Stalin's ally against Trotsky, but then joined Bukharin's right-wing group and supported the NEP. After Bukharin's downfall, Rykov was sacked from the Politburo and all other posts. He was executed in 1938 after a show trial.

CROSS-REFERENCE

Sovnarkom (the Council of People's Commissioners) is introduced in Chapter 4, page 31.

KEY TERM

The Red International of the Trade Unions: (sometimes called 'Profintern'), this was set up by the Comintern in 1921 as a communist rival to the Social Democratic International Federation of Trade Unions, established in 1919 with its headquarters in Amsterdam

KEY PROFILE

Fig. 9   *Tomsky was popular in the Party*

Mikhail Tomsky (1880–1936) was from a working-class background. He was in charge of the trade unions from 1920 but fell out with Lenin over the role of the unions under the NEP. Later, Lenin rehabilitated him and he was elected to the Politburo in 1922; he was one of the pall-bearers at Lenin's funeral. Tomsky was hostile to the Left and allied himself with Bukharin. He was expelled from the Politburo in 1930. He committed suicide in 1936 to avoid being killed in Stalin's Great Terror.

Summary

The first phase of the power struggle that would follow Lenin's death in 1924 was already underway before Lenin died, as the 'Triumvirate' of Zinoviev, Kamenev, and Stalin, the General Secretary, moved to block the ambitions of Trotsky. Lenin's Testament criticised leading colleagues in the Party and did not make clear who should follow him as leader. This left the leading communists, including Stalin and Trotsky, to manoeuvre for power and influence. Party alliances shifted as Zinoviev and Kamenev, anxious about Stalin's growing power, switched their support to Trotsky and the Left. The power struggle was to be a lengthy and confused political process of bitter ideological disputes, personal rivalries and shifting alliances between the men who saw themselves as Lenin's successors and guardians of his legacy.

ACTIVITY

Summary

Look back through this chapter and write down reasons for and against the proposition that: 'By 1924, Lenin's actions had created the conditions for Civil War within the Party leadership'.

STUDY TIP

This question requires a balanced assessment of the main contenders for power in 1924, looking at their strengths and weaknesses as potential leaders of Russia. However, you must ensure that the essay is well planned and does not turn into a list. One approach would be to think of the qualities needed to be an effective leader of Russia and draw on what you know about each leader to show which possessed the suggested quality and which did not, also providing examples to support your views. You should also ensure you make it clear whether you agree with the quotation (in whole or in part) as a result of your analysis.

AS LEVEL **PRACTICE QUESTION**

'None of the contenders for power in 1924 possessed the qualities needed to be an effective leader of Russia.' Explain why you agree or disagree with this view.

10 Ideological debates and issues in the leadership struggle

Fig. 1 *Lenin and Stalin together at Gorky, 1922. During Lenin's last years, Stalin made great efforts to be close to Lenin at every opportunity, posing as Lenin's loyal and 'indispensable' comrade*

LEARNING OBJECTIVES

In this chapter you will learn about:

- NEP and industrialisation
- 'permanent revolution' versus 'socialism in One Country'
- how and why Stalin became party leader
- the outcome for the other contenders.

NEP and industrialisation

From 1921, the Party was badly split over economic policy, but the split was not only about economics. The question of how to manage the economy was inseparable from the ideological debates about Marxism and Leninism. When Lenin introduced the **New Economic Policy** in 1921, it was a radical divergence from Marxist theory because it allowed private enterprise to continue, in contradiction of revolutionary socialism. Lenin said in 1921 that NEP was a necessary compromise, to be implemented 'seriously and for a long time'. Lenin's successors had to grapple with this legacy: Was it a temporary tactic to be discarded as soon as possible? Or was it permissible, given the backward conditions of Russia, to stick to the NEP to build the economy as a precursor to full socialism?

The 'Left', led by Trotsky, Zinoviev and Kamenev, wanted to abandon NEP. The 'Right', led by Rykov, Tomsky and Bukharin, believed NEP should continue. Stalin's attitude was inconsistent, fluctuating from a left-leaning position up to 1925, then support for the continuance of the NEP up to 1928, finally switching back in 1928 to 1929 to a policy of replacing the NEP with a revolutionary surge towards rapid industrialisation and collectivisation of agriculture.

'Permanent revolution' or 'Socialism in One Country'

The ideological issue that overshadowed all other debates was the question of the world revolution. All theories of Marxism-Leninism had assumed it was impossible for revolution to survive in a single country; the capitalist countries would gang together and strangle the revolution at birth. Thus it was not just desirable but essential for the Bolshevik Revolution in Russia to trigger a chain reaction of other revolutions. But Marxist theory was contradicted by events: the revolutions in Germany, Hungary and elsewhere

ACTIVITY

Evaluating primary sources

Look carefully at Fig 1, then read the section in this chapter on 'How and why Stalin became party leader'. Make a brief evaluation of the importance of personal proximity to Lenin for Stalin's rise to power. (You may find it helpful also to consider the opening section of Chapter 12.)

CROSS-REFERENCE

Lenin's introduction of the **New Economic Policy** in 1921 is discussed in Chapter 7, page 62.

ACTIVITY

Using the evidence of this chapter, consider the following possible explanations of Stalin's inconsistency towards economic policy. Was it simply due to political calculation, fitting his ideas to the needs of the power struggle? Was he was just reacting to short-term economic pressures, such as the bread shortages and high food prices of 1928? Or was Stalin driven, all along, by committed leftist ideology?

CROSS-REFERENCE

permanent revolution is discussed on page 19.

KEY TERM

Socialism in One Country: the concept that efforts should be concentrated on building the socialist state in USSR irrespective of what went on elsewhere in the world. This broke with the previously held Marxist position that socialism had to be established globally

CROSS-REFERENCE

Stalin's **position in the Party leadership** is discussed in Chapter 9, page 80.

CROSS-REFERENCE

The **cult of Leninism**, by which Lenin was elevated to god-like status, is discussed in Chapter 12, page 104.

ACTIVITY

Extension

Find and read Stalin's funeral oration on the death of Lenin online. Pick out phrases that would help contribute to the 'Cult of Lenin'.
Consider whether this oration is really a piece of Stalinist propaganda.

A CLOSER LOOK

Trotsky's hesitation in 1924

Robert Service, in his biography of Stalin, suggests that Trotsky was correct in his judgement to hold back at the 1924 Party Congress. Service argues that at the time there was still an inbuilt majority against Trotsky, and that any move he made to remove Stalin from the Politburo would have awakened fears of Trotsky bidding for supreme power.

were crushed, and defeat in the Russo-Polish War in 1920 blocked the revolutionary way to the West. In the 1920s, the USSR existed as the only communist state in the world. How to react to this theoretically impossible situation was a burning question for the Party.

Trotsky and the Left still held to the line that the Soviet Union should commit to '**permanent revolution**'; maximum support should be given to the Comintern in fomenting revolutions across the world until a truly socialist society was achieved everywhere. From 1923, however, Stalin came to the more pragmatic view that there *could* be '**Socialism in One Country**' and that Bolshevik Russia should aim to build a 'workers' paradise' in the Soviet Union as an example to the world. NEP had been a compromise with economic reality; 'Socialism in One Country' would be a compromise with the realities of the international situation. This approach appealed to many in the Party who wanted stability, and who feared the continuous revolutionary turmoil that Trotsky was advocating.

How and why Stalin became Party leader

By 1924, Stalin had established a central **position in the Party leadership**. Lenin's funeral enabled Stalin to entrench his position further. Stalin was placed in charge of arrangements for the funeral and seized the opportunity to promote the **cult of Leninism** by making the funeral a state occasion, marked by reverend adoration for the Great Leader. Stalin insisted that Lenin's body was embalmed and placed on public view. It has been said that Stalin was making Leninism into a religion, with the loyal comrade Stalin as its High Priest. **Trotsky was absent** – far away in Sukhum on the Black Sea, convalescing from a serious bout of influenza.

A CLOSER LOOK

Trotsky's absence from Lenin's funeral

Trotsky's failure to attend Lenin's funeral gave a political advantage to Stalin. Afterwards, it was widely suspected that Stalin had cunningly 'arranged' Trotsky's absence by misleading messages, but this was not the case. Trotsky chose to stay at Sukhum because he was ill and a long way away. At the time, missing the funeral did not seem as important as was later realised.

During 1924 and 1925, the power struggle shifted into a new phase. Until this time, Stalin's political skills had been underrated by other, more flamboyant, leaders – just as they had underrated the importance of Stalin's bureaucratic power as General Secretary. With their more obvious and pressing concern to 'stop Trotsky', Stalin's ambitions had gone unnoticed. However, as Trotsky's position became weaker, perceptions of Stalin changed and the Triumvirate began to fall apart.

The defeat of the Left Opposition, 1924–1927

It was perhaps surprising that Trotsky did not make a decisive move against Stalin early in 1924. This was the time when Stalin's control of the bureaucracy was gradually being perceived as a threat to his rivals; the Thirteenth Party Congress in May 1924 seemed to offer the perfect occasion to move against Stalin. **Trotsky hesitated**, possibly because he was nervous of being blamed for causing a split in the Party, possibly because he thought there would be a better opportunity later. Stalin also had valuable support from Kamenev and Zinoviev at the Congress, who protected Stalin from criticisms arising from Lenin's Testament. The Triumvirate seemed strong.

Trotsky never found a better opportunity to challenge Stalin. His position, seemingly so powerful at the time of Lenin's death, slid slowly backwards. Trotsky was not a natural conspirator like Stalin; he lacked an instinct for bureaucratic infighting, or the patience needed to mobilise his supporters, or to win over potential allies until it was too late. Stalin, however, showed a single-minded focus on building up a personal following of loyal supporters such as **Vyacheslav Molotov** (the Assistant General Secretary) **Lazar Kaganovich** (first secretary of the Party in Ukraine), **Kliment Voroshilov** (an ally of Stalin since they had worked together as Political Commissars fighting in the Civil War) and **Sergei Kirov**, a youthful rising star in the Leningrad party leadership, and placing them in key positions. According to Robert Service, 'Stalin demanded efficiency as well as loyalty from the gang members. He created an ambience of conspiracy, companionship and crude masculine humour. In return for their services he looked after their interests'.

KEY PROFILE

Molotov's real name was **Vyacheslav Mikhailovich Skryabin (1890–1986)**. The son of a shop assistant, he joined the Bolsheviks in 1906, was twice exiled to Siberia, and was involved in the Bolshevik seizure of power in Petrograd in 1917. A loyal ally of Stalin, he was Second Secretary from 1922. Often seen as a boring mediocrity (Trotsky referred to him as 'Stone Arse') he played a key role in Stalin's rise to power. He replaced Rykov as Party Chairman in 1930 and was then Minister of Foreign Affairs from 1939 to 1949. He was ousted by Khrushchev in 1956.

Fig. 2 *Stalin and his 'gang members'.*

After the Thirteenth Party Congress of 1924, tensions grew within the Triumvirate as Kamenev and Zinoviev became frustrated by their failure to control Stalin. Bukharin became an ally of Stalin against the others. This was the time when the debate over 'permanent revolution' or 'Socialism in One Country' was particularly intense, and the mood of the Party was moving towards Stalin's view that stability within the USSR was more important than 'reckless adventures' fomenting revolution abroad. Similarly, the future of the NEP was fiercely debated; many in the Party disagreed with Bukharin's enthusiastic support for **peasants** 'enriching themselves'. In these shifting

KEY PROFILE

Lazar Kaganovich (1893–1991) was often known as 'Iron Lazar'. From 1917, he rose through the ranks to become First Secretary of Ukraine. He was a loyal supporter of Stalin in the 1920s, running the party bureaucracy. He joined the Politburo in 1930. His role in forced collectivisation was very brutal; he has been blamed as the chief cause of the Great Famine in 1932 to 1933; he continued to be a central figure managing industry, railways and the war effort. He lost influence after Stalin's death.

KEY PROFILE

Kliment Voroshilov (1881–1969) was a member of the Politburo from 1925 to 1961. He was a loyal supporter of Stalin from 1921 and became People's Commissar for Military and Naval Affairs in 1925. He was made a Marshal of the Soviet Union in 1935. Voroshilov became a Second World War commander and remained a powerful figure in the regime until after Stalin's death.

KEY PROFILE

Sergei Kirov (1886–1934) was active in the revolutions of 1905 and 1917, and was a flamboyant military commander in the North Caucasus in the Civil War. He became prominent in the party organisation in Azerbaijan; in 1926, he was handpicked by Stalin to replace Zinoviev as Party boss in Leningrad. He was very popular with the Party membership and seen as a rising star. This is probably the reason why he was assassinated, on Stalin's secret orders, in 1934.

CROSS-REFERENCE

The economic policies pursued by Bukharin and Stalin, regarding the **peasants**, are covered in Chapter 14.

alliances, Stalin almost invariably placed himself in the 'golden middle', avoiding extreme positions.

From a private letter from Zinoviev to Kamenev, 30 July 1924:

You're letting Stalin make a mockery of us. You want facts? Examples? Allow me! The National Question: Stalin makes all the appointments of the Central Committee instructors. The Comintern: V.I. (Lenin) dedicated a good 10 per cent of his time to the Comintern. Stalin just turns up, takes one quick look, and makes a decision. Bukharin and I are never asked about anything.
Pravda: This morning, Bukharin was told the entire editorial board of the paper had been sacked without him being asked. We can't tolerate this any longer.
If the party is doomed to go through a period (probably very brief) of Stalin's personal despotism, then so be it. But I for one do not intend to keep quiet about all this swinish behaviour by Stalin. People talk about the 'triumvirate' in the belief that I am not the least important member of it. But in reality there is no triumvirate, only Stalin's dictatorship.

A statement by Kamenev, as part of his and Zinoviev's attack on Stalin at the Party Congress, in December 1925:

We are against creating a theory of 'the Leader'; we are against making anyone into 'the Leader'. We're for the idea that our leadership should be internally organised in such a way that there is a truly all-powerful Politburo uniting all our party's politicians, and that the Secretariat should be subordinate to it, carrying out the Politburo's decrees. Personally, I suggest our General Secretary is not the kind of figure who can unite the old Bolshevik high command around him. It is precisely because I've often said this personally to comrade Stalin, and precisely because I've often said this to a group of Leninist comrades, that I repeat it now to the Congress. I have come to the conclusion that comrade Stalin is incapable of performing the role of unifier of the Bolshevik high command.

You should be able to comment on the provenance of each source, reflecting on its author, date and audience, and referring to its tone and context. In evaluating the content, you need to quote from the sources to support the points made about Stalin's position and also apply your own historical knowledge to explain your points.

 PRACTICE QUESTION

Evaluating primary sources

With reference to Sources 1 and 2 and your understanding of the historical context, which of these two sources is more valuable in explaining Stalin's position in 1924–1925, during the struggle for power after Lenin's death?

By the beginning of 1925, the balance within the Party was swinging further away from Trotsky. At the Central Committee in January, Trotsky was forced out of his post as People's Commissar for War. Zinoviev proposed that Trotsky should be expelled from the Party but Stalin, determined to keep his image as a moderate, rejected this. Trotsky was thus isolated but not yet defeated. Without fears of Trotsky to keep it together, the Triumvirate became even more fractious; Kamenev and Zinoviev opposed Stalin in the Central Committee in September 1925 and the battle lines of the power struggle were redrawn at the Fourteenth Party Congress in December 1925. Kamenev and Zinoviev launched a direct attack on Stalin.

They found it very hard to do this effectively. They had, after all, been allied to him for the previous year and had frequently backed Stalin's view of the dangers of 'factionalism'. From 1925, they were easily painted as factionalists endangering the security of the USSR at a precarious time. The result was that Kamenev and Zinoviev were gradually pushed towards joining their former enemy, Trotsky, in the Left Opposition. Stalin and Bukharin formed a partnership, sometimes called the 'Duumvirate', that was virtually running the country in 1926 and 1927.

Fig. 3   *Bukharin, Stalin and Trotsky at the funeral of Felix Dzerzhinsky, 1926*

The power struggle was far from over in 1926 and the Party leadership was still unstable. Stalin and Bukharin still feared Trotsky, and even more so when Kamenev and Zinoviev joined Trotsky in mid 1926. The Left Opposition became the United Opposition. The bitter infighting in the first half of 1926 was theoretical as well as political: there was a war of words fought out by the main contenders in a flood of books and pamphlets sometimes known as the '**Literary Discussion**'. This was an important episode in the power struggle. Trotsky did not win the war of words as he had expected; Stalin's line appealed to a majority of party members. Even if Trotsky had won, it would not have compensated for his weaker position in bureaucratic politics.

The clash between Trotsky and his allies on one side, against Stalin and Bukharin on the other, continued through 1926. Although Stalin generally had the upper hand, he still faced continuous criticism and, in December 1926, his frustrations led him to offer to resign as General Secretary. Trotsky and the United Opposition increased the pressure in the spring and summer of 1927, at a time when Stalin was blamed for the crushing of the **Chinese Communists** in Canton and Shanghai.

Stalin and Bukharin fought back strongly, backed by their inbuilt majorities in Party committees. In October 1927, the Central Committee voted to expel Trotsky, Zinoviev and Kamenev from the CC. In November, Trotsky and Zinoviev were expelled from the Party altogether. At the Fifteenth Party Congress in December 1927, the expulsions were confirmed, and dozens of other 'oppositionists' were expelled also. Stalin and Bukharin were seemingly triumphant.

The defeat of Bukharin and the Right

Outwardly, the 'Duumvirate' of Stalin and Bukharin was secure and harmonious. The two families lived near each other and private relations

A CLOSER LOOK

The 'Literary Discussion'

Trotsky's writings were the most impressive of those produced in the Literary Discussion; Bukharin, Kamenev and Zinoviev also contributed books and articles. But Stalin was an active theorist, too. His book *On Questions of Leninism* argued the case for 'Socialism in One Country' with thoroughness (though misrepresenting what Lenin had actually said). His opponents continued to underrate Stalin's understanding of revolutionary theory but his book and his speeches were well prepared.

CROSS-REFERENCE

Stalin's policies in relation to China in 1927 are covered in Chapter 12, page 105.

CROSS-REFERENCE

Stalin's aims in terms of economic **policy** are discussed in Chapter 11.

CROSS-REFERENCE

The **first Five Year Plan** is discussed in Chapter 11, page 98 and Chapter 14, page 117.

between them were friendly. But political tensions began to emerge in 1928. Partly, these tensions were about power: Stalin's long-term aims did not extend to sharing power. Partly, they were about **policy**, especially in relation to the NEP and the peasants.

At the beginning of 1928, Russia was facing a serious food shortage; the regime had difficulty buying enough grain from peasant producers. This crisis intensified dissatisfaction with the NEP among Party members keen to see Russia industrialise more quickly. There was an undercurrent of criticisms of Bukharin, always likely to be seen as 'soft' on the peasant question. Stalin's instincts were in favour of tough action to compel the peasantry to increase grain supplies; it is also possible Stalin had always favoured such policies but had held back while he was fighting his political battles with the Left. As Stalin moved to harsh measures in the countryside, divisions between him and Bukharin widened.

Stalin personally supervised stern measures against the peasants in western Siberia in January and February 1928. It is significant that he did not discuss this with Bukharin beforehand, but took unilateral action. At the same time, Stalin was preparing the way for a rapid surge in industrialisation – what later became the **first Five Year Plan**. Again, this led to friction with Bukharin, who wanted industrialisation, but at a slower pace. In April 1928, Bukharin protested against 'excesses' by officials. Bukharin expected other Party leaders to support him, but they did not. He and Stalin clashed repeatedly in the Politburo. Bukharin's numerous speeches and articles in favour of 'sensible' policies made little impact. Bukharin was now isolated and vulnerable to Stalin's attacks.

SOURCE 3

Bukharin defending himself against attacks by Stalin at a meeting of the Politburo, 9 February 1929:

Serious, urgent questions are not discussed. The entire country is deeply troubled by the grain crisis and supply problems. But conferences of the proletarian ruling party are silent. The entire country feels that all is not well with the peasantry. But conferences of the proletarian party, *our party,* are silent. The entire country sees and feels the changes in the international situation. But conferences of the proletarian party are silent. Instead, there is a hail of resolutions about 'deviations'. Instead, there are millions of rumours and gossip about the 'rightists' Rykov, Tomsky, Bukharin, etc. This is petty politics, not the politics needed in a time of difficulties to tell the working classes the truth of the situation, the politics that trusts the masses and hears and feels the needs of the masses.

STUDY TIP

Consider each source in turn to evaluate both what it says or implies about faction-fighting and whether the provenance of the source would make it more or less valuable. You will need to comment on the tone and emphasis of the sources and apply your own knowledge of the context to explain and assess what is said.

 PRACTICE QUESTION

Evaluating primary sources

With reference to Sources 1, 2 and 3 and your understanding of the historical context, assess the value of these three sources to an historian studying the faction-fighting in the leadership struggle after Lenin's death.

Stalin, formerly the moderate in the 'golden middle', was reverting to radical revolutionary policies in many areas: war in the countryside against the 'kulaks', sudden and rapid industrialisation, even a new emphasis on interventionist foreign policies and aggressive support for the Comintern. These new policies were followed through with increasing severity through 1928 and into 1929. Bukharin ceased to be a partner and became an enemy, along with other 'rightists' such as Rykov and Tomsky.

By February 1929, Bukharin was desperate enough to consider making an alliance with Trotsky (he did not go through with it, but Stalin was aware of the contacts between them). In April 1929, Bukharin was deprived of several of his government posts, including editorship of *Pravda*; in November 1929, he was expelled from the Politburo. In December 1929, Stalin made a speech that revealed the harsh nature of the policies he now intended to follow. The era of Stalin the Revolutionary was over; the era of **Stalin the Despot** was just beginning.

ACTIVITY

It has been claimed that Stalin's emergence as leader of the Soviet Union followed a series of carefully crafted steps. Construct a timeline in the grid below to pick out key stages in this process.

Phases	Dates	Key events
'Stop Trotsky' 1922–1924		
Defeat of the Left 1924–1927		
Defeat of the Right and the Rise of a Despot		

The outcome for the other contenders

Few of the Old Bolsheviks died peacefully in their beds. Of those who contended for power in the 1920s, Stalin was the only one to live beyond 1940. The rest died through violence, on Stalin's orders.

Their elimination was gradual after 1929. Some, like Trotsky, went into exile and criticised Stalin's dictatorship from afar. Most attempted to reconcile themselves to Stalin's rule by making humiliating confessions of past 'errors' and accepting subordinate positions in the Party. Zinoviev and Kamenev gave in to Stalin in 1928, but they lost their high posts and their place in the Politburo. Rykov was sacked and replaced by Molotov in 1930. Tomsky was removed from his role with the trade unions. Even Bukharin, the most committed opponent of Stalin, admitted 'my mistakes' in November 1930 in a desperate effort to preserve some limited influence in the Party. He hated Stalin but still retained faith in the revolution and could not make a complete break with it.

But they did not save themselves; Stalin neither forgot nor forgave his former rivals. As his regime tightened its grip on all aspects of politics and society in the 1930s, and as Stalin himself became ever more paranoid about real and imaginary threats to his position, he set about purging any remnants of opposition. In a series of arrests and show trials in the later 1930s, those who had once opposed Stalin (and those who knew the truth about his earlier career) were targeted, denounced and executed.

Stalin was not satisfied with just defeating his rivals. Most were forced into humiliating confessions of past 'crimes' of conspiring against the USSR; their families were often victimised. The memory of their contribution to the Bolshevik revolution was systematically expunged by the **falsification** of the documentary or photographic record of their place in history.

A CLOSER LOOK

Why Stalin won the power struggle

Whether Stalin was an opportunist who manipulated ideology or was driven by genuine convictions, he certainly knew how to deal with ideological issues and debates, always promoting the idea that he was following the principles laid down by Lenin. Stalin's ability to pick a middle path through Party debates while also exploiting developments, such as the change from elections to appointments within the party hierarchy, the growth of central authority during the Civil War, and the ban on factionalism, provided the framework within which Stalin was able to rise to power.

ACTIVITY

Extension

One of the finest books about Soviet Russia is by Stephen F. Cohen, *Bukharin and the Bolshevik Revolution*. Professor Cohen also contributed many fascinating comments to *Revolutionary*, the first episode of the 1990 Thames television documentary on Stalin. Try to view this on YouTube.

CROSS-REFERENCE

For more on the **falsification** of history, look ahead to Chapter 15, page 131.

The fates of the contenders

Zinoviev: submitted to Stalin, 1928; expelled from the Party, 1932; executed after a show trial, 1936

Kamenev: submitted to Stalin, 1928; expelled from the Party, 1932; executed after a show trial, 1936

Tomsky: forced out as leader of the trade unions, 1929; removed from Central Committee, 1934; killed himself in 1936 to avoid trial and execution

Rykov: expelled from Politburo, 1930; removed from Central Committee, 1934; executed after a show trial, 1938

Bukharin: expelled from the Politburo, 1929; rehabilitated, 1934; executed after a show trial, 1938

Trotsky: expelled from the Party, 1927; exiled 1929; murdered by one of Stalin's agents, 1940

ACTIVITY

Divide into pairs or small groups and take one of the leadership contenders each: Stalin, Trotsky, Zinoviev, Kamenev, Bukharin, Rykov or Tomsky. Using Chapters 9 and 10, create a poster to show your contender in the leadership struggle and what happened to him down to 1929.

STUDY TIP

This question requires you to examine the means by which Stalin rose to the top in the power struggle after Lenin's death. However, you must be careful to avoid a narrative of the power struggle with comment. You should plan your argument beforehand, drawing on examples to support comment on Stalin's displays of ruthless ambition and the importance of policy disagreements at key stages. Remember that there were several different policies being considered at this time. Decide which was key to Stalin's success and argue accordingly.

Summary

By December 1929, Stalin's dictatorship was at last fully established. Politically, Stalin had outmanoeuvred and marginalised all his rivals. Ideologically, Stalin had made himself dominant and free to uphold his key themes: Socialism in One Country, centralised control, Stalin's own role as Lenin's true successor, and the need to rush through the economic transformation of the Soviet Union. The forces of revolution were channelled into the ideas of what was now 'Marxism-Leninism-Stalinism' – as interpreted by Stalin. Internal party dissent was obliterated. The key personalities who had opposed Stalin were swept aside.

 PRACTICE QUESTION

'Stalin's success in the power struggle by 1929 was due more to his ruthless ambition than to his policies.' Assess the validity of this view.

11 Economic developments

Fig. 1 *Soviet collective farming*

LEARNING OBJECTIVES

In this chapter you will learn about:

- the reasons for and impact of the 'Great Turn'
- the economic shift and the launch of the first Five Year Plan
- the decision to collectivise.

The 'Great Turn'

In 1924, the Soviet economy was based on the continuation of the **NEP**. The great **compromise of 1921** had swerved away from war communism towards a partial return of free markets and private economic activity; this had achieved a degree of economic stability. Many in the Party saw NEP as the way forward for the foreseeable future. Between 1927 and 1929, however, there was a dramatic shift in economic policy: the 'Great Turn'. NEP was abandoned as the regime committed itself to rapid industrialisation whatever the costs, and previous policies towards the peasantry were scrapped to make way for the brutal enforcement of collectivisation of agriculture. This change of direction marked the end of the first, Leninist phase of the Bolshevik state, and the start of Stalinism.

The problems of the Russian economy

Industrialisation in Russia had taken place at some speed in tsarist Russia in the years before 1917, but the industrial economy was badly hit by the impact of war and Civil War. There was a degree of industrial recovery after **1921** but this was slow and patchy, despite the elaborate central planning organisations, Veshenka and Gosplan. Production was weakened by strikes, managerial inefficiency and low levels of mechanisation. Officials blamed Nepmen (private traders) for obstructing central planners; factory managers blamed government officials for interfering and demanding unrealistically low prices.

The problems of industrialisation were closely linked to agriculture and **collectivisation**. The regime required sufficient food to supply the needs of industrial workers, and also wanted a grain surplus to help pay for industrial investment and machinery. It was hoped that *kolkhozes* and *sovkhozes* (voluntary collectives and state farms) would achieve what was needed, but the growth of collective farms was extremely slow. Even by 1928, less than 5 per cent of the peasant population was working on collective farms, and there was little enthusiasm for them among the peasants.

CROSS-REFERENCE

The establishment of the **NEP** is discussed in Chapter 7, page 62.

The **compromise of 1921** is discussed in Chapter 7, page 63.

The ideological debate surrounding compromise of **1921** and the context of the power struggle, are outlined in Chapter 10.

Collective farms

Collectivisation had existed to a limited extent since 1918 (see Chapter 7, page 62); collective agriculture was a key aspect of communist ideology. There were two types of collective farm: the *kolkhoz* (people's farm) and the *sovkhoz* (state farm). The *kolkhoz* was similar to peasant communes in tsarist Russia, with around 75 peasant families working as 'brigades' in a farm' cooperative. The *sovkhoz* was a state-run farm (often operating on land confiscated by the state from estate owners) that was given to landless peasants who became state-controlled workers.

KEY TERM

command economy: Marxist theory demanded that the state should control the 'commanding heights of the economy' to enforce socialism on business and eliminate capitalism; the term 'command economy' expresses this top-down approach to managing the economy

SOURCE 1

Adapted from a letter sent to the Society of Former Political Prisoners by a peasant farmer in December 1924 (the farmer was a long-standing supporter of the Social Revolutionaries):

The land-hungry hate the state farms. They desperately want work and they blame the central government for cutting back coal production in the Donbass. In their opinion the October Revolution gave them nothing and they want some other sort of reform that would give them all work. They don't want tsarism, landowners or capitalists back, but in their opinion, the leadership of the state is in incompetent hands – hence all the calamities of the present time. Of course, all those peasants who owned land prior to the revolution want private land ownership. The peasants' greatest wish is a bit more land and a guaranteed wage as well. If we judge the mood of the peasants by the decrees issued by Soviets, conferences and the like, we will not see the true face of the peasant.

SOURCE 2

Adapted from a report to Moscow party activists by Nikolai Bukharin, April 1925 (Bukharin was a leading member of the Politburo, widely regarded as the Party's greatest expert on economic questions, especially agriculture):

Advanced technology has become a matter for conspiracy. Thus, on the one hand, the prosperous peasant is unhappy because we prevent him from accumulating wealth and from hiring peasant labourers; on the other hand, the village poor, the victims of overpopulation, sometimes grumble at us for preventing them from hiring themselves out to this same prosperous peasant. An excessive fear of hired labour, fear of accumulation, fear of the emergence of a prosperous peasant class, could lead us to adopt an incorrect economic strategy in the countryside. We are too eager to tread on the toes of the prosperous peasant. But this means the middle peasant is afraid to improve his farm; while the poor peasant complains we are preventing him from selling his labour to the rich peasant. Overall, we need to say to the entire peasantry: enrich yourselves, accumulate wealth, develop your farms.

SOURCE 3

Adapted from a private letter sent by an industrialist to the magazine *Enterprise* in March 1927 (the industrialist, who was an experienced mining engineer, did not expect his letter to be published):

You are asking me how to bring prices down? Why are our prices so high? What is wrong with Soviet industrial organisation? By asking such questions you are raising the old arguments about the advantages and disadvantages of the **command economy** – something writers have been arguing about for decades. There has been a lot of talk recently about worn-out equipment and out-of-date factories, and the need for capital investment. From my own experience I can tell you straight that it is a load of rubbish. The equipment is not half as bad as the maintenance and management. They appoint as director somebody who has nothing to do with the factory, knows nothing about production and how his machines work. What can the poor man do? He bashes his machinery until the factory stops working because of all the breakdowns and accidents. Then he moans about his equipment being worn out. How do you bring down prices under such crazy conditions?

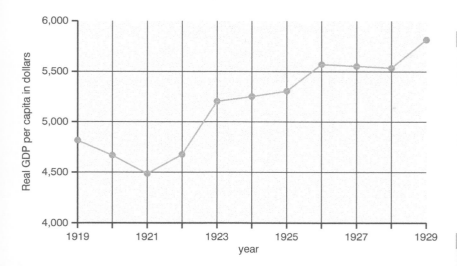

Fig. 2 *GDP in the Soviet Union 1919–1929*

KEY TERM

GDP (Gross Domestic Product):
measured by adding together the output of all economic sectors to estimate total wealth over one year; it is sometimes labelled GNP (Gross National Product)

 PRACTICE QUESTION

Evaluating primary sources

With reference to Sources 1, 2 and 3 and your understanding of the historical context, assess the value of these three sources to an historian studying the arguments surrounding economic change in Russia in the mid 1920s.

STUDY TIP

Consider the arguments raised in each source about the need (or otherwise) for change. Also consider who is putting this view forward and assess whether the author would present a fair case or perhaps distort the factors to suit his own viewpoint? A thorough consideration of provenance should enable you to make some sensible comments on the value of each source to an historian.

The reasons for the 'Great Turn'

By 1927, several key factors were pushing the regime towards a shift in policy:

- There were serious weaknesses in industrial management, and more efficiency was needed to increase production, to improve the quality (and lower the price) of industrial goods. The problems of industry and agriculture were closely intertwined. Both the peasants and the urban workers were facing harsh economic conditions, including shortages, unemployment, and low living standards.
- The drive towards industrialisation was perceived to be going too slowly. By 1927, the NEP was failing to produce the growth that many leading communists had expected; they wanted to increase the USSR's military strength and develop its self-sufficiency, so that it was less reliant on foreign imports.
- There was a huge crisis in grain procurement in the winter of 1927 to 1928. The amount of grain purchased by the government was 25 per cent down on the previous year's total. Grain prices were low and peasant producers were concentrating on other goods for which they could obtain higher prices. Party officials sent a stream of complaints to Moscow, blaming the peasants for 'hoarding' grain while they hoped for higher official prices.
- Many in the Party were impatient to revert to 'true' communist ideology in managing the economy. To move towards 'true socialism' it was essential to develop industry and not have a state dependent on procuring grain by purchasing it from peasant producers. 'True socialism' also demanded state control over production, not dependence on the peasantry for good grain harvests.
- Stalin's attitude to economic policy was also changing. Having previously supported the NEP he was now ready to be more radical. This may have been because economic circumstances pushed him to look for new solutions, or because he now felt secure enough in power to push through the policies had always wanted.

A CLOSER LOOK

Historians and the debate about the 'Great Turn'

There is a wide range of historical interpretation about the NEP and the 'Great Turn'. Stephen F. Cohen's *Bukharin and the Bolshevik Revolution* (1973) emphasises all-party support for the NEP and suggests Bukharin's policies of continuing support for the richer peasants was economically correct. Alec Nove's *An Economic History of the USSR* (1969) claims the NEP was working well in the 1920s but industrial production was distorted by the Party's policy of forcing down prices to an unrealistically low level. Other historians, including R.W. Davies in 1998, have put forward the view that the NEP had saved the economy from disaster in the beginning but *had* to be changed by the late 1920s because it could not provide the framework for large-scale industrialisation.

The evolution of policy in these years is summarised below:

Table 1

1925	Fourteenth Party Congress (the 'industrialisation congress') called for 'the transformation of our country from an agrarian into an industrial one, capable by its own efforts of producing the necessary means.'
1926	The NEP was maintained although concerns were raised as more investment was needed to drive industry forwards.
Dec 1927	At the Fifteenth Party Congress there was an announcement of the end of the NEP and beginning of the First Five Year Plan for rapid industrialisation — known as 'The Great Turn'.

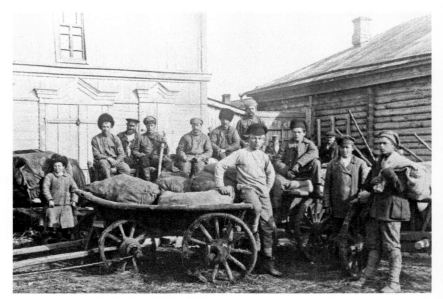

Fig. 3 *Private enterprise under the NEP*

ACTIVITY

Look at the various reasons for the Great Turn. Arrange them under the headings: Political, Ideological and Economic. Which do you think was Stalin's most important reason?

CROSS-REFERENCE

The **clash of opinion** between Stalin and Bukharin, and the consequent defeat of Bukharin, are covered in Chapter 10, page 91.

STUDY TIP

You might find the chart you prepared in the activity above helpful in planning this essay. You will need to evaluate the economic reasons for Stalin's decision to abandon the NEP and press ahead with rapid industrialisation and collectivisation, but, to provide balance, other factors will also need to be looked at. These could be grouped into factors linked to ideology and factors linked to the political rivalry and the leadership struggle.

The impact of the Great Turn

The Great Turn of 1928 to 1929 began an economic and social revolution. Both its successes and its failures were to have a massive and lasting impact on the Soviet economy and on the lives of the people, both in industrial towns and cities and in the countryside. The new shift in policy also had a major impact on debates and power struggles within the Party. During 1928 and 1929, the **clash of opinion** (and wills) between Stalin and Bukharin intensified and relations between the two former allies broke down completely. The NEP was over; the era of rapid industrialisation was beginning.

 PRACTICE QUESTION

The launch of 'Stalin's Great Turn' was primarily motivated by economic factors.' Explain why you agree or disagree with this view.

The launch of the first Five Year Plan

In 1928, Stalin launched his programme for rapid industrialisation through the first Five Year Plan. This was envisaged as only the beginning of a sustained industrial transformation through a series of further Five Year Plans. Centralised planning was to be maximised, setting systematic targets were set for ambitious increases in output. The main aims were to:

- develop heavy industry (coal, iron, steel, oil and machinery)
- boost overall production by 300 per cent

- improve the transport system, especially railways
- transform society and the economy by electrification; the target was to generate six times more electric power by 1933 than the total in 1928
- feed the expanding industrial workforce through big increases in agricultural production
- Light industry (chemicals, household goods etc) was given low priority, but was still expected to double its output.

These ambitious targets were intended to force managers and workers to devote maximum effort to the fulfilment of the Five Year Plan; the launch of the Plan was accompanied by a tidal wave of propaganda to whip up enthusiasm. The propaganda was full of grandiose predictions of future success. Stalin claimed **the targets of the first Five Year Plan** would be fulfilled by the mass enthusiasm of the workers, all pulling together for a great cause. There was to be massive new investment in the infrastructure, especially in railways and energy production. Vast new industrial complexes were planned, such the new 'steel city' of **Magnitogorsk**, near Chelyabinsk, and Stalinsk, situated in the coal basin of Kuznetsk. Plans were made for new tractor factories Stalingrad on the Volga, and Kharkiv in Ukraine.

A CLOSER LOOK

Magnitogorsk

In 1928, a Soviet delegation travelled to Cleveland in Ohio in order to discuss with experts at the US Steel Company how to copy the best American technology in order to build a new steel city as a great showpiece of Soviet industry. The Magnitaya area, in western Siberia, was chosen because of its vast reserves of iron ore. It was to be named Magnitogorsk.

CROSS-REFERENCE

The **effects of the first Five Year Plan** in the 1930s are discussed in Chapter 14, page 117.

Fig. 4 *An enhanced sketch of the proposed steel production complex of Magnitogorsk*

Stalin's rush to transform Russia through industrialisation and collectivisation aroused much enthusiasm and high expectations in many sections of society. Many elements in the Party membership were pleased to see a commitment to radical social change and an end to the compromises of the NEP. The propaganda from the regime was often overblown and exaggerated but it nevertheless had a considerable impact. Urban workers hoped for better employment prospects and higher living standards. Many poor and 'middle' peasants were led to hope they would benefit from further land reform and the introduction of more modern methods.

From the start, however, the 'Stalin Revolution' provoked opposition and pessimism. Many in the party saw the kulaks as the backbone of the agricultural economy; they were fearful that the harsh imposition of collectivisation would result in less food being produced. Many of those managing industrial production were already critical of the adverse impact of central planning and were not persuaded that a huge new emphasis on central planning would magically solve the problems of industry; they regarded the new policy as a high-risk gamble.

ACTIVITY

Complete the following chart with notes to record key facts about the launch of the first Five Year Plan.

Position in 1928/9	Detail and Comment
Attitude of different groups and individuals to the launch of rapid industrialisation	
The vision and scale of the first Five Year Plan	
The problems that were likely to hold back the success of the first Five Year Plan	

The decision to collectivise

The decision to commit the USSR to collectivisation was not a single, sudden decision. Collective farms were already a feature of Soviet agriculture before 1927, though there were few of them. Between late 1927 and December 1929, intense **debates within the Party** culminated in the decision to push through a massive acceleration of collectivisation, to be imposed by force if necessary.

A CLOSER LOOK

Stephen F. Cohen, in his book *Bukharin and the Bolshevik Revolution* (1973), comments that 'Before 1928, Stalin was largely a **Bukharinist** in economic philosophy; in 1928–29 he groped towards policies that were in effect counter-Bukharinist; he began to become a Stalinist.'

A CLOSER LOOK

Party debates about collectivisation

Many in the Party would have liked to see a massive expansion of state farms; but the relatively few existing state farms were unproductive and very unpopular with the peasantry. For Bukharin and his allies, helping the peasantry was the key to economic success; it was important to give them incentives to produce more. Bukharin believed prices should be allowed to rise, encouraging peasant farmers to sell more. His supporters, the '**Bukharinists**', included many members of the Party, of which some were academic experts in the Institute of Red Professors. But Bukharin's opponents wanted faster progress towards modernisation and the growth of industry – and they regarded the peasants as an obstacle in the way of achieving this.

Three interrelated factors were behind the drive towards collectivisation:
- the grain procurement crisis in the winter of 1927 to 1928
- the need for increased food supplies to support the expansion of the industrial workforce for the Five Year Plan
- an ideological conviction that collectivisation was the right socialist path to follow, and that the 'rich peasants' were an obstacle in the way of progress.

In dealing with the grain procurement crisis, Stalin focused special attention on west Siberia and the Urals, where the harvest had been generally good but grain procurement was down by one-third on the previous year. Stalin's officials and police went across the region, closing free markets, using the criminal law (Article 107) to stop '**speculation**', and pressuring local officials and police to seize grain by force. This aroused intense opposition from many peasants, which provoked Stalin into even sterner measures.

Stalin was convinced that his tough action in 1928 had been effective and was ready to use his 'Urals-Siberia method' as a weapon of choice in the battle of grain procurement. Officials not ready to enforce this harsh approach were sharply criticised, not least by Bukharin.
- By the summer of 1928, however, **Bukharin's political position** was weakening; he found himself outvoted more and more often, both in the Politburo and in the Central Committee.

KEY TERM

'**speculation**': in the peasant economy, 'speculation' meant buying up grain and hoarding it while hoping for the price to rise

CROSS-REFERENCE

To recap on **Stalin's actions against Bukharin** in the power struggle, look back to Chapter 10, page 92.

- In October, the 'Bukharinists' lost the majority they had previously held in the Moscow party.
- In November, Stalin felt strong enough to make direct attacks on Bukharin, charging him with 'Right deviation'.

During 1929 the drive for forced collectivisation steadily gained momentum. It was popular with many Party members and local officials; it was pushed ever more strongly from the centre. Molotov was particularly active in issuing central directives in the summer of 1929; there was a 'chain reaction' between these directives and enthusiastic support from officials in the localities. At the same time, the Central Committee introduced a policy of sending 25,000 industrial workers into the countryside to accelerate the development of collective farms. In December 1929, Stalin announced to the Party Congress his readiness to impose forced collectivisation without any restraint: to 'smash the kulaks as a class'.

SOURCE 4

Stalin, announcing the intensification of 'deKulakisation' in his speech to the Party Congress, 27 December 1929:

To launch an offensive against the kulaks means that we must smash the kulaks, eliminate them as a class. Unless we set ourselves these aims an offensive would be merely pinpricks, phrase-mongering, not a true Bolshevik offensive. We must strike at the kulaks, strike hard to prevent them from ever rising to their feet again. Could we have undertaken such an offensive five or three years ago? No, we could not. It would have meant certain failure, strengthening the position of the kulaks, and leaving us without enough grain. But what is the position now? We have the material base that enables us to break the resistance of the kulaks, to eliminate them as a class so that we can replace them with state farms and collective farms. That is why we have recently passed from the policy of restricting the exploiting tendencies of the kulaks to the policy of eliminating the kulaks as a class. When the head is cut off, no one wastes tears on the hair.

ACTIVITY

Draw a spider diagram to show the reasons behind the decision to collectivise.

 PRACTICE QUESTION

Evaluating primary sources

With reference to Sources 2 and 4 and your understanding of the historical context, which of these two sources is more valuable in explaining Stalin's decision to attack the kulaks?

KEY CHRONOLOGY

Collectivisation: the defeat of the Bukharinists

1927	Dec	Concerns in the Party about the grain procurement crisis
1928	Jan	Stalin's demand for 'extraordinary measures' in grain crisis
	Apr	Bukharinists outvoted in the Politburo on agricultural policy
	Nov	Bukharin attacked by Stalin for 'Right deviation'
1929	Apr	First Five Year Plan launched at Party conference
	Nov	Bukharin removed from Politburo
	Dec	Stalin's 'war against the kulaks' speech to the Party Congress

STUDY TIP

These two sources provide different perspectives on why the wealthier peasants (kulaks) were attacked. Try to consider carefully which is more valuable in providing an explanation on Stalin's behaviour.

Fig. 5 *Peasants on their way to work at a collective farm*

Summary

The ideological and economic compromises of the early 1920s were
thrown aside by 1928 to 1929 in favour of a rush to industrialisation and
forced collectivisation. In 1924, the Soviet economy had been based on the
continuation of the NEP. Between 1927 and 1929, however, there was a dramatic
shift in economic policy, the 'Great Turn': a move away from the NEP to rapid
industrialisation through the Five Year Plans, and the accelerated collectivisation
of agriculture. This entailed central planning and a 'command economy', to bring
new industrial growth, to build national self-sufficiency, and to bring about a
truly 'socialist' state. The implementation of the Great Turn was accompanied by
the renewal of intense debates about the economy within the Party leadership.
By December 1929, Stalin had achieved political dominance; the way was open
for him to impose 'revolution from above' on the Soviet economy.

12 Government, propaganda and foreign relations

ДУХ ВЕЛИКОГО ЛЕНИНА И ЕГО ПОБЕДОНОСНОЕ ЗНАМЯ ВДОХНОВЛЯЮТ НАС ТЕПЕРЬ НА ОТЕЧЕСТВЕННУЮ ВОЙНУ... (И. Сталин)

Fig. 1 *Soviet poster of Stalin in Lenin's shadow*

LEARNING OBJECTIVES

In this chapter you will learn about:

- Stalin's style of government
- propaganda and the beginning of the Stalinist cult of personality
- Stalin's attitude to foreign powers including China, Germany and the Treaty of Berlin
- changes in the Comintern.

ACTIVITY

Consider the image of Stalin in Fig 1. Using the evidence that follows in this chapter, how might this image be used to explain Stalin's leadership by 1929?

Stalin's style of government

Stalin had shown great political skill in his rise to power, successfully handling difficult alliances and rivalries, always managing to present a moderate image. Stalin always understood the advantages of his central position in the Party, especially his grip on the bureaucracy through his post as General Secretary; and '**bureaucratic centralism**' was the key to his style of government. In Stalin's system, '**factionalism**' was a crime against the Party. Once the 'Party line' had been set out by the leader, backed by majorities in Party committees and the Politburo, dissent equated to disloyalty. Stalin's government was always presented as a continuation of Lenin's legacy, with all-pervasive reminders to politicians and to the people that Stalin had been Lenin's closest comrade.

Stalin's style of government was also built on the politics of divide-and-rule. Stalin's success in the power struggle owed much to his ability to build up a group of **loyal supporters** in the lower levels of the party leadership, men who were of crucial importance in helping Stalin to outmanoeuvre his high-placed rivals, but who owed their political position entirely to Stalin.

Stalin's loyal henchmen were essential to his dictatorship, but they were constantly in fear, not only of Stalin, but also of each other. Fear was perhaps *the* driving force in Stalin's system of government. Fear permeated the imposition of Stalin's policies, in the way collectivisation was imposed, in the way officials were intimidated, in the extensive use of the secret police, in the growth of forced labour camps. The sinister role of the secret police and its army of informers was nothing new in 1929; Lenin and **Felix Dzerzhinsky** had ruthlessly used the Cheka as a political weapon from its foundation in 1917. But the role of the secret police (re-named **OGPU** in 1926) became more pervasive under Stalin and Dzerzhinsky's successor Vyacheslav Menzhinsky.

KEY TERM

bureaucratic centralism: government controlled from the Centre; this includes the central appointment of district officers and other party officials (the bureaucracy)

CROSS-REFERENCE

The **ban on factions** imposed by Lenin is outlined in Chapter 7, page 62; its continuation under Stalin is discussed in Chapter 10.

CROSS-REFERENCE

Stalin's success in building up a support base of **loyal supporters** is described in more detail in Chapter 10, page 89.

CROSS-REFERENCE

Felix Dzerzhinsky is profiled in Chapter 3, page 24.

A CLOSER LOOK

OGPU (Joint State Political Directorate) was reorganised in 1926 as the secret police organisation to succeed the Cheka. Its new boss, Vyacheslav Menzhinsky, had been a member of the Presidium of the Cheka since 1919; he became Chairman after the death of Felix Dzerzhinsky. Menzhinsky was loyal to Stalin and very efficient; but he was often ill and left a lot of the work to his deputy, Genrikh Yagoda. Menzhinsky died in 1934, probably from natural causes, although Yagoda later 'confessed' to having poisoned Menzhinsky.

CROSS-REFERENCE

For detail on **industrial trials** under Stalin, look at Chapter 17, page 142.

ACTIVITY

How did Stalin's style of government differ from Lenin's? Make a chart to show the similarities and differences.

ACTIVITY

Look online for images of Stalin or propaganda posters between 1924 and 1929. What impression of the developing Stalinist state do they give?

CROSS-REFERENCE

To find out about the development of the **Stalin cult in the 1930s**, look ahead to Chapter 15, page 130.

Along with propaganda, repression was a constant theme in Soviet government. **The use of terror** reached even greater heights in the 1930s but was used from the beginning to eliminate opponents and intimidate the people. Lenin had frequently spoken frankly about the need to use terror; Stalin claimed, with justification, that he was continuing Lenin's rule in this regard. Repression was not only the business of the secret police; it was often used by government officials enforcing government policies on peasants and workers.

Propaganda and the beginning of the Stalinist cult

Like Lenin, Stalin relied heavily on the propaganda machine to harness support for his policies. Images of happy, productive workers reinforced the socialist message behind industrialisation and collectivisation. New initiatives, such as the launch of the first Five Year Plan in 1928 were 'sold' as the inspiration of the all-knowing Great Leader, Stalin; frequently presenting him alongside Marx or Lenin. Stalin lost no opportunity to reinforce his own position through using his associations with Lenin, backed by slogans such as 'Stalin is the Lenin of Today'. (Another trick of Soviet propaganda was to connect with the tsarist past, using the imagery and icons that were familiar to traditional peasant society).

ПОД ВОДИТЕЛЬСТВОМ ВЕЛИКОГО СТАЛИНА–ВПЕРЕД К КОММУНИЗМУ!

Fig. 2 *Soviet poster showing a typical representation of the Stalin cult*

By 1929, the basis of the **Stalin cult** was already established. Stalin's image was fixed as the 'Great Helmsman' steering the ship of state through the dangers threatening Russia and as Lenin's true successor. Lenin had never sought to create a 'cult' himself, but a Lenin cult grew rapidly after his death, largely through the efforts of Stalin, who wanted to appear as Lenin's disciple and heir. By the late 1920s, Lenin was being treated like a god, whose words held the answer to all Russian problems. Stalin even insisted (against the wishes of Lenin's wife Krupskaya) on having the body embalmed and Lenin's tomb turned into a shrine. Such actions increased Stalin's own status.

'By 1929 it was clear that the Stalinist state would be very different from Lenin's.' Assess the validity of this view.

Stalin's attitude to foreign powers

Stalin's main aim in foreign affairs was to keep Russia safe while concentrating on domestic affairs to build '**Socialism in One Country**'. But complete isolation from the outside world was not possible. Stalin had to deal with pressing concerns abroad, especially in relation to **China** and Germany. He also had to take into account the **Comintern** and its continuing influence. To Stalin, the Comintern was an unwelcome nuisance, a hangover from the failed dreams of achieving 'permanent world revolution' – but he could never state this openly.

Stalin's chief representative in foreign affairs was **Georgii Chicherin**, backed by his able deputy, **Maksim Litvinov**. Both Chicherin and Litvinov were polished diplomats with a moderate and reassuring image; they were regarded by Stalin as very useful in maintaining 'safe' relations with foreign powers, especially Germany.

A CLOSER LOOK

Instability in China, 1925–1927

China had been very unstable after the collapse of the old Imperial China in 1911; this instability flared up again after the death of President Sun Yat-sen in 1925. The rise of an industrial working class led to militant action; there were mass strikes in Shanghai and Canton.

China

The Chinese Communist Party (CCP), formed in 1921, hoped to carry through a communist revolution in China and expected support from Stalin and the Comintern. However, Stalin preferred to back Jiang Jieshi, leader of the revolutionary-nationalist movement, the **Guomindang (GMD)**, whom he believed was more likely to bring stability to a key strategic area on Russia's eastern borders. Stalin was also suspicious of the independent interpretation of Marxist ideology developed by the Chinese communists. Stalin therefore pushed the CCP to join forces with the Guomindang in an 'alliance from within'. However, this did not happen; there was bitter conflict:

- March 1926, the GMD massacred striking workers in Canton and established a military dictatorship
- April 1927, GMD viciously suppressed a communist-led workers' revolt in Shanghai and thousands of workers were killed
- 1927, GMD massacred striking workers in the city of Wuhan; c30,000 workers were killed by the GMD in 1927.

In responding to the events in China in 1925 to 1927, Stalin's concern was for stability in Russia, not spreading revolution to other countries. Since Stalin believed the Guomindang was the strongest force in China, he gave Jiang Jieshi financial backing and military help; Stalin also pressured the Politburo into accepting the Guomindang as a member of the Comintern. In Stalin's eyes, anything that had gone wrong in China was the fault of the communists who moved away from supporting the urban working class and focused on the peasantry. Links between the CCP and the Soviet Union became weaker.

STUDY TIP

To answer this question you will need to consider the similarities and differences between Lenin and Stalin's approaches to government, the economy, industry and agriculture (it could be useful to use your knowledge on Stalin's changes from Chapter 11) and propaganda. In addition, it could be helpful to look back at Section 2 of this book to remind yourself of what Lenin's state was like.

CROSS-REFERENCE

For the debate surrounding '**Socialism in One Country**' versus 'permanent revolution', look back to Chapter 10, page 88.

The establishment of the **Comintern** to promote world revolution is covered in Chapter 8, page 70, and its development under Stalin is discussed below, on page 107.

CROSS-REFERENCE

Georgy Chicherin is profiled in Chapter 8, page 74.

KEY PROFILE

Maksim Litvinov (1876–1951) was from a wealthy family of Lithuanian Jews. He was active in revolutionary politics from 1898 and joined the Bolsheviks in 1903. He was in exile from 1906 mostly in Britain (he married an English girl); in 1918 Lenin appointed him Soviet envoy to Britain. His social background made him very effective in dealing with Western diplomats. He was Chicherin's deputy, and replaced Chicherin as People's Commissar for Foreign Affairs in 1930.

Guomindang (GMD): often known as the Kuomintang (KMT), the GMD was led by Jiang Jieshi (Chiang Kai-shek) and was essentially a right-wing nationalist movement that claimed to be revolutionary; the GMD fought a long political battle with the Chinese communists from 1926 until it was defeated by the 1949 communist revolution

ACTIVITY

Extension

Look on YouTube for the 'Latest Pictures from Shanghai 1927' which is part of a Pathé newsreel, a collection of news films which used to be shown in cinemas to inform the audience about world events.

ACTIVITY

Evaluating primary sources

What is Trotsky's view of Stalin's behaviour towards Jiang Jieshi and the GMD in 1926–1927?
Would this account by Trotsky be of value to historians studying Stalin's attitude to China in 1926 to 1927?

CROSS-REFERENCE

The **Treaty of Rapallo** is outlined in Chapter 8, page 74.

Stalin's 'betrayal' of the CCP was bitterly criticised by Trotsky and the Left Opposition. But Stalin's policy of 'Socialism in One Country' had wide support in the Party and Trotsky's influence was waning; although the Communist Party Congress of December 1927 was the occasion for much criticism of Stalin's actions over China, it was also the Congress that expelled Trotsky from the Party.

Fig. 3   *GMD guards rounding up Communist prisoners in Canton, 1927*

SOURCE 1

Adapted from a publication of Leon Trotsky, written in August 1930, when Trotsky was in exile on the island of Prinkipo, near Istanbul in Turkey. This concerns Stalin's support to the Guomindang in 1926 to 1927:

In 1926, Jiang Jieshi came forward to insist on the acceptance of the Guomindang into the Comintern: in preparing himself for the role of an executioner, he wanted to have the cover of world Communism and — he was given it. At the Politburo everybody accepted the Guomindang, led by Jiang Jieshi, into the Comintern, with only one vote against (mine). While engaged in the preparation of a decisive counter-revolutionary action in April 1927, Jiang Jieshi, at the same time, took care to exchange portraits with Stalin. This strengthening of the ties of friendship was prepared by one of Stalin's agents who visited Jiang Jieshi at Canton. The Chinese Communists were forced to submit and keep quiet.

Germany and the Treaty of Berlin, 1926

The first breakthrough in 'normalising' relations between the USSR and the wider world had been the **Treaty of Rapallo** with Weimar Germany, signed in 1922. Germany and Russia continued to have good relations after Rapallo. The German foreign minister from 1923 to 1929, Gustav Stresemann, was keen to maintain cooperative relations with Russia; and the Soviet foreign minister, Georgy Chicherin, was committed to a pro-German foreign policy.

In 1925, Stresemann's attempts to restore Germany's diplomatic position in Europe led to the Locarno treaties, a wide-ranging set of agreements aimed at ensuring the post-war peace settlement would not be altered by force. In the mid 1920s, prosperity and peace seemed to be returning to Europe, and the terms of the Treaty of Berlin of 1926 reflected this mood, especially on the German side.

Fig. 4 *Chicherin with Gustav Stresemann and his wife, during negotiations for the Treaty of Berlin, 1926*

The German government stated that the Treaty of Berlin was adapting the German-Russian agreement at Rapallo to a 'new political situation'. The consolidation of relations with Russia was popular in Germany; on the Russian side, Maksim Litvinov spoke approvingly of the Berlin agreement as 'an amplification of the Treaty of Rapallo'.

The text of the treaty talked in general terms about 'trustful cooperation between the German people and the peoples of the USSR'; and about 'promoting general peace'.

- Article 1 re-stated the importance of Rapallo as the basis for friendly German-Soviet relations with regard to all political and economic questions affecting their two countries.
- Article 2 stated that if either country was attacked by a third power, the other would remain neutral in the conflict.
- Article 3 contained a joint promise not to join any economic boycott that might be launched against either Germany or Russia.
- Article 4 stated that the treaty would remain in force for five years; and that the two states would discuss 'in good time' the future their political relations.

The USSR also gained economic benefits from the Berlin treaty; in June 1926, the USSR received large financial credits from German banks. Good relations continued until the death of Stresemann in 1929 which coincided with the beginnings of the world economic crisis. Also, 1928 to 1929 was the time when Stalin began to take a radically different line on the role of the Comintern.

Changes in the Comintern

Between 1924 and 1929, the Comintern had been a low priority for Stalin. He had been far more concerned with internal affairs: winning power, and developing the policies of 'Socialism in One Country'. Stalin's attitude and actions relating to China in 1925 to 1927 were typical of his general approach at that time. As his grip on power tightened during 1929, however, Stalin was moving towards a radical new policy in foreign affairs, as part of his 'Stalin Revolution'. The beginnings of Stalin's 'revolution from above' were most obviously to be seen in the high tempo set for the programme of

ACTIVITY

Look back at Chapter 8 and make a timeline to show the evolution of Russo-German relations between 1918 and 1929. Add a sentence of comment to each event you record.

CROSS-REFERENCE

Stalin's actions against the kulaks are described in Chapter 10, page 92.

KEY TERM

'social-fascism': many in the Comintern, including Zinoviev, put forward the view that social democratic parties in Western Europe were actually assisting fascism because they compromised with capitalism and prevented progress towards class revolution

STUDY TIP

The contrast between these two sources is explained by their provenance and you will need to explain how the author, time and audience of each make the source more or less worthwhile. Consider also the content and use your own knowledge to assess whether or not it is to be directly trusted or whether its value lies in conveying a particular opinion.

industrialisation, and the brutal imposition of forced collectivisation through Stalin's '**war against the kulaks**'. But it was also apparent in Stalin's sudden switch to more aggressive ambitions abroad.

At the Sixth Comintern Congress in July 1928, Stalin put forward his view that the world situation was changing, that world capitalism was facing a terminal crisis, and that the time was right for an all-out attack on anti-communist social democratic parties in Europe – Stalin termed them '**social-fascists**', and the deadliest enemies of socialism. Stalin pushed the Comintern to purge 'weak elements' (as well as Trotskyists) and to prepare for a return to fight to spread revolution across the world.

SOURCE 2

Adapted from Stalin's speech to the Sixth Comintern Congress, August 1928:

Since the first world imperialist war, the international labour movement has passed through three phases of development. The *first* phase was the period of extremely acute crisis in the capitalist system, and direct revolutionary action by the proletariat. This phase reached its peak in 1921, with the victory of the USSR over the forces of foreign intervention and internal counter-revolution. But it ended with severe defeats for the proletariat in Western Europe. Then came a period of gradual stabilisation of the capitalist system; at the same time, this period saw the rapid restoration of the USSR, and the building up of socialism. Finally has come the *third* phase, which will give rise to a fresh series of imperialist wars, and to gigantic class battles.

SOURCE 3

Adapted from Russia and the West under Lenin and Stalin, by the American, George Kennan; the writer held diplomatic roles in Russia in the 1930s and became an American expert on Soviet affairs; he wrote his book in 1961:

In the 1920s, Stalin portrayed Russia as 'threatened' – and took pains to confuse, in the public mind, the two dangers involved – the danger of capitalist intervention against Russia and the danger of opposition to himself from foreign socialists and communists. He did this because one fear was respectable and the other was not. He hid the measures he took to defend himself from foreign socialism and communism behind an apparent concern for the security of the Soviet Union. This is why he constantly exaggerated the possibility of hostile military intervention against the USSR. This is why he worked so hard to identify socialist and communist rivals with hostile bourgeois forces.

(AS LEVEL) PRACTICE QUESTION

Evaluating primary sources

With reference to Sources 1 and 2 and your understanding of the historical context, which of these two sources is more valuable in explaining Stalin's attitude to Western powers in the 1920s?

It is hard to know why Stalin pushed more aggressive policies in 1928. Understandably, Trotsky and his supporters condemned Stalin for being hypocritical. But Stalin had been a man of genuine revolutionary instincts in 1917 to 1919, and he may have been simply reverting to type once the need for 'socialism in one country' had passed. There is another possible reason, in that the strongest opponent of Stalin's new line was **Bukharin**; it could be that Stalin's main purpose was to pick a political fight with him.

Soviet control over the Comintern became tighter. Stalin put loyal yes-men in place to run the Comintern for him. Strict discipline was imposed on the communist parties in countries such as France, Germany and Italy. Soviet agents were sent abroad to infiltrate foreign communist parties and report back to Moscow. Many foreign communist leaders were encouraged to come to the USSR, ostensibly to join in the great drive to sharpen communist ideology and unity; in reality, it was just a way of controlling them. Any illusions that the Comintern was an international brotherhood were dropped; the Comintern became a tool of Stalin's 'top-down' foreign policy.

CROSS-REFERENCE

Bukharin is profiled in Chapter 9, page 84; his political defeat by Stalin is discussed in Chapter 10.

Fig. 5 *Poster praising the Comintern*

Summary

By December 1929, Stalin's control over the political system of the USSR was virtually absolute. Internal dissent within the Party, previously in the public arena, was now confined to the inner circles of power. Stalin had become the personification of ideology, policy and authority. He was therefore able to put his stamp on the methods of dictatorial government; and to present himself through the cult of Stalin as the true, unchallenged successor to the great Lenin. In relations with the outside world, Stalin had followed a 'safe' foreign policy, playing down the importance of 'world revolution' in the 1920s in favour of securing internal stability through 'Socialism in One Country'. By 1929, abroad as at home, Stalin was in full control and ready to push through the 'Stalin Revolution'.

 PRACTICE QUESTION

To what extent was Stalin's attitude to foreign powers before 1929 driven by ideology?

STUDY TIP

In order to answer this question you will need to reflect on what attitudes might be expected from a ruler who claimed to follow Marxist-Leninist ideology. Having established what principles you might expect Stalin to follow, look at his actual dealings with foreign countries and assess how far he lived up to the ideal. You might want to consider that an alternative factor was more important to him. Remember to give precise examples to support your ideas.

4 Economy and society, 1929–1941

13 Agricultural and social developments in the countryside

LEARNING OBJECTIVES

In this chapter you will learn about:

- voluntary and forced collectivisation

- state farms and mechanisation

- the impact of collectivisation on the kulaks and other peasants and the famine of 1932–1934

- the success of collectivisation.

CROSS-REFERENCE

Viktor Serge is profiled in Chapter 7, page 58.

ACTIVITY

Evaluating primary sources

What impression of developments in the countryside after 1929 is given in Source 1?

SOURCE 1

Adapted from **Viktor Serge**'s *Memoirs of a Revolutionary*, published posthumously in 1951. The chapter from which this source is taken is entitled the 'Years of Resistance, 1928–1933':

The women came to deliver the cattle confiscated by the collective farm, but made a rampart of their own bodies around the beasts: 'Go on, bandits, shoot!' And why should these rebels not be shot at? Terror reigned in the smallest hamlets. There were more than 300 centres of peasant insurrection going on simultaneously. Trainloads of deported peasants left for the icy North, the forests, the steppes, the deserts. These were whole populations, denuded of everything; the old folk starved to death in mid-journey, new-born babies were buried on the banks of the roadside, and each wilderness had its crop of little crosses of boughs or white wood. Other populations, dragging all their mean possessions on wagons, rushed towards the frontiers of Poland, Rumania and China, and crossed them – by no means intact, to be sure – in spite of the machine guns.

Voluntary and forced collectivisation

Fig. 1 *A meeting of kolkhoz workers at harvesting; the poster reads, Farm workers say "Go to the collectives", 1929*

Stalin had committed the USSR to collective farming as a result of his **Great Turn** of 1928. Initially, the emphasis had been on voluntary collectivisation – persuading peasants of the benefits of working communally through posters, leaflets and films. Such an approach, however, had limited effect. Moreover, the 'Ural-Siberian method' of grain requisitioning, involving the forcible seizure of grain and the closing down of private markets, had brought unrest in rural areas. By 1929, less than 5 per cent of all farms had been collectivised and Stalin believed that some of the grain procurement problems had been caused by the richer kulaks holding back supplies. Consequently, in December 1929, Stalin announced that he would 'annihilate the kulaks as a class'.

Collectivisation Stage 1, 1929–1930

The government began the campaign with the issue of new procurement (delivery) quotas, with punishments for peasants who did not keep up with deliveries. At the same time, a deliberate propaganda campaign was waged against the kulaks, in an attempt to create a rift within the peasant class between poor and better-off farmers. By the end of 1929, the government had begun a programme of all-out, forced collectivisation. Peasants were driven into collectives by local party members (often students from the cities, filled with fervour to create a new socialist society) with the support of the OGPU and Red Army where necessary.

Stalin declared that kulaks must be 'liquidated as a class' and they were not permitted to join collectives. The Red Army and OGPU were used to identify, execute or deport **kulaks**, who were said to represent 4 per cent of peasant households. However it was not always easy to distinguish between peasant-types and in practice, c15 per cent of peasant households were destroyed and c150,000 peasants forced to migrate north and east to poorer land. Not surprisingly, some tried to avoid being labelled as kulaks, by killing their livestock and destroying their crops, but this only added to rural problems.

In January 1930, Stalin announced that 25 per cent of grain-farming areas were to be collectivised that year. The brutal treatment meted out to kulaks was used to frighten poorer peasants into joining the collectives and, by March 1930, 58 per cent of peasant households had been collectivised through a mixture of propaganda and force, in the face of mounting peasant disquiet. The speed with which this operation was carried out led even Stalin to say that local officials were being too rigorous and confrontational in their methods; Party members were, he wrote in an article, becoming 'dizzy with success'. Consequently, a brief return to voluntary collectivisation was permitted until after the harvest had been collected that year, and peasants were allowed to leave collectives and had their livestock returned to them, provided they were not kulaks. This immediately reduced the collectives' numbers; in October 1930, only c20 per cent of households were still collectivised.

Collectivisation Stage 2, 1930–1941

Stalin's climb down was only a temporary tactic. Once the peasants had sown the spring crop, in 1931, the process of collectivisation speeded up again and the rate of collectivisation gradually increased, to reach 100 per cent of households by 1941.

Year	Percentage of collectivised households
1931	50%
1934	70%
1935	75%
1937	90%
1941	100%

A CLOSER LOOK

Reasons for collectivisation

There were good reasons for launching the collectivisation programme in 1929. This coincided with the launch of Stalin's first Five Year Plan for industry, the success of which depended on regular supplies of food to support town workers and plenty of grain for export to finance industrial development. However, for Stalin, collectivisation was as much a social as an economic crusade.

CROSS-REFERENCE

To recap on Stalin's **Great Turn**, look back to Chapter 11, page 95.

The **decision to collectivise** is discussed in Chapter 11, page 100.

CROSS-REFERENCE

For an explanation on the **kulaks**, see the Closer Look in Chapter 7, page 58.

ACTIVITY

Create a timeline/chart to show the stages by which the collectivisation process was carried out. You could begin with the 'Great Turn' (see Chapter 11).

The *kolkhoz*

The typical collective farm, known as a *kolkhoz*, was created by combining small individual farms together in a cooperative structure. Many comprised a single village, in which the peasants lived in the same houses as before and had a plot of land of their own to work on, as well as farming in the communal fields. The average *kolkhoz* comprised c75 families, and their livestock (cattle, sheep, goats, pigs, and chickens).

However, the creation of such a *kolkhoz* was not easy. Communal fields had to be mapped out and work parties had to join the peasants to dig new ditches, erect new fences and sometimes establish communal buildings. In some of the larger *kolkhozes*, schools and clinics were also established.

Each *kolkhoz*:
- had to deliver a set quota of produce to the State. Quotas were high: up to 40 per cent of crops. A low purchase price was set by the government but the farm was not paid if the quotas were not met
- shared any profit or goods left after procurement among the collective farm members, according to the number of 'labour days' he or she had contributed to the farming year. (From 1932 *kolkhozes* were able to sell any 'left-over' produce in a collective farm market: the only free market permitted in USSR.)
- was under the control of a Communist Party member who acted as the Chairman of the collective. This ensured communist control of rural areas
- forbade peasants from leaving the *kolkhoz* through a system of internal passports (from 1932).

State farms and mechanisation

The *sovkhoz*

A relatively small number of farms were run as state farms *(sovkhozes)* rather than *kolkhozes*. Some state farms had been created in the early 1920s as an example of 'socialist agriculture of the highest order' and they were still seen by communist purists as the 'ideal' form of farming. In these, the labourers were classified as 'workers' rather than 'peasants' and they were paid a wage directly by the State. Their movement was, however, just as restricted as those of the *kolkhoz* peasants.

The *sovkhozes* were usually larger than the *kolkhozes* and were created on land confiscated from former large estates. The *sovkhoz* workers were recruited from landless rural residents and the farms were organised according to industrial principles for specialised large-scale production. This type of organisation was deemed particularly suited to the grain-growing areas of the Ukraine and southern Russia, but peasant opposition to becoming wage-labourers forced Stalin to permit most farms to be of the *kolkhoz* type in the 1930s. Nevertheless, the official expectation was that all *kolkhozes* would be turned into *sovkhozes* in the longer term.

Machine Tractor Stations

Since the collectives were intended to provide more efficient farming, the establishment of the *kolkhozes* and *sovkhozes* was accompanied by a drive towards greater mechanisation and the use of more modern farming methods. The use of tractors and agricultural machinery also had the added bonus of reducing the number of peasants needed on the land (so releasing them to work in the industrial cities).
- **Machine Tractor Stations** (MTS) were set up from 1931, to provide seed and to hire out tractors and machinery to collective and state farms; 2500

ACTIVITY

Create a Venn diagram of two overlapping circles. Label the first circle '*The kolkhoz*' and the other '*The sovkhoz*'. Complete with as many details of both that you can think of, putting common characteristics in the overlap.

were established (although there was still only one MTS for every 40 collective farms by 1940).

- The state farms generally received more and better machinery (for example combine harvesters) and chemical fertilisers.
- Agronomists, veterinary surgeons, surveyors and technicians were sent to the countryside to advise on how to use the machinery and improve farming methods; again the state farms were offered the most support.

Fig. 2 *A machine tractor station*

By 1938, 95 per cent of threshing, 72 per cent of ploughing, 57 per cent of spring sowing and 48 per cent of harvesting were carried out mechanically but other farm operations were less mechanised and many of the machines that were used were still labour intensive. The type of harvesting reapers generally used in the collectives, for example, merely cut grain, which was then removed from the reaper and bound by hand. Other tasks such as weeding also continued to be largely manual work. There were also limited numbers of lorries in use for the transport of goods. By the end of 1938, there were 196,000 lorries being used in Soviet agriculture compared with over a million in the USA.

A CLOSER LOOK

Machine Tractor Stations

The MTS acted as a Party prop in rural areas. Officials ensured that quotas were collected from the farms and that the correct propaganda messages were conveyed. They acted as 'spies' too, reporting any local troubles.

The impact of collectivisation on the kulaks and other peasants and the famine of 1932–1934

There was widespread and violent opposition to the process of collectivisation, amounting to civil war in the countryside. Although some, mainly poorer peasants, joined collectives voluntarily, most peasants did not. Peasants from more fertile agricultural areas like the Ukraine were particularly hostile. Peasants, fearing they would be labelled kulaks, burned their farms and crops and killed their livestock rather than hand them over.

The armed forces dealt brutally with the unrest, sometimes burning down whole villages. Any peasant who resisted was classified as a kulak and a class enemy and in centres and millions of peasants were deported, usually to remote areas such as Siberia, where they would be herded into labour camps although sometimes as 'work-gangs' to the new industrial towns. 'Dekulakisation' thus removed some of the most successful and skilled farmers from the countryside.

Probably over 10 million peasants died as the result of resistance or the effects of deportation. By 1939, about 19 million peasants had migrated to towns: in effect, for every three peasants who joined a collective, one left the countryside and became an urban worker.

Those peasants that joined the collectives were, all too often, left with a sense of betrayal and hostility towards the regime, regarding their condition as a 'new serfdom'. By a law of August 1932, anyone who stole from a collective (even just taking a few ears of corn) could be gaoled for ten years. (This was subsequently made a capital crime.) Further decrees gave ten-year sentences for any attempt to sell meat or grain before quotas were filled. Internal passport controls were introduced, largely to prevent peasants fleeing from famine-stricken areas.

Furthermore, although peasants were supposed to receive a share of the 'profits' of their collective farm, the quotas were so high that there rarely was any 'profit' and therefore little incentive to work hard. Most peasants were only interested in their private plots, where they could keep some animals and grow vegetables not only to provide for their own families but also, from 1935, to sell in the market place. Since food was desperately needed, a government decree allowed this practice that had previously been happening illegally to continue, and it has been estimated that 52 per cent of vegetables, 70 per cent of meat and 71 per cent of milk in the Soviet Union was produced this way by the late 1930s.

Although some peasants benefitted from more education, rural Russia was the poor relation of the new urban USSR. In effect, the peasantry was sacrificed in the name of Soviet ideology, to meet the needs of industry.

The famine of 1932–1934

Fig. 3 *Starving peasants during the Great Famine*

ACTIVITY

Extension

Try to get hold of a copy of *Virgin Soil Upturned (Book One: Seeds of Tomorrow)* by Mikhail Sholokhov, originally published in 1932. Sholokhov was a communist who disapproved of dekulakisation. He wrote about collectivisation in two novels. *Book Two: Harvest on the Don* was not published until 1960.

In October 1931, drought hit many agricultural areas. Combined with kulak deportations, this brought a severe drop in food production and by the spring of 1932, **famine** appeared in Ukraine. Over 1932 to 1933 the famine spread to Kazakhstan and parts of the Northern Caucasus. This was one of the worst famines in Russian history (and in some areas it continued to 1934).

The success of collectivisation

Overall, the state seemed to achieve its purposes in promoting collectivisation. The industrial workforce was fed and exports of grain increased, while many peasants left the countryside to swell the workforce in the towns. Nevertheless, such achievements were at the expense of the peasants themselves who, at best, endured an upheaval that destroyed a way of life and, at worst, were forced to starve and die in the interests of 'economic socialisation'.

ACTIVITY

Extension

Find out more about collectivisation in Ukraine and the famine. Was government action a deliberate policy of genocide, as many Ukrainian nationalists allege?

During the period of peasant opposition, agricultural production fell dramatically (sometimes even to 1913 levels), and recovery did not take place until the late 1930s. Grain and livestock were destroyed (25 to 30 per cent of cattle, pigs and sheep were slaughtered by peasants between 1929 and 1933). Grain output did not exceed pre-collectivisation levels until after 1935, while it took until 1953 before livestock numbers were back to where they had been pre-collectivisation. The collectives were often poorly organised in the early years as well. The party activists who helped establish them knew nothing of farming and there were also too few tractors, insufficient animals to pull ploughs and a lack of fertilisers. Collectivisation was thus a slow and brutal way of achieving Stalin's economic goals.

The political impact of collectivisation was equally important for Stalin. For the first time, the Soviet regime had extended its political control over the countryside, mainly through Party management of the collectives. Never again would peasants be able to resist the regime. This reinforced Stalin's control within the USSR and over the Communist Party. **Those on the right** who opposed collectivisation, such as Bukharin and Rykov, lost power and influence as the USSR moved further along the road towards Stalin's version of socialism. Class differences in the countryside were abolished and apart from the existence of small private plots, any remains of capitalism, based on private enterprise, had been destroyed.

ACTIVITY

Create your own record of the success of collectivisation by completing the following chart, in which you are invited to consider the strengths and weaknesses of this policy thematically:

Results of collectivisation	Strengths	Weaknesses
Economic		
Social		
Political		

A CLOSER LOOK

Government responsibility for the famine

Despite the drop in grain production, the state continued to demand its requisitions. Government policy, therefore, contributed to the deaths from famine. Historian Robert Conquest believes that there was a deliberate policy to take unrealistic grain quotas in areas that had opposed collectivisation (particularly Ukraine), thus condemning millions of peasants to starvation.

CROSS-REFERENCE

The views of **right-wing members** of the Communist Party, such as Bukharin and Rykov, are introduced in Chapter 9, page 84; the developing split between them and Stalin is discussed in Chapter 10, page 88.

STUDY TIP

In order to answer this question, you will need to consider what is meant by success. It is possible for collectivisation to be politically successful but economically disastrous. You should also consider for whom it was a success and who lost out.

 PRACTICE QUESTION

'Collectivisation in the USSR, in the years 1929 to 1941, was a success.' Assess the validity of this view.

Summary

- Collectivisation was partly voluntary, but most was compulsory, and by the end of the 1930s most of the countryside was either collectivised or comprised of state farms.
- The process was brutal because many peasants resisted the process. They were branded 'kulaks' and were killed, deported, or went to work in the towns.
- Peasants (particularly in Ukraine) suffered horrendously during the famine of 1932–3. Their lot may have been made worse by deliberate government policy.
- Agricultural production fell back in the early years of collectivisation, although levels eventually rose and greater mechanisation was introduced so that the process ensured the success of Stalin's economic plans.
- Collectivisation gave the communist state control over the countryside for the first time since the revolution of 1917.

14 Industrial and social developments in towns and cities

SOURCE 1

Adapted from a speech given by Stalin to the first all-Union Congress of managers of Socialist industry in February 1931. The title of the speech is 'the Tasks of the Economic Executives':

To slacken the tempo would mean falling behind. And those who fall behind get beaten. But we refuse to be beaten. One feature of the history of old Russia was the continual beatings she suffered because of her backwardness – her military backwardness, cultural backwardness, political backwardness, industrial backwardness, agricultural backwardness. Do you want our socialist fatherland to be beaten and to lose its independence? If you do not want this, you must put an end to its backwardness in the shortest possible time and develop a genuine Bolshevik tempo in building up its socialist economy. There is no other way. That is why Lenin said on the eve of the October Revolution: 'Either perish, or overtake and outstrip the advanced capitalist countries. We are fifty or a hundred years behind the advanced countries. We must make good this distance in ten years. Either we do it, or we shall be crushed.'

Gosplan and the organisation, aims and results of the first three Five Year Plans

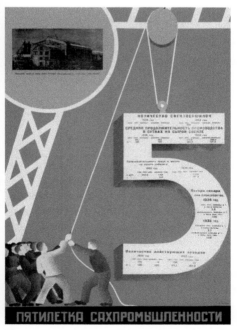

Fig. 1 *Soviet poster depicting the first Five Year Plan*

Stalin chose to advance his economic programme for industry (already launched in 1928), through a series of 'Five Year Plans' which set attainment targets for industrial enterprises. **Gosplan**, the State Planning Agency, was given responsibility for drawing up the plans and establishing output targets for every economic enterprise in accordance with Party directives.

ACTIVITY

Evaluating primary sources

1. What evidence is provided by Source 1 of factors affecting Stalin's economic decisions in the 1930s?
2. What are the strengths and weaknesses of this source as a piece of historical evidence?

CROSS-REFERENCE

The establishment of **Gosplan** in 1921 is covered in Chapter 7, page 62.

The work of Gosplan

Gosplan's job was to ensure that overall economic objectives of the Five Year Plans were met, by matching input against output. It firstly calculated how much 'input', (i.e. the necessary raw materials) was available by looking at statistics of production minus exports plus imports. It then matched this 'input' to 'output' targets to identify any mismatches. Using these calculations, it established priorities for the use of resources, organised supply and distribution and took steps to ensure the necessary investment and reorganisation to 'balance' the economy.

It was no easy task, given that the Communist government made the overall decision as to what should be produced, and when, over a five-year period, while regional Party leaders competed to put forward ambitious projects and argue with **Gosplan** as to why their region should have first call on resources. Gosplan also suffered from a lack of reliable information (particularly on the cost of imports or the price that exports might command) and faced the difficulty of planning for many variable and changing commodities.

The targets set were usually very ambitious. They were intended to force managers and workers to devote their maximum effort to the programme – and the launching and fulfilment of these plans were accompanied by much propaganda. Since failure to achieve a target was deemed a criminal offence, all those involved in administering and carrying out the plans went to great lengths to ensure that the reported statistics showed huge improvements – often way above the targets originally set. Thus, corruption and faulty reporting was built into the system from the outset.

Gosplan was placed in the unenviable position of working from deliberately falsified statistics and if things went wrong, its officials could be held responsible. Indeed, once the plans got underway, thousands of State employees were dismissed, including members of Gosplan's own offices, on the grounds that they were not sufficiently class-conscious, enthusiastic or free from corruption.

The first Five Year Plan, 1928–1932

The first Five Year Plan was approved by the Sixteenth Party Congress in April 1929, although the plan was backdated to October 1928. It was not based on very secure data and was extremely over-ambitious. The ambitious target system included:

Table 1 *Targets for industrial output during the first Five Year Plan*

Output targets	1927–1928 actual production	1932–1933 target production
Coal (million tonnes)	35.4	75
Oil (million tonnes)	11.7	22
Steel (million tonnes)	4	10.4
Pig iron (million tonnes)	3.3	10

Soviet statistics adapted from A. Nove, An Economic History of the USSR, 1969

While it is easy to criticise the imperfections in the plan model, it should be emphasised that the first Five Year Plan was a great experiment and there was no obvious example elsewhere from which to learn – particularly at a time of economic collapse in the West following the **Wall Street Crash**. One major problem was, however, that people were afraid to question anything about it as Stalin's regime became more authoritarian and criticism might easily be labelled as disloyalty, sabotage or treason.

Wall Street Crash

The American stock market (on Wall Street) collapsed in October 1929, bankrupting many enterprises both in USA and in Europe, which had relied on American loans. It heralded the 'Great Depression', a time of low productivity and widespread unemployment in the capitalist West.

Fig. 2   *Booming industrial scene in Stalin's industrial Russia*

This plan focused on the development of heavy industries (sometimes called producers' goods or capital goods) such as coal and steel – raw materials that were a means of making other products.

Aims were to:
- increase production by 300 per cent
- focus on the development of coal, iron, steel, oil and machinery
- boost electricity production by 600 per cent
- double the output from light industry such as chemicals.

The publicity surrounding its launch provoked an enthusiastic response. Such was its success that Stalin claimed that the targets had been met in four years rather than five, but this was probably due to 'over-enthusiastic' reporting by local officials, keen to show their loyalty and effort. In reality, none of the major targets were actually met, although investment brought some impressive growth. Electricity output trebled, coal and iron output doubled and steel production increased by a third. New railways, engineering plants, HEP schemes and industrial complexes sprung up.

However, for all Stalin's claims, the targets for the chemical industry were not met and house-building, food-processing and other consumer industries were woefully neglected. There were too few skilled workers and too little effective central coordination for efficient development, while smaller industrial works and workshops lost out in the competition from the bigger factories.

The second Five Year Plan, 1933–1937

This built on the infrastructure provided by the first plan. It gave more attention to **consumer goods** than the first plan, but heavy industry still remained as the overall priority.

Aims were to:
- continue the development of heavy industry
- promote the growth of light industries, such as chemicals, electricals and consumer goods

KEY TERM

consumer goods: products such as clothing and furnishings, which are wanted by the people rather than by other manufacturing industries

- develop communications to provide links between cities and other industrial areas
- foster engineering and tool-making.

The plan had some success, particularly during the 'three good years', 1934 to 1936. The Moscow Metro was opened in 1935, the Volga canal in 1937 and the Dnieprostroi Dam producing hydro-electric power, which had just been completed in 1932, was extended with four more generators to make it the largest dam in Europe. Electricity production and the chemical industries grew rapidly and new metals such as copper, zinc and tin were mined for the first time. Steel output trebled, coal production doubled and by 1937, the Soviet Union was virtually self-sufficient in metal goods and machine tools. In 1936, the focus of the plan changed slightly as a greater emphasis was placed on **rearmament**, which rose from 4 per cent of GDP in 1933 to 17 per cent by 1937.

Nevertheless, oil production failed to meet its targets and despite some expansion in footwear and food-processing, there was still no appreciable increase in consumer goods. Furthermore, an emphasis on quantity, rather than quality, which had also marred the first Five Year Plan, continued.

A CLOSER LOOK

Armaments production

A provision, which did not appear in the published military budget, was the development of at least one secret workshop devoted to weapons production in each industrial complex. Such workshops are thought to have provided almost half of Soviet military production and the high priority given to defence, where output rose by almost 300 per cent between 1933 and 1938, was largely at the expense of the advertised consumer targets.

ACTIVITY

What can we learn about Stalin's first two Five Year Plans from this table?

The following table enables a comparison to be made between the target figures for the first and second Five Year Plans and actual production of certain key products:

Economic area	1932–1933 target production	1932 actual production	1937 target production	1937 actual production
Coal (million tonnes)	75	64.4	152.5	128
Oil (million tonnes)	21.7	21.4	46.8	28.5
Steel (million tonnes)	10.4	5.9	17.0	17.7
Pig iron (million tonnes)	10	6.2	16.0	14.5
Electricity m.kWh	22,000	13,540	38,000	36,000
Machine tools (thousands)		19.7	40.0	45.5
Tractors (thousands)		50.6	166.7	66.5

We can get some idea of the frenzied pace of industrialisation in the USSR from accounts of travellers in the 1930s.

SOURCE 2

Adapted from the writings of Louis Fischer, an American who visited Russia in 1935 and recorded his observations in a book, *Soviet Journey*, published the same year:

Moscow is encircled by a broad ring of new factories and housing estates. Eight miles from the heart of the city stands the Freezer Cutting Tool Plant, finished in 1931. In sight of it are six new factories. From the outside it looks like a modern European or American factory, but on its walls, in large letters, slogans have been painted, 'Long live the World Revolution'. From Moscow you take a train to see the Dnieper Dam. Nearby is a new town. In 1931, wheat still grew where factories now stand. An industrial centre at this point enjoys the advantages of cheap local electric power. Only a fraction of the plant is now ready, but the city is already a busy metal centre. The aluminium works are producing goods which, unfortunately, do not reach Soviet citizens' kitchens. You visit a blast furnace and in just 30 seconds you are choking, breathless, out of action. How can men stand it six hours a day?

The third Five Year Plan, 1938–1942

This plan had a particular focus on the needs of the defence sector, in light of the growing threat that **Nazi Germany** posed to the USSR. The plan was disrupted by the approach of war in 1941.

Aims were to:
- place a renewed emphasis on the development of heavy industry
- promote rapid rearmament
- complete the transition to communism.

Again, heavy industry was the main beneficiary, with some strong growth in machinery and engineering, although the picture varied across the country and resources were increasingly diverted to rearmament, on which spending doubled between 1938 and 1940. This had an adverse effect on other areas. Steel production stagnated, oil failed to meet targets, causing a fuel crisis, and many industries found themselves short of raw materials. Consumer goods were also relegated, once again, to the lowest priority.

The biggest problem with the third Five Year Plan was the dearth of good managers, specialists and technicians following Stalin's **purges**. There was also an exceptionally hard winter in 1938 and the needs of defence played a part. Furthermore, the plan was disrupted and finished early because of the German invasion of 1941.

New industrial centres and projects and the involvement of foreign companies

The plans involved some 'showpiece' projects, designed to show the modernity and capabilities of the Soviet State. Some of the main ones are described below.

ACTIVITY

Evaluating primary sources

What impression does Source 2 give of industrial change in Russia in the 1930s?

A CLOSER LOOK

The Nazi threat

Hitler came to power in 1933 and set about rearming and expanding Germany. He made no secret of the fact that he sought *Lebensraum* (living space) for German people to the East. This threatened Soviet territory.

CROSS-REFERENCE

For Stalin's **purges**, in which many citizens lost their jobs and sometimes suffered deportation or even execution, look ahead to Chapter 18.

ACTIVITY

Make a diagram to show the economic successes and failures of the first three Five Year Plans. Provide a concluding paragraph giving your view on the plans' success. You might like to research some further statistics to support your conclusions, but remember, 'official' figures may have been doctored.

Project	What it was	Additional details
Dnieprostroi Dam –construction began in 1927 and it opened in October 1932	The largest hydro-electric power station on the Dnieper River, placed in Zaporizhia, Ukraine. Generating some 560 MW, the station became the largest Soviet power plant at the time and one of the largest in the world.	The power station was built on deserted land in the countryside. It was planned to provide electricity for several aluminium production plants and a high quality steel production plant that were also to be constructed in the area. It began generating electricity during the first Five Year Plan. After four further generators were installed during the second Five Year Plan, it increased Soviet electric power fivefold in 1932. The industrial centres of Zaporizhia, Kryvyi Rih and Dnipropetrovsk grew from the power provided by the station.
The Turksib (Turkestan to Siberia) Railway –built between 1926 and 1931; passenger service began in 1929	Also known as the Central Asiatic Railway, this connected Central Asia with Siberia. It ran from Tashkent to Novosibirsk, where it met the West Siberian portion of the Trans-Siberian railway.	This was a huge construction project built for political as well as economic reasons. Heralded as the 'forge of the Kazakh proletariat', it was designed to create a working class in the steppes and semi-deserts of Central Asia. This costly railroad was built by nearly 50,000 workers. The line also facilitated the transport of cotton from Turkestan to Siberia and cheap Siberian grain from Russia to the Fergana Valley. Viktor Alexandrovitch Turin directed a 1929 Soviet documentary film about the building of the railway.
Moscow Metro – opened in 1935	Opened with one 11-kilometre line and 13 stations. It was the first underground railway system in the USSR. It was extended in a second stage, 1938, but a third stage was delayed by the Second World War.	This was part of the second Five Year Plan, which focused on urbanisation and needed to cope with the influx of peasants to the city in the 1930s. It was an ambitious architectural project designed to prove that a socialist metro could surpass capitalist designs. The project drew resources and specialist workers from the entire USSR; massive recruitment campaigns were launched for the unskilled labourers. Artists and architects were employed to produce a system that reflected 'a radiant future'. This included marble walls, high ceilings, grand chandeliers and the use of steel: itself a sign of the USSR's industrial achievement.
Moscow–Volga Canal – constructed between 1932 and 1937	Connects the Muskva and Volga rivers. One of the world's tallest statues of Lenin, 25 metres high, was built in 1937 at the confluence of the Volga River and the Canal.	The canal was built by prisoners from the Dmitlag labour camp – which grew to be the largest of its kind in 1934. During the construction almost 200,000 prisoners were employed, of which c22,000 died. (Those fulfilling their work quotas were given 600 grams of bread per day; those that did not received 400 grams; and those who were being punished, 300 grams.) The White Sea Baltic Canal of 1933 was similarly built by forced labour.

Fig. 3 *Magnitogorsk complex, on a morning during the first Five Year Plan*

Other major projects involved the construction of completely new industrial cities such as Magnitogorsk in the Urals and Komsomolsk in the Far East of Russia. Such new industrial complexes were intended to showcase socialism in action.

At Magnitogorsk, a gigantic steel plant and a town of 150,000 people was created from nothing. Here, workers lived in communal barracks beneath imposing pictures of Lenin and Stalin, and were subject to constant lectures and political discussions.

SOURCE 3

Adapted from *Beyond the Urals* by John Scott, who, as an American student, joined the Communist Party and volunteered to work at Magnitogorsk:

Brigades of young enthusiasts from every corner of the Soviet Union arrived in the summer of 1930 and did the groundwork of railroad and dam construction necessary. Later groups of local peasants and herdsmen came to Magnitogorsk because of bad conditions in the villages, due to collectivisation. Many of the peasants were completely unfamiliar with industrial tools and processes. A colony of several hundred foreign engineers and specialists, some of whom made as much as one hundred dollars a day, arrived to advise and direct the work. From 1928 until 1932, nearly a quarter of a million people came to Magnitogorsk. About three-quarters of these new arrivals came of their own free will, seeking work, bread-cards, better conditions. The rest came under compulsion.

ACTIVITY

Evaluating primary sources

Using Source 2 and additional photographs, information and propaganda material you can discover online, create a large poster to capture the essence of Magnitogorsk. You might also like to read Stephen Kotkin's *Magnetic Mountain: Stalinism as a Civilization* (1995), which gives a vivid picture of the town.

CROSS-REFERENCE

Komsomol, the Communist youth organisation, is discussed in Chapter 19, page 160.

Komsomolsk was the result of a government decision in 1931 to construct a shipyard on the River Amur in East Russia, to open up this area. It was largely built using volunteer labour from the Communist youth organisation, **Komsomol**, which gave it its name. However, the construction also used penal labour from the prison camps in the area. By the end of the 1930s, several shipyards and heavy plant had been completed and the city became a regional centre for industries such as metallurgy, machinery, oil refining and shipbuilding.

The use of foreigners

To provide the necessary expertise for these vast projects and others like them, the USSR was forced to turn to foreign companies and individuals with both managerial and technical skills. For example, the American, Henry Ford, advised on the car industry, training Russian engineers in the USA and helping to design the car-plant at Gorky.

The Dnieprostroi Dam project used the experience gained from the construction of hydro-electric power stations in Canada and, in 1932, six American engineers (including Colonel Hugh Cooper who masterminded the Russian construction and G. Thompson, an engineer from General Electric) were awarded the 'Order of the Red Banner of Labour' for 'outstanding work in the construction of DniproHES'.

Walter Rukeyser, a consultant engineer, helped develop the asbestos industry at 'Asbest' in the Urals, while the development of the Moscow Metro relied on construction engineers from Britain. Although built and decorated by native workers, the engineering designs, routes, and construction plans were handled by specialists recruited from the London Underground.

Sometimes ordinary labourers travelled to the USSR from the West to work on these new plants. At a time of Depression, communism presented an attraction and some foreigners genuinely believed they were contributing to a new world order.

CROSS-REFERENCE

More detail on the **deportations** that took place during the purges of the 1930s can be found in Chapter 18, page 152.

STUDY TIP

You should consider both agricultural and industrial change in your response to this question, so it could be helpful to look back at Chapter 13 as well as the material covered here. Identify what you understand by a socialist economy in your opening paragraph. Rather than writing a fully chronological essay, which could become over-narrative, try looking at those aspects of the economy where there were successful moves to 'economic socialisation' and balance these against ways in which the economy was not efficiently socialised.

However, foreigners were sometimes looked upon with suspicion and it was easy to scapegoat them when things went wrong. The secret police arrested numerous British engineers working in Moscow because they had gained an in-depth knowledge of the city's geographical layout. Engineers for the Metropolitan-Vickers Electrical Company (Metrovick) were also arrested and **deported** in 1933, ending the role of British business in the USSR.

> **A LEVEL PRACTICE QUESTION**
>
> How successful was Stalin in creating a 'socialist economy' in the years 1929 to 1941?

The Stakhanovites and working and living conditions for managers, workers and women

Stakhanovites

The Stakhanovite movement emerged after Aleksei Stakhanov, a coal miner in the Don Basin, cut an extraordinary 102 tonnes of coal with his pneumatic pick in 5 hours 45 minutes in August 1935. This was the amount of coal normally expected from a miner in 14 times that length of time. He was therefore hailed as an example of how human determination and endeavour might increase productivity. He was declared a Soviet hero and given a large bonus and honorary awards, and competitions were arranged for others to emulate Stakhanov's achievement. It was ideal propaganda for a Party trying to create a new proletarian culture based on teamwork and selfless sacrifice. By December 1935, the number of broken records had entered the world of make-believe and filled two volumes. The Stakhanov movement became a way of forcing management to support their workers so as to increase production.

The Stakhanovite movement was not universally popular with all workers at the time. There was no doubt some jealousy attached to the Stakhanovites' receipt of superior accommodation and other material benefits. There are records of Stakhanovites being victimised or even attacked by colleagues who were less enthusiastic and resented campaigns to persuade them to work even harder.

A CLOSER LOOK

The Stakhanov propaganda stunt

Many years later, it was revealed that much of Stakhanov's feat had been a propaganda stunt. Stakhanov had been given a support team of several workers who had done everything possible to support him, carrying out a range of tasks that miners were normally expected to do for themselves, such as propping up the roof. This enabled Stakhanov to focus exclusively on cutting coal.

Fig. 4 *A propaganda poster celebrating Stakhanovite workers*

Managers

Industrial enterprises were placed under the control of directors or managers who had the unenviable task of ensuring that the output targets set by regional administrators (working under the Commissariat for their particular economic area) were met. Fulfilling quotas, while having limited control over their own resources, prices, wages and other costs, was not an easy task. Of course, managers did their best to negotiate the largest workforce and wage fund possible but once this was established a factory manager had little choice but to focus on attaining or surpassing the output target. The manager received a bonus that could be as much as 40 per cent of his income if he did better than expected. So, while managers received high salaries and status as part of the new industrial elite, the production quota was always an overriding concern.

Indeed, such was the pressure faced by managers, that it became quite normal to falsify statistics. A manager could be put on trial, imprisoned or even executed if he failed to meet targets. He also had to ensure that his books balanced, so as not to be charged with '**wrecking**'. From 1936, factories had to pay for their own fuel, raw materials and labour from their 'profits' so managers had to account carefully – or at least appear to have credible figures. In such conditions, it is little wonder that bribery and corruption became embedded within the system.

Managers were also expected to apply state regulations in the workplace. There were national 'work norms' which governed how much work a labourer should be expected to do and rules, such as those on absenteeism, to be enforced. These made it difficult for the manager to earn the good will of his labour force and some (bravely) tried to ignore the rules, proving keener to pay bonuses than to punish, lest their production levels fall. When work norms were raised in 1936 by between 10 per cent and 50 per cent, it became even harder for managers to deal with protesting workers – yet any attempt to bypass regulations or lower the norm, could result in accusations of sabotage. Stakhanovites posed a particular problem to managers. Too much effort from the Stakhanovites could lead to factory targets being revised upwards, creating new problems for output in the following year. Furthermore, workers, keen to show their prowess (and earn medals and other benefits), sometimes accused managers of wrecking their Stakhanovite attempts by failing to supply good tools or resources.

As well as a slump in trade in the late 1930s as a result of the worldwide Depression, managers faced labour shortages as conditions on collective farms improved, reducing immigration to the cities, and as increasing numbers of young men were conscripted into the military. Indeed, military demands also exacerbated shortages of raw materials (particularly oil, coal and wood) at a time when consumer demand was growing.

Workers

Despite the communist talk of '**proletarianisation**' and the creation of the '**socialist man**', the living and working conditions experienced by most industrial workers were far from a 'socialist paradise'.

The drive for industrialisation brought some tough measures: a seven-day working week and longer working hours. Arriving late or missing work could

A CLOSER LOOK

Living conditions for managers

The manager who managed his books well could enjoy a reasonably comfortable life but most kept any illicit gains well hidden for fear of being reported. For the honest manager, living conditions were not far removed from those of his workers.

KEY TERM

wrecking: acts perceived as economic or industrial sabotage, such as failing to meet economic targets, lowering morale in the workplace (by failing to uphold Stalinist propaganda), lack of effort, or incompetence

KEY TERM

proletarianisation: turning the mass of the population into urban workers; ridding society of selfish capitalist attitudes and developing a cooperative mentality

result in dismissal, eviction from housing and loss of benefits. Damaging machinery or leaving a job without permission was a criminal offence and strikes were illegal. From 1938, labour books (in addition to internal passports) recorded workers' employment, skills and any disciplinary issues.

Nevertheless, there was a certain degree of enthusiasm among workers in the early years of industrialisation. An extensive training programme was set up and opportunities for advancement by learning new skills meant some workers did well. From 1931, wage differentials were introduced, to reward those who stayed in their jobs and worked hard. By allowing managers to vary wages, award bonuses, pay by the piece (in order to increase productivity) and offer better housing to reward skills and devoted application, the proletariat became more diverse in its experience – some thriving, while others struggled. Stalin's industrialisation drive also produced new opportunities for social advancement. His **purges** in the 1930s hit hardest at intellectuals and white-collar workers, so reducing the numbers competing for jobs and creating plenty of vacancies 'at the top'. Nevertheless, even though in 1933 Stalin could announce, 'life has become better, comrades, life has become more joyous' the realities of daily life remained grim throughout this period.

The numbers that poured into the industrial cities, particularly in the early 1930s, left workers living in extremely cramped communal apartments where they had to cope with inadequate sanitation and erratic water supplies. Public transport was overcrowded, shops were often empty and queues and shortages were an accepted feature of life.

Although **real wages** increased during the second Five Year Plan, they were still lower in 1937, than they had been in 1928 (and in 1928 they had been little better than in 1913). Rationing was phased out in 1935 but market prices were high and, while those in positions of importance in the socialist system (for example, Party officials) could obtain more goods more cheaply, this was not the case for **ordinary workers**, whose living standards stagnated and may even have fallen slightly in the last years before the war.

CROSS-REFERENCE

The concept of '**socialist man**' is examined in Chapter 19, page 163.

The **purges** of the 1930s are discussed in Chapter 18.

KEY TERM

real wages: what can actually be bought with money wages, taking into account the varying price of goods

ACTIVITY

Which would you rather have been in the 1930s, an urban manager or an urban worker? Share your thoughts with a partner.

A CLOSER LOOK

Convict labour

Thousands of convicts in the labour camps died in the brutal conditions, yet it is far from certain how useful this labour force actually was. It is likely that the State spent more on resources and guarding the prisoners than they got back in productive work.

A CLOSER LOOK

Labour discipline

Government attitudes towards workers became harsher in 1939 and 1940 as the prospect of war loomed. Discipline was tightened: being 20 minutes late for work became a criminal offence. Furthermore, a decree of 1940 ended the free labour market: skilled workers could be directed anywhere, while others needed permission to change jobs. Social benefits were also cut.

There were also workers who were forced to labour for the state in order to fulfil Stalin's grandiose projects – **prison camp inmates** whose work and living conditions could be grim indeed. The Belomor Canal, for example, was built almost entirely by manual labour between 1931 and 1933. The labour force employed on this project reached c300,000 at its peak, and many died of overwork, poor treatment, lack of food and disease. The death rate was 700 per day; but new prisoners came into the camps in the canal area at the rate of 1500 per day. The average survival time was just two years.

SOURCE 4

Adapted from the recollections of D. P. Vitkovsky, a prisoner who worked as a supervisor on the Belomor Canal in 1933:

They were sent to the canal in tens of thousands at a time, and right off they gave them norms of shingle and boulders that you'd be unable to fulfil even in summer. No one was able to warn them; and in their village simplicity they gave all their strength to their work and weakened very swiftly and froze to death. At the end of the workday there were corpses left on the work site. The snow powdered their faces. One of them was hunched over beneath an overturned wheelbarrow; he had hidden his hands in his sleeves and froze to death in that position. Someone had frozen with his head bent down between his knees. Two were frozen back to back leaning against each other. At night the sledges went out and collected them. The drivers threw the corpses onto the sledges with a dull clonk. And in the summer bones remained from corpses which had not been removed in time, and together with the shingle they got into the concrete mixer.

PRACTICE QUESTION

Evaluating primary sources

With reference to Sources 2, 3 and 4 and your understanding of the historical context, assess the value of these sources to an historian studying industrial development in Russia in the 1930s.

Women

Fig. 5 *Women working in a textile factory 1929–41*

KEY TERM

Zhenotdel: the women's section of the Secretariat of the Central Committee of the Communist Party

Despite communist doctrines of 'equality', in 1929 female workers (representing c29 per cent of the workforce) were largely concentrated in the lowest paid jobs requiring the least skills – particularly in textiles and other light industry. Women were routinely discriminated against and were paid less than men for fulfilling the same work norms. This did not immediately change with the launching of the first Five Year Plan. Indeed, **Zhenotdel**, the department of the Russian Communist Party devoted to women's affairs, was closed down in January 1930 and there was no drive to increase female labour.

However, women workers began to enter Soviet industry in unprecedented numbers and by 1935, women constituted 42 per cent of all industrial workers. As prices rose, urban working class women flooded into industry and also found jobs in education, healthcare and administration in order to sustain their families. The desperate attempts of factory managers to reach their quotas led them to employ the wives, widows and teenage daughters of their male workers. These women not only proved a valuable labour resource, they were more reliable than victims of collectivisation from the countryside. Furthermore, the employment of urban women reduced the need for further housing development to cope with migration into cities – so female employees indirectly helped in the accumulation of capital for further industrial growth.

During the second Five Year Plan, the Party took note of the value of female workers and sent orders for more women to be employed in heavy industry. However, many factory managers continued to hire women for the jobs requiring fewest skills, and were reluctant to offer promotions or train women to take on skilled work. On the factory floor, females might be harassed, both physically and sexually, by their male co-workers and with the abolition of the Zhenotdel, there was no institution to fight inequality in the workplace.

Nevertheless, from 1936, the Party made more effort to enrol women in technical training programmes, and even made women's entry into management positions easier. Consequently, increasing numbers of women found their way into well-paid skilled positions, including work in heavy industry such as lumber, metal and machine production. The provision of state nurseries, crèches, canteens and child-clinics enabled these women to cope with work and family. Although, on average, women still earned 40 per cent less than men, advances were certainly made. A little over 43 per cent of the industrial workforce was female by 1940.

ACTIVITY

Extension

You may be interested to read more about the role of women in industry in *Women at the Gates: Gender and Industry in Stalin's Russia* by Wendy Goldman.

The success of the Five Year Plans

For all their weaknesses, the Five Year Plans undoubtedly helped to transform the USSR into a modern industrial economy. Some targets were over-ambitious and the emphasis on quantity meant that products were often of poor quality; but the relentless drive to achieve certainly stimulated economic growth and increased output. The Soviet economy probably grew at 5 to 6 per cent each year between 1928 and 1940: an impressive result. The USSR became a major industrial power in little over ten years.

The first Five Year Plan saw impressive gains in several areas of heavy industry, for example engineering, several branches of which were begun almost from nothing, while the second Plan additionally brought a huge growth in construction and transport. Between 1928 and 1932, the industrial workforce doubled and, between 1926 and 1939, the urban population increased from 26 to 56 million people.

After some initial dislocation, the workers enjoyed three 'good years' between 1934 and 1936, with an increase in consumer goods. Some of these goods, such as gramophones, made virtually their first appearance in the USSR for the ordinary citizen. Productivity and wages both rose, while prices fell.

However, the gains did not last and the third Plan was interrupted by the approach of war so that the original targets could not be met. Shortages recurred and resources were diverted. Nevertheless, the plans had permitted a huge growth in the armaments industry with tanks, aircraft and guns produced that were the equal of, and in some cases superior to, anything produced elsewhere in the world. The ability of the USSR to gear itself for war is, in itself, a reflection of the plans' successes.

There were, of course, social downsides and other specific stumbling blocks – particularly the shortage of skilled labour (which was only partially addressed). Even more important was USSR's inability to extract sufficient oil to meet their needs. Some relief was gained by the Soviet occupation of eastern Poland in late 1939, and the Baltic States in 1940, which added to the USSR's economic potential.

Nevertheless, the Party had achieved something of what it had set out to do. The plans advanced the proletarianisation of the Russian people and transformed the basis of the Soviet economy. They also helped to foster a sense of pride and belief that the communist system was superior to Western capitalism, which suffered greatly in the Depression of the 1930s.

Summary

- Gosplan organised the process by which industry was transformed under the Five Year Plans.
- Industrialisation was managed through a centralised 'command economy'; managers had to fulfil quotas.
- Ambitious targets drove achievement, and propaganda reinforced the message.
- The focus was on heavy industry. Other sectors were comparatively neglected although there was some consumer development during the second Five Year Plan.
- Living and working conditions were harsh, but there was some marginal improvement by 1941 and skilled workers generally did well.

A LEVEL **PRACTICE QUESTION**

To what extent had the Five Year Plans fulfilled Stalin's aims by 1941?

ACTIVITY

Look back at your chart of the successes and failures of the three Five Year plans. Extend it to provide some detail on the achievements and weaknesses of this period of industrialisation for

a. Soviet Society and
b. the Party.

ACTIVITY

Extension

Try to look at Soviet Economic Development from Lenin to Khrushchev (1994) by the economic historian R. Davies. Davies provides an excellent overview of the USSR's economic performance, which also takes into account the changes in agriculture that accompanied industrialisation.

STUDY TIP

It would be a good idea to identify Stalin's aims at the outset of your answer. You will probably want to distinguish between his political, economic and social aims, and these themes could provide the basis for your answer. Try to make a balanced assessment of the strengths and weaknesses of the plans and their impact in relation to each of these themes, as well as providing an overall judgement.

15 The development of the Stalin cult

ACTIVITY

Evaluating primary sources

What qualities does Avdienko attribute to Stalin in this speech?

SOURCE 1

Adapted from a speech by the Soviet author and poet, A. O. Avdienko, to the Seventh Congress of Soviets in February 1935. It was subsequently published in *Pravda* in August 1936:

Thank you, Stalin. Thank you because I am joyful. Thank you because I am well. Centuries will pass, and the generations still to come will regard us as the happiest of mortals, as the most fortunate of men, because we lived in the century of centuries, because we were privileged to see Stalin, our inspired leader. Yes, and we regard ourselves as the happiest of mortals because we are the contemporaries of a man who never had an equal in world history.
I write books. I am an author. All thanks to thee, O great educator, Stalin. I love a young woman with renewed love and shall perpetuate myself in my children — all thanks to thee, great educator Stalin. I shall be eternally happy and joyous, all thanks to thee, great educator, Stalin. Everything belongs to thee, chief of our great country. And when the woman I love presents me with a child the first word it shall utter will be: Stalin.

The cult of personality

From December 1929, and his fiftieth birthday celebrations, the cult of Stalin grew conspicuously; Stalin became the leader who inspired confidence during a period of rapid change. Every new initiative was 'sold' as the work of the all-knowing leader and portraits showed Marx, Engels, Lenin and Stalin in continuous progression, bringing enlightenment to the Russian people. Paintings, poems, posters and sculptures were produced to glorify Stalin's role as the 'mighty leader', 'father of the nation', 'universal genius' and 'shining sun of humanity'.

SOURCE 2

Adapted from 'Song About Stalin', a poem by Mikhail Izakovsky, a communist from a poor peasant background who had begun writing in praise of the regime in the 1920s. This was written in 1936:

For the sake of our happiness
He marched through all storms
He carried our Holy banner
Over our enormous land.
And fields and factories rose,
And tribes and people responded
To the call of our leader

He gave us for ever and ever
Youth, glory and power
He has lit the clear dawn of Spring
Over our homes
Let us sing, comrades, a song
About the dearest person
About our sun, about the truth of nations
About our Stalin, let's sing a song

ACTIVITY

Choose one phrase from the poem in Source 2 and provide some evidence that could support it.

The Stalin cult was fully established in the years 1933 to 1939, although it did not reach its height until after the Second World War. *The History of the All-Union Communist Party* (or the 'Short Course') was published as the main historical textbook for all educational institutions in 1938. In this Stalin assumed a major role in the October/November revolution and subsequent Civil War, while Trotsky and other old Bolsheviks were portrayed as 'enemies of the people' or assigned to minor roles. **Photographs were doctored** to remove Stalin's enemies and show Stalin at the side of Lenin. History became the History of Communist success, with all paths leading to the glories of Stalinism. The book had sold 34 million copies in the Soviet Union by 1948.

The adulation Stalin received was on a scale and of an intensity rarely seen before. Although it was 'manufactured', it showed the strength of support he had acquired within the Soviet Union. Some praised him because they had benefitted from his rule – or hoped to benefit in the future and needed to be assured of his patronage. However, for many, a very real sense of emotional attachment to Stalin reflected the tradition of loyalty to the leader. Just as the peasantry had once shown unwavering loyalty to their Tsar, who could do no wrong, so Stalin was seen as a father to his people. Peasants and workers even created their own 'red corner' of the great leaders in their homes, in the same way that they might have created a saints' corner in tsarist times.

SOURCE 3

Adapted from the memoirs of the poet and novelist Yevgeny Yevtushenko, who grew up in Siberia during the 1930s. In this excerpt, Yevtushenko recalls his feelings when he was five:

I went with my father and mother to watch the holiday parades, organised workers' demonstrations, and I would beg my father to lift me up a little higher. I wanted to catch sight of Stalin. And as I waved my small red flag, riding high in my father's arms above that sea of heads, I had the feeling that Stalin was looking right at me. I was filled with a terrible envy of those children my age lucky enough to be chosen to hand bouquets of flowers to Stalin and whom he gently patted on the head, smiling his famous smile into his famous moustache.

Stalin's own role in the development of the cult is somewhat ambiguous. It has been claimed that he did not encourage it and that it was not of his own making. At the same time, he did little to stop it. His successor, Nikita Khrushchev, revealed in 1956 that when Stalin read a pre-publication version of the official *Short Biography* of his own life, he insisted that it be revised to praise his qualities and achievements even more.

 PRACTICE QUESTION

Evaluating primary sources

With reference to Sources 1, 2 and 3 and your understanding of the historical context, assess the value of these three sources to an historian studying the cult of Stalin.

Literature, the arts and socialist realism

Although Lenin had personally been a traditionalist, freedom of expression had been encouraged in the 1920s, provided that art was not used to express counter-revolutionary sentiments. However, Stalin viewed **cultural pursuits** in much the same way as he viewed pure propaganda. Literature, art, architecture,

CROSS-REFERENCE

The idea that **cultural pursuits** should influence 'the human soul' is discussed in Chapter 19, page 163, where the concept of the 'socialist man' and the impact of cultural change are explored.

KEY PROFILE

Andrei Aleksandrovich Zhdanov (1896–1948) was an old Bolshevik who had worked his way up through Party ranks to replace Kirov as Party Secretary in Leningrad in 1934. He became a member of the Politburo in 1939 and led the defence of Leningrad in 1941 to 1944. In 1946, he was appointed to direct cultural policy and he promoted the **Zhdanovshchina**. He died suddenly in 1948; there were rumours that Stalin had deliberately had him removed but there is no actual evidence for this.

CROSS-REFERENCE

For more detail on the **Zhdanovshchina** look ahead to Chapter 23, page 201.

CROSS-REFERENCE

The impact of **cultural change** is discussed in Chapter 19, page 164.

ACTIVITY

Extension

Find a copy of *Quiet Flows the Don* by M. A. Sholokov. It is a love story written in 1934 and describes the relationship of two Russian peasants who are trying to support the establishment of communism in Russia.

sculpture, the theatre, film and music alike were all considered only valuable and legitimate if they supported socialist ideology. 'Art for its own sake' had no place in the Soviet State and writers were expected to be 'engineers of the human soul'. The creativity of the 1920s, thus gave way to conformity in the 1930s.

From 1932, all writers (whether of newspapers, magazines, plays, novels or poems) had to belong to the 'Union of Soviet Writers', while painters and art critics were required to join the Union of Artists. Similar bodies were established for musicians, film-makers and sculptors. These exerted control over both what was created and who was allowed to create, because non-membership meant artistic isolation with no opportunity for commissions or the sale of work. Individual expression was deemed politically suspect.

The new norms demanded adherence to the doctrine of 'socialist realism'. According to the writers' union this meant 'the truthful, historically concrete representation of reality in its revolutionary development'. In simpler terms, it meant that writers and all other artists were not to represent Soviet life exactly as it was at that time, but were to show what it might become (and was moving towards) in the future. In this way people were to be led to appreciate 'socialist reality' and see a foreshadowing of the future in the present. Literature and Art thus became the media by which citizens learned that the 'march to Communism' was inevitable.

The frame of reference for writers was laid down by **Andrei Zhdanov** in April 1934 at the first Congress of the Union of Soviet Writers, although the principles applied to all art forms. Works were expected to glorify the working man, and particularly communities working together and embracing new technology. The messages conveyed were to be uplifting, optimistic and positive. One popular novel was Nikolai Ostrovsky's *How the Steel Was Tempered*. The message was one of happy endings.

While new artistic endeavour was constrained by political demands, there was also much interest in Russian works of the nineteenth century. Although Soviet **culture** was designed to be for the 'ordinary people' (the proletariat), there was no attempt to create a new 'proletarian culture' that was in any way distinct

Fig. 1 *Nature being tamed by Soviet industrial endeavour*

from the 'upper class/bourgeois' culture of the pre-revolutionary era. So, the great works of the nineteenth century were much read, seen, heard and copied, since it was believed that the 'ordinary people' could understand and relate to these. The Stalinist era thus brought recognisable 'real' subject matter in painting, and solid and imposing classical forms in architecture. Landscape art was revived as a favoured medium – particularly scenes that showed nature being tamed by Soviet industrial endeavour. In music there was a return to the Russian classical composers, Glinka and Tchaikovsky; in literature, to Pushkin and Tolstoy.

Folk culture was also promoted. Traditional peasant arts and crafts were praised and museums of folklore were set up. Folk choirs and dancing troupes appeared, supposedly representing a Russian 'national culture' and performing in folklore festivals. The theme tied in well with Stalin's commitment to 'national' values, and praise for Russia's great heritage, but, in practice, much of this was pure Stalinist invention.

ACTIVITY

According to your own personal interests, undertake some further research into the life and work of one or more of the artists, musicians, writers or other cultural figures that lived and worked in Russia before the Second World War. Each member of the group should prepare a presentation and share their findings.

A CLOSER LOOK

Moscow

The transformation of Moscow epitomised socialist realism in architecture. The style was monumental, with Lenin's mausoleum 'shrine' on the Red Square 'parade ground' in the shadow of the Kremlin; and on the Kremlin, in 1935, five red stars replaced the imperial eagles which had been removed. The new **Moscow Metro**, also opened in 1935, had stations designed as 'palaces of light' – symbols of 'all-victorious socialism'. Mosaic designs, marble-pattern floors and stained-glass panels were designed to inspire pride and reverence. The grandest design of all (but one that was never completed) was for a 'Palace of the Soviets'. It was intended as the tallest building in the world, topped with a gigantic statue of Lenin.

CROSS-REFERENCE

The building of the **Moscow Metro**, which was viewed as a great socialist industrial project, is outlined in Chapter 14, page 123.

CROSS-REFERENCE

To recap on the 'heroic' exploits of Aleksei **Stakhanov**, and the resulting Stakhanovite movement, look back to Chapter 14, page 124.

Propaganda

Stalin relied heavily on his propaganda machine to harness support for his policies. Military illusions were sometimes used; collectivisation of agriculture, for example, was termed a 'full-scale socialist offensive on all fronts'. Treacherous class enemies (portrayed as agents of foreign, imperialist powers) were damned, while pictures of happy, productive workers reinforced the socialist message of Stalin's collectivisation and industrial policies. The hardships associated with economic change were romanticised to emphasise the glories of the new socialist society in which all workers' dreams were coming true. Indeed, it has been suggested that Stalin's Soviet regime was the first state to attempt to create a new type of humanity, transmitting social and political values in the hope of affecting people's thinking, emotions and behaviour.

The 'worker-hero' became a common propagandist theme and **Stakhanov** was extolled as a role model. Young men who accomplished heroic endeavours actually appeared on the front page of *Pravda* more often than Stalin himself between 1937 and 1938. Female Stakhanovites also featured and 25 per cent of all female factory workers were described as 'norm-breaking' – although the 'Mother-heroines' who had large families were also glorified. Idealised workers also appeared in sculpture. Vera Mukhina produced a massive stainless steel sculpture, 'Worker and Kolkhoz Woman', for the 1937 World Trade Fair in Paris; 24.5 metres high, it depicted two figures with a sickle and a hammer raised over their heads in workers' solidarity.

Soviet aviators and Arctic explorers were also treated as heroes and given wide publicity in the press and in cheap books that were produced in bulk to help an increasingly literate population lap up propaganda stories of model

A CLOSER LOOK

Socialist propaganda in Pravda

Pravda published a series of articles and cartoons in a section entitled 'With Us' and 'With Them'. 'With Us' featured stories about the opening of new factories, scientific discoveries and so on, while 'With Them' provided dreary descriptions of the hardships in the West, unemployment and disasters.

A CLOSER LOOK

Pavlik Morozov

Pavlik Morozov was a 13-year-old boy whose exploits are probably fictitious. He supposedly denounced his own father as a friend of the kulaks in 1932, whereupon his grandfather brutally murdered him and his younger brother. Pavlik was upheld as a model for all children to follow and his story publicised all over Russia. It was a subject of reading, songs, plays, a symphonic poem, a full-length opera and six biographies.

citizens. The story of the heroic **Pavlik Morozov**, who denounced his father as a kulak and was killed by angry relatives, was a particular favourite children's story, providing an example of sacrifice in the socialist cause.

However, for the illiterate there were also ubiquitous wall posters, propagandistic films and radios, with receivers in communal locations so that all could hear the news.

Fig. 2 *Vera Mukhina's stainless steel sculpture, 'Worker and Kolkhoz Woman'*

ACTIVITY

Create your own Stalinist propaganda poster.

STUDY TIP

This essay requires you to consider the extent to which Stalin prevented creativity and free expression in the arts. You could consider to not only support the quotation but also criticise it too.

A LEVEL | PRACTICE QUESTION

'There was no such thing as freedom of expression in the arts in Russia in the 1930s.' Assess the validity of this view.

Summary

- The Stalin cult was considerably developed in the 1930s; not only was Stalin glorified as a person but his pronouncements and policies were regarded as godlike.
- Literature and all the arts had to follow the dictates of socialist realism and to present a political message glorifying Soviet achievements and attacking 'negative influences' from within or outside the USSR.
- Any intellectual or artist who did not conform was banned from working and could be imprisoned, exiled or even 'disposed of'.
- The Soviet regime had always relied heavily on propaganda as a way of controlling its subjects' minds and actions, but it was taken to new heights under Stalin.

16 The social and economic condition of the Soviet Union by 1941

A Soviet joke from the 1930s:

Q. What would happen if you built Communism in the Sahara Desert?
A. Everything would be fine for the first three years, but then there would be a serious shortage of sand.

- the strengths and weaknesses of the economy of the Soviet Union by 1941

- the strengths and weaknesses of social conditions in the Soviet Union by 1941.

The strengths and weaknesses of the economy by 1941

What sort of people do you think might have made up jokes like this? Can you make up your own Soviet joke?

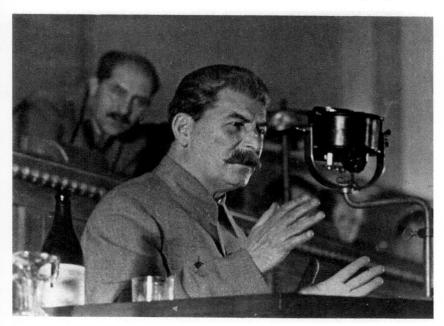

Fig. 1 *Stalin speaking at the Kremilin*

By 1941, Stalin's Five Year Plans had transformed Russia into a highly industrialised and urbanised nation, while all Russian farms had been collectivised and the free market brought to an end. Although Soviet claims and statistics were often exaggerated, there is no doubt that a remarkable transformation had taken place. In 1926, 17 per cent of the population lived in towns, but by 1939, 33 per cent did so and by 1940, the USSR had overtaken Britain in iron and steel production and was not far behind Germany.

Stalin himself was very proud of his industrial achievements, as can be seen from this speech.

Adapted from a speech by Joseph Stalin, delivered on 17 May 1938 at a reception in the Kremlin for those working in higher education, and published two days later in *Pravda*:

Comrades, permit me to propose a toast to science and its progress. To the progress of that science whose devotees, while understanding the power of

ACTIVITY

Evaluating primary sources

What message is Stalin trying to convey in Source 2? How accurate do you think the message is?

established scientific traditions are not willing to be slaves of these traditions; the science which has the courage to smash old traditions and is able to create new standards and new views.

Sometimes it is not well-known men of science who lay the new roads, but plain, practical men, innovators in their field. Here, sitting at this table, is Comrade Stakhanov.

He is unknown in the scientific world. He has no scientific degree. But who does not know that in practical work in industry Stakhanov and the Stakhanovites have upset the existing standards, which were established by well-known scientists and technologists, have shown that they were antiquated, and have introduced new standards which conform to the requirements of real science and technology?

By emphasising heavy industry and rearmament, Stalin had helped lay the foundation for victory in the Second World War. Coal and oil production were vastly stepped up in the third Five Year Plan, nine aircraft factories were constructed in 1939 and, between 1938 and 1941, spending on rearmament rose from 27.5 billion roubles to 70.9 billion roubles. On the eve of war, Soviet industry was producing 230 tanks, 700 military aircraft and more than 100,000 rifles per month.

Table 1 Proportion of budget devoted to defence

1933	3.4%
1937	16.5%
1940	32.6%

However, there were crucial weaknesses. Economic development was uneven. Heavy industry had grown massively by 1941, but, after a brief rise under the second Five Year Plan, consumer production had been cut back and consumer goods were scarcer than they had been under the NEP. The quality of goods was poor, even though labour productivity had increased as bureaucrats were set on figures and targets at the expense of all else. Bureaucracy also hindered the implementation of economic schemes, and whilst massive investment permitted growth under the Five Year Plans, the organisation at local level was at times chaotic. Furthermore, the economy was not geared for imminent war in 1941 and, when war broke out, deficiencies in both the quality and quantity of equipment and problems of supply were soon apparent.

The following tables provide figures for 1940 (the last date for which they are available before the outbreak of war in 1941):

Table 2 Comparative statistics of USSR and other major powers in 1940 (figures are in million tonnes)

Country	Pig iron	Steel	Coal
USSR	14.9	18.4	164.6
USA	31.9	47.2	359.0
Great Britain	6.7	10.3	227.0
Germany	18.3	22.7	186.0
France	6.0	6.1	45.5

Table 3 The Soviet economy in 1928 and 1940 – all animals and products are in millions (shoes = million pairs); grain, oil, coal and steel in million tonnes; electrical power in billion kwh; '0' denotes less than a million

Product	1928	1940
Agriculture		
grain	73	95
cows	29	28
pigs	19	27
Industrial		
electrical power	5	48
crude oil	11.7	31
coal	35.4	165
steel	4	18
trucks	0.7	14
tractors	0.1	3
Consumer goods		
automobiles	0	0.5
washing machines	0	0
cameras	0	35
radios	0	16
shoes	58	211

ACTIVITY

Do these statistics prove the success of Stalinist economic policies?

The strengths and weaknesses of society by 1941

Fig. 2 *A poster commending Stalin's socialism*

The 1930s had also seen a good deal of social change as a result of Stalin's economic drive. On the positive side, Stalin could claim to have made further progress towards true socialism as a result of the economic changes of the 1930s because, by the Soviet definition, socialism meant 'social' ownership of the means of production. In other words, all people collectively 'owned' factories and fields (or rather the State did on people's behalf), so that there were no profits being made by some people at others' expense. The Soviets claimed that State ownership was just a particular form of 'social' ownership since the State was protecting the individual against the exploitation of the citizen by profit-seeking capitalists, which was the hallmark of capitalist countries whose economies were based on private enterprise. In this sense, Stalin had carried through a highly successful economic programme and in so doing had furthered communist ideology.

He had also acquired a much greater control over the people. Communist control was, for example, considerably strengthened in the countryside. From 1929, peasants were supervised by Party officials attached to each *kolkhoz* and secret police units were stationed at each Motor Tractor Station to check up on the rural population. In the cities, the factory managers were subject to the controls of the Party (on pain of demotion or even execution), while the workers were kept in strict order through labour books and internal passports and with the threat of the denial of ration cards, eviction from lodgings and even penal sentences for misdemeanours.

However, what had emerged in the industrialisation drive of the 1930s was actually very different from the original socialist ideals. Rather than a classless society, Stalin had helped to create a hierarchical society dominated by a privileged Party elite. The peasants were at the mercy of the collectives, and the urban and rural working classes, no longer exploited by capitalist employers, were instead ruthlessly driven by their Soviet masters. Instead of 'withering away' (in accordance with **Marxist stage theory**) the State had become more formidable, extensive and brutal.

CROSS-REFERENCE

To refresh your understanding of **Marxist stage theory**, look back to the Introduction, page xv.

A CLOSER LOOK

The USSR and Marxist stage theory

The Soviets never claimed to have achieved complete communism under Stalin because to get to that stage, the State with all its organising and governing bodies would have to have 'withered away'. Instead, the Soviet claim to have reached 'socialism' was based on the fact that the few remaining private factories were closed in 1930, while the collectivisation of agriculture was completed during the 1930s.

Critics asserted that the USSR was not a socialist state, because 'social' ownership under Stalin did not exist for the good of the people. Rather, it was a form of dictatorial or totalitarian power in which all activity, including economic activity, was determined by what the unelected leaders decided was good for the Party and the State, without taking the needs of individual citizens into account.

KEY TERM

Cold War: the state of hostility that existed between the communist Soviet Union and its satellite states and the liberal/democratic and capitalist Western powers between 1945 and 1990

Even Stalin appears to have been aware of the social downside of his economic policies, if the following source is to be believed:

SOURCE 3

Adapted from *The Second World War* by Winston Churchill, published in 1951, Churchill recalls his first private conversation with Stalin over dinner in Moscow in 1942 about collectivisation in the 1930s. Stalin and Churchill were allies in the Second World War, although Churchill was strongly anti-communist and by 1951, the two leaders took opposing sides in the **Cold War**:

I asked, 'have the stresses of this war been as bad to you personally as carrying through the policy of the collective farms?' 'Oh, no,' he said, 'the Collective Farm policy was a terrible struggle.' 'I thought you would have found it bad,' said I, 'because you were dealing with millions of small men.' 'Ten millions,' he said, holding up his hands. 'It was fearful. Four years it lasted. It was absolutely necessary for Russia, if we were to avoid periodic famines, to plough the land with tractors. Only Collective Farms with workshops could handle tractors. We took the greatest trouble to explain it to the peasants. After you have said all you can to a peasant, he says he must go home and consult his wife. After he has talked it over, he always answers that he does not want the Collective Farm and would rather do without the tractors.' 'These were what you call kulaks?' 'Yes,' he said, 'It was all very bad and difficult – but necessary.'

As well as the destruction of the kulaks and the dislocation caused to Russia's peasants, many of whom moved to the industrial cities, little regard was given to the welfare of urban workers in the relentless drive to industrialise. Even those at managerial level were expendable and the treatment meted out to this important social group is indicative of the overriding concern of the state to force change at any cost. Huge pressure was put on management. For example, in July 1940, a decree was issued making poor quality production a criminal offence, so that, in theory at least, enterprises had to worry about quality as well as meeting quantitative targets. This interference breached a Central Committee directive of 1929 to the effect that enterprises such as factories should be managed by one person, free from interference by the party organisation.

Thus the quality of life for all non-Party personnel suffered from the economic drive. The low rations, poor housing and constant pressure, were largely the offshoot of Stalin's own determination to sacrifice the people in the interests of his economic vision. Indeed, for Stalin and his followers, the ideological motive for industrialisation appears to have been as important as building national strength. Stalin promoted the industrialisation campaign as one of class warfare, and far from trying to unite the nation, deliberately split it, for example using committed groups like the Communist youth group, **Komsomol**, to preach against 'class enemies' who were trying to hold up progress.

The situation on the outbreak of war in 1941

Fig. 3 *Soviet tanks rolling towards the battle front June 1941*

The principle of central authority and the development of the command economy were to prove vital in the organisation of the Soviet war effort in 1941. It has even been suggested that the harshness of the labour laws and the severity of working conditions in both town and country in the 1930s, helped build resilience among the Soviet labour force and made them more ready to suffer for the greater good – so enabling them to cope with the hardships of war.

ACTIVITY

Evaluating primary sources

How does Stalin justify state-led collectivisation in Source 3? How convincing do you find his argument?

CROSS-REFERENCE

Komsomol is discussed in Chapter 19, page 160.

Nevertheless, while economic and social developments by 1941 gave the USSR a much stronger basis from which to mount a defence and fight-back than would have been the case in 1928, the third Five Year Plan was left incomplete and by 1941 the nation was still producing less grain than under the NEP. No wonder the coming of war left Stalin in a state of panic – as is apparent from his radio broadcast of 1941.

ACTIVITY

Evaluating primary sources

In what ways does Source 4 show the importance of central control for wartime USSR?

SOURCE 4

Adapted from Stalin's first radio broadcast of the war, delivered to the Soviet people on 3 July 1941:

The issue is one of life and death for the Soviet State; of life and death for the peoples of the USSR. We must mobilise ourselves and reorganise all our work on a new wartime footing. All our industries must be made to work with greater intensity, to produce more rifles, machine-guns, cartridges, shells, planes; we must organise the guarding of factories, power stations, telephonic and telegraphic communications and arrange local air-raid protection. In case of forced retreat, all rolling stock must be evacuated, the enemy must not be left a single engine, a single railway car, not a single pound of grain or gallon of fuel. The collective farmers must drive off all their cattle and turn over their grain to the safe-keeping of the State authorities for transportation to the rear. All valuable property, including non-ferrous metals, grain and fuel that cannot be withdrawn must be destroyed without fail.

 PRACTICE QUESTION

Evaluating primary sources

With reference to Sources 2, 3 and 4 and your understanding of the historical context, assess the value of these three sources to an historian studying the economic and social condition of the USSR in 1941.

STUDY TIP

Each source offers some detail on economic and social change in the USSR by 1941 and in that respect they are all valuable for an historian. However, their varying provenances give you plenty of scope to evaluate just how reliable the evidence they provide is, and by applying your own knowledge you should be able to make an informed judgement on the value of each.

Summary

ACTIVITY

Summary

With reference to what you have read in this section, complete the following chart:

USSR in 1941	Strengths	Weaknesses
Economic		
Social		

 PRACTICE QUESTION

'The USSR was in a weak economic condition when war broke out in 1941.' Assess the validity of this view.

STUDY TIP

You will need to define what you understand by a 'weak' economic condition in order to answer this question. You may, for example, feel that there were economic weaknesses in the Soviet economy in 1941, but that the economy could not be described as 'in a weak condition' overall. Remember also that the economy includes both agriculture and industry and you may choose to address each separately. The first row of your summary chart could prove a useful starting point for your planning.

17 Dictatorship and Stalinism

Fig. 1 *A 1935 French cartoon depicting Stalin controlling the USSR; the sign says 'We are very happy'*

The machinery of state terror, the NKVD and the early purges

The machinery of **state terror** had emerged under Lenin, so the USSR was already a police state in 1928. The Soviet people were kept under strict surveillance by Party activists and informers, and the General Secretariat kept extensive records on the population. Lenin had established the Cheka in December 1917, to act as his 'sharp sword of the revolution' and from 1922 to 1934 security functions were carried out by the Department of Political Police – the OGPU. The OGPU also supervised a network of labour camps, which had been built up since 1918 to replace the old tsarist prison camps.

Stalin extended the use of terror during his rise to the leadership position (for example in 1929 Trotsky was expelled from the USSR and Bukharin removed from the Politburo) and to enforce collectivisation through the destruction of the kulaks. Furthermore, in 1930, Stalin expelled some of his former supporters from the Party for criticising the excesses of collectivisation and, in 1931, put a group of former Mensheviks and SRs on trial. In pushing through his Five Year Plans for industry, he also sent specialists and engineers, whom he accused of machine-breaking and sabotage, to labour camps.

LEARNING OBJECTIVES

In this chapter you will learn about:

- the machinery of 'state terror', the NKVD and the early purges
- Kirov's murder
- the show trials
- the Stalin constitution.

KEY CHRONOLOGY

1929	Trotsky is expelled from the USSR
	Bukharin is removed from the Politburo
1930	Collectivisation and the coercion of the kulaks
	The Industrial Party show trial for sabotage and treason
1931	The trial of several former Mensheviks and SRs
1932	Stalin's wife Nadezhda Alliluyeva commits suicide
	Ryutin is denounced for opposing Stalin
1933	The Metro-Vickers trial of British engineers for 'sabotage'
1934	The Seventeenth Party Congress
	OGPU is replaced by NKVD
	Kirov is murdered
1936	The show trial of 16 August

KEY TERM

state terror: a means to control the population and remove opposition through control and fear; Stalin made terror an instrument of government

purge: literally a 'cleaning out of impurities'; this term was primarily used to describe forcible expulsions from the Communist Party but in the later 1930s it came to mean the removal of anyone deemed a political enemy; a *chistka* is a Russian word for a political purge

KEY PROFILE

Martemyan Ryutin (1890–1937) had become a member of the Central Committee in 1927 and was a supporter of moderate agrarian policies. He was expelled from the Party in 1930 for criticising collectivisation. On release from gaol he circulated documents which blamed Stalin for the USSR's economic problems. He was arrested in 1932 and given a ten-year prison sentence. Ryutin was ultimately executed in January 1937 as part of the **Yezhovshchina** (Great Purge).

CROSS-REFERENCE

The **Yezhovshchina** is discussed in Chapter 18.

CROSS-REFERENCE

Kirov is profiled in Chapter 10, page 89 and his murder is outlined on page 143.

Zinoviev and **Kamenev** are profiled in Chapter 3, pages 23 and 18. For their executions, look ahead to Chapter 18, page 155.

CROSS-REFERENCE

Beria is profiled in Chapter 18, page 153.

A CLOSER LOOK

The Shakhty Trial of 1928 and other industrial trials

In 1928, managers and technicians at the Shakhty coal mine who had questioned the pace of industrialisation were accused of 'counter-revolutionary activity'. They were given a public 'show trial' in which they were forced to confess. Five were executed and others received long prison sentences. Gosplan was subsequently purged of critics and ex-Mensheviks, and further trials took place throughout the USSR. In the 'Industrial Party' show trial of November 1930, a random group of industrialists, Mensheviks and SRs were accused of sabotage and in the 1933 Metro-Vickers trial, British specialists were found guilty of wrecking activities.

By the end of the first Five Year Plan in 1932, there were renewed signs of opposition to Stalin's leadership, particularly since forced collectivisation had culminated in the 1932–3 famine. This weakened Stalin's position and led to a further **purge** of the party.

Martemyan Ryutin, (former Moscow Party Secretary and a 'rightist' who had been expelled from the party in 1930) led the call for changes in policy. He circulated a 200-page document entitled 'Stalin and the Crisis of the Proletarian Dictatorship' among Party members in March 1932. This became known as the 'Ryutin Platform', and was followed by another urging Stalin's removal. Stalin called for the execution of these 'traitors' and although he was over-ruled (not least by **Kirov**, the popular Leningrad Party leader who had been tipped as a likely successor to Stalin), Ryutin was imprisoned for ten years, while **Zinoviev**, **Kamenev** and 14 others were expelled from the Party for failure to report the existence of the document. There were 24 further expulsions the next month and, by 1934, a fifth of the Party had been branded 'Ryutinites' and expelled in a non-violent purge or *chistka*.

ACTIVITY

You might like to find out about the suicide of Stalin's wife Nadezhda Alliluyeva, which took place in 1932 at a time when Stalin was under great pressure.

In 1934, the USSR's internal security was passed to the NKVD (People's Commissariat of Internal Affairs), led in turn by **Yagoda**, **Yezhov** and **Beria**. In the same year, the ordinary police was also put under the control of the NKVD, and the labour camps reorganised into a national network, known as the Gulags. In this way, the whole system of policing and state repression was unified under the NKVD.

KEY PROFILE

Genrikh Yagoda (1891–1938) had joined the Cheka at the end of the Civil War and became head of the secret police (NKVD) in 1934. He was responsible for preparing the first major show trial in 1936, but was accused of being insufficiently thorough, arrested, tried, and executed in 1938.

Fig. 2 *Sergei Kirov, Bolshevik revolutionary leader and Soviet politician, who was assassinated in Leningrad on 1 December, 1934*

Kirov's murder, 1934

At the Seventeenth Party Congress in 1934, a split formed between Stalin, who wanted to maintain the pace of industrialisation, and others within the Politburo who spoke about stopping forcible grain seizures and increasing workers' rations. Only two of the Politburo firmly supported Stalin (Molotov and **Kaganovich**), while Kirov, who spoke out in opposition, received a long, standing ovation. Furthermore, the title of 'General Secretary' was abolished and Stalin and Kirov (along with **Zhdanov** and Kaganovich) were all given the title 'Secretary of Equal Rank'. Stalin may have been in favour of this (in order to spread the responsibility for the economic crisis) but it meant, in theory at least, that Stalin was no more important than the other secretaries.

Kirov was murdered in December 1934. The circumstances were suspicious and Stalin was quick to claim that this was part of a Trotskyite plot to overthrow the Party. A decree was published a day after the assassination, giving Yagoda, as head of the NKVD, powers to arrest and execute anyone found guilty of 'terrorist plotting'. Over a hundred Party members were shot and thousands more arrested and sent to prison camps. In January 1935, Zinoviev, Kamenev and 17 others were arrested, accused of instigating terrorism and sentenced to between 5 and 10 years imprisonment. Shortly afterwards, 12 NKVD members in Leningrad were found guilty and imprisoned and in a further round up. In June 1935, the death penalty was extended still further – to anyone aware of subversive activity.

KEY PROFILE

Nikolai Yezhov (1895–1939) had been a political Commissar during the Civil War and afterwards worked for the Party and Komsomol. He joined the OGPU and in 1936 replaced Yagoda as head of the NKVD. During his time in this role, from September 1936 to December 1938, he was responsible for the Yezhovshchina – a period of purges and terror. Yezhov was one of Stalin's protégés – intelligent, hard working and loyal – and affectionately referred to by Stalin as, 'my blackberry'. However, he had a more sinister side as a tension-riddled, alcoholic, drug-addicted deviant who personally supervised torture. In 1939, when Stalin wished to end the terror, Yezhov was quietly removed from office and shot, being made a scapegoat for the excesses of the purges.

ACTIVITY

Imagine yourself in the position of a young Party activist in the early 1930s. What would have been your view of the use of state terror?

CROSS-REFERENCE

Kaganovich is profiled in Chapter 10, page 89.

Zhdanov is profiled in Chapter 15, page 132.

A CLOSER LOOK

Kirov's murder

As he approached his office in the Leningrad Party headquarters on 1 December 1934, Kirov was shot in the neck by Leonid Nikolayev. Nikolayev was a disgruntled Party member (once expelled, but reinstated) whose wife may have been having an affair with Kirov. However, he was not linked to the Left opposition and when questioned, Nikolayev suggested the NKVD 'knew' all about the murder. Kirov's bodyguard and some NKVD men were mysteriously killed in a car accident before

We do not know whether Stalin was implicated in Kirov's murder or not (Stalin's daughter maintained that the assassination was actually the work of the NKVD and Laventri Beria). Prepare a case either for Stalin's complicity or against it. You could hold a 'court session' in your classroom in which some give prosecution and defence speeches and others ask questions and participate in a vote.

Evaluating primary sources

Discuss the intention of the letter quoted in Source 1 with a partner. Try to identify the different purposes it might serve.

they could give evidence and although some leading NKVD men were sentenced for failure to protect Kirov, their terms were short and their treatment lenient. In 1938, Yagoda pleaded guilty to allowing Nikolayev to reach Kirov; however, since Yagoda himself was then on trial, he may well not have been telling the truth.

SOURCE 1

Adapted from a confidential letter from the Central Committee of the Communist Party to all Party organisations, 18 January 1935:

We must put a stop to the opportunistic complacency which arises from the mistaken assumption that as we grow in the strength of our forces, our enemies become ever more tame and harmless. Such an assumption is fundamentally wrong. It is an echo of the Right deviation, which assured all and sundry that the enemies would quietly creep into Socialism, that they would become real Socialists in the end. Bolsheviks must not rest on their laurels and become empty-headed. We do not need complacency, but vigilance, real Bolshevik, revolutionary vigilance. We must remember that the more hopeless the position of the enemies becomes, the more readily they will clutch at extreme measures as the only measures of the doomed in their struggle against Soviet power. One must remember this and be vigilant.

The assassination became the signal for the regime to tighten its hold over the country and begin widespread purges. Stalin's intense suspicion, verging on paranoia, of rivals and potential plots, his vindictiveness towards those who had crossed him in the past, his determination to allow no limits to his power or his policies and to exercise total control over both party and country can be dated from this time.

The show trials

Show trials became a political tool in Stalinist Russia. These were public trials to which foreign journalists were invited and their function was to 'prove' that the USSR and Stalin were facing opposition from 'enemies of the state', whose crimes might well have been previously hidden behind a veneer of loyalty, and that the disposal of such enemies was entirely justified. Of course, a more likely interpretation is that the show trials were a means by which Stalin could remove his enemies and, in particular, those who challenged (or might, in the future, challenge) his authority, while still retaining his own popularity.

The show trials were meticulously staged. The verdict was never in doubt and the purpose of the trial was to demonstrate the accused's guilt, preferably with a public admission of betraying the revolution and people. In the months preceding the trial, it was the task of the NKVD to extract a signed confession. Every conceivable form of interrogation was used, ranging from subtle pressure and promises, to starvation, physical and mental torture and threats to the defendant and his family. In April 1935, a new law decreed that children over the age of 12 who were found guilty of crimes would be subject to the same punishments as adults, including the death penalty. This provision allowed NKVD to coerce confessions by suggesting that false charges would be brought against the accused's children.

The first major show trial was in August 1936 when Stalin decided that Kamenev and Zinoviev (who had already been secretly tried in 1935) should be made to undergo a show trial for propagandist purposes. Both were accused of alliance with Trotsky (who had been expelled from the USSR in 1929), stirring up discontent and plotting to kill Stalin. Fourteen others were accused alongside them and Yagoda oversaw the interrogation proceedings.

SOURCE 2

Adapted from a Central Committee circular, 'On the Terrorist Activities of the Trotskyite-Zinovievite Counter-revolutionary bloc', 29 July 1936. This document was read by top Party members only and was kept secret until after the trial:

Trotsky, Zinoviev and Kamenev joined forces with the most desperate and embittered enemies of Soviet power, and turned into the organising force of the remnants of the classes which have been smashed in the USSR and which, in desperation, are resorting to the terror — the basest instrument of struggle against the Soviet government. They have become the leading detachment of the counter-revolutionary bourgeoisie, voicing its will and its aspirations. They have no political motivations for struggling against the Party other than naked and undisguised careerism and the desire to get into power at whatever cost. Their principal motive for adopting terror is the successes of our Party of socialist construction — successes which arouse resentment in them and incite them to revenge for their own political bankruptcy.

Fig. 3 *The Show Trials*

The trial was held from 19 to 24 August, 1936. No material evidence was presented, and the defendants confessed their guilt. Zinoviev announced, 'I am fully and utterly guilty. I am guilty of having been the organiser, second only to Trotsky, of that block whose chosen task was the killing of Stalin. I was the principal organiser of Kirov's assassination.' Kamenev declared, 'I Kamenev, together with Zinoviev and Trotsky, organised and guided this conspiracy. We were actuated by boundless hatred and by lust of power.'

The prosecutor, Vishinsky, closed his speech by proclaiming, 'I demand that these mad dogs be shot, every last one of them.' All the defendants were sentenced to death and were subsequently executed in the cellars of Lubyanka Prison in Moscow on 25 August 1936. Trotsky was sentenced to death in absentia.

A CLOSER LOOK

The Show Trial of 16 August 1936

Witnesses later reported that when Stalin was told, before the trial, that Kamenev refused to confess, he became enraged and told the official not to return until he had a signed confession. Half-way through the trial, Stalin visited the former Politburo member, Tomsky, carrying a bottle of wine. Tomsky, Bukharin and Rykov were under investigation for complicity with Zinoviev. Tomsky ordered Stalin to leave, and promptly shot himself.

ACTIVITY

Evaluating primary sources

What are Trotsky, Zinoviev and Kamenev accused of in Source 2? Can you explain why this document was written?

ACTIVITY

Draw a diagram to show the various motives which led to the purges and show trials.

Evaluating primary sources

Summarise the view conveyed by Hook in Source 3.

SOURCE 3

Adapted from the autobiography of Sidney Hook, a Jewish American who had been attracted to communism as a young man and had visited the USSR in 1929. His views changed in the 1930s. Hook's autobiography, *Out of Step: An Unquiet Life in the 20th Century* was published in 1987:

The charges against the defendants were mind-boggling. They had allegedly plotted and carried out the assassination of Kirov and planned the assassination of Stalin and his leading associates – all under the direct instructions of Trotsky. This, despite their well-known Marxist belief that terrorism was an inappropriate agent of social change. In addition, they were accused of sabotaging the five-year plans in agriculture and industry by putting nails and glass in butter, inducing disease in pigs and wrecking trains. Despite the enormity of these offences, all the defendants in the dock confessed to them with eagerness and at times went beyond the criticisms of the prosecutor to defame themselves. This spectacular exercise in self-incrimination, unaccompanied by any expression of defiance, was unprecedented in the history of any previous Bolshevik political trial. Equally mystifying was the absence of any significant material evidence. Although there were references to several letters of Trotsky, allegedly giving specific instructions to the defendants to carry out their wicked deeds, none was introduced into evidence.

STUDY TIP

In order to assess the value of the sources it is important that you examine the provenance, tone and emphasis as well as the content. The sources offer comment on the reasons for state terror, how it was carried out and its effects, so you should consider how these sources would work together to support a historical study. Don't forget to use your own knowledge to comment on the strengths and weaknesses of the sources as evidence.

In September 1936, Yagoda was replaced by Yezhov. It was alleged publically that Yagoda had not been active enough in uncovering the 'conspiracy'. However, more importantly, he failed to secure the confessions of Rykov and Bukharin, whom Stalin was determined to implicate. The trial of the latter had to be called off – but this proved only a brief respite.

 PRACTICE QUESTION

Evaluating primary sources

With reference to Sources 1, 2 and 3 and your understanding of the historical context, assess the value of these three sources to an historian studying state terror in the USSR in 1935 to 1936.

CROSS-REFERENCE

The **progression towards true socialism** is explained in Chapter 16.

KEY TERM

former people: the old noble and bourgeois elites who lost their social status after the 1917 Revolution; they also included the imperial military and the clergy

The Stalin constitution, 1936

In the same year as the first great show trial, a new constitution, drafted by Bukharin, was introduced. It was intended to mark the progress towards socialism and to celebrate the triumphs of previous years. The constitution declared that **socialism had been achieved**. (The next stage would be to achieve true communism.)

Stalin claimed that his constitution was 'the most democratic in the world'. It proclaimed the USSR to be a federation of 11 Soviet Republics (replacing the former 7). The (All-Russian) Congress of Soviets was replaced by a new 'Supreme Soviet' made up of the 'Soviet of the Union' and the 'Soviet of Nationalities'. Each republic also had its own supreme soviet. The new constitution promised local autonomy to ethnic groups and support for national cultures and languages ('nationalist in form, socialist in content'). It also promised four-yearly elections with the right to vote for all over the age of 18 (although this was raised to 23 in 1945), including the **'former people'** who had previous been deprived of voting rights. Also, it was accompanied by an extensive statement of civil rights, such as freedom from arbitrary arrest, the freedom of the press and religion and the right of free speech. Citizens were expected to work, and were guaranteed the right to work, education and social welfare. Elections would involve all citizens and not just be dominated by representatives from Party branches. The republics of the USSR were given some rights of jurisdiction in their own territories, including primary education.

The new constitution did, indeed, look democratic and its main intention may have been to impress foreigners. In practice, the promised rights were largely ignored, and the central control exercised over the republics' budgets ensured the primacy of Union laws and little real regional independence. Although the constitution acknowledged the right of any Union-republic **to leave the union**, Stalin did not in practice, allow this to happen.

ACTIVITY

Look back at the details of the 1918 Constitution (Chapter 5, page 43) and draw parallel diagrams of the 1918 and 1936 Constitutions. Identify the similarities and differences.

Summary

- Purging of real or suspected opponents of the communists had been carried out from the early days of the new regime in 1918, but became much greater in scope in the 1930s.
- Kirov's assassination in 1934 started a new wave of purges, which included show trials of leading communists, some of whom had been Stalin's rivals in the past.
- The NKVD, along with a network of informers and other security services, implemented the terror.
- Stalin issued a constitution in 1936 that confirmed a series of constitutional rights for the Soviet people, but was largely a paper propaganda exercise.

A LEVEL | PRACTICE QUESTION

How significant was the murder of Kirov in 1934 for the Stalinist government in the USSR in the years 1934 to 1936?

A CLOSER LOOK

The 1936 Constitution in practice

When Party leaders in Georgia allegedly planned **secession** in 1951, they were purged.

Furthermore, elections were not contested so that the right to vote was merely to affirm a choice of representative and, in any case, the Supreme Soviet only met for a few days twice a year. This was said to be so that members could continue regular employment, but it meant that the body provided more of a sense of participation than any actual involvement in policy making. It was viewed by the Party as a forum for imparting decisions back to the localities rather than for electors to present their views to the centre.

STUDY TIP

You will need to think of various ways in which the murder might be considered 'significant' (important) and assess the degree of importance. You must also assess the extent of governmental change produced by this event. You will also want to consider some limitations, and the 1936 Constitution could be of relevance.

18 The Yezhovshchina

LEARNING OBJECTIVES

In this chapter you will learn about:

- mass terror and repression at both central and local levels
- the gulags and the treatment of national minorities
- the end of the purges and the death of Trotsky
- the responsibility for and impact of the terror and purges.

ACTIVITY

Evaluating primary sources

In what ways would Source 1 be of value to an historian studying the Stalinist Terror?

KEY CHRONOLOGY

1937	Jan	Trial of 17
	May–Jun	Purge of the military
	Jul	Order 00447 orders the removal of 'Anti-Soviet elements'
1938	Mar	Trial of 21 Beria replaces Yezhov as security chief
1939		Pace of terror slows down
1940		Assassination of Trotsky in Mexico

CROSS-REFERENCE

Nikolai Yezhov is profiled in Chapter 17, page 143.

SOURCE 1

Adapted from a speech by **Nikolai Yezhov**, a member of the Central Committee who became head of the NKVD in 1936, to NKVD agents in March 1936. Yezhov was noted for his short height:

I may be small in stature but my hands are strong — Stalin's hands. There will be some innocent victims in this fight against Fascist agents. We are launching a major attack on the Enemy; let there be no resentment if we bump someone with an elbow. Better that ten innocent people should suffer than one spy get away. When you chop wood, chips fly.

Fig. 1 *Original photo with Yezhov standing next to Stalin's left*

Fig. 2 *Photo altered by censors to remove Yezhov when he fell out of favour*

Fig. 3 *Stalin and his companions, a satirical cartoon in the newspaper Aux Ecoutes*

Fig. 4 *Segei Korolkov's pictures depict the fate of those sent by the NKVD to 'corrective' labour camps called the gulags*

Fig. 5 *At the court of justice of the Moscow district, c1930*

Mass terror and repression at local levels

From July 1937, Stalinist terror took on a new intensity with the issue of NKVD Order 00447. This was drawn up by Nikolai Yezhov and approved by the Politburo who ordered the establishment of small NKVD committees at regional levels as well as at Republic level, to search out 'former kulaks, criminals, and other anti-Soviet elements'. The committees were to:

- classify kulaks and other 'anti-Soviet elements' into two categories
- subject the first category to death by shooting
- send the second category to the **gulag** labour camps
- work to a system of quotas – with upper quotas established by area and social classes (for example proletarians, peasants, kulaks, members of the bourgeoisie).

An arrest list was drawn up, including artists, musicians, scientists and writers as well as managers and administrators. In theory, the quotas could not be exceeded, but in practice it proved easy to obtain Yezhov's personal approval to exceed the limits and in some cases Stalin intervened personally to allow more arrests. Within a month, over 100,000 had been arrested and 14,000 sent to the gulags and, by the autumn of 1937, the pressure to achieve arrests was so great that the NKVD committees began selecting individuals almost at random – targeting those who might most easily be persuaded to confess.

KEY TERM

gulag: the acronym for the 'Main Camp Administration'; this agency administered the Soviet forced labour camps from 1930, and 'gulag' came to be used to describe the camps themselves

CROSS-REFERENCE

The purges of **Party officials** are discussed later in this chapter, on page 153.

The NKVD was particularly keen to root out those considered dangerous to society, such as those belonging to 'suspect groups' like 'gypsies' or former members of other political parties. **Party officials** were often denounced, but thousands of ordinary people too, were also swept up in the **arrests**. Everyone was encouraged to root out 'hidden enemies' – to check up on neighbours or fellow workers, and even watch their friends and family for signs of oppositional thoughts.

A CLOSER LOOK

Arrests and confessions

The NKVD relied on informers to keep up their quotas of arrests, so an atmosphere of suspicion and fear was created. Modern historians have estimated that there was only one informer to every 400 inhabitants, but the concentrations of informants varied and perception was often stronger than reality. Confessions were extracted from victims by threats or physical and mental torture. Beatings and the 'conveyor belt' system, whereby a victim was passed from one interrogator to another until he or she was mentally or physically broken, were commonplace.

A CLOSER LOOK

The Trial of 17

The accused included Grigorii Pyatakov (who was said to have caused explosions in mines in Siberia), **Karl Radek** (editor of *Izvestiya* and one of the framers of the 1936 Soviet constitution) and Gregorii Sokolnikov (Commissar of Finance).

Radek and Sokolnikov received ten years imprisonment although Radek died in prison in 1939, almost certainly killed by an NKVD officer. Radek's colleague, Grigorii Ordzhonikidze, Commissar of Heavy Industry, took his own life in 1937, although his death was officially reported as a heart attack.

Mass terror and repression at central level

This spread of 'Red Terror' coincided with a further series of national show trials, often referred to as the Great Purges.

The Trial of 17, January 1937

This was a show trial of 17 prominent communists who were accused of plotting with Trotsky (who was living in exile abroad), spying and sabotaging industry. They were proclaimed 'vipers, liars, clowns and insignificant pygmies'. After delivering their 'confessions', 13 were sentenced to death.

CROSS-REFERENCE

Karl Radek is profiled in Chapter 8, page 71.

ACTIVITY

Evaluating primary sources

Comment on Trotsky's explanation for the Trial of 17 in Source 2. How convincing is his argument?

SOURCE 2

Adapted from the writings of Leon Trotsky in exile in Mexico, on hearing of the Trial of the 17. His account was intended for publication:

How could these Old Bolsheviks, who went through the jails and exiles of Tsarism, who were the heroes of the civil war, the leaders of industry, the builders of the party, diplomats, turn out at the moment of the 'the complete victory of socialism' to be saboteurs, allies of fascism, organisers of espionage, agents of capitalist restoration? Who can believe such accusations? How can anyone be made to believe them? And why is Stalin compelled to tie up the fate of his personal rule with these monstrous, impossible, nightmarish juridical trials? First and foremost, I must affirm the conclusion I had previously drawn that the top rulers feel themselves more and more shaky. The degree of repression is always in proportion to the magnitude of the danger. The unremitting repressions are precisely for the purpose of preventing the masses from the real programme of Trotskyism which demands first of all, more equality and more freedom for the masses.

CROSS-REFERENCE

Marshal Mikhail Tukhachevsky is profiled in Chapter 6, page 61.

Military purge, May–June 1937

Some officers had been incriminated in the show trials of 1936 and 1937. Fearing they might try to mount a military coup, Stalin struck first and, in May 1937, ordered the arrest of **Marshal Mikhail Tukhachevsky** (Chief of Staff and Deputy Commissar for Defence) and Yan Gamarnik (Head of the Red Army's political commissars). They were accused of espionage and plotting with Trotsky and, together with six other top military commanders were executed in June 1937.

This trial opened the way for a 'Great Purge' of the Red Army, which included two further '**Marshals of the Soviet Union**', 11 war commissars, all 8 admirals (and those that replaced them) and all but one of the senior air force commanders. Approximately 50 per cent of the officer corps in all three services, as well a substantial number in military intelligence, were also executed or imprisoned, although around a quarter of the imprisoned were reinstated by the middle of 1940.

Very few dared voice concerns about the trials and purges. In June 1937, Osip Pyatnitsky (Comintern official and member of the Central Committee), spoke out and the following morning Yezhov 'unearthed' evidence that Pyatnitsky had been an agent of the tsarist secret police. He was removed from the Central Committee, stripped of Party membership, arrested, imprisoned for a year and executed in October 1938. It is also known that during 1937 to 1938 up to 74 military officials were shot for refusing to approve the execution of people whom the officials believed innocent.

The Trial of 21, March 1938

A group of 21 prominent communists, accused of belonging to a rightist and Trotskyite bloc were interrogated in the third show trial of March 1938. Among these were **Nikolai Bukharin** and **Andrei Rykov** (both of whom had been rearrested in February 1937) and **Genrikh Yagoda**, former head of the secret police. **Mikhail Tomsky** was to have been put on trial, but he committed suicide beforehand.

This group of 'old Bolsheviks' faced wild and fabricated claims of, for example, plotting to kill Lenin in 1918 and conspiring with the Germans and Japanese to dismember the USSR. Bukharin proved a tough opponent for the NKVD interrogators. He held out for three months (and sent 34 personal letters to Stalin) but threats to his young wife and infant son eventually wore him down. While others made full confessions at the trial, Bukharin would only admit to the 'sum total of crimes', and refused to confess to specific allegations. He professed his loyalty to the end, but he and 17 others were executed.

SOURCE 3

Adapted from Bukharin's 'confession' at his show trial in March 1938:

I am perhaps speaking for the last time in my life. I am explaining how I came to realise the necessity of capitulating. I refute the accusation of having plotted against the life of Lenin, but my counter-revolutionary confederates, and I at their head, endeavoured to murder Lenin's cause, which is being carried on with such tremendous success by Stalin. The logic of this struggle led us step-by-step, into the blackest quagmire; siding with political counter-revolutionary banditry. We repent our frightful crimes.

I am kneeling before the country, before the Party, before the whole people. The monstrousness of my crimes is immeasurable. May this trial be the last severe lesson, and may the great might of the USSR become clear to all. Everybody perceives the wise leadership of the country that is ensured by Stalin. What matters is not the personal feelings of a repentant enemy, but the flourishing progress of the USSR and its international importance.

Similar trials occurred throughout the USSR at which Party members were often denounced by their colleagues. The purges provided an opportunity to settle old scores, to remove those who stood in the way of a promotion or simply to show an individual's zealous devotion to Stalin. The order of July 1937 against 'anti-Soviet elements' led lower-ranking Party members to

A CLOSER LOOK

Marshal of the Soviet Union

The rank of Marshal of the Soviet Union was created in 1935 as the highest military rank. It was conferred on Kliment Voroshilov (People's Commissar for Defence), Alexander Yegorov (Chief of the General Staff of the Red Army), and three senior commanders, Vasily Blyukher, Semyon Budyonny, and **Mikhail Tukhachevsky**.

Blyukher, Tukhachevsky and Yegorov were subsequently executed as a result of the Great Purge of 1937–8.

A CLOSER LOOK

Tukhachevsky's family

Tukhachevsky's wife was jailed and executed in 1941, his mother and one sister died in prison. Three other sisters managed to survive prison, but their husbands were executed, as were Tukhachevsky's two brothers.

CROSS-REFERENCE

To remind yourself of the roles of the prominent Communists mentioned here, start by looking at their Key Profiles:
Nikolai Bukharin: Chapter 9, page 84.
Andrei Rykov: Chapter 8, page 85.
Genrikh Yagoda: Chapter 17, page 142.
Mikhail Tomsky: Chapter 9, page 85.

A CLOSER LOOK

Yagoda was tried and executed in 1938, possibly by his own successor Yezhov. Yagoda's family members were shot, imprisoned or exiled. Yagoda's removal ensured that Stalin had full control of the NKVD.

KEY TERM

Yezhovshchina: the period 1936–40 when Yezhov led the NKVD and there was a large number of purges

ACTIVITY

Evaluating primary source

Do you find the confession in Source 2 surprising? It has been suggested that confessions were given:

a. in order to save the victims' families

b. because the accused were so reduced by torture they hardly knew what they were saying

c. because committed communists actually believed their confession was serving the best interests of the USSR.

Discuss Bukharin's confession in Source 2 with a partner and try to account for what he said.

A CLOSER LOOK

Trotsky in exile

Although in exile abroad since 1929, living in Turkey, France, Norway and Mexico, Trotsky had maintained a high profile with a constant output of writing, which justified his past behaviour and criticised Stalin. In *The Revolution Betrayed* (1937) Trotsky wrote of the 'rapid degeneration' of the Communist Party and claimed that Stalin had perverted and destroyed the gains of the Russian Revolution and created an over-bureaucratic State.

A CLOSER LOOK

The nationalities and economic change

Collectivisation had a devastating effect on the economies of some republics. For example Uzbekistan's agriculture was decimated when it was forced to produce cotton to supply Russian industry, while Ukraine suffered terribly from famine during collectivisation. Furthermore, because of resistance to economic change, Stalin adopted a ruthless policy of centralisation in the 1930s; for example, Russian was made compulsory everywhere (although basic education could still be in the native language).

denounce those above them, while higher officials and secretaries accused those on the ground. A third of all Party members had been purged by the end of 1938, many of which were accused of '**Trotskyite** conspiracy'.

ACTIVITY

Complete this diagram to record key facts about those who were purged during the **Yezhovshchina**. You could divide the groups in the left-hand column between the members of your class, undertake some further research, and prepare an illustrated poster that shows why the group suffered and what happened to it.

The purged	Key facts
Party members	
Leaders of the Republics	
Members of the Armed forces	
Managers, engineers and scientists	
NKVD men	
People related to those who had been purged	
Industrial workers	
Peasants	
Others	

The gulags and the treatment of national minorities

From the 1930s more gulags were built to provide cheap labour for Stalin's huge industrial projects, as well as to house political prisoners and 'class enemies' such as the kulaks. However, from 1937 with the Great Purges and spread of the terror, the gulags took on a new and even more sinister aspect.

There was another huge surge in inmate numbers, from c800,000 in 1935 to anything between 5.5 and 9.5 million by the end of 1938 (according to the modern British-American historian Robert Conquest). The numbers of intelligentsia in the gulags swelled and the gulags became places in which prisoners were deliberately worked to death or actually murdered outright. The term, 'class enemies' gave way to 'anti-Soviet enemies' who were accorded no mercy. Prisoners were no longer regarded as being capable of 're-education' and the possibility of early release for good behaviour disappeared. Even the camp commandants themselves were not immune to the persecution of these years and many were purged.

For those inmates who did not face immediate execution, conditions in the camps were appalling. There were meagre rations (which could be reduced further on the slightest provocation), inadequate clothing, poor and overcrowded accommodation, and a dearth of health care or medical provision. Work expectations were high, the physical demands excessive and the hours of work far in excess of those of town workers. Unsurprisingly, mortality rates were between four and six times higher than those in the rest of the USSR.

Stalin's rule was a very difficult time for the various **nationalities** that made up the USSR. The republics were hit by Stalin's economic changes and suffered greatly in the Terror, with a wave of national deportations from c1937. In 1937, a large Korean minority was deported from the Far Eastern region to Central Asia when war with Japan threatened. Poles and Germans were also deported from near the Western frontiers and extensive purges were carried out in the newly annexed parts of Poland and the Baltic States in 1939 and 1940. In 1941, over 400,000 Volga Germans were deported to Siberia and Central Asia.

Those 'national communists' within the republics who showed distaste for centralising policies were purged, and virtually the entire Party leadership of the non-Russian republics was replaced in 1937 to 1938 by those more prepared to bow to Moscow's wishes.

The years of the Yezhovshchina also saw anti-Semitic attitudes revive, especially in rural areas during the campaigns against 'saboteurs'. When 2 million Jews were incorporated into the Soviet Union in 1939 to 1940, as a result of the invasion of Eastern Poland and the Baltic republics, many rabbis and religious leaders were arrested in these areas.

Although there is no evidence of mass national minority discontent at this time (and that would have been very difficult to organise), life for Soviet citizens outside Russia became increasingly difficult. Stalin's **anti-religious campaigns**, for example, spread into Ukraine and Belorussia and there was direct persecution of Muslims in the Central Asian republics after 1928.

The end of the purges and the death of Trotsky

Although purges of Stalin's opponents continued until well into the Second World War, the pace slowed down after the end of 1938. The Yezhovshchina had threatened to destabilise the State and both industry and administration suffered. Stalin used Yezhov as a scapegoat, accusing him of excessive zeal and the Eighteenth Party Congress declared that the 'mass cleansings' were no longer needed. Yezhov was subsequently arrested, tortured, secretly tried and shot in February 1940. He was replaced by **Lavrentii Beria**.

In August 1940, Stalin settled a final score. **Trotsky** had been tracked down by Stalinist agents, living in a fortified house on the outskirts of Mexico City. In May, hired assassins had broken in and opened fire, but Trotsky had escaped unharmed. It was left to another agent, Ramon Mercador, to carry out a successful assassination. Mercador gained admittance to the house by posing as an admirer, keen to seek Trotsky's views on a political paper he had written, but once in his study, he plunged an ice pick into Trotsky's head. Mercador received a sentence of 20 years for the attack, but his mother was awarded the 'Order of Lenin' in honour of her son's service. Stalin thus ensured that the last of the old Bolsheviks who might have had a greater claim to leadership had gone.

The responsibility for and impact of the terror and purges

Responsibility for the Terror and purges

Although there has long been a historical debate about the exact extent of Stalin's role in the Terror there can be little doubt that he was crucial both in starting the purges and ending them (at least temporarily: they resumed again both during and after the Second World War).

Stalin was no stranger to violence. From his earliest Bolshevik days he had been a man of action. Nevertheless, there was little to anticipate the scale of the terror in the 1930s, other than Stalin's ruthless persecution of the peasantry once collectivisation had begun. A key moment that led to the institutionalisation of the Terror may have been the **suicide of Stalin's wife**, Nadezhda Alliluyeva, in 1932.

Stalin's personality made him suspicious, vindictive, and even paranoid. He was obsessed with reinforcing his own position, eliminating possible rivals, and wreaking revenge on fellow Bolsheviks (the 'Old Guard') who had been his rivals or opponents before the 1930s. He was personally responsible for promoting and then ending the purges. Many Soviet citizens apparently believed the official Party line that Stalin was a heroic leader, protecting his people from a nest of traitors trying to hold back Soviet progress or even

CROSS-REFERENCE

Stalin's **anti-religious campaigns** are outlined in Chapter 19.

ACTIVITY

Extension

You can read more about the gulags in Anne Applebaum's book *Gulag: A History of the Soviet Camps*, which draws on memoirs, writings and the author's personal research into the NKVD archives.

KEY PROFILE

Lavrentii Pavlovich Beria (1899–1953) was, like Stalin, from Georgia. From 1935 he became part of the Moscow Party elite; he replaced Yezhov as NKVD chief in 1938, and played a key role in Stalin's purges. During the war he organised mass deportations of 'suspect' nationalities, including the Crimean Tatars in 1944. He also organised the use of workers in the gulags for war production. In 1945, he was put in charge of developing the Soviet atomic bomb. He was also central to 'High Stalinism' and renewed purges. In 1953, he was overthrown and killed in a coup led by Khrushchev and Zhukov, after Stalin's death.

A CLOSER LOOK

Warnings to Trotsky

Trotsky's son, Leon Sedov had been murdered in Paris in 1938 and the decapitated body of another close friend, Rudolf Klement, had been found floating in the River Seine.

CROSS-REFERENCE

The **suicide of Stalin's wife** is outlined in Chapter 17.

Stalin and 'fear'

In 1931, Yagoda reputedly asked Stalin whether he would rather people followed him out of conviction or fear. To his surprise, Stalin replied, 'Fear.' When asked to explain, Stalin replied, 'People are always afraid. But convictions can change.'

Evaluating primary sources

Which aspect of the terror does Khrushchev condemn the most in Source 4?

The **Treaty of Rapallo** is covered in Chapter 8, page 74.

The **Treaty of Berlin** is covered in Chapter 12, page 106.

In small groups, discuss who or what was to blame for the Terror and prepare a reasoned argument to deliver to your class. You should look at a range of factors and back your judgements with evidence to show why your chosen factor was the most important.

These sources have very different provenances and you should be able to comment on their value as evidence with reference to their authors, audiences and dates, as well as considering the tone and emphasis of each. You must also evaluate the content and identify how each contributes to an understanding of the reasoning behind the Terror. To do this you will need to apply your own contextual knowledge.

destroy the country. Many of those who were anxious about excesses during the Terror persuaded themselves that Stalin was not personally responsible.

Adapted from the 'Secret (de-Stalinisation) Speech' of Nikita Khrushchev, delivered to the Twentieth Party Congress in February, 1956. Khrushchev had been a provincial party secretary in the 1930s, secretary of the Ukrainian Communist Party in 1938 and a Politburo member in 1939. He became Soviet leader after Stalin's death. In 1956, he spoke out against Stalin's 'crimes':

Stalin acted not through persuasion, explanation and patient cooperation with people, but by imposing his concepts and demanding absolute submission to his opinion. Whoever opposed this concept or tried to prove his viewpoint, and the correctness of his position, was doomed to removal from the leading collective and to subsequent moral and physical annihilation. This was especially true during the period following the Seventeenth Party Congress, when many prominent Party leaders and rank-and-file Party workers, honest and dedicated to the cause of communism, fell victim to Stalin's despotism.

Stalin originated the concept 'enemy of the people'. This term automatically rendered it unnecessary that the ideological errors of a man or men engaged in a controversy be proven; this term made possible the usage of the most cruel repression, violating all norms of revolutionary legality, against anyone who in any way disagreed with Stalin, against those who were only suspected of hostile intent, against those who had bad reputations.

Other explanations for the Terror are:

- Terror was an integral part of the communist system, and indeed of earlier Russian regimes. The 1917 Revolution and its aftermath, the Civil War, saw the communist regime born in terror, and then maintained by terror. **Stalin simply applied terror** more ruthlessly and on a larger scale. Any means were justified in order to ensure that the first socialist state remained intact in the face of a hostile world.
- Terror was a necessary part of the process of economic change taking place from the late 1920s. It was needed to remove the kulaks, provide slave labour and to provide scapegoats for mistakes and failures.
- Terror was the work of over-zealous officials in the provinces, who acted ruthlessly and followed their own independent agenda. Therefore, the drive to terror did not come exclusively from Stalin. Local Party activists promoted terror, confident that this is what their leader wanted, and their actions would not be checked.
- Terror was a response to the real threat of a military coup involving the Germans. (The contacts between the Red Army and Nazis that arose from the **Rapallo and Berlin treaties** had made Stalin suspicious.)
- The Terror was self-escalating; it almost took on a life of its own as it was used by individuals to settle personal scores, get rid of rivals or open avenues of promotion. Fear fed on fear. For those in fear of being denounced, it was better to prove loyalty by denouncing someone else first.

 PRACTICE QUESTION

Evaluating primary sources

With reference to Sources 2, 3 and 4 and your understanding of the historical context, assess the value of these three sources to an historian studying the reasons for the Terror in the USSR in the 1930s.

The impact of the Terror and purges

By the end of the purges, Stalin was in a position of supreme power. He was a dictator, with absolute control over the Party and a subservient populace. He had removed potential rivals (although it must be remembered that most of the high-profile victims, such as Zinoviev, Kamenev and Bukharin, had actually lost power and influence before the Terror) and the Party was turned into a compliant tool of Stalin. The Central Committee, for example, which had, before 1936, controlled membership through expulsions of those who failed to match the high standards of discipline that Party membership demanded, lost this power. The expulsion of 850,000 members between 1936 and 1938 was due to the personal interventions of Stalin and Yezhov's NKVD, and the reasons for dismissal were more arbitrary. By 1939, less than 10 per cent of the Party membership had joined before 1920; less than a quarter of recruits since 1920 survived the purges.

Although the expulsion of many Party bureaucrats and administrators was a major development, possibly of still greater impact was the loss of experienced army officers. Around 23,000 officers were shot or dismissed (some were later reinstated) and many new officers had to be recruited to match the increase in **the size of the Red Army** in the late 1930s. It was a major task to find and train this number of officers and **military failures** evident in the first months of the war in 1941 must, at least in part, be attributed to the effect of the purges.

Other areas of society were also deprived of skilled personnel. Teachers, engineers and specialists were all persecuted at a time when rapid industrial change demanded their expertise. However, it is dangerous to generalise. Different areas suffered to greater and lesser degrees depending on the zeal of local officials. Also, while some elements of society suffered more greatly than others, there was also the positive outcome that 'ordinary people' had been given an opportunity to 'shake up' their managers and officials – making them more accountable and therefore more responsive to needs.

A CLOSER LOOK

The **size of the Red Army** increased from just under 1 million in 1936 to 5 million by 1941.

CROSS-REFERENCE

The **military failures** at the beginning of the Great Patriotic War against Germany in 1941 are discussed in Chapter 21, page 178.

Summary

- The Yezhovshchina, between 1936 and 1938, affected all sections of society in the USSR, bringing mass terror and repression at **central and local levels**.
- The labour camps became gulags; conditions became more extreme and death and execution more commonplace.
- National minorities within the USSR suffered badly from persecution.
- When industry and administration suffered, from the end of 1938, the pace of the Terror slowed with the removal of Yezhov.
- The assassination of Trotsky in 1940 removed the last of Stalin's potential rivals.
- Stalin's personal responsibility for, and the impact of, the Terror and purges are both open to debate.

 PRACTICE QUESTION

'The most significant outcome of the Terror and purges of the Yezhovshchina was an increase in Stalin's political dominance.' Assess the validity of this view.

STUDY TIP

This question invites you to consider a range of consequences from the Yezhovshchina and provide a judgement as to the most significant. It is important to show an understanding of the interrelationship of factors. You will not only need to assess the strengths and weaknesses for Stalin's political position but look at the outcome for others and show how these changes also had repercussions for Stalin's position.

19 Culture and society

LEARNING OBJECTIVES

In this chapter you will learn about:

- the impact of Stalinism on the Church, women, young people and working men
- urban/rural differences
- 'socialist man'
- the impact of cultural change
- similarities and differences between Lenin's and Stalin's USSR.

Fig. 1 *A satirical anti-religious cartoon*

The impact of Stalinism on the Church, women, young people and working men

The Church

Marx had described religion as 'the opium of the people' and claimed it was used to justify the power of the upper classes over the people, but Lenin had allowed freedom of religious worship while destroying much of the 'earthly' power of the Russian Orthodox Church. Church lands were seized; births, marriages and deaths as well as schools, secularised; priests persecuted; atheistic propaganda circulated. In 1927, Sergius, the **Patriarch of the Orthodox Church**, made a promise to stay out of politics in return for State recognition of the Orthodox Church.

Under Stalin, the Orthodox Church found itself under more direct attack when religious schools were closed down and the teaching of religious creeds forbidden. Worship was restricted to 'registered congregations' only, and many churches were physically destroyed or deconsecrated. Between 1929 and 1940, the holy day of Sunday was itself abolished. Workers were employed for six of the seven days of the week, with a sixth of workers having each day off.

Although there was a brief relaxation of the anti-religious campaign in 1935, it was vigorously renewed as the Terror was extended. Stalin's 1936 Constitution criminalised the publication or organisation of religious propaganda, although priests regained the right to vote (which they had lost in 1918). Many priests

KEY TERM

Patriarch of the Orthodox Church: the head of the Russian Orthodox (Christian) Church

were victims of the purges, accused of political involvement, and large numbers went to the gulags in the later 1930s. Nevertheless, Orthodox congregations survived, with priests supported by voluntary donations.

Soviet Muslims also suffered as their property and institutions (land, schools and mosques) were seized and their **Sharia** courts were abolished. This produced a split within the Islamic Church with the 'New Mosque' movement taking a pro-Soviet line. Nevertheless, pilgrimages to Mecca were forbidden from 1935, the frequency of prayers, fasts and feasts reduced and the wearing of the veil forbidden. This led to a backlash in some of the central Asian Muslim communities where traditionalists murdered those who obeyed the Soviet injunctions. Many Muslim priests were imprisoned or executed.

The anti-religion drive also extended to Jewish schools and synagogues, which were closed down. In addition, there were attacks on Buddhist institutions and the Armenian and Georgian Churches. In each case, while the power of the Church as an institution was broken, faith remained strong.

By 1941, nearly 40,000 Christian churches and 25,000 Muslim mosques had been closed and converted into schools, cinemas, clubs, warehouses, museums and grain stores. Nevertheless, there was plenty of evidence of strong religious belief, and this was possibly strengthened by attacks during the period of collectivisation and the purges. Despite the pressure on believers and the dangers of expressing 'controversial' views, in the 1937 census, over half a million Soviet citizens described themselves as religious believers. The real number of believers was certainly much higher. For all its efforts, the regime found it impossible to kill off religious belief and observance.

Women

Soviet propaganda under Lenin had extolled the new 'liberation' of women, where sex discrimination was outlawed, divorce and abortions made easier, the family was regarded as a relic of bourgeois society and women took jobs alongside men.

However, in the 1930s, a fall in population growth (not helped by the purges, nor by living conditions on the collectives and in the overcrowded urban apartments), combined with the disruption caused by **family break-ups** and fears of war, led Stalin to revert to more traditional policies. This 'Great Retreat' was a conscious rejection of the social experiments of the post-revolutionary period. The 'family' became the focus of a new propaganda wave, in which Stalin was presented as a father figure and ideal 'family man', and divorce and abortion were attacked. The importance of marriage was re-emphasised, wedding rings were reintroduced and new-style wedding certificates were issued. Even in films and art, women were portrayed in a new way – less the muscular, plainly dressed women who had helped to build Soviet Russia in the 1920s, more the feminine family women with adoring children.

A new 'family code' was put forward in May 1936 and made law in June, following a decision of the Central Committee:

- Abortion became illegal. This had the impact of increasing the birth rate in the late 1930s.
- It was made more difficult to get a divorce; large fees were introduced and both parties had to attend the proceedings.
- Contraception was banned and only permitted on medical grounds.
- Mothers with six or more children received tax exemptions and bonus payments for every additional child under ten in the family.
- Child support payments by fathers were fixed at 60 per cent of income, although they were difficult to collect because many men married several times.
- Children who committed violent crimes were to be treated like adults from the age of 12.

- Adultery was criminalised (and the names of male offenders published in the press).
- New decrees were to be enforced against prostitution and homosexuality (although in practice the authorities regarded these as 'capitalist vices' and were reluctant to acknowledge their existence or extent).

Fig. 2 *Propaganda poster from 1936 that reads 'Thanks to a dear Stalin for a happy childhood'*

SOURCE 1

Adapted from a leading article in *Pravda*, 28 May 1936, entitled 'Public discussion on the law on the abolition of legal abortion, etc'. This law was subsequently enacted in June 1936:

The published draft of the law prohibiting abortion and providing material assistance to mothers has provoked a lively reaction throughout the country. It is being heatedly discussed by tens of millions of people and there is no doubt it will serve as a further strengthening of the Soviet family. Parents' responsibility for the education of their children will be increased and a blow will be dealt at the light-hearted, negligent attitude towards marriage. When we talk of strengthening the Soviet family we are speaking precisely of the struggle against the survivals of a bourgeois attitude towards marriage, women and children. So-called 'free love' and all disorderly sex-life are bourgeois through and through, and have nothing to do with either socialist principles or the ethics and standards of conduct of the Soviet citizen.

The elites of our country, the best of Soviet youth, are, as a rule, also excellent family men who dearly love their children; the man who does not take his marriage seriously and abandons his children to the whims of fate, is usually also a bad worker and a poor member of society.

ACTIVITY

Evaluating primary sources

Discuss with a partner: Would Source 1 have come as a surprise to Soviet women?

CROSS-REFERENCE

For the numbers of **women working** in industry, and for the working and living conditions of women workers, look back to Chapter 14, page 127.

Despite the new emphasis on family life, and encouragement for women to give up paid employment when they married, the numbers of **women working** in factories continued to increase and large numbers also worked on the collective farms, where status and conditions were poor. Furthermore, the divorce rate remained high (37 per cent in Moscow in 1934) and there were over 150,000 abortions to every 57,000 live births. Indeed, although encouraging traditional marriage meant that in 1937, 91 per cent men and 82 per cent of women in their thirties were married, the years 1929 to 1940 saw a falling rate of population growth. Single and divorced women were also more likely than men to be left unemployed and not get compensation. Women in this position often appeared on the fringes of society: for example, the number of prostitutes in cities rose. The failure of women to get injustices overturned in the courts led to several strikes and protests but only the most committed women were prepared to give up time for activities such as attending Party-organised meetings in the workplace, and female participation in high Party politics actually declined in the 1930s.

Overall, it is fair to say that there was no significant improvement for women in 1930s. Poorer women were still expected to look after their children and homes even though they had the additional burden of contributing more to the full-time work force as part of the drive to construct socialism. Women in the Asian Islamic Republics had even lower status.

SOURCE 2

Adapted from Nina Popova's, 'Women in the Land of Socialism'. Popova was the daughter of a worker and a Soviet Party member and official from 1932. She became President of the Soviet Women's Committee in 1945. This paper was published in Moscow in 1949:

It is the Soviet system that has opened before women all opportunities for developing their native abilities and displaying initiative, and that has secured them the happiness of cloudless motherhood. As stated in the Central Committee decision of June 1936, 'In no other country in the world are women, as mothers and as citizens, who bear the great responsibility of giving birth to and bringing up citizens, so respected and so protected by law as in the USSR.' The Stalin Constitution gives legislative embodiment to women's freedom and to the conditions which enable them to take real advantage of their freedom. The concern shown by the Party and the Government for mothers, for the health and education of the rising generation of builders of Communism, and the all-embracing protection of the interests of mother and child are most noteworthy features of our Socialist State. Lofty Soviet humanism, the concern for the human being taught by Lenin and Stalin, underlies all the efforts of the Soviet State for the protection of the interests of mother and child.

Young people

Education

Education was seen as crucial in building a socialist society. Free education was offered at all levels in co-educational schools in the **1920s**.

Stalin regarded the results of these experiments as disastrous. An industrialising USSR needed a better-educated and skilled workforce. The new-style education was failing to produce the skilled workers, scientists and technicians the country needed. Consequently, the Central Committee decided on a significant change in policy in the 1930s, introducing a more organised **school structure** and reverting to traditional methods of teaching and discipline.

A CLOSER LOOK

The school structure

Centralised control of education was provided by Narkompros (the People's Commissariat for Education) which provided nursery schools for children at 3 years, infant schools until 7 years and secondary school until at least 15 years. Parents were expected to contribute towards the cost of secondary schooling. Many adult education institutions were also established.

ACTIVITY

Evaluating primary sources

In the light of your own contextual knowledge, write a critical appraisal of Source 2.

A CLOSER LOOK

Education in the 1920s

In the 1920s, an emphasis on acquiring knowledge was despised. Ideology was more important, and children were expected to do socially useful work. More traditional teachers were driven out and replaced by more committed communists. Students from a proletarian background were given priority on higher education courses, although some students were of poor quality and there was a high dropout rate. Examinations were abandoned.

CROSS-REFERENCE

The economic planning agency **Veshenka** is introduced in Chapter 4, page 34.

A CLOSER LOOK

Selective secondary schools in the 1930s

The selective secondary schools had a rigid academic curriculum, formal teaching, report cards tests and uniforms. Some were single-sex. The core subjects were reading, writing and science with 30 per cent of time devoted to Russian language and literature, 20 per cent to maths, 15 per cent to science and 10 per cent to Soviet-style history. Nationalism was promoted and military training was incorporated in the years before the war.

CROSS-REFERENCE

To recap on the **Stakhanovite system**, look back to Chapter 14, page 124.

KEY TERM

Komsomol: the all-Leninist Union Young Communist League; the youth division of the Communist Party, which was represented in its own right in the Supreme Soviet

CROSS-REFERENCE

The huge complex at **Magnitogorsk** is discussed in Chapter 11, page 99 and Chapter 14, page 122.

Many schools became the responsibility of the collective farms or town enterprises while the universities were also seen as agencies for delivering economic growth and put under the control of the economic planning agency, **Veshenkha**.

The quota system, whereby a high proportion of working-class children were given places at secondary school, was abandoned in 1935 and **selection** reappeared for all, including non-proletarians. This meant the able received a strong academic education.

More emphasis was put on the higher training of specialists who could help in the industrialisation drive, with courses in mathematics, science and technology. For the less able, increasing amounts of 'practical' work (linking to the Five Year Plans) were encouraged. The importance of duty and loyalty to the Party and the State was fostered at all levels. Teachers were given a higher status and were increasingly likely to be Party members. However, teachers and university lecturers were closely watched and could be arrested if they failed to live up to the expected high standards. They were encouraged to set high targets for themselves and their students under the **Stakhanovite system**, and if students failed to do well they could be blamed and purged.

One of the striking successes of education in the 1930s was the spread of literacy, especially in rural areas. Only about 65 per cent of the population had been literate before the revolution. By 1941, 94 per cent of the 9 to 49-age group in the towns was literate and 86 per cent in the countryside. For the communists, this was particularly desirable, because a literate population could more readily absorb the all-pervasive propaganda. There were also marked improvements at university level and the USSR turned out particularly strong science graduates, even though the numbers of working-class students reaching university and the higher classes at secondary level fell when the quota system was abandoned.

Youth organisations

From 1926, the youth organisation '**Komsomol**' catered for those aged 10 to 28 years. This organisation grew and became more significant under Stalin.

The organisation taught communist values. Smoking, drinking and religion were discouraged, while volunteer social work, sports, political and drama clubs were organised to inspire socialist values. Special 'palaces' were built to serve as community centres for the 10 to 15-year-old 'Young Pioneers', and free summer and winter holiday camps were organised.

Komsomol had close links to the Party, and became directly affiliated in 1939. Members took an oath to live, study and fight for the Fatherland and helped carry out party campaigns and assisted the Red Army and police. *Komsomolskaia Pravda* was published as a youth newspaper, encouraging young people to respect their parents. Many members of Komsomol became very enthusiastic about the industrialisation drive, and joined activist groups, flocking to projects such as the building of **Magnitogorsk**.

SOURCE 3

Adapted from an interview given to an American in Munich by a soviet refugee, born in 1914, shortly after the end of the Second World War, explaining his reason for joining Komsomol and becoming a party activist:

In spite of material difficulties, such as the constant food shortage which was particularly acute at the time, neither I nor the young people around me had any anti-Soviet feelings. We simply found in the heroic tension involved in the building of a new world an excuse for all the difficulties. The atmosphere of undaunted struggle in a common cause – the completion of the factory – engaged our imagination, roused our enthusiasm, and drew us into a sort of front-line world where difficulties were overlooked or forgotten. Of course, it was only we, the younger generation, who accepted reality in this way. Our parents were full of muted but deep discontent. The arguments of our elders, however, had little effect upon us, being, as they were, wholly concerned with material things, while we found in the official justification of all these difficulties, a superficial idealism which had considerable appeal to the young.

Membership of Komsomol and the Young Pioneers demanded full-time commitment, but also offered a chance for social and educational advancement. The uniform, with a red neckerchief and rank badges, singled these young people out, and helped ensure they were favoured within the Soviet system.

ACTIVITY

Evaluating primary soures

In what ways does Source 3 suggest that there was a generational difference in reactions to Stalinism? Can you explain why this difference might exist and in what ways it might be considered surprising?

Fig. 3   *Meeting of Komsomol youth organisation members in uniform and with banner*

Of course, not all young people wanted to become involved in these youth movements. Some were more interested in Western culture, such as cinema, fashion and jazz, despite the regime's condemnation of such pre-occupations as 'hooliganism'. Some simply opted out, others joined small secret 'oppositional' youth organisations, but direct confrontation with the Soviet system was rare.

 PRACTICE QUESTION

Evaluating primary sources

With reference to Sources 1, 2 and 3 and your understanding of the historical context, assess the value of these three sources to an historian studying women and the family in the 1930s.

Working men

The establishment of the Soviet state had been undertaken in the name of the proletariat, and, in general, urban **working men** were enthusiastic about Stalin's policy of rapid industrialisation. They hoped this would bring more jobs and raise their standards of living. Aspiring workers saw the advantages

STUDY TIP

Consider the provenance of each source very carefully and make sure you address issues such as the purpose and audience in order to evaluate these sources. Use your own knowledge to examine what they say and back all comments with reference to the source material.

CROSS-REFERENCE

The working and living conditions of **working men** are also discussed in Chapter 14, page 124.

of the attack on foreigners and bourgeois managers as offering more opportunities for advancement.

Those who did best out of Stalinist policies were the skilled workers. With the spread of technical education and more opportunities for training, the introduction of wage differentials from 1931 and the Stakhanovite movement, determined and loyal workers found new ways to improve themselves. The acute skills shortage suffered in the 1930s meant that those who were ready to acquire expertise could, provided they were prepared to conform to the harsh labour laws, command good pay. Such men were able to raise their living standards in the later 1930s, although as war approached in 1940 to 1941, and resources were diverted elsewhere, their income fell back.

However, life for the mass of unskilled working men, many of whom were former peasants forced into the towns by collectivisation, was harsh. Unused to the strict labour discipline, they were likely to move around from job to job, trying to avoid staying too long in one place so as not to acquire a bad working record. Conditions of living were tough; overcrowding strained family life and meant there was little, if any, privacy. Petty crime and hard drinking proliferated and in the time of the Terror they could be deprived of all they had for the smallest misdemeanour or unguarded word.

Urban and rural differences

Despite the emphasis on the urban proletarian workers, the Stalinist changes from 1929 brought more changes to the rural than urban population. Areas which had been relatively untouched before collectivisation found themselves under strong central control as the regime policed the countryside more closely and enforced compulsory schooling for the first time. The rise in literacy also provided more opportunities for propagandists to try to influence rural minds.

It was a time of dislocation as some of the basic 'certainties', which had dominated rural life (religion, friendship and traditions), were questioned and changed. It was also a time of movement into new regions and towns. Since the Party was everywhere and the fear induced by the Terror bred a lack of trust, the old traditions of openness and cooperation in the countryside were strained.

During the 1930s, collectivisation came to be grudgingly accepted. Some peasants benefitted from having access to machinery like tractors, and villages often had schools and even clinics for the first time. Nevertheless, the disparity between life in the cities and countryside never went away and peasants were invariably viewed by the Party as inferior citizens. For many rural workers, especially the younger ones, their dream was to be able to move to a city.

Life in urban communities was far from 'paradise'. The Great Famine of 1932–3 not only caused millions of deaths in the countryside but also caused major problems in towns as they were swamped by refugees and the rationing system, which continued until 1935, often broke down. There was a shortage of housing and practically no privacy in the *kommunalka*. People learned to whisper in case their neighbours overheard conversations that could result in denunciations to the authorities and a visit from the security police. Apartment blocks were supervised by concierges whose task was partly to spy on individuals. Some workers lived in barracks or in their factories. Only favoured Party members had the right to more substantial and private accommodation.

Many cities were without sewage, street lighting and public transport, despite show projects such as the Moscow Metro. Water was rationed. There was also considerable 'hooliganism' or urban violence. Living standards dropped considerably, with 1933 being the worst year: overall food consumption was lower than in 1900 and meat consumption was only a third of the 1928 figure. Many depended on the black market for survival.

Problems for working men

Some found it difficult to find work because of something in their or their family's history. Coming from a 'bourgeois' family could be a real disadvantage, as was belonging to a family in which someone had been purged; it automatically created suspicion as a possible 'enemy of the people'. Workers learned to conceal their backgrounds or even lie about them.

kommunalka: a communal dwelling, or housing bloc, where most urban families lived; space was allocated according to family size; typically, two to seven families shared a hallway, kitchen and bathroom, while each family had its own room, serving as a living/dining room and bedroom

Conditions improved from 1935, with 1937 being probably the best year for living standards. It became legal for some small trades to operate privately: shoe repair, hairdressing and plumbing activities. This was because the State just could not resolve the shortages (buying shoes was a particular problem). However, problems increased again after 1937 as the bad harvest of 1936, and the continued increase in the urban population, put further strains on public services.

ACTIVITY

Divide your group in two. One half should draw up a balance sheet of the advantages and disadvantages of living in the countryside during the 1930s; the other should do the same for the towns. Choose a spokesperson to deliver the group's findings and discuss as a whole which manner of living was preferable.

Overall, urban workers probably coped better in the 1930s than the peasants in the countryside. Changes were fewer and at least factory workers had regulated hours and wages and could benefit from workplace canteens and even shops, providing goods for the employees to purchase. In rural communities, these were troubled times, and peasants had most of their produce taken from them. When war came in 1941, however, there was a reversal. Conditions in both urban and rural communities became very harsh and rationing was reintroduced, but the peasants, at least, had their private plots to fall back on.

Socialist man and woman

Building socialism was partly about economic change but the regime was also intent on creating a new type of citizen: new **socialist man** and woman. Such a person was dedicated to the Party and lived and worked for the community. Although well educated and intelligent, socialist men and women were not independent thinkers, but people who willingly accepted what the State said because they knew that what they were told was best for all. Independent thought or attitudes were regarded as a curse, not a virtue to be admired.

New socialist man or woman was an urban creature, not an ill-educated, backward peasant who might be distracted by outdated religious beliefs and superstitions. The building of the new industrial city-complexes was much influenced by this concept. Here, an environment could be created in which the 'socialist man' could flourish; one where the community took precedence over the individual, and behaviour was held up to the scrutiny of neighbours. From the Komsomol Youth Organisation to the state-run and state-supervised clubs and societies, there was no room for a private life. There were also periodic events, such as Stalin's birthday to celebrate – with processions and festivals glorifying the triumph of socialism.

Scientists studied how this ideal citizen could be groomed. The most famous scientist was **Trofim Lysenko**. He believed that if human beings acquired the right characteristics, they could be passed on to the next generation. In theory, this would make the task of the State in promoting a well-ordered socialist society easier, as the characteristics of the old class enemies (aristocracy, bourgeoisie and rich peasants) would disappear and it would take much less effort for the State to indoctrinate new generations. The science behind Lysenko's theories was, not surprisingly, widely discredited by reputable scientists outside the USSR. It was also, in part, undermined by Stalin's own warnings that as the Soviet State became more successful, the State needed to redouble its vigilance over the population as its enemies would become more desperate.

KEY TERM

socialist man: a person who was publicly engaged and committed to the community; 'Soviet man' willingly gave his service to the State (in the factory, on the fields or in battle) and had a profound sense of social responsibility

KEY PROFILE

Trofim Lysenko (1898–1976) was a Soviet biologist and agronomist who exercised considerable influence over Soviet policies. His genetic theories influenced agricultural practices in the 1930s and were extended to account for the evolution of Soviet man. Lysenko received unconditional backing from Stalin; those who opposed his views were silenced. His doctrines were not discredited until after 1964.

ACTIVITY

Extension

Read George Orwell's *1984,* in which Orwell criticised the whole notion of 'programming' a population, and conveyed his doubts that a totalitarian State would ever have the confidence to allow itself to 'wither away' of its own accord (which was Marx's utopian vision, not Stalin's).

The impact of cultural change

CROSS-REFERENCE

Cultural change in the USSR in the 1920s and the 1930s (including the development of socialist realism) is also discussed in Chapter 15, page 131.

KEY PROFILE

Maxim Gorky (1868– 1936)

Already a renowned author in tsarist Russia, Gorky had become disillusioned by the Civil War and lived abroad between 1921 and 1928. Stalin persuaded him to return to Russia because of his reputation and he helped in the development of socialist realism, He received many honours and had a major street in Moscow named after him, as well as the town where he had been born. He died while undergoing medical treatment. It is possible that he was murdered on Stalin's orders.

CROSS-REFERENCE

The treatment of **Pasternak** and **Akhmatova** in the post-war years is discussed in Chapter 23, page 201.

KEY PROFILE

Boris Pasternak (1890–1960) was a leading Russian poet who had initially welcomed the revolution but, by the 1930s, was considered 'bourgeois' for his failure to embrace socialist realism. Stalin is said to have had Pasternak's name removed from a list of intellectuals to be purged because he admired his translations of Georgian classics. Pasternak found it impossible to write in the atmosphere of the 1930s. Although he became internationally famous for his semi-autobiographical *Doctor Zhivago*, written in the war years, he continued to be persecuted in the USSR during Stalin's later years.

Fig. 4 *The Moscow metro showing Soviet realism in architecture*

The attempt to mould culture to the creation of the new 'socialist man' met with a varied response. Komsomol members were generally the most enthusiastic. They were the ones who led the attack on 'bourgeois' values, revelling in criticising, and sometimes burning or vandalising non-socialist books and artworks, heckling actors and mocking religion. They also helped spread 'proletarian culture' as they participated in the 'shock brigades', used in collectivisation and industrialisation, and worked on literacy schemes.

A CLOSER LOOK

Cultural change and the churches

The Christian cultural heritage was placed under threat as churches were raided and priests persecuted. By 1941, only around 1 church in 40 was still working as a church (the rest had been destroyed or converted to secular use) and 152 of the 168 bishops in place in 1930 had been killed or incarcerated. Jewish and Islamic culture also suffered from persecution.

Some cultural figures toed the Party line and 'artistic brigades' were organised that exhorted others to fight for socialist realism. The author **Maxim Gorky**, for example, declared that under Stalin, Russian writers had 'lost nothing but the right to be bad writers'. Nevertheless, the leading figures in the arts in the 1930s, for example the photographic artist Isaak Brodsky, were not generally accepted as artistic 'greats' outside the USSR.

Many were silenced by the regime or, like the novelist **Boris Pasternak** and the poet **Anna Akhmatova**, remained silent of their own accord. Some writers were sent to work on industrial or agricultural sites; this was not necessarily a punishment but a way of trying to ensure that they were fully imbued with socialist values.

The mid 1930s saw a ruthless attack on the avant-garde. In 1936, for example, *Pravda* published a damning critique of **Shostakovich's** opera *Lady Macbeth of the Mtsensk District*, under the headline, 'Chaos instead of Music'.

Stalin had recently heard this modernist work and, despite the popularity the opera had enjoyed since the premiere in 1934, the composer was accused of 'leftist distortions'. Although Shostakovich himself avoided arrest, a theatre director who spoke in his defence was seized, brutally tortured by the NKVD and shot; the director's wife was also stabbed to death.

Dmitri Shostakovich (1906–75) was a world-famous composer of symphonies, chamber music and choral works. He was often in disgrace with the Soviet regime, particularly during the **Zhdanov cultural purge** after 1946. During the war he was treated as a hero for his 'Leningrad' symphony, composed during the siege of Leningrad, but he never felt safe until after Stalin's death in 1953.

CROSS-REFERENCE

For detail on the **Zhdanov cultural purge**, look ahead to Chapter 23, page 201.

CROSS-REFERENCE

Nikolai Ostrovsky's book **How the Steel Was Tempered** is introduced in Chapter 15, page 132.

Overall, the attempt to impose new cultural values seems to have fallen well short of the hopes. By far the most popular cultural activity among the Russian people was visiting the cinema, where Hollywood movies were enjoyed far more than Soviet propagandist films. Although *How the Steel Was Tempered* was the most frequently borrowed book from the Magnitogorsk library, that new industrial city can hardly be held as representative of the whole USSR. The modern Cambridge historian Dr John Barber has suggested that only around a fifth of workers wholeheartedly supported the Stalinist regime and its politics; this leaves four fifths on whom all the attempts at indoctrination and the spread of new cultural values had little impact.

 PRACTICE QUESTION

To what extent did the proletariat benefit from Stalinist rule in the 1930s?

STUDY TIP

To answer this question you will need to consider working men, women and children and the influences on their lives – living, working and their personal 'freedoms'. It could be helpful to begin with a plan in which you identify areas of improvement and areas of stagnation or deterioration.

Similarities and differences between Lenin's and Stalin's USSR

Lenin's reputation always stood very high in the USSR and lasted much longer after his death than Stalin's, yet Stalin had as great an impact on the USSR as Lenin, perhaps more so. Historians and commentators have been much more critical of Stalin, claiming that Stalin undermined Lenin's work rather than continuing it. For Stalin's enemies like Trotsky, Stalin turned the USSR into a perversion of what was intended to be the first workers' state.

However, this is too simple an explanation. Lenin was a ruthless leader. Some apologists have excused the excesses under Lenin, such as the Red Terror, as a response to the desperate situation in which Russia found itself after the revolution. Stalin's excesses, especially the widespread purges, seem far less excusable by comparison. However, Lenin signed death warrants with as little thought as Stalin.

Stalin used methods established by Lenin – especially the setting up of internal security services and the emphasis on class warfare – but took them to much greater extremes. His terror was on a much greater scale. Stalin's hold on the Party was achieved to a large extent by fear and terror, as well as individuals' hopes of advancement, whereas Lenin's hold had depended much more on his personal reputation. Both Stalin and Lenin adapted their policies to what they perceived were the needs of the regime at any particular time, and both were prepared to come up with an ideological justification for any policy changes.

ACTIVITY

Create a spider diagram to show the various influences to which a worker was subjected in the 1930s in an attempt to create a 'socialist man'.

The chart below shows some of the key similarities and differences between Lenin's and Stalin's USSR. Copy this table, adding examples to support the points and adding any other similarities and differences that you can think of.

Lenin's USSR by 1924	Stalin's USSR by 1941
One-party State; limited Party membership	Strong Party control; large membership
Leading communists debated policy in the Politburo	Policymaking directed by Stalin; Party organs often bypassed
Old Bolsheviks carried authority	Old Bolsheviks had gone; new generation owed everything to Stalin
Centralisation and bureaucracy had emerged in the Civil War; Lenin feared it would stifle progress	Highly centralised state with large bureaucracy which was privileged, self-perpetuating and resistant to change
Mixed economy – NEP	Nationalised industry; emphasis on heavy industry
Predominantly agricultural and limited progress towards collectivisation	Agriculture collectivised
Secret police (Cheka) established	Secret Police (NKVD) had wide powers
Terror used against real or potential enemies	Widespread terror and purges used in seemingly arbitrary way (although the worst had passed by 1940)
Censorship and control but some opportunity to experiment in arts, freedom in schools and limited Party influence in rural areas	Strong elements of totalitarianism in all aspects of society and culture; little opportunity for independent thought and action

Stalin made relatively few contributions to Marxist theory after 1929, except possibly in his ideas on the role of the State in a socialist but still pre-communist society. Basically, Stalin continued and extended Leninism, with a particular focus on carrying out economic and social changes. Russia under Stalin also found itself in an international situation in the 1930s that could not have been foreseen earlier by Lenin, and this led Stalin to fuse Russian nationalism with Soviet socialism in conditions which Lenin had not experienced.

This quotation requires you to look at the purpose behind the social and cultural policies. You need to consider whether they were driven by a concern to strengthen the USSR or the Marxist ideology which Stalin claimed to follow. You will probably want to approach the answer thematically, although you should aim to provide an overall conclusion too.

(A LEVEL) PRACTICE QUESTION

'In his social and cultural policies, Stalin was less interested in Marxist theory than in the strength of the USSR.' Assess the validity of this view.

Summary

- Soviet culture and society were affected by Stalinist changes in the 1930s; there was an attempt to control every aspect of people's lives, not just political life.
- The Churches were weakened, although their spiritual hold was not destroyed.
- Women were given legal equality with men, but in practice were still 'second class' citizens.
- There were changes in education and the development of a youth organisation –all designed to support Soviet economic growth and influence young people in the way of Soviet thinking.
- Working men were subject to a barrage of decrees; for some workers, life got better thanks to the industrialisation drive which raised real wages.
- Life was hard for many, but more so for many peasants than town and city dwellers.
- There was a conscious drive to create the 'new' Soviet man and woman, with varying degrees of success.
- Several features of Stalinism in the 1930s had already been present under Lenin's regime, but Stalin took certain aspects, such as terror and the drive for an all-embracing totalitarian state, to new extremes.

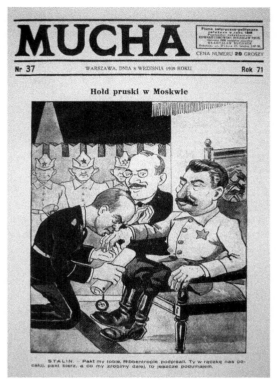

Fig. 1 *'Prussian tribute in Moscow': A Polish cartoon satirising German 'surrender' to Stalin in the August 1939 Nazi-Soviet Pact, showing Soviet Foreign Minister Molotov gloating as German foreign minister Ribbentrop kneels before Stalin*

LEARNING OBJECTIVES

In this chapter you will learn about:

- Soviet cooperation with Germany
- Soviet entry into the League of Nations
- pacts with France and Czechoslovakia, and Soviet intervention in the Spanish Civil War
- Soviet reaction to Western appeasement and Japanese aggression
- The Nazi-Soviet Pact and its outcome, 1939–41.

CROSS-REFERENCE

The **Treaty of Rapallo** is covered in Chapter 8 page 74.

The **Treaty of Berlin** is covered in Chapter 12 page 106.

Stalin and international relations, 1929–41

Cooperation with Germany

Cooperation between the USSR and Germany had been established by the 1922 **Treaty of Rapallo**, and consolidated by the **Treaty of Berlin** in 1926. The most intensive period of Soviet military collaboration with Germany was from 1929 to 1932. The Soviet Union benefitted from German technical expertise for the modernisation of industry and armaments production; Stalin made agreements with German armaments manufacturers in order to acquire modern weapons. In 1931, Germany and Russia negotiated the continuation of the Berlin treaty. But by then the Soviet-German relationship was beginning to come under strain.

A CLOSER LOOK

After the 1928 **Comintern** Congress, Stalin attacked democratic socialist movements, calling them 'social fascists'; this meant that the German Communist Party (KPD) should never cooperate with the German Social Democratic Party (SPD).

A CLOSER LOOK

Soviet-German military cooperation

The vastness of Russian territory enabled the German Army (Reichswehr) to carry through military developments that were forbidden under the Versailles Treaty. Areas of operation included: the Junkers aircraft factory at Fili, near Moscow; a training school for German pilots at Lipetsk in Ukraine; a facility for practising tank warfare at Kazan; and a secret joint facility at Samara for developing poison gas weapons.

Soviet–German trade slowed significantly in the early 1930s. Relations were also affected by changes in the policies of the **Comintern.** By 1932, with the Nazi Party gaining mass electoral

CROSS-REFERENCE

The changed policies of the **Comintern** are covered in Chapter 12.

CROSS-REFERENCE

The **rise of Hitler** and the ensuing threat to the USSR is outlined in Chapter 14, page 121.

support, it seemed certain that political upheaval in Germany would force a change in Soviet policy. Stalin was slow to react to the **rise of Hitler**; indeed it has been claimed he was pleased about it because it would accelerate the collapse of capitalism. But in 1933 and 1934 the 'Rapallo period' of cooperation with Germany was put to one side as Stalin showed interest in collective security and improved relations with the Western democracies. Even then, despite the ideological divide between Nazism and communism, Stalin kept his options open for a possible return to cooperation with Germany.

A CLOSER LOOK

Assessing Stalin's foreign policy

Stalin's foreign policies in the 1930s were complicated and contradictory. It has often been suggested that Stalin pursued a 'zig-zag' policy, frequently changing direction according to circumstances. An alternative view is that Stalin had a single-minded obsession with security; the tactics were unpredictable, but the overall strategic objective was always the same. The Soviet historian Alexandr Nekrich claimed in his 1997 book *Pariahs, Partners, Predators* that there was a consistent **'Stalin Doctrine'** in the 1930s, wanting a war between Germany and the capitalist West that would weaken both sides while the USSR remained neutral.

A CLOSER LOOK

The **'Riga Watchers'** were American foreign policy experts, including able young men such as George Kennan and Charles Bohlen, who used Riga, the capital of independent Latvia, as a 'listening post' from which to observe developments inside Russia.

CROSS-REFERENCE

Maksim Litvinov is profiled in Chapter 12, page 105.

CROSS-REFERENCE

Russia's absence from the **League of Nations** and concept of **collective security** are discussed in Chapter 8 page 74.

Soviet entry into the League of Nations

The Soviet Union moved away from diplomatic isolation. In 1933, diplomatic relations were established with the United States. An American Embassy was opened in Moscow, allowing US diplomats to operate within the USSR instead of depending on the **'Riga Watchers'** who previously reported on the Soviet Union from nearby Latvia. US diplomatic recognition was important in opening the way for the USSR to join the League of Nations; so was the personal diplomacy of the Foreign Commissar, **Maksim Litvinov.**

Litvinov was well established by 1933 as the 'acceptable face' of the Soviet regime. His long experience of the West, and his polished social background, gave him credibility with Western diplomats. It was a visit to Washington by Litvinov in November 1933 that finalised the agreement to re-open formal relations. Apart from skilful diplomacy, there was also a pressing issue pushing the two powers towards recognition: both Stalin and the Americans were worried about the **rise of Japan**, the country that had invaded Manchuria in 1931 and seemed set for further militaristic expansion. Bringing the USSR into the **League of Nations** appealed to the Western powers as a desirable step towards strengthening **collective security** against threats of Japanese or German aggression.

A CLOSER LOOK

Fears of Japanese aggression

Russia was deeply involved in the Far East from the 1890s, with the building of the Trans-Siberian Railway and expansionist Russian ambitions in Manchuria, to exploit the weakness of the Chinese empire. Japan also had ambitions in Manchuria; and fought a war against China in 1894 to 1895. This rivalry led to the Russo-Japanese War, in 1904, settled by American mediation in 1905. The continued rise of Japanese military power, and Japan's occupation of Manchuria in 1931, was a major concern for Stalin, and also for the Western powers, especially the United States.

Outwardly, entry into the League was a radical change in Soviet policy. By 1934, however, the international situation was very different. Both **Germany and Japan** had withdrawn from the League of Nations and there was renewed interest in collective security. The major powers were anxious for the USSR to join the League, and Stalin saw advantage in doing so; in September 1934, the USSR was admitted to the League.

SOURCE 1

Adapted from an article by **Karl Radek** and published in **January 1934**. Radek was an experienced revolutionary who had been an ally of Trotsky in the 1920s but had reconciled with Stalin in 1930:

The object of the Soviet Government is to protect the soil of the world's first proletarian state from the criminal folly of a new war. To this end the Soviet Union has struggled with the greatest determination and consistency for sixteen years. The defence of the peace and of the neutrality of the Soviet Union against all attempts to drag it into the whirlwind of a new world war is the central problem of Soviet foreign policy. The Soviet Union pursues the policy of peace because peace is the best condition for building up a socialist society.

In 1934 and 1935, Stalin took further steps towards supporting collective security; the hard-line policy enforced on the Comintern from 1928 was scrapped. Stalin now announced a new official policy to support broad-based **'popular fronts'** in other countries. Soviet communism was to cooperate with democratic socialists in the fight against fascism. Stalin announced this new line in *Pravda* in 1934. It became official policy at the Comintern Congress in Moscow in 1935.

ACTIVITY

Make a list of reasons as to why you think the USSR was admitted to the League of Nations in 1934. Exchange views with a partner and agree on an order of importance.

Pacts with France and Czechoslovakia

Stalin was slow to react to the rise of Hitler; he did little to protest against the repression of the German KPD by the Nazi regime, and he was willing to continue military and naval cooperation with Germany. But he did seek to find new allies, in addition to gaining US recognition and entering the League of Nations. In December 1932, the USSR negotiated a non-aggression pact with Poland; this was made into a ten-year agreement in 1934. A similar non-aggression pact was signed with France in November 1932; this was the basis of a Franco-Soviet Pact of Mutual Assistance, negotiated in December 1934 and signed in May 1935.

France was a willing partner in this new diplomatic approach. The French were worried about the rise of Nazism, especially by Hitler's public announcement of German rearmament in March 1935. But the Franco-Soviet Pact did not have specific clauses on military cooperation, and was vague on the circumstances in which it might be activated. Many observers in Western countries were sceptical about the pact; they regarded it as a rather hollow threat of a two-front war on Germany.

The Franco-Soviet Pact was quickly followed by a similar pact between the USSR and Czechoslovakia, in which the USSR gave an undertaking to intervene militarily, if Czechoslovakia was attacked by 'a third party' (that is,

A CLOSER LOOK

Germany, Japan and the League of Nations

Germany had been allowed to join the League of Nations in 1926 at a time when the German government appeared to be cooperating in fulfilling the terms of the Versailles treaty. However, Hitler had withdrawn his country again in 1933, and Japan, a founder member of the League, having mounted a war against China in the Far East, also withdrew from the League in 1933.

CROSS-REFERENCE

Karl Radek is profiled in Chapter 8, page 71.

ACTIVITY

Evaluating primary sources

In what ways does Radek's article, in Source 1, support the concept of the 'Stalin Doctrine'?

KEY TERM

popular fronts: the rise of fascist Italy and Nazi Germany led to calls for 'anti-fascist solidarity' – setting aside divisions and rivalries to provide united action by liberals and the Left. A popular front government was formed in France in May 1935, and there were calls for popular fronts in many other countries. Under Stalin's orders, support for popular fronts became the official policy of the Comintern in August 1935.

"LOVE ME, LOVE MY BEAR."

Madame La République. "C'EST MAGNIFIQUE!"
Kino Leopold. "MAIS CE N'EST PAS LA PAIX."

Fig. 2 *'Love me, love my bear': a cartoon satirising the 1935 Franco-Soviet Pact*

ACTIVITY

Draw a diagram to show the position of the USSR in 1935 and the international position and influences on the State.

A CLOSER LOOK

Remilitarisation of the Rhineland

In March 1936, Hitler ordered German troops to march into the Rhineland, territory that had been declared a de-militarised zone at the Treaty of Versailles in 1919. France and Britain did not intervene; Hitler's remilitarisation of the region succeeded. George Kennan argued in *Russia and the West under Lenin and Stalin,* that: 'from the moment of the German entry into the Rhineland, Stalin must have reckoned that it was only a matter of time before he must either fight Hitler or make a deal with him'.

Germany), as long as the French did also. Czechoslovakia was encouraged into the pact by France, who had a traditional policy of seeking allies in Central Europe, and also by Britain, whose foreign secretary, Anthony Eden, visited Moscow in 1935. From the Russian side, the smooth diplomacy of Litvinov was very influential; and Stalin put pressure on the French Communist Party to support the pact.

Soviet intervention in the Spanish Civil War

Stalin's new approach to international affairs and collective security received a serious setback in March 1936, when Hitler's forces occupied and **remilitarised the Rhineland**, directly contravening the terms of the Versailles treaty. The passive response of France to Hitler's 'calling the bluff' of Versailles weakened Stalin's faith in the value of the Franco-Soviet Pact of 1935. It also seemed an alarming indication for the future: if France was not going to enforce Versailles on an issue so close to France itself, then France was hardly likely to be bold in resisting German attempts to in East Central Europe.

Germany's remilitarisation of the Rhineland set the context for Stalin's reaction to the Spanish Civil War, which began in July 1936, when right-wing army officers led by Francisco Franco launched a nationalist rebellion against the Spanish Republic. Both fascist Italy and Nazi Germany sent military support to the Francoists. The Popular Front government of France wanted to prevent the Civil War in Spain from becoming internationalised; in August 1936, France proposed a general agreement on non-intervention in Spain. At first, Stalin went along with this policy but was anxious about what he perceived as French and British weakness in combating fascism. In September 1936 Stalin took the decision to intervene in Spain.

This intervention was on a large scale and rapidly implemented, with hundreds of Soviet 'advisers' sent to Spain, backed by troops, tanks and aircraft. The intervention was political as well as military; Soviet forces operated independently of the Spanish Republican government, and Soviet political agents followed orders from Moscow, not from Madrid. Soviet propaganda went into overdrive in support of the 'anti-fascist crusade' in Spain: with a flood of posters and cinema newsreels, and a mass rally in Leningrad in 1937.

Soviet intervention had a significant impact on the war; it probably saved Madrid from falling to Franco. After the early months of 1937, however, Stalin's policy changed. Direct military commitment was scaled down. The Soviet aim was no longer to help the Republic to victory; it was to prolong the war, in order to wear down Italian and German forces. Politically, Soviet priorities in Spain focused on internal feuds and rivalries against left-wing elements in Spain opposed to the domination of Soviet communism. Stalin was seemingly concerned with internal security, driven by a fear of a revolutionary idealism he could not directly control. Many of the Soviet personnel who served in Spain were repressed after returning home.

Another reason for Stalin's changed policies in Spain from 1937 was disillusionment with France and Britain. The Western democracies did little to prevent the victory of the Francoists in Spain. They also showed growing suspicion of Stalin's intentions in Spain. Liberal public opinion in the West admired the willingness of the USSR to intervene in Spain; but, on a governmental level, Soviet intervention exacerbated fear and dislike of Soviet communism, weakening the prospects for future collaboration.

Soviet reaction to Western appeasement and Japanese aggression

Western appeasement and the Munich conference

By 1938, the Soviet Union was facing dangerous threats to its security. Stalin knew from secret intelligence reports from Germany that Hitler had told his generals in November 1937 to prepare for a war of aggression and territorial expansion against Czechoslovakia and Poland. Also in 1937, Japan had launched a war of aggression in China. Collaboration with the Western powers and reliance on collective security for defence against these threats did not seem likely to be effective. The League of Nations had proved toothless in dealing with aggression, for example the Japanese invasion of Manchuria in 1931. The policies of France and Britain were increasingly dominated by **appeasement**.

In March 1938, German forces invaded Austria and imposed the *Anschluss,* incorporating Austria into the German Reich. France and Britain protested but took no action. It was obvious Czechoslovakia would be Hitler's next target; in the summer of 1938, there was Nazi-inspired agitation for the German-speaking Sudetenland to be transferred from Czechoslovakia to Germany. This crisis was exactly the threat the 1935 Soviet pacts with France and Czechoslovakia had been intended to guard against; but there was little chance of the pacts being activated. Although France was the country most directly concerned, it was Britain's prime minister, Neville Chamberlain, who took the lead in 1938.

Chamberlain had a strongly anti-communist stance, and he firmly believed that the way to save the peace was negotiating directly with Hitler. This approach led to the Munich conference in September 1938, attended by Germany, France, Britain and Italy. This four-power conference excluded Czechoslovakia, despite it being the country whose fate was being decided. Although the Soviet Union had signed a mutual defence pact with France in 1935, the USSR was not invited either. The pact between Czechoslovakia and the USSR was not activated, as it depended on the French taking action, and they did not.

Soviet feuds and rivalries with left-wing elements in Spain

Many different groups fought on the Republican side in Spain's civil war. Volunteers from many countries fought with the International Brigades. POUM (Workers Party of Marxist Unification) was a Trotskyist party hostile to Stalinism. The PCE (Spanish Communist Party) and the PSUC (United Socialist Party of Catalonia) were intensely loyal to Stalin and the Comintern. There were other leftist splinter groups. Many people were killed in the bitter disputes within the Left.

Fig. 3 *A Soviet propaganda poster on the alliance between Spanish Republic and Russian people*

appeasement: a term widely used in the 1930s to denote the policies of the Western democracies in response to demands from Hitler's Germany to revise the Treaty of Versailles; rather than relying on military alliances to enforce the post-war peace, the 'appeasers' believed in negotiations to 'meet legitimate German grievances'

The Soviet Union drew the obvious conclusions from the actions of the Western powers at Munich. Any hopes of an anti-Hitler alliance containing the USSR were severely dented. After Munich, the danger of Stalin turning his back on the West and making a cynical deal with Hitler should have been plainly apparent – as was shown by the comments of Joseph Davies, the former US Ambassador in Moscow, in a confidential letter to Washington in January 1939.

Fig. 4 *'What, No Chair For Me?' A cartoon by Low from 1938, imagining Stalin's reaction to the Munich conference*

ACTIVITY

Evaluating primary sources

Look carefully at Figure 4, and then consider the evidence of the former US ambassador to Moscow in Source 2. How far do these sources corroborate each other?

SOURCE 2

Adapted from a letter by Joseph E. Davies to President Roosevelt's adviser, Harry Hopkins, in January 1939. Davies had been US Ambassador in Moscow from 1936 to 1938:

Brussels, 18 January 1939
My dear Harry,
Conditions are hell over here. Chamberlain's peace is a flop. That is the overwhelming opinion in diplomatic circles here. There is one thing that can be done now in my opinion, and that is to give some encouragement to Russia to remain staunch for collective security and peace. The Soviets have got enough to digest in Russia. That is Stalin's policy — peace to consolidate Russia's position economically, is what they need, and they know it. The Chamberlain policy of throwing Italy, Poland, and Hungary into the arms of Hitler may be completed by so disgusting the Soviets that it will drive Russia into an economic agreement and an ideological truce with Hitler. That is not beyond the bounds of possibility or even probability — the Soviets did it for ten years from 1922.

The Soviet response to Japanese aggression

The problem of Japan was a major concern for Stalin in the 1930s. Japan's military dictatorship had built up a powerful war machine. The Japanese occupation of Manchuria in 1931, and Japan's invasion of the rest of China in 1937, presented a serious threat to the position of the USSR. (Many historians believe Stalin was more worried about the rise of Japan in the 1930s than he was about Hitler's Germany.) The threat from Japan was made more urgent by the **Anti-Comintern Pact** between Japan and Germany.

Anti-Comintern Pact

The Empire of Japan and Nazi Germany signed the first Anti-Comintern Pact in November 1936; an agreement to take joint action against 'interference' in their internal affairs by the Comintern – though the real enemy was the Soviet Union. Italy joined the Anti-Comintern Pact in November 1937, forming the three-power alliance that later became known as the 'Axis'.

The USSR stationed substantial military forces on the Manchurian frontier; from the summer of 1938 there were numerous border confrontations. These tensions spilled over into a major war that raged from May to September 1939, involving over 100,000 troops and 1000 tanks and aircraft. The decisive battle was at Khalkhin Gol in Soviet Mongolia in August 1939, where the Japanese army was encircled and defeated by Soviet forces led by **General Georgy Zhukov**; 75 per cent of the Japanese troops in the battle were killed.

The 1939 war between Japan and the USSR was almost a 'forgotten war', little noticed internationally, but it had significant consequences for both sides. Japan had underrated Soviet military strength and suffered a heavy defeat; afterwards Japanese expansionists left the Soviet Union severely alone, concentrating on targets in the Pacific instead. For the USSR, the war confirmed the need to remain militarily strong in the Far East; and it also coincided with a major shift in policy towards Western Europe. On 23 August 1939, while the battle at Khalkhin Gol was still in progress, Stalin's foreign minister, **Vyacheslav Molotov**, was signing the Nazi-Soviet Pact in Moscow.

Georgy Konstantinovich Zhukov (1896–1974) was a career soldier in the Red Army. He won medals for bravery in the First World War and in the Russian Civil War. He was promoted to senior positions in 1937 and 1938, during the army purges. In 1939, he was given command on the Mongolia front; his victory at Khalkhin Gol led to his being made a Hero of the Soviet Union. Zhukov was probably the most important of all Stalin's generals in the Great Patriotic War from 1941 to 1945, though the two men often clashed. He was demoted in 1948 but was restored to favour by Khrushchev after Stalin's death in 1953.

Vyacheslav Molotov is profiled in Chapter 10, page 89.

Fig. 5   *Soviet tanks in action in the 1939 war between Japan and the USSR*

The Nazi-Soviet Pact and its outcome, 1929–41

Origins of the Nazi-Soviet Pact

Seen through the newspaper headlines at the time, the signing of the Nazi-Soviet Pact by the German and Soviet foreign ministers, Ribbentrop and Molotov, on 23 August 1939, was a stunning surprise: a diplomatic revolution agreed by bitter ideological enemies. It should not have been such a surprise, because it was in many ways the logical outcome of the situation facing Hitler and Stalin. By the summer of 1939, it was clear that Europe was sliding towards war. Hitler was already committed to the invasion of Poland; what he wanted was freedom to do this without having to fight against a British-French-Soviet alliance in support of Poland. Stalin's nightmare, to be avoided at all costs, was a two-front war against Germany and Japan; what he wanted was for the fascist/militarist capitalists (Germany, Italy, and Japan) to fight a war against the bourgeois/democratic capitalists (Britain and France), leaving the Soviet Union safely neutral.

Thus, for Hitler, making a deal with Stalin gave him a free hand to invade Poland; the non-aggression pact also provided Germany with vital raw materials from Russia, on very favourable terms. For Stalin, the pact offered territorial gains, in eastern Poland and the Baltic States; more importantly, it guaranteed Stalin a breathing space, allowing time to consolidate the great economic changes within Russia. The pact also built on previous cooperation between the USSR and Germany, a relationship that had been put on one side after Hitler's rise to power, but never completely forgotten.

Outwardly, Stalin remained open to a possible military alliance with the West. He allowed Litvinov to continue negotiations with the Western democracies; and the Soviet propaganda war against the evils of Nazism continued. In March 1939, after Germany occupied Prague, France and Britain gave guarantees to Poland (which was plainly Hitler's next target) that they would go to war if Germany invaded. But practical military assistance to Poland would require the help of the USSR, and the Poles were reluctant to permit Soviet forces to enter their country (which was essential in order to block any German invasion).

Britain and France were not only hindered by Polish reluctance to cooperate with the USSR; they also completely failed to realise **the need for urgency** until it was too late. The Anglo-French Military Mission did not reach Moscow until August 1939. By then, it had no possibility of success, because Stalin had already made up his mind; the Nazi-Soviet Pact was already being negotiated.

French-British lack of urgency

The Anglo-French Military Mission seemed to be operating on the assumption that urgency was not required. It was slow in preparation, lacked the presence of high commanders, and travelled to Moscow by a leisurely route. In any case, it was almost certainly too late to make any difference. The fact that Litvinov, the pro-West foreign commissar, had been replaced by the hard-line Vyacheslav Molotov, should have provided a clear sign of Stalin's probable intentions.

ACTIVITY

Evaluating primary sources

What reason does Stalin give for the signing of the 1939 Nazi-Soviet pact in Source 3?

STUDY TIP

The three sources provide a variety of suggestions as to the aims of Soviet foreign policy, and your job is to evaluate the suggestions critically in the light of your own knowledge. You must also look carefully at the provenance of each source, considering the author, date, audience, tone and emphasis, and commenting on whether these add to or detract from the value of the sources as evidence.

SOURCE 3

Adapted from Stalin's speech to the Politburo, 1 August 1939; the speech was kept secret, and never published until 1999:

If we accept Germany's proposal and sign a non-aggression pact with her, Germany will attack Poland, and the intervention of France and Britain in that war will become inevitable. In these conditions we will have a great possibility of remaining on the sidelines in the conflict, and we can reckon on our successful entry into that war later. We are making our choice and it is clear. We must accept the German proposal and politely send back the Anglo-French mission. The first advantage we will gain is the destruction of Poland right up to the gates of Warsaw. Comrades! It is in the interests of the USSR, the homeland of workers, that war breaks out between the German Reich and the capitalist Anglo-French bloc. We must do everything we can to help the war last as long as possible, to ensure the exhaustion of both sides.

 PRACTICE QUESTION

Evaluating primary sources

With reference to Sources 1, 2 and 3 and your understanding of the historical context, assess the value of these three sources to an historian studying the aims of Stalin's foreign policy in the years 1929 to 1939.

Outcome of the Nazi-Soviet Pact, 23 August 1939

The Nazi-Soviet Pact seemed like a master stroke by Stalin:

- It gave him protection from war against Germany, at a time when the USSR was militarily weak (as was shown later in 1939 during the **'Winter War'** with Finland).

- It gave him the breathing space he wanted in order to concentrate on internal affairs.
- It enabled huge territorial gains for the USSR, and the destruction of Poland, 20 years after the Red Army had been halted on the **Vistula** in the first Russo-Polish War.
- With Hitler's invasion in the West in 1940, Stalin was able to seize control of the Baltic States, Estonia, Latvia and Lithuania.
- Stalin could look forward to the prospect of a long war in which Britain, France and Germany would all be economically and militarily exhausted, as had happened between 1914 and 1918.

CROSS-REFERENCE

The halting of the Red Army in the 'Miracle of the **Vistula**' of the first Russo-Polish War is outlined in Chapter 8, page 73.

However, Stalin's optimism about the consequences of his deal with Hitler was based on two faulty assumptions. His first miscalculation was about the strength of the French Army, and the nature of modern warfare. He believed that the coming war would last for years, like the war of 1914–18. The rapid fall of France in June 1940 was a nasty surprise for Stalin, putting Hitler in complete control of Western Europe, with the German war machine not weakened and exhausted, but stronger than ever.

A CLOSER LOOK

Soviet military weakness and the 'Winter War' 1939–40

Soviet forces invaded Finland in November 1939. Despite having much larger forces, the war went badly for the USSR at first, partly because Stalin's purges had weakened the Red Army. A peace agreement was signed in Moscow in March 1940 (10 per cent of Finland's territory was ceded to the USSR). When Germany invaded Russia in 1941, war between Finland and the USSR resumed: the Continuation War, which lasted until an armistice was agreed in September 1944.

Fig. 6 *Map of Europe in 1940, after German conquests in the West and the occupation of the Baltic States by the USSR*

KEY CHRONOLOGY

The Nazi-Soviet Pact

1938	Sept	Exclusion of the USSR from Four-Power Conference at Munich
1939	Mar	British and French guarantees to Poland
	Apr	Polish-German non-aggression pact of 1934 ended
	May	Litvinov replaced by Molotov as Foreign Commissar
	Aug	Anglo-French military mission to Moscow Molotov-Ribbentrop Pact signed in Moscow
	Sept	Invasion of Poland by German and (later) Soviet armies New German-Soviet border agreed by Molotov and Ribbentrop
1940	Jun	Soviet occupation of the Baltic States
1941	Jun	Nazi-Soviet Pact broken by German invasion of USSR

Stalin's second miscalculation was that he thought he could trust Hitler. From June 1940, knowing he was in a weak position, Stalin strictly observed all the terms of the Nazi-Soviet Pact. Trade agreements were further developed; the USSR always paid promptly and in gold. Trainloads of foodstuffs and raw materials continued rolling west into Germany. But by October 1940, Hitler had already begun preparing to invade the USSR in 1941. Allied intelligence services picked up evidence of this and sent private warnings to Stalin, but he refused to believe them. When the invasion came, at 03:15 on 22 June 1941, the Soviet Union was badly unprepared to defend against it. The 'triumph' of the 1939 Nazi-Soviet Pact turned into a disaster.

Summary

Between 1929 and 1941, Stalin's foreign policy seemed to be inconsistent. The USSR's relationship with Germany went from cooperation, to violent ideological hostility, to a non-aggression pact, to total war. The Comintern switched from a hard-line policy against 'social fascists', to participation on Popular Fronts', to 'friendship' with Germany, to alliance with the West in 1941. The USSR went from diplomatic isolation, to membership of the League of Nations, to a prospective alliance with the Western powers, to total hostility against the West from August 1939, and then to wartime alliance with the West from 1941.

Yet this was in many ways a very consistent inconsistency. Stalin's aims in the 1930s can be seen as a coherent obsession with defending the Soviet state against the enemies that encircled it: capitalism, rival ideologies, a resurgent Germany, Japan. These enemies represented real external dangers; and they were intertwined in Stalin's mind with internal dangers, to his political control and to the economic transformation of Russia. Stalin would ultimately succeed in his aims; but he might not have done so. If Japan had, as Stalin feared, gone to war with the Soviet Union in December 1941, instead of the United States, the outcome would have been very different.

 PRACTICE QUESTION

'The signing of the Nazi-Soviet Pact in 1939, reflected the total failure of Stalin's foreign policy.' Assess the validity of this view.

21 The Great Patriotic War and its impact on the Soviet Union, 1941–1945

Fig. 1 *A patriotic painting of the Battle of Kursk, which turned the tide of war on the Eastern Front in the summer of 1943*

LEARNING OBJECTIVES

In this chapter you will learn about:

- Operation Barbarossa and the Stalinist reaction
- the course of the war
- the USSR under occupation and during the fight-back
- the Soviet economy: mobilisation and evacuation of industry; foreign aid.

Operation Barbarossa and the Stalinist reaction

Operation Barbarossa

By the summeEr of 1941, Hitler was poised for the invasion of Russia; he had been preparing his strategy since October 1940. Britain had refused to make peace after the German conquest of France and Western Europe, but was not able to offer a military threat. Hitler knew that the Soviet Union was badly unprepared for war. The German armed forces were experienced, battle-hardened and well equipped. Hitler's planners were confident of achieving a rapid and decisive victory.

The invasion was originally scheduled for 1 June, but was delayed for three weeks, because the policies of Hitler's Italian allies had caused a crisis in Yugoslavia. This compelled Hitler to invade Yugoslavia in another

KEY CHRONOLOGY

1941	Jun	Operation Barbarossa; German invasion of USSR
	Sept	Beginning of Siege of Leningrad
	Dec	Battle of Moscow; German advance halted
1942	Jul	Renewed German offensive, south towards Caucasus oil fields
	Nov	German army surrounded at Stalingrad
1943	Feb	Surrender of German army at Stalingrad
	Jul	Battle of Kursk; start of long German retreat
1944	Jan	End of Leningrad siege
1945	May	Soviet victory in the Battle for Berlin

Fig. 2 *Operation Barbarossa*

KEY TERM

blitzkrieg ('lightning war'): was the term widely used to define the rapid victories achieved by German armies in conquering Poland in September 1939 and France in 1940, using fast-moving armoured units, backed by close air support; the invasion of the USSR was intended to be another such 'lightning war'

CROSS-REFERENCE

The outcome of the **Nazi-Soviet Pact** is covered in Chapter 20, page 174.

A CLOSER LOOK

Soviet unpreparedness for war

Soviet military strength had been undermined by the **army purges of 1937 to 1939**, as had been shown by the poor performance of the Red Army in the **'Winter War' against Finland**. Soviet resources were also stretched by the need to keep substantial forces in the Far East, after the **1939 war against Japan**. The total size of the Soviet armed forces had been greatly increased between 1939 and June 1941, but these forces lagged well behind Germany in efficiency, equipment and leadership. The extensive territories in eastern Poland and the Baltic States that had been seized in 1939 and 1940 to provide a 'buffer zone' against attack, provided no defence and were overrun in a matter of weeks.

CROSS-REFERENCE

Revisit the detail on the **1937 to 1939 army purges** in Chapter 18.

The **'Winter War' against Finland** is discussed in Chapter 20, page 175.

Read the section on the **1939 war against Japan** in Chapter 20, page 172.

blitzkrieg campaign; the launch of Operation Barbarossa (codename for the invasion of the USSR) was re-set for 22 June. At the time, this delay did not seem significant, but it did cut short the time-window for completion of the operation, before winter weather conditions intervened.

Three huge army groups spearheaded the German invasion plan: north through the Baltic States towards Leningrad; south and east into Ukraine; and a central thrust towards Moscow. (Some of Hitler's senior advisers wanted all forces to be concentrated in the central drive on Moscow, but he overruled them.) The aims behind Barbarossa were not just military victory – it was also an attempt to seize control over the entire Soviet economy, and to eradicate communism. Hitler also believed that many Soviet citizens would welcome the German invaders as 'liberators'.

The Stalinist reaction

Stalin's miscalculation about the effectiveness of the **Nazi-Soviet Pact** left the Soviet Union **unprepared for war** in June 1941. Even when foreign sources warned Stalin that a German invasion was imminent, he took no action – partly because he preferred not to believe them, partly because he dared not take any visible steps against an invasion in case those steps provoked Hitler into launching it.

The weakness of the Soviet position in June 1941 was reflected in Stalin's actions. He shrank away from making a radio broadcast to the people; that task was left to Molotov. Stalin seems to have lost his nerve, expecting that the people, and the Party leadership, would blame him and turn against him. It was nearly two weeks before Stalin dared to make a radio speech to the nation on 3 July. When he did so, it was a startling change in tone from the terror of the 1930s: Stalin appealed to patriotism and religion, and to unity among the nationalities. 'Friendship' with Nazi Germany was replaced by ideological hatred; Stalin's new friend was the British prime minister, Winston Churchill. This new tone, of a Great Patriotic War linked to national struggles of the Russian past, was to be a lasting feature of Soviet war propaganda.

SOURCE 1

Adapted from a radio speech to the nation on the outbreak of war, given by the foreign minister, Vyacheslav Molotov on 22 June 1941:

Now that the attack against the Soviet Union has taken place, our troops have been ordered to repel this villainous assault and drive the German invaders from the territory of our Motherland. This is not the first time our people have had to deal with an aggressive enemy. During Napoleon's campaign against Russia our people responded with the Patriotic War, and Napoleon suffered defeat and ruin. The same will happen to that puffed-up Hitler, who has instigated a new invasion of our country. The Red Army and our people will once again wage Patriotic War for the Motherland, honour, and freedom. Citizens of the Soviet Union! The government calls upon you to once again close ranks around our glorious Bolshevik Party, around our Soviet Government, and around our great leader, Comrade Stalin!

SOURCE 2

Adapted from a speech by Stalin in a radio broadcast to the people, 3 July 1941 (this was the first time Stalin had made a public address to the people since the German invasion two weeks earlier):

The enemy is tireless and cruel. He aims to secure our lands, grain, and oil. He aims to bring back the power of the landowners and restore Tsarism, to destroy the national culture and statehood of Russians, Ukrainians, Belorussians, Lithuanians, Latvians, Estonians, Uzbeks, Tatars, Moldovans, Georgians, Armenians, and other free peoples of the Soviet Union. A war with fascist Germany is no ordinary war; it is a great war of the whole Soviet people. The aim of this people's patriotic war against the fascist oppressors is not just to get rid of the danger threatening our country, but also to help all those peoples of Europe groaning beneath the yoke of German fascism. We shall not be alone in this war of liberation. Our war to free our Fatherland will merge with the struggle of the peoples of Europe and America for their independence and democratic freedoms.

Fig. 3 *Soviet propaganda poster of 1942, showing the Red Army aligned with heroes of Russia's past: Alexander Nevsky fighting the Teutonic Knights in 1242; General Suvorov fighting Napoleon in 1812; Vasily Chapayev killed in Russia's Civil War in 1919*

Stalin was guilty of errors and poor leadership in the early stages of the war:

- He had a panic attack after the invasion and failed to give leadership in the first weeks; he prepared to move the government away from Moscow, to Samara on the Volga, and only decided at the last moment to stay in Moscow.
- He relied for too long on many inferior commanders, who had been promoted for political reasons after the purge of the army.
- In September 1941, he helped to cause a massive defeat of his southern armies at Kiev by refusing to allow them to retreat until it was too late; he also showed no urgency in defending Leningrad after it was besieged.

It was only after a long series of defeats and disasters that his 'war cabinet', **Stavka**, became an effective mechanism to run the war.

Stalin was saved by the size of Russia, with its huge population, and vast distances; by the severity of the Russian winter; and by the patriotism of the Soviet people. He also learned from his mistakes, and eventually was to receive accolades as the 'Great War Hero'. Stalin was helped by advance information about the **intentions of Japan**, provided by a 'master spy', Richard Sorge. As a result, Stalin was saved from having to fight a two-front war. When Japan attacked the US naval base at Pearl Harbor in Hawaii in December, this brought the United States into the Grand Alliance against the Axis Powers (Germany, Italy and Japan).

KEY TERM

Stavka: the top-level military command of the USSR in the Great Patriotic War; the name originated in Tsarist times, but Stavka was formed under Stalin on 23 June 1941; it comprised key generals such as Timoshenko and Zhukov, as well as key politicians, like Molotov and Voroshilov. Stavka was subordinate only to GKO (the State Defence Committee), which was the supreme political war cabinet

Avoiding war against Japan

The USSR had fought a major war against Japan in 1939 and feared that Japan (allied to Hitler in the 'Axis') would invade the USSR in 1941. But Stalin was tipped off by Richard Sorge, a Soviet double agent who ran a spy ring in Japan, that the target of Japanese aggression would be the United States, not Russia. This foreknowledge enabled Stalin to transfer high quality troops from Siberia in time to strengthen the defence of Moscow. (Sorge was a Comintern agent active in Germany from 1929 and in Japan from 1933. He was executed in Tokyo in 1944.)

Adapted from *I Chose Freedom,* by Viktor Kravchenko. The author was an engineer who worked in collectivisation of Ukraine in the 1930s, and was a captain in the Red Army during the Great Patriotic War. He asked for political asylum in the United States in 1944 and spent the rest of his life there. His book was published in 1947:

During the period of the Nazi-Soviet Pact, Stalin helped Hitler to conquer Europe by providing him with metals, ores, oil, grain, meat, butter, and every conceivable material, in accordance with their economic pact. Even after the invasion, Stalin helped Hitler by leaving him immense riches in military goods and productive capacity, and – most shameful of all – tens of millions of people. Failure to prepare for war will be held against the Stalin regime by history, despite the ultimate victory. It was to blame for millions of unnecessary casualties, for human wretchedness beyond calculation. Why was the population of Leningrad not evacuated? This 'oversight' is ignored by the hallelujah-shouters, but up to May 1943, more than 1.3 million died of hunger and cold in three successive winters of terrifying siege.

Look carefully at the provenance of each source and also examine the tone and emphasis of each speechmaker/writer in order to evaluate this material as evidence for an historian. Apply your own knowledge to the evaluation of the content too.

(A LEVEL) PRACTICE QUESTION

Evaluating primary sources

With reference to Sources 1, 2 and 3 and your understanding of the historical context, assess the value of these three sources to an historian studying the Stalinist reaction to the German invasion of the Soviet Union in 1941.

The course of the Great Patriotic War

There were three distinct phases in the course of the Great Patriotic War:

1. **June 1941 to the summer of 1942:** Soviet Russia struggled to survive against successive German offensives, suffering massive losses of people and territory.
2. **1942 to summer of 1943:** Soviet Russia stabilised its war effort, built a powerhouse war economy, and halted German advances.
3. **1943 to summer 1945:** Soviet armies moved on to the offensive, recaptured vast areas that had been occupied, and achieved total victory.

The USSR was part of a Grand Alliance, with Britain (from June 1941, after the German invasion of Russia) and with the United States (from December 1941 after the Japanese attack on Hawaii). The Western allies played a massive role in the ultimate defeat of Germany and Japan; they also supplied crucial supplies to aid the USSR's war effort. But it was the Soviet Union who suffered worst from the war, with enormous human and material losses, and years of brutal occupation. The Great Patriotic War was the defining experience of the Soviet people under Stalin's rule.

Copy the chart below on an A3 sheet. As you read the following section, complete it to record the course of the war:

Stage	Key events with dates	Detail of key events	Significance
June 1941– summer 1942			
Summer 1942– summer 1943			
Summer 1943– summer 1945			

The struggle for survival, June 1941 to October 1942

The speed of **the German advance** was astounding. Vast distances were covered in days. Huge Soviet armies were encircled and defeated: at Minsk and Smolensk, on the central front, and near Kiev, where 665,000 Soviet troops were captured. Soviet forces were rapidly expelled from the Baltic States. On all fronts, there were catastrophic losses of Soviet aircraft. After two weeks, German generals believed that the war was virtually won and that Moscow would be captured before the end of August. Hitler was convinced victory was close.

Leningrad was encircled early in September. Forces were in place for a final advance on Moscow. Half a million Soviet troops surrendered after the fall of Kiev on 19 September. On 15 October, the Soviet leadership offered negotiations for a **compromise peace**. Hitler disregarded this and kept pursuing total victory. In November, the weather worsened and the Soviet defences hardened, with some desperate counter-attacks pushing German forces back from the outskirts of Moscow. By December, German victory was tantalisingly close but had not been achieved. On 5 December, the advance on Moscow was halted.

Stalin's peace offer

By October 1941, huge territories had been lost, and German forces were driving towards Moscow; if they succeeded, Stalin knew Japan was likely to invade from the east.

Stalin therefore authorised Molotov and **Beria** to open secret negotiations with Germany. Nothing came of these, although the possibility remained open until early 1942; Hitler was convinced he would win anyway. The peace offer remained a hidden secret until after the collapse of the USSR.

Draw a flow diagram to illustrate the progress of Operation Barbarossa, with key dates and events coupled with comments on their significance.

Even after Operation Barbarossa had failed to win decisive victory, the Soviet Union was still involved in a desperate war for survival. There was limited fighting in the early months of 1942, but by May Germany was ready to launch another offensive designed to knock Russia out of the war. This offensive was not, as expected, towards Moscow, but south and east, towards the Caucasus oilfields. As in 1941, German forces made rapid advances after the launch of

1941	22 Jun	Operation Barbarossa
	8 Sept	Start of Siege of Leningrad
	19 Sept	Fall of Kiev and loss of Ukraine
	18 Oct	Transfer of troops from Siberia to defend Moscow
	27 Nov	German forces halted 20 km from Moscow
	5 Dec	German drive on Moscow halted
1942	31 May	Big German victories in eastern Ukraine
	28 Jun	*Case Blue,* German offensive towards Caucasus oilfields
	24 Jul	Fall of Rostov on the Don
	23 Aug	Start of bombardment of Stalingrad
	12 Oct	German advance at Stalingrad halted

The German advance

German victory depended absolutely on speed; Hitler always knew the military balance would turn against Germany if it became a long war of attrition. Most of German military resources went into the invading army groups; there were no mass forces in reserve. Transport behind the advance was stretched over vast distances. Hitler's generals also began to realise that they had underestimated the number of Soviet divisions: when Barbarossa began, the Germans believed they faced 200 Soviet divisions; by August they had identified at least 360.

Beria is profiled in Chapter 18, page 153.

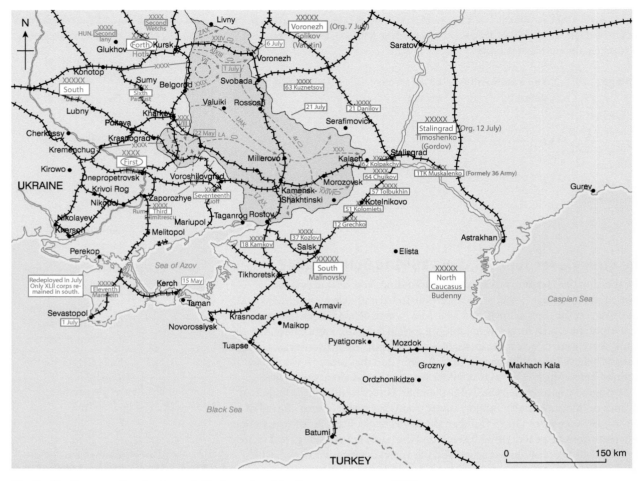

Fig. 4 *The German offensive towards Stalingrad and the Caucasus, summer 1942*

Case Blue (codename for the Caucasus plan), with massive victories in eastern Ukraine. The fall of Rostov on the Don in July was one of the lowest moments for the USSR in the whole Great Patriotic War.

But Case Blue was sidetracked by Hitler's decision to divert forces to the capture of **Stalingrad**, on the Volga. Originally a sideshow, Stalingrad became a symbolic battle: Stalin put immense efforts into defending the city; Hitler became obsessed with taking it. In August and September, Soviet forces desperately defended Stalingrad; from October the balance changed. German forces began to pull back from the Caucasus, and the German Sixth Army at Stalingrad was cut off and encircled.

A CLOSER LOOK

Defence of Stalingrad

For many weeks in the late summer of 1942, it seemed certain Stalingrad would fall to the Germans; nine-tenths of the city was in their hands. Soviet forces held one enclave on the Volga, supplied at night by boats across the river. Stalin had refused to evacuate the civilian population, saying: 'they will fight harder for a live city than for a dead one'. But the USSR was building up new armies and new weapons. By October 1942, it was the Germans who were on the defensive, fighting for survival, and, on Hitler's direct order, forbidden to retreat.

Turning the tide, October 1942 to August 1943

Hitler's strategic mistake in persisting with defending Stalingrad to the death made the battle into a catastrophic German defeat, psychologically as well as militarily. The war had become the long war Germany had always wanted to avoid. Vast new Soviet armies had a decisive impact on the final outcome at Stalingrad; and on the regaining of Rostov on the Don, three weeks later.

By early 1943 Hitler was running out of men, resources, and time. He launched Operation Citadel, a great offensive near Kursk in July. But the offensive was halted by massive Soviet firepower at the Battle of Prokhorovka, the biggest tank battle in history, decisively won by the Red Army, with its massed force of **T-34 tanks**. Hitler called off the Kursk offensive on 13 July but the battle became a springboard for Soviet forces to counter-attack and to regain huge territories from German occupation. The road to Berlin was open.

A CLOSER LOOK

The T-34 tank

By 1943, the USSR had fully **mobilised its economy**. There was a surge in production of guns, tanks and aircraft, mostly from vast armaments factories east of the Urals. This surge equipped the Red Army with a key military asset, the T-34 tank. Compared with the most advanced German tanks, the T-34 had less sophisticated design and engineering, but it was immensely durable and easy to maintain and repair. Mass production of the T-34 was the foundation of victory in the great tank battle at Kursk in 1943.

ACTIVITY

Members of your group could undertake some further research into the key events of the war on the Eastern Front and create illustrated presentations for the rest of the group. Alternatively, you might like to create an illustrated wall poster showing the course of the war in visual representations with captions.

The road to Berlin, August 1943 to December 1944

After Kursk, final Soviet victory was all but certain. The war was no longer about the desperate defence of the USSR, but rebounding into a great Soviet offensive that would drive the Germans all the way back to Berlin. From August 1943 to December 1944, there was a chain of Soviet victories stretching across Eastern Europe: reconquering Ukraine, lifting the siege of Leningrad, invading Poland, Lithuania, Romania and Hungary.

In November 1943, Stalin, Roosevelt and Churchill met at Tehran – the first summit conference of the 'Big Three' – to discuss what to do with the Allied victory that was now inevitable. This victory, however, was neither swift nor easy. The retreating German forces proved to be resilient defenders. Even after the bomb plot that nearly killed Hitler in July 1944, Germany continued to fight and millions more lives were lost. When Stalin met Churchill in Moscow in October 1944, victory was still far off. It was April 1945 before the Red Army reached Berlin.

KEY CHRONOLOGY

1942	22 Dec	Start of German retreat from the Caucasus
1943	2 Feb	Surrender of German Sixth Army at Stalingrad
	24 Feb	Rostov liberated by Red Army
	4 Jul	Delayed launch of Operation Citadel
	12 Jul	Battle of Prokhorovka
	13 Jul	Kursk offensive called off by Hitler

CROSS-REFERENCE

The **mobilisation of the economy** is covered below, on page 186.

KEY CHRONOLOGY

1943	6 Nov	Liberation of Kiev
	28 Nov	Tehran summit: Stalin, Roosevelt and Churchill
1944	4 Jan	Entry of Soviet forces into Poland
	27 Jan	Siege of Leningrad ends after 972 days
	13 May	Crimea liberated by Red Army
	13 Jul	Capture of Vilnius in Lithuania
	29 Dec	Start of Soviet siege of Budapest

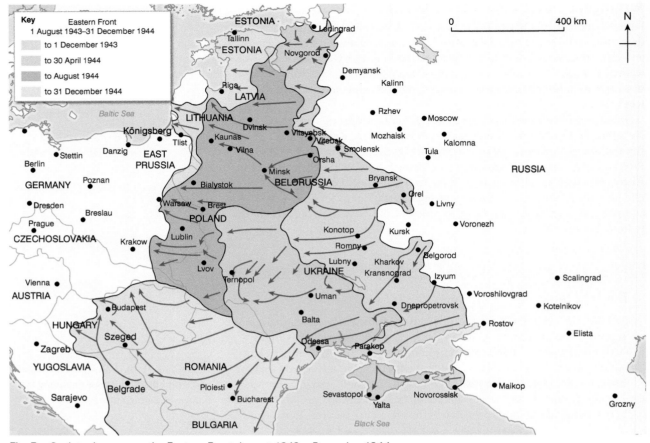

Fig. 5 *Soviet advances on the Eastern Front, August 1943 – December 1944*

The USSR under occupation and during the fight-back

The Soviet Union was ravaged by war: first by massive destruction during the German advance, and by Soviet 'scorched earth' tactics as the Red Army retreated. During the Soviet fight-back, the same areas that had been smashed by invasion and occupation were fought over again. The tides of war washed over some places many times: the city of Kharkiv in Ukraine was first overrun in October 1941, briefly recaptured in February 1942, and lost again in March. It was the scene of massive battles in May 1942 and finally liberated in August 1943. But Kharkiv was only one of 1700 Soviet towns and cities devastated by the war, along with 70,000 villages.

Life for civilians on the Home Front was unrelentingly harsh. Food, fuel and shelter were all in short supply. Leningrad was under siege from autumn 1941 to spring 1944; 600,000 people died of hunger and cold. It is estimated that by 1945 civilian deaths totalled more than 12 million. There was massive destruction of factories, hospitals and urban housing. Normal life was dislocated: by the displacement effect of the German invasion, by mobilisation for the armed forces or work in munitions factories, by mass deportations. Many hardships were the side effects of military conflict; but here were other causes: atrocities by the German occupiers, and repressive measures by the Soviet dictatorship against its own people. In enduring these hardships, there was also a strong sense of making sacrifices to fight in a great national cause.

When launching the invasion, Nazi leaders had talked grandly about 'liberating' the subject nationalities in the USSR from a communist system they hated, and there were some examples of the Germans being welcomed in parts of Ukraine, and in the Baltic States. But this did not last. The Germans (and Stalin himself) were surprised by the residual loyalty of Soviet citizens; and local populations were rapidly alienated by the repressive actions and atrocities committed by the German occupiers. Thousands of Soviet soldiers were held as prisoners of war; few ever came home. Thousands of Soviet workers were conscripted to work in German war factories. Right from the start, Hitler ordered the instant execution of captured Soviet commissars. There were massacres and deportations of Jews, such as at **Babi Yar** near Kiev. And there were vicious reprisals against the bands of partisans who harassed German forces behind the lines.

ACTIVITY

Extension

The siege of Leningrad was an epic event. To research it further, look at one of the many TV documentaries about the siege available on YouTube; for those who like historical fiction, there is a splendid novel, *The Siege,* by Helen Dunmore.

Fig. 6   *Siege of Leningrad, winter 1942–1943*

A CLOSER LOOK

Babi Yar

Hitler saw the war in the East as a racial war; invading the USSR was accompanied by widespread deportations and massacres of Jews. Soon after the occupation of Kiev in September 1941, the SS began to round up the Jewish population for extermination; 34,000 were taken to Babi Yar, a ravine outside the city, shot, and put into mass graves.

A CLOSER LOOK

The mass deportation of the Crimean Tatars

The Tatars had seen themselves as a nation since the fifteenth century, strongly influenced by the Ottoman Empire. After the end of Tsardom, many Tatars died in the Civil War, and during forced collectivisation and the Great Famine in the 1930s. Stalin was suspicious of their separate national identity, even though many Tatars had served in the Red Army. In May 1944 Beria organised the deportation of the entire Tatar population (240,000) to Uzbekistan in Soviet Central Asia. Their descendants returned to live in Crimea after Ukraine became independent in 1991.

Soviet citizens also suffered at the hands of their own government. Commissars and secret police were obsessed about hunting down 'slackers', 'deserters', and 'defeatists'; thousands of people were arrested or executed. The regime was intensely suspicious of ethnic minorities who might collaborate with the Germans, such as Chechens, and the **Crimean Tatars**, who were expelled to Central Asia in May 1944. When western areas of the USSR were liberated from occupation, Stalin's regime treated harshly those citizens who had been POWs, or who had worked for the Germans.

A great national myth emerged out of the Great Patriotic War: of a united Soviet people pulling together through shared sacrifices, following the Great Leader, Stalin, to heroic victory. This myth, of course, was not entirely true. Many people criticised the regime, and many were punished by it. There were many examples of cowardly and corrupt behaviour by selfish Party officials. But the myth *was* underpinned by a solid basis of truth. The experiences of total war, and the massive propaganda campaigns that shaped them, did bring people together. There were powerful unifying factors: fear and hatred of the Germans; a deep patriotism in defending the Motherland; an underlying faith in the revolution – and in Stalin.

A CLOSER LOOK

20,000 trains

Evacuation of industrial plants became urgent in August 1941. Many factories were dismantled and moved to the Urals. Railroads made the evacuation possible: 3000 wagons per day took steel factory equipment from the Dnieper area; 3000 per day the electrical industry; 25,000 wagons in one week shifted factories from Ukraine; 80,000 wagons moved 500 factories from Moscow. The relocation was a vital success, even though it was often disorganised, and conditions for workers were harsh.

KEY PROFILE

Andrei Tupolev (1888–1972) was a talented engineer who had a prominent role in the design and development of Soviet military aircraft, especially bombers. From 1929 he was chief designer, basing his work on the Junkers factory near Moscow that was part of Soviet-German military cooperation after Rapallo. In 1935, Tupolev designed the biggest-ever aircraft, the *Maxim Gorky*. In 1937 he was arrested during the purges but released in 1941 to work in war production. He was not fully rehabilitated until 1956 after Stalin's death.

A CLOSER LOOK

In a similar way, **Cold War historians** in the West played down the significance of the Eastern Front in the Second World War, focusing attention on great British and American victories, like D-Day.

The Soviet war economy

Mobilisation and evacuation of industry

The German invasion and occupation of the Western regions of the USSR in 1941 and early 1942 destroyed the basis of the Soviet economy, in industry and in agriculture. Vast areas were occupied. Whole sectors of industry were ruined by bombardment, or deliberately destroyed before Soviet forces had to retreat. Much of the new productive capacity that had been gained in the drive to industrialise in the 1930s was lost. If the Soviet Union could not build a new industrial base to replace the losses, then the war would be lost also.

The solution was to relocate in order to rebuild. Equipment, workers, whole factories, were packed up, put on **20,000 trains** and shifted hundreds of miles to the east, beyond the reach of German bombs. In other countries, such as Germany and Britain, the civilian population was mobilised for 'total war' – but nowhere was total war as total as it was for the Soviet people.

Fig. 7 *Building for victory: Soviet munitions factory east of the Urals, 1943*

The mobilisation of Soviet industry was vital for the war effort. It was another industrial revolution to match the Five Year Plans of the 1930s. In the 1930s, a centrally-controlled command economy had often proved inefficient and ill-suited to peacetime conditions; but that centralised system was very well matched to the needs of total war. During 1942, the Soviet Union began to build a huge industrial base for war production: especially, guns, tanks, and aircraft. (The foundations of a Soviet aircraft industry had been laid in the 1920s and 1930s by **Andrei Tupolev**, but the huge losses in 1941 made it necessary to start all over again.)

Foreign aid to the USSR

After 1945, **during the Cold War**, news reports and school textbooks in the Soviet Union said little about the aid poured into the USSR by the Allies under Lend-Lease. In fact, the scale of foreign aid to Soviet Russia was vast. The United States sent to Russia huge quantities of armaments, industrial goods, and foodstuffs.

Fig. 8   US lend-lease supplies to the Allies, January to March 1943

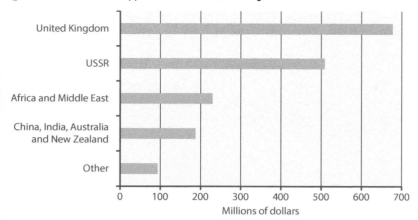

There were two main routes for this vital supply line: the Arctic convoys, and the so-called Persian Corridor. The Arctic convoys were at the end of a fragile maritime lifeline: across the Atlantic to Britain, and then via the North Sea and north Russia to Murmansk. The Persian Corridor was a safer, more roundabout route, through the Persian Gulf and across Iran to the Caspian Sea. From here it was easy to transfer goods to Baku and the Volga River region, or eastwards to war factories beyond the Urals. A wide range of goods was supplied; one vital aspect was more than **300,000 American trucks**. The flow of these war supplies was a significant factor in the Soviet war effort throughout, but especially in the winter of 1942 to 1943, when the USSR was recovering from the heavy losses earlier in the war.

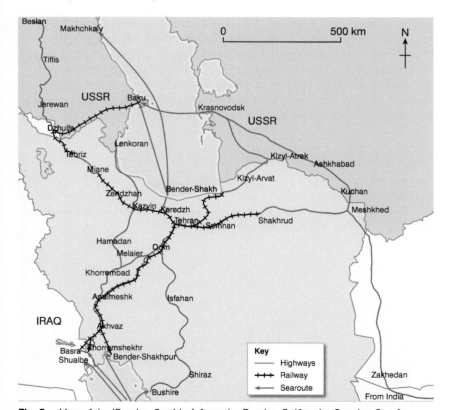

Fig. 9   *Map of the 'Persian Corridor', from the Persian Gulf to the Caspian Sea for foreign aid into the USSR*

300,000 trucks

The Soviet rail network was badly hit early in the war and heavy-duty trucks were essential for transportation. Lend-Lease supplied them in huge numbers – mostly Studebaker Us6 models, known to Soviet troops as 'Studer'. Two books, *The Road to Berlin*, by John Erickson, and *Russia's War*, by Richard Overy, give an excellent insight into Soviet war production and how it was helped by Lend-Lease. There are also two excellent TV documentaries: *Generalissimo* (Thames TV 1992) and *Red Star* (Episode 17 of *World at War* (1970).

ACTIVITY

Look back through the chapter so far and create a summary diagram. Divide this into political, social and economic sections to show the overall impact of the war on USSR 1941–5.

Fig. 10 *Supply convoy en route to USSR, passing through the 'Persian Corridor', Iran 1944*

Summary

The Soviet Union was transformed into a military-industrial superpower by the Second World War. This was a war that Stalin's Russia did not want, and nearly lost; but it was the defining experience of the Soviet Union. The war had left its mark on the entire population: men and women, old and young, soldiers and civilians, the millions who died and those still living. In the process, the war created a great national myth of shared heroism and sacrifice. By April 1945, the Red Army had liberated the Soviet people from German occupation, and fought its way to the edge of Berlin. Victory over the Axis was simply a question of time. Already by the end of 1944, Stalin was preparing for the USSR to share with its Western allies in making a new world order.

STUDY TIP

You will need to reflect on Stalin's leadership in wartime, including his inspiration, his diplomacy, his military strategies and his economic policies. Try to evaluate his contribution and it could be beneficial to assess whether the title (which was much used in USSR in the years after the war) was truly deserved or merely another piece of propaganda.

 PRACTICE QUESTION

To what extent does Stalin deserve the title, 'the Great War hero' for his leadership of the USSR between 1941 and 1945?

22 The defeat of the Germans

Reasons for the defeat of Germans and the results of victory

Fig. 1 *Raising the Soviet flag on the roof of the Reichstag in Berlin, 2 May 1945*

A CLOSER LOOK

Unconditional surrender

The Allies considered it essential to inflict total defeat and total surrender on ending the Second World War. Stalin also feared that his allies might make a separate peace; the insistence on unconditional surrender was partly to reassure him about this.

A CLOSER LOOK

The 'race for Berlin'

Stalin showed great urgency in his desire for the Red Army to push westwards at maximum speed. The Allied Supreme Commander, General Eisenhower cooperated. He wanted to minimise casualties, and avoid any clashes with Soviet forces. On 27 March, Eisenhower gave an order for the Allied advance in the West to be slowed down, to let the Red Army reach Berlin first.

CROSS-REFERENCE

General Zhukov is profiled in Chapter 20, page 173.

The final defeat of Germany took an unexpectedly long time. By late 1944, it had seemed imminent, with German armies retreating on all fronts. However, victory was delayed through the Allied insistence on Germany's **unconditional surrender**. There was no possibility of an agreed armistice, and the Germans fought to the bitter end.

Stalin wanted the Red Army to win the **'race for Berlin'** before the Americans did. As Soviet forces gradually pushed the Germans back, the capital cities of East Central Europe were liberated: Warsaw, Budapest, Prague and Vienna. This process was very costly but Stalin repeatedly ordered all-out frontal assaults, regardless of the very high casualties.

By early 1945, Germany's war effort had been badly weakened by the effects of mass bombing – Dresden, for example, was destroyed in February 1945. In April 1945, the Red Army reached the outskirts of Berlin; a few days later, Soviet forces met up with American forces, at Torgau on the Elbe. This culminated in the final battle for Berlin, in which **General Zhukov** used tactics that meant exceptionally severe losses of men. For Stalin, the final defeat of the Germans was driven by political as well as military motives. He wished to control as much as possible of Central Europe and Germany, to provide a buffer zone against any future threats to the USSR. The symbol of Soviet victory in the Great Patriotic War was the storming of the German parliament building (the Reichstag) on 2 May 1945.

ACTIVITY

Compose a letter that an ordinary Red Army soldier might have sent to his family back in the USSR to describe the experience of mingling with American soldiers at Torgau.

CROSS-REFERENCE

The **'command economy'** is introduced in Chapter 11, page 96.

The **mobilisation** of resources is discussed in Chapter 21, page 186.

KEY CHRONOLOGY

The defeat of the Germans on the Eastern Front, 1945

17 Jan	Entry of Soviet forces into Warsaw
13 Feb	Destruction of Dresden by mass Allied bombing
25 Apr	Meeting of Soviet and US forces at Torgau on the Elbe
2 May	Storming of the Reichstag; end of the Battle for Berlin
8 May	German surrender; end of war in Europe

Reasons for the defeat of the Germans

Soviet strengths

- The Soviet Union's vast geographical size made it almost impossible for Germany to strike a decisive, knock-out blow against it. German forces constantly faced the problems of dangerously overstretched lines of communication. The size of the USSR enabled whole new armies, and a whole new industrial base, to be built up in the East, beyond Germany's reach.
- The population of the USSR (171 million in 1941) was nearly three times greater than Germany's (although Hitler could also exploit the manpower of occupied countries between 1938 and 1941). The USSR could replace losses in a way that was impossible for the Germans.
- The USSR had vast natural resources (such as oil) that were unleashed by the war. The longer the war went on, the stronger Soviet military-industrial power became. In 1943, especially, the USSR simply out-produced German war industries.
- The Soviet **'command economy'**, already established before the war, was well-suited to the needs of total war and the emergency **mobilisation** of workers and resources.
- After a bad start, the military leadership of the USSR became ruthlessly effective. Stalin proved himself to be a very capable war leader. Stalin's generals became highly competent. Propaganda and patriotism motivated the armed forces and **civilians** to fight and endure.

A CLOSER LOOK

Women and Russia's war

All countries fighting the Second World War enlisted women in the war effort; but the USSR did so to a greater extent than any. Women fought as infantry soldiers; as tank captains at the Battle of Kursk; as skilled workers in munitions factories; and in a wide range of auxiliary uniformed organisations. After the devastation of Soviet cities, towns and villages, it was women who held daily life together.

Fig. 2 *Women front-line soldiers were prominent in the Red Army's liberation of Eastern Europe*

German weaknesses

- Hitler was not able to achieve the rapid initial victory he had hoped for.
- From December 1941, Germany had to fight a two-front war.
- Germany lacked self-sufficiency in raw materials. By 1943 to 1944, war production in Germany depended on all-out exploitation of dwindling economic and human resources.
- Hitler made crucial strategic mistakes and sacked many of his best generals, replacing them with yes-men.
- The Germans alienated peoples in occupied countries, provoking resistance movements and partisans.

The contribution by the Allies

- Stalin's allies presented a dangerous threat to Hitler on other fronts, preventing him from focusing on the war in the East.
- Mass bombing campaigns by the British and Americans from 1943 inflicted huge damage on Germany's war effort, weakening the resources available to fight on the Eastern Front.
- Allied secret intelligence, gained by code-breaking, undermined Germany's war effort at crucial times (though Stalin was never informed about it directly).
- Enormous amounts of vital military and economic aid poured into the USSR.

ACTIVITY

Look back at Chapter 21 and, together with the suggestions above, try to make an ordered list of reasons for the Soviet success in war under the following headings: geographical reasons; military reasons; political reasons; international reasons; other factors.

PRACTICE QUESTION

'Stalin's victory in the Great Patriotic War owed more to luck than to his good leadership.' Assess the validity of this view.

Results of victory for the USSR

Fig. 3 *Victory Parade in Moscow, 1945*

CROSS-REFERENCE

The **German weaknesses** are also discussed in Chapter 21.

STUDY TIP

This question requires a balanced assessment of the reasons for Stalinist victory in the Great Patriotic War. You should find your chart, prepared in response to the activity above, helpful here. Try to identify a number of factors to illustrate Soviet strengths (and, in particular Stalin's own strengths) as well as noting other reasons for the victory. It could be useful to look back at Chapter 21 to help in the exemplification. Consider the degree to which the various factors on both sides were well thought out decisions and policies or simply 'luck'. The latter is a concept which historians tend to be very suspicious of, so use the word with care!

A CLOSER LOOK

The new world superpower

Along with the United States, the USSR had emerged as a superpower by 1945. Before 1941, the Soviet Union had been regarded as a lesser military power, vulnerable to foreign aggression. The pressures of the Second World War forced the USSR to build up huge military-industrial strength, and to maximise its economic potential. The war also greatly weakened other powers.

CROSS-REFERENCE

To see a map of the 'Soviet bloc' that arose as a result of the **territorial expansion**, look ahead to Chapter 24, page 206.

Victory in the war established the Soviet Union as a **superpower**. The war galvanised the USSR and unleashed its huge economic potential. The war badly weakened the other European powers, and made the USSR by far the dominant military power on the continent. Germany, the main enemy, was under occupation, economically destroyed and likely to be de-militarised. The war strengthened Stalin's regime by the glow of victory. The war seemed to vindicate communist ideology, offering the 'road to socialism' as a replacement for fascism, and an alternative system to capitalism.

The war brought about massive **territorial expansion** of the Soviet Union. The previously independent Baltic States, Estonia, Latvia and Lithuania, and parts of East Prussia, were incorporated into the USSR as Soviet republics. Beyond the borders of the USSR, the Red Army had occupied many of the countries of East Central Europe, and was in position to establish pro-Soviet regimes there. Soviet victory in the war also caused one of the great mass migrations in history: 12 million refugees, many of them ethnic Germans, fled westwards in 1944 to 1945 as the Red Army advanced.

Despite the extent of Soviet victory, fears and insecurity remained. Stalin was anxious about the economic power of the United States and how it might be used in Europe. Stalin feared a resurgence of Germany. He feared and distrusted many of his own people; Stalin's regime was ruthless in repressing any Soviet citizens who had been outside the USSR during the war (for example as forced labour in the Third Reich, or even as prisoners of war). There were already disagreements about the **Four-Power occupation of Berlin** after the German surrender. Even at the moment of victory in May 1945, it was obvious that agreeing an overall peace settlement would be very difficult.

A CLOSER LOOK

The Four-Power occupation of Berlin

Defeated Germany was divided into four occupation zones: Soviet, American, British and French. Even though Berlin was entirely within the Soviet Zone, the city was also divided into four zones, ruled by a joint Allied Control Commission. This led to recurrent disputes between the USSR and the Western Allies.

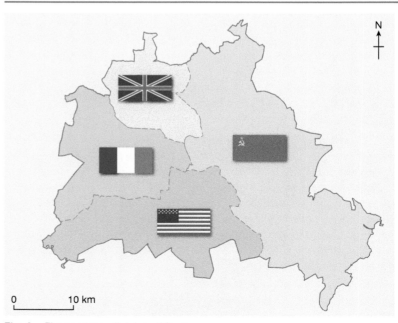

Fig. 4 *The post-war division of Germany*

Victory in the war had also been achieved at a terrible price. Approximately 20 million Soviet citizens died: 7.5 million in the armed forces and more than 12 million civilians. Large sections of the USSR were utterly devastated. The post-war reconstruction of the infrastructure, of industry, and of agriculture presented a massive challenge.

Post-war reconstruction

ACTIVITY

Discuss with a partner: What was the most important result of victory for the USSR? Justify your choice and share your ideas with your group.

Fig. 5 *Cleaning up and rebuilding after the destruction caused by war*

The impact of the war on the Soviet economy was **devastating**. Between 1941 and 1945, the war killed one in eight of the population and caused massive dislocation. But Stalin promised in 1945 that the USSR would be the leading industrial power by 1960. In August 1945, Gosplan was instructed to prepare a new Five Year Plan for economic recovery. The fourth Five Year Plan set ambitious targets, for industry and agriculture. One third of the Plan's expenditure was to be spent on Ukraine, which had been one of the areas most devastated by war, and was a very important region both for industry and for agriculture.

CROSS-REFERENCE

The physical **devastation** of the USSR during the war is covered in Chapter 21, page 185.

SOURCE 1

Adapted from Stalin's speech about his fourth Five Year Plan to voters in the electoral district of Moscow, February 1946:

The main tasks of the new Five Year Plan are to rehabilitate the devastated regions of our country, to restore industry and agriculture to the pre-war levels, and then to exceed those levels to a considerable extent. The rationing system is to be abolished in the very near future. Special attention will be given to expanding the production of consumer goods, and to raising the standard of living of the working people. As regards long-term plans, our Party intends to organise another powerful upswing in our national economy that will raise our industry to a level, say, three times as high as before the war. It can be done and we must do it (*loud applause*).

ACTIVITY

Evaluating primary sources

With reference to Source 1, list the main aims of the fourth Five Year Plan. Which do you think would have been the most welcome to his audience?

Industry

When the war ended, much of Soviet industrial production had to be switched away from military needs to the civilian economy. Industry struggled to adjust to peacetime conditions in 1945 and 1946. Mining production was running at less than half the 1940 level; electric power at 52 per cent; and steel at 45 per cent. The transport infrastructure was still badly disrupted. The workforce was exhausted after the colossal efforts and sacrifices demanded by the war. Many of these problems were intensified by the sudden ending of **foreign aid** through Lend-Lease in August 1945.

In spite of the difficulties, by 1950 there was a considerable industrial recovery under the fourth Five Year Plan. Many of the plan's targets were equalled or exceeded. These successes were due to several factors, including **war reparations**, central planning, and the committed efforts of the Soviet people. The post-war Soviet economy proved itself to be very resilient, and its rapid growth from 1946 reflected a 'rebound effect' from a long series of disasters stretching back well before the 1941 to 1945 war. Long-term growth trends were slower than in Western Europe but in the post-war years there was considerable scope for the Soviet economy to improve on its past performance.

CROSS-REFERENCE

The extent of **foreign aid** is covered in Chapter 21, page 186.

Table 1 Industrial production (in millions) under the fourth Five Year Plan

	1940	1945	1950
Coal (tons)	165.9	149.3	261.1
Oil (tons)	31.1	19.4	37.9
Steel (tons)	18.3	12.3	27.3
Cement (tons)	5.7	1.8	10.2
Electricity (kilowatts)	48.3	43.2	91.2

A CLOSER LOOK

War reparations and industrial recovery in the USSR

The Soviet Union insisted on the fulfilment of war reparations from enemy countries, even though many of them had pro-Soviet governments. Huge amounts of equipment and materials (including great quantities of scrap metal) were transported to the USSR, especially from Soviet zone of occupation in Germany. Sometimes whole factories, together with their workers, were shifted to Russia. How much difference this made to economic recovery is still disputed among economists and historians; but it was not a decisive factor.

A CLOSER LOOK

Famine in the Soviet Union, 1946–7

Famine began in parts of Ukraine and central Russia in July 1946. The main cause was the dislocation caused by the war, especially shortage of agricultural labourers, and the lack of machinery. This was intensified by severe drought. Thousands died of hunger, though nothing like on the same scale as in the **Great Famine of the early 1930s**. (In his memoirs, Nikita Khrushchev claimed that the 1946 to 1947 famine was made worse by Stalin's policies, and that grain was exported abroad, not used to relieve the famine.)

Under the fourth Five Year Plan, Soviet economic recovery from the war was far more impressive than had been the case after the First World War and the Civil War. Alongside the necessary rebuilding of heavy industry, there was (unlike the 1930s) improved production of consumer goods and some steady growth in living standards. As early as 1948, average Soviet incomes had climbed back up to the 1938 levels. This relatively rapid recovery was part of a wider trend: all over Europe there was a prolonged growth in prosperity in the 1950s.

This did not mean that all economic problems in the USSR were solved. The economy was overloaded by military expenditure, which went up sharply because of the intensification of the Cold War. The size of the armed forces increased from 2.8 million in 1948 to 4.9 million by 1953. Military spending was 18 per cent of total expenditure in 1950, but rose to 25 per cent in 1952. Among other problems there continued to be an acute housing shortage, and the recovery of Soviet agriculture was slow and plagued with difficulties. By 1953, there were growing pressures to reform the economy.

Agriculture

Agriculture in the USSR had been devastated by the war. Officially, 98,000 collective farms had been ruined, with the loss of 137,000 tractors, 49,000 combine harvesters, 7 million horses, 17 million cattle, 20 million pigs and 27 million sheep. Food production was 60 per cent of the 1940 level. The prospects for recovery were hindered by a severe labour shortage, and by the fact that far less land was under cultivation than before the war (the 1945 total was only 75 per cent of what it had been in 1940). To make matters worse, 1946 was the driest year since 1891, and the harvest was poor. In some regions, there was **famine**.

CROSS-REFERENCE

Revisit detail on the **Great Famine of 1932–4** in Chapter 13, page 114.

SOURCE 2

Adapted from a letter sent to their local Politburo representative by the management of a collective farm in Western Siberia, 13 September 1948:

We'd like you to explain to us why year in year out we have to hand over our whole harvest and don't get a single gram back. This is undermining the economy of collective farms and the incentive of farmers to work. We realise that during the war more grain was needed to supply the army, and we gladly and uncomplainingly gave up everything to defeat the enemy. As there were poor harvests, in 1945, '46 and '47, we also handed over everything to rebuild the economy as quickly as possible. For 1948 we hoped that once we had achieved our state grain delivery, we could distribute about one kilo each per work day. But the district committees have given us instructions to deliver much more than the quota, so there's nothing left to give out; and there's not even enough seed to sow for 1949. We don't see a crumb of bread and live off potatoes.

ACTIVITY

Evaluating primary sources

What do you imagine the Politburo representative would have said or written in response to this letter? Try to write a paragraph of reply.

There was a recovery in agriculture, though it was slow and patchy. The fourth Five Year Plan brought some increases but failed to reach most of its targets. By the time of Stalin's death in 1953, the agricultural sector was still unsatisfactory, though some regions were progressing much better than others. (On the other hand, the age-old cycle of famines in Russian and Soviet history was broken; there was never another one after 1947.) One problem holding back reforms in agriculture was Stalin himself. A book by Stalin, *Economic Problems of Socialism in the USSR,* was published in 1952; as with other topics, Stalin's writings were seen as incontrovertible, and this discouraged any tendencies towards innovation and change. After Stalin's death, his successors felt they had to introduce reforms and concessions to peasant farmers to alleviate the problems in agriculture.

Table 2 Agricultural production (in millions) in the USSR, 1940–1952

	1940	1947	1948	1949	1950	1951	1952
Grain (tons)	95.6	65.9	67.2	70.2	81.2	78.7	92.2
Potatoes (tons)	76.1	74.5	95.0	89.6	88.5	58.7	69.2
Cotton (tons)	2.2	1.7	2.2	2.5	3.5	3.7	3.8
Cattle (m head)	28.0	23.0	23.8	24.2	24.6	24.3	25.0

ACTIVITY

Compare the statistics on industry and agriculture in Tables 1 and 2, and use them to make an evaluation of the achievements of the fourth Five Year Plan.

SOURCE 3

Adapted from a report of the speech to the Supreme Soviet by **Georgii Malenkov**, published by the official Soviet news service *Izvestia*, 9 September 1953:

Up to now we have not had an opportunity to develop light industry and the food industry at the same tempo as heavy industry. At the present time we can, so we are obliged to ensure more rapid improvement in the people's living standards. We must significantly increase investment in light industry and the production of food and fish; we need a big increase in the output of consumer goods, and rapid growth in the production of grain. We need to sharply reduce compulsory deliveries from the personal plots of land on collective farms and to reduce agricultural taxes.

CROSS-REFERENCE

Georgii Malenkov is profiled in Chapter 23, page 198.

STUDY TIP

You should be able to comment on the provenance of each source, reflecting on its author, date and audience and referring to its tone and context. In evaluating the content, you need to quote from the sources to support the points made about the aims, efforts successes and failures of post-war reconstruction.

 PRACTICE QUESTION

Evaluating primary sources

With reference to Sources 1, 2 and 3 and your understanding of the historical context, assess the value of these three sources to an historian studying post-war reconstruction in the USSR between 1945 and 1953.

Summary

- Victory in the Great Patriotic War was achieved at great cost, but it represented a vindication of Stalin's role as leader.
- Post-war economic reconstruction by 1953 was more successful than might have been expected amid the ruins of 1945.

'High Stalinism', 1945–1953

Fig. 1   *The cult of personality: celebrations of Stalin's seventieth birthday*

LEARNING OBJECTIVES

In this chapter you will learn about:

- dictatorship and totalitarianism in Stalin's USSR
- renewed terror and the NKVD under Beria
- Zhdanovism and the cultural purge
- Stalin's cult of personality
- the Leningrad affair, purges and the Doctors' plot.

Dictatorship and totalitarianism

'High Stalinism' was the culmination of Stalin's regime in the years from 1945 to 1953. It was in these years that Stalin's authority over state, party and people, and the cult of personality that was the face of the **dictatorship**, reached its peak. Stalin's dictatorship seemed unchallengeable, the embodiment of **totalitarianism**. As the heroic leader of the Great Patriotic War, basking in the glow of victory presiding over a new world superpower, Stalin ruled supreme while those around him competed for the privilege of fulfilling his will.

Not even **High Stalinism** could make the USSR in every respect a totalitarian state. Despite his fearsome authority, 175 million people could never be entirely controlled by one man. Like most dictatorships, Stalin's rule rested on complex bureaucratic structures, a balancing act between the Party and the government; and playing off key subordinates against each other.

During the war, many aspects of Stalin's dictatorship had been relaxed. Persecution of religion was slackened. There had been many appeals to patriotism, national unity, and the 'spirit of the people'. Fear of Stalin's regime, so intense in the Great Terror, had been overtaken by fear of the German invaders. Wartime propaganda promised a 'better world' after victory. But after the war any tendencies towards liberalisation were obstructed. Wartime institutions were dismantled and the GKO (State Defence Committee) was dissolved in September 1945. The military hierarchy was also downgraded, with Marshal Zhukov demoted to a minor command at faraway Odessa. The grip of the dictatorship was tightened, and the Stalin cult intensified.

High Stalinism appeared to be a new, more extreme form of dictatorship. In the years from 1945, Stalin became more reclusive, capricious and unpredictable. Stalin was ageing (66 years old in 1945) and had been at the centre of power for 25 years. He suffered a mild stroke in 1946 and this may have been partly responsible for his increasing paranoia in the post-war years. On the other hand, many historians have explained High Stalinism as a reversion to the past, and not radically new. His irrational behaviour seemed different from his wartime leadership, but it was in keeping with personality traits that had always been present.

KEY TERM

dictatorship: a form of government in which absolute power is exercised by a single person or small clique

KEY TERM

totalitarianism: a political system that demands absolute obedience to the state and that each and every citizen is subject to central state authority; this means that individual rights and freedoms cannot exist; all forms of human expression must be dictated by the state and everything individual must be submerged into one mass identity

ACTIVITY

Extension

You might like to read *Stalin: The Court of the Red Tsar* by Simon Sebag Montefiore in which Stalin's 'reclusive', 'capricious' and 'irrational behaviour' (including the endless wild drinking parties of his inner circle) is described in vivid detail.

Using the evidence of this chapter, draw up a table of evidence and arguments for and against the proposition that Stalin's USSR was a totalitarian state. (You might do some brief online research on specific historians who agree or disagree.)

CROSS-REFERENCE

Molotov is profiled in Chapter 10, page 89; **Beria** in Chapter 18, page 153 and **Zhdanov** in Chapter 15, page 132.

KEY PROFILE

Georgii Malenkov (1902–88) rose through the Party ranks from 1924, when he was put in charge of keeping files on party members in the Orgburo. He took part in the purges and show trials; he joined the Politburo in 1941. He supervised aircraft production during the war and, after 1945, worked with Beria on rockets and atomic weapons. Malenkov was a bitter opponent of Zhukov. In 1948, with Beria, Malenkov organised the purge of the Party leadership in Leningrad. He was briefly leader of the USSR after Stalin died, but was displaced by Khrushchev (backed by Zhukov and the army).

KEY PROFILE

Anastas Mikoyan (1895–1978) was a great survivor: the only Old Bolshevik to remain high in the governing elite all the way through the rule of Lenin, Stalin, and their successors. Of Armenian descent, Mikoyan first met Stalin during the Civil War, and backed him in the power struggle. He joined the Politburo in 1935, and was a member of GKO during the war. In 1952, along with Molotov, he became a target of Stalin's intended purge, but was saved by Stalin's death. He died peacefully in his bed in 1978, 25 years after Stalin.

A CLOSER LOOK

The historians and High Stalinism

Although High Stalinism is a term usually applied to Stalin's last years, many historians have taken the view that the developments after 1945 were not really new but a reversion to what had already existed in the 1930s. Moshe Lewin, author of a well-reviewed book on collectivisation, suggested in 1992 that High Stalinism began in 1934, after the murder of Kirov; Stephen F. Cohen, the biographer of Bukharin, took a similar view. Robert Service, in his definitive 2004 biography of Stalin, also noted how much post-1945 Stalinism was a continuation of pre-1941 Stalinism.

Stalin had always played leading figures in the regime off against the other; this continued after 1945. Men like **Molotov**, **Malenkov**, **Mikoyan**, **Beria** and **Zhdanov** all came in and out of favour according to Stalin's whims and the scheming of their rivals. When Zhdanov challenged the policy of Stalin's closest war-time aide, Malenkov, an investigation under Mikoyan was set up which condemned Malenkov's actions. Malenkov lost his position as Party secretary and Zhdanov became Stalin's closest adviser, until Malenkov and Beria schemed against Zhdanov and engineered his political downfall in 1948. Molotov held great power in the regime during and after the war but fell out of favour in 1949. These rivalries and petty jealousies helped to confirm Stalin's dominance. The Central Committee and the Politburo met regularly but Stalin was often able to bypass both government and Party and exert direct central authority.

The Party and its institutions were undermined. No Party congresses were held between 1939 and 1952. The Politburo was reduced to an advisory body, which waited to be told by Stalin or his spokesmen what 'official' line was to be followed. The big decisions were taken in *ad hoc* gatherings of Stalin's inner circle. Membership of the Party and its organisations remained high, but members were less likely to be committed ideologists from the ranks of peasants or workers. The 'new men' were obedient **bureaucrats**, who did not show initiative and avoided ideological debates. Inertia, leaving things as they were, was a key feature of High Stalinism.

ACTIVITY

Extension

The 'faceless' Russian **bureaucrats** that emerged in this period were caricatured by George Orwell in *Animal Farm* (1945) and *1984* (1949). Try to read one of these novels and give a short presentation to your class on Orwell's allegories.

SOURCE 1

Milovan Djilas was a Yugoslav Communist who knew Stalin well during the war. After 1948, Yugoslavia broke away from the Soviet Bloc and Djilas became disillusioned with Stalin. This is adapted from his book, *Conversations with Stalin*, first published in 1962:

An ungainly dwarf of a man passed through gilded and marbled imperial halls, and a path opened up before him; radiant, admiring glances followed him, while the ears of courtiers strained to catch his every word. And he, sure of himself and his works, obviously paid no attention to all this. His country was in ruins, hungry and exhausted. But his armies and his generals, heavy with fat and medals, and drunk with vodka and victory, has already trampled half of Europe under their feet, and he was convinced they would soon trample over the other half. He knew that he was one of the cruellest, most despotic figures in human history. But this did not worry him one bit; for he was convinced he was carrying out the will of history.

Renewed Terror

High Stalinism was also characterised by a revival of terror. Stalin ruthlessly enforced isolation from the non-Soviet world. This was partly out of concern for national security at a time of the emerging Cold War, but also because of an obsessive fear of ideological contamination. One sign of this fear was Stalin's **harsh treatment of returned prisoners of war** and his purge of **former army officers**; even the relatives of those who had spent time outside the USSR were considered suspect. Anyone with knowledge of the world outside was liable to come under suspicion.

Within the USSR, especially in areas newly incorporated into it (such as the Baltic States and Western Ukraine) people needed to show unwavering loyalty, even in the small minutiae of daily life. A careless word or brief contact with a foreigner could get a person denounced and arrested, possibly sent to the gulag. Anyone, even friends, or colleagues, might be possible informers against an individual to be singled out and subsequently condemned. In February 1947, a law was passed outlawing marriages to foreigners. Hotels, restaurants and embassies were under surveillance with police watching for meetings between Soviet girls and foreign men. Terror was pervasive. Being innocent was no defence in a **secret police** state.

A CLOSER LOOK

Dangerous knowledge

One example of harsh treatment after returning to the USSR was Leopold Trepper, a Polish Communist who risked his life as a key leader of Red Orchestra, the left-wing spy ring inside Nazi Germany. When he returned, Trepper was awarded a medal as a Hero of the Soviet Union; immediately afterwards he was arrested and deposited in the gulag. He was released in 1955.

CROSS-REFERENCE

Stalin's treatment of **prisoners of war** and his **purge of former officers** are discussed in Chapter 19, page 160.

SOURCE 2

Recollections of Harrison Salisbury, an American journalist who had worked in Moscow during the war and made a return visit to the USSR in 1949. His comments appear in the third episode of the 1992 Thames TV documentary on Stalin: *Generalissimo*:

I'd first gone to Moscow in 1944, during the war. At that time, of course, we were still allies; there was still certain camaraderie and a feeling of being together. All that was gone when I returned in 1949. I had many friends in Moscow, from the war. I telephoned several of them. Either the telephone did not answer or they hung up when they heard my voice. As I walked along Gorky Street, I would meet people I knew. At first, I tried to speak to them, but they would look right through me. I quickly understood that it was too dangerous for them to talk to me. I was regarded at that time by the police and the government, I suppose, as a dangerous spy. And for any Russian to have any contact with me would almost certainly lead to arrest, and possibly a one-way ticket to Siberia.

The NKVD under Beria

At the head of the security apparatus in the post-war years was the sinister figure of Lavrentii Beria, who was not only NKVD chief, but also, deputy prime minister, a full member of the Politburo, and the man in charge of developing a Soviet atomic bomb. As head of the NKVD, Beria presided over a vast expansion of prison labour camps in the Gulag. His sadistic, psychopathic personality cast a long shadow over the USSR.

CROSS-REFERENCE

The **secret police** had been at the forefront of the Bolshevik state since the formation of the Cheka by Lenin and Dzerzhinsky in 1918, and had been central to the Great Terror in the 1930s. To recap on its development, look back to Chapter 12, page 101 and Chapter 18, page 151.

Fig. 2 *Family man: Lavrentii Pavlovich Beria taking a break from power and terror*

The NKVD was itself strengthened and reorganised as two separate ministries: the MVD (Ministry of Internal Affairs) controlled domestic security and the gulags; the MGB (Ministry of State Security, forerunner of the KGB) handled counter-intelligence and espionage. Although far fewer people were killed than in the Great Terror of the 1930s, tens of thousands were arrested annually for 'counter-revolutionary activities' during the last years of Stalin. In total, around 12 million wartime survivors were sent to the labour camps, suffering appalling conditions.

SOURCE 3

Adapted from the 'Secret Speech' to the Twentieth Party Congress, by Nikita Khrushchev, 1956. The speech was made by Khrushchev to a closed session of the Congress, after the international delegates and journalists had left the meeting:

We must state that after the war the situation became even more complicated. Stalin became even more capricious, irritable, and brutal; in particular his suspicions grew. His persecution mania reached unbelievable dimensions. It seemed to him as if many ordinary people were becoming enemies before his very eyes. After the war Stalin separated himself from the collective leadership even more. Everything was decided by him alone, without any consideration for anyone or anything. This unbelievable suspicion was cleverly taken advantage by the abject provocateur and vile enemy, Beria, who had murdered thousands of Communists and loyal Soviet people.

 PRACTICE QUESTION

Evaluating primary sources

With reference to Sources 1, 2 and 3 and your understanding of the historical context, assess the value of these three sources to an historian studying Stalin's dictatorship in the years 1945 to 1953.

Zhdanovism and the cultural purge

Complementing Stalin's unparalleled authority in government were new controls over intellectual life. The period became known as the Zhdanovshchina, as it was **Andrei Zhdanov** who coordinated the great cultural purge launched by Stalin in 1946. This was typical of the 'totalitarian' approach to culture, to promote the 'right' ideology by using culture as a medium for propaganda, and to suppress dissent and creative individualism. At this time, Stalin also feared the spread of 'bourgeois and decadent' western values because of the war.

The Zhdanovshchina began with a purge of two literary works published in Leningrad: *The Adventures of a Monkey*, by the satirist Zoshchenko, and a collection of poems by Anna Akhmatova. The publishers were purged and the authors expelled from the Union of Soviet Writers. Another writer, **Boris Pasternak**, was condemned for his 'apolitical' poems; his girlfriend was sent to the gulag. Even long-dead giants of Russian literature such as Dostoevsky were attacked for lacking 'socialist qualities'.

Socialist realism, promoted as 'true' Soviet art in the 1920s and 1930s, was re-asserted as the norm in literature, art, and cinema. The great film director, Sergei Eisenstein, was attacked for his epic film *Ivan the Terrible* because he portrayed the tsar's bodyguards as thugs rather than a 'progressive army'. Condemned artists had to make public recantations of their 'errors' in order to continue working. Novels, plays and films that denigrated American commercialism, or extolled Soviet achievements, and the cult of Stalin were favoured. Anti-Semitism was also prevalent: many Jewish artists were suppressed or ignored, Jewish newspapers closed down, and Nazi wartime atrocities were portrayed as 'fascist crimes', without mentioning Jews.

Soviet music suffered badly from the Zhdanov purge. The great composers **Shostakovich** and **Prokofiev** came under vitriolic criticism; for 'rootless cosmopolitanism' and 'anti-socialist tendencies'. They found it difficult to get their music performed, and were removed from their teaching posts. Prokofiev's wife was imprisoned as a way of intimidating him.

In addition to the arts, science and scholarship were victimised. In August 1948, the regime gave **Trofim Lysenko** complete dominance over the Academy of Sciences. 'Lysenkoism' crippled Soviet scientific development and the study of maths, physics, chemistry and economics was badly affected by spurious ideas based on 'Marxist principles'.

Western influence was completely blocked. Non-communist foreign papers were unobtainable, foreign radio transmissions were jammed, only a few 'approved' foreign books were translated into Russian. Only pro-Soviet foreign writers and artists were allowed into the USSR; and very few Soviet citizens allowed to visit the West.

ACTIVITY

Compose a literary or art piece that would have been acceptable in the Zhdanovshchina — perhaps a poem, article or painting in praise of Stalin. (You might like to read the section on the 'cult of personality' below before attempting this.)

Stalin's cult of personality

The **Stalin cult** was raised to new heights after 1945. Building on his reputation as saviour of Russia in wartime, Stalin was portrayed as the world's greatest living genius, equally superior in all areas of philosophy, science, military strategy and economics. This image was cultivated in newspapers, books, plays, films, radio and speeches; it became customary for the first and last paragraphs of any academic article or book to acknowledge Stalin's genius on the subject. According to the historian Gregory Freeze, 'Stalin was accorded

CROSS-REFERENCE

Andrei Zhdanov is profiled in Chapter 15, page 132.

Boris Pasternak is profiled in Chapter 19, page 164.

Socialist realism in the 1930s is covered in Chapter 15, page 131.

Shostakovich is profiled in Chapter 19, page 165.

KEY PROFILE

Sergei Prokofiev (1891–1953) was a young composer who left Russia in 1918 to live in the United States. He returned to the USSR in 1935. From 1946, he was a target for Zhdanov's cultural purge, along with Shostakovich and Khatchachurian. Many of Prokofiev's works were banned from performance. In 1948, Prokofiev's wife Lina was arrested for 'espionage'; she was not released until 1953, after Stalin's death. Prokofiev was partly rehabilitated after 1949 but never fully regained his position. He died in March 1953, on the same day as Stalin.

CROSS-REFERENCE

Trofim Lysenko is introduced, with a Key Profile, in Chapter 19, page 163.

CROSS-REFERENCE

The **Stalin cult** in the 1930s is discussed in Chapter 15.

god-like veneration in the post-war years: he was the hero of plays, folksongs and symphonies; canals and dams were named after him; he was praised as 'the father of all the peoples' and 'the best friend of all children'.

Even though Stalin had not visited a peasant village or kolkhoz for 25 years and spent most of his later years at his dacha outside Moscow, he was portrayed as a 'man of the people' who knew what everyone was doing and thinking. In reality, he relied on others to provide him with information, and was often misled by his own propagandists. The Stalin cult reached a climax on his **seventieth birthday**, when Moscow's Red Square was dominated by a giant portrait of Stalin, suspended in the sky and illuminated by halo of search lights.

Towns competed with each other for the privilege of re-naming themselves after him: this happened to Stalingrad, Stalino, Stalinsk, Stalinabad and Stalinogorsk, but the proposal to rename Moscow 'Stalinodar' was never implemented. 'Stalin prizes' were introduced to reward artistic or scientific work (to counter-balance the western Nobel prizes). The Great Leader enjoyed everlasting ovations. Photographs were retouched to remove the pockmarks from his face. Monuments to him appeared all over the USSR. Paintings were commissioned to celebrate mythic great moments in his earlier career.

CROSS-REFERENCE

A photograph of the celebrations of **Stalin's seventieth birthday** appears at the start of this chapter on page 197.

ACTIVITY

Search online for examples of Stalin statues, monuments and other depictions of his cult and create a Stalin poster for display.

Fig. 3 *A patriotic painting of the public adulation of the Great Leader, c1950*

The Stalin cult was never enough for Stalin: neither the adulation from the people nor slavish obedience and flattery from his subordinates reduced his obsessive fear for his personal power. Throughout his last years, Stalin made sure that the men around him were kept in a permanent state of fear: of Stalin, and of each other. Stalin deliberately engineered an atmosphere of poisonous jealousies and personal rivalries. His motives for doing this were mixed: paranoia about possible conspiracies against him; the tactic of 'divide-and-rule' to prevent any of his subordinated becoming too powerful; and simple megalomania. More purges were on the way.

The Leningrad affair, purges and the Doctors' plot

The Leningrad affair

There had always been party rivalries between Leningrad and Moscow (not least because Leningrad was formerly the capital of Russia). Stalin always took care to prevent politicians with a power-base in Leningrad from becoming too powerful. Trotsky had been prominent in 1905 and again in 1917 as leader of the Petrograd Soviet. Zinoviev controlled the Leningrad Party until he was removed from power and replaced by Kirov. When Kirov became too powerful and too popular by 1934, he was eliminated. There were many reasons why Zhdanov was pushed aside in 1948, but one key factor was his power-base in Leningrad. Another was Stalin's resentment of the pride Leningrad took from its heroic role in the **great siege** of 1941 to 1944.

In 1949, Stalin decided to follow up the removal and death of Zhdanov by purging the Leningrad Party in 1949. Many 'Leningraders' had been promoted to senior posts in Moscow during the time of Zhdanov's ascendancy, including Nikolai Voznesenski, an economic expert who was a rising star in the Politburo. Stalin, egged on by Malenkov and Beria, wanted to bring the Leningraders to heel. The Leningrad affair escalated from attacks on Voznesenski to a major purge of leading officials. The accusations against them were organised by Malenkov and Beria. All were executed in October 1950. By that time, more than 2000 officials from the city had been dismissed from their posts, exiled, and replaced by pro-Stalin communists.

Purges

The Leningrad affair was a return to the methods of political control of the late 1930s: this was the first major purge within the Party since 1938. It was not the last. More purges followed, and the climate of fear deepened.

In reality, the Leningraders were never a direct political threat to Stalin. But his default political approach was to set rival elements within the regime against each other. This was shown in the next purge: the 'Mingrelian Case' (Georgian Purge) launched in 1951. The target was Party officials in Georgia, who were accused of collaboration with Western powers. These officials were mostly Mingrelians, an ethnic group in Georgia; what made the accusations against them significant was the fact they were followers of Beria, who was of Mingrelian origin.

The Mingrelian Case rumbled on into 1952 and had not finally been settled by the time Stalin died in March 1953. But it served its purpose as a way of limiting Beria's power. Another aspect of the Mingrelian Case was the suppression of non-Russian nationalities. The purge also had anti-Semitic overtones because the Mingrelians were charged with having conspired with 'Jewish plotters'. Later in 1952, anti-Semitism was a driving force in the most menacing purge of Stalin's last years, the Doctors' plot.

The Doctors' plot

The trigger for action against the Doctors' plot was a 'conspiracy' revealed by Lydia Timashuk, a female doctor (and also a secret police informer) who wrote to Stalin accusing the doctors who treated Zhdanov in 1948 of sloppy methods contributing to his death. At the time, nothing was done, but in 1952, Stalin used the file as an excuse to arrest many doctors for being part of a 'Zionist conspiracy' to murder Zhdanov and other members of the leadership. Stalin made an issue of '**anti-Zionism**', claiming that Jewish doctors, in the pay of the United States and Israel, were abusing their positions in the medical profession to harm the USSR. The conspiracy had also supposedly infiltrated the Leningrad Party, and the Red Army.

The fantastic accusations against the doctors were driven along on a wave of anti-Semitism, which had deep roots in Russia, and was stirred up in the post-war years. The director of the Jewish theatre in Moscow was mysteriously killed in a car crash in 1948, almost certainly arranged by the secret police. The Jewish wives of Politburo members Molotov and Kalinin were arrested in 1949, in the same year as a new campaign against 'anti-patriotic groups' in the arts and the universities began. But the Doctors' plot was also an excuse for political action; men high in the regime (Beria, Mikoyan, Molotov and Kaganovich) all feared becoming victims of a new Stalin terror.

A CLOSER LOOK

Leningrad's pride concerning the great siege

The three-year defence of Leningrad was one of the mythic events of the Great Patriotic War. Leningrad was officially declared a 'hero-city'; Shostakovich's iconic Seventh Symphony, the 'Leningrad', had been composed and performed during the siege, as a symbol of patriotic defiance. The view of many in Leningrad was that this great victory was the special achievement of the defenders of the city, not the USSR as a whole. Such talk offended Stalin.

A CLOSER LOOK

Anti-Zionism

Anti-Zionism was a term directed against the idea of a Jewish state of Israel; but it was really a code word for anti-Semitic hatred. Stalin had initially favoured the creation of a Jewish state in Palestine after the war, but he soon regarded Israel as a pro-American puppet state. He reverted to his long-standing anti-Semitic prejudices, fearing that any Jews in the USSR were potential enemies. This feeling was reinforced by the arrival of the Israeli ambassador to the USSR, Golda Meir, in 1948, who was enthusiastically cheered by Soviet Jews wherever she went.

ACTIVITY

Extension

Read the novel *The Betrayal* by Helen Dunmore, which evokes the atmosphere of suspicion in Stalin's last years, and the helplessness of the doctors. One of those who survived, Yakov Rapoport, eventually wrote his memoirs in 1988, at the age of 90; his story can be found online in a news report from the *New York Times,* 13 May 1988.

Fig. 4 *Anti-Semitic Soviet poster issued at the time of the Doctors' plot, 1952*

Stalin threatened his Minister of State Security, Nikolai Ignatiev, with execution if he did not obtain confessions. Hundreds were arrested, several of them tortured. Thousands of ordinary Jews were also rounded up and deported to the gulag. Anti-Jewish hysteria was also whipped up by the press, so that non-Jews feared to enter hospitals and shunned all Jewish professionals. Nine senior doctors were condemned to death – but they survived. Before the executions took place, Stalin died. The world began to change.

Summary

- The glow of victory did not last very long in Soviet Russia. The sense of national unity engendered by the war effort, and the sense that the grip of the dictatorship had been relaxed, proved temporary and illusory.
- Under High Stalinism the dominance of Stalin's regime was ruthlessly re-asserted. A climate of fear like that of the 1930s was re-introduced, with renewed terror, purges, and cultural repression.
- Political and economic development was suffocated by Stalin's cult of personality, and by the iron hold of Stalin over the feuding politicians in his inner circle. By 1953, Stalinism had paralysed the Soviet Union, a country waiting for one man to die in order to allow any hope of change.

STUDY TIP

You will need to consider what is meant by totalitarian and the ways in which the regime did, and did not, meet these criteria. Plan your answer carefully. You might like to revisit the activity at the opening of this chapter to help assemble a good range of examples to support your comments.

 PRACTICE QUESTION

To what extent did Stalin lead a totalitarian regime in the years 1945 to 1953?

24 The transformation of the Soviet Union's international position

The emergence of a 'superpower'

Fig. 1 *Stalin with Attlee and Truman at Potsdam, August 1945. Six months earlier, at the Yalta conference, a similar official photograph showed Stalin with Roosevelt (who died in April 1945) and Churchill (voted out of power in July 1945); at Potsdam Stalin was the senior world statesman*

Before 1941, the Soviet Union had not wanted to be a superpower; Stalin's main ambition was for the Soviet Union to be left alone, allowing time for the transformation of the Soviet economy to be completed. However, during the war, a vast new **military-industrial war machine** was built up. By May 1945, the armed forces of the USSR consisted of 7.5 million well-equipped troops and the USSR had increased its territory, by absorbing the Baltic States and large areas of eastern Poland. The Red Army remained in control of the nation states in east central Europe it had liberated (such as Romania, Hungary and Poland) and had occupied eastern Germany, including Berlin. The European great powers had all been seriously weakened by the war. Alongside the other, **American superpower,** the USSR was poised to dominate the post-war world.

The rise of the Soviet superpower was reflected in the diplomacy of the Grand Alliance between the USSR, Britain and the United States. Once it was clear, by the summer of 1943, that the war would eventually be won, a series of wartime summit meetings took place to decide what would happen after the war was won:

- The first summit to include Stalin was at Tehran in November 1943.
- Churchill met Stalin in Moscow in October 1944.
- The 'Big Three' met at Yalta in February 1945.
- The three Allies met at Potsdam in July 1945, after Germany had been defeated but while the war in the Far East was still continuing. By this stage it was becoming clear that Britain, exhausted and bankrupted by the war, was an empire in decline and would be overshadowed by the two 'superpowers'.

In 1945, the US revealed that it had developed an atomic bomb – and this was used to end the war against Japan. This placed the USSR at an obvious disadvantage in the power stakes and Stalin placed Beria in charge of accelerating

CROSS-REFERENCE

The build-up of the **military-industrial war machine** is the subject of Chapter 21, page 186.

A CLOSER LOOK

The other superpower

The American rise to world power had many parallels with the USSR. Before 1941, the US was broadly isolationist. Like the USSR, the US was forced into the war involuntarily, by sudden aggression; then built a huge war machine, exploiting previously untapped potential; and then was drawn into the heart of Europe to defeat Nazism. US economic power financed two wars of its own, in Europe and the Pacific, financed the wars of its allies, and enabled a consumer boom at the same time.

ACTIVITY

Extension

From 1945, a nuclear 'arms race' began between USA and USSR. Find out about the early stages of that race between 1945 and 1953. Who was winning in 1953?

KEY TERM

satellite states: countries that retained their national identity but had pro-Soviet governments (sometimes called 'puppet states'); from 1949 onwards these came increasingly under Soviet control

buffer states: a term used to describe the satellite states of Eastern Europe, which emphasises Stalin's intention that these should provide security for the USSR's western borders

the development of a Soviet atomic bomb. He committed huge resources to the project and the first successful test was in August 1949. Possession of nuclear weapons finally confirmed the Soviet Union's superpower status. This status was reflected in the United Nations, formed in 1945 in the hope it would be more effective than the League of Nations had proved after 1919. The USSR was one of the five permanent members of the UN Security Council.

The formation of a Soviet bloc

The outcome of Second World War led to Soviet military domination of eastern and central Europe. This led to the formation of a Soviet bloc (or 'Soviet Empire'). The territory of the USSR was extended, and in the neighbouring national states the USSR used its military presence, and its political influence over local communist parties, to encourage the formation of governments that were 'friendly' to the Soviet Union. By 1948, most of these countries became **satellite states** closely linked to the USSR. This created a zone of **buffer states**, which Stalin hoped would protect the USSR against future invasion from the west.

Fig. 2 *'Buffer Zone': the expanding Soviet bloc after 1945, showing (i) areas of eastern Poland and the Baltic States absorbed into the USSR (including areas of eastern Poland and the Baltic States), and (ii) neighbouring states such as Bulgaria, Romania, Poland, Hungary and Czechoslovakia, which became satellite states*

A CLOSER LOOK

The Katyn Forest Massacre

From September 1939, Beria was responsible for about 40,000 Polish prisoners; those deemed 'pro-Soviet' were allowed to live; the rest were killed, to eliminate 'nationalist counter-revolutionaries'. At Katyn, near Smolensk, 22,000 were shot and put in mass graves. In 1943, these graves were 'discovered' by Soviet forces; a propaganda campaign blamed the Nazis. The 'secret' of Katyn was maintained in communist Poland until the 1980s. Under Gorbachev, the USSR expressed its 'regret' in 1990.

The formation of the Soviet bloc had deep roots. In 1939, under the terms of the Nazi-Soviet Pact, the USSR invaded and occupied eastern Poland. In 1940, by the secret protocols of the pact, Soviet forces occupied the Baltic States. These annexations were part of a long-term plan, ruthlessly implemented. In April to May 1940, 22,000 captured Polish army officers were killed by the NKVD in the **Katyn Forest Massacre,** to eliminate Polish nationalist elements who might oppose communism. The same aim was ruthlessly applied in 1944 when the Red Army was ordered to halt its advance to allow time for the **Warsaw Uprising** to be crushed by the Nazis.

In several states, 'friendly' communist regimes were quickly established. From the 1930s, exiled communist party groups from European countries had been trained in Moscow, ready to infiltrate post-war governments after liberation. As soon as the Red Army entered Poland, a provisional government was set up in Lublin, dominated by pro-Moscow communists. In Yugoslavia, communist partisans led by Josip Tito gained control of the post-war government, and Tito's regime was expected to be an important part of the Soviet bloc. Communist regimes also controlled Bulgaria and Romania. The eastern region of Germany became a Soviet zone of occupation and a group of Moscow-trained Communists gained political control by 1946.

Extending the Soviet bloc in east central Europe took longer. In countries where democratic national governments were elected, communist parties were instructed by Moscow to join with non-communists, especially socialists and 'bourgeois liberals', in order to gain a political foothold that could be slowly built upon. These **'salami tactics'** enabled pro-Soviet governments to gain power in Hungary in 1947, and Czechoslovakia in 1948, where it was suggested that the communists had even stooped to the murder of the pro-Western Minister, Jan Masaryk. The creeping expansion of the Soviet sphere of influence caused growing diplomatic tensions and fears of open conflict between the USSR and the capitalist West.

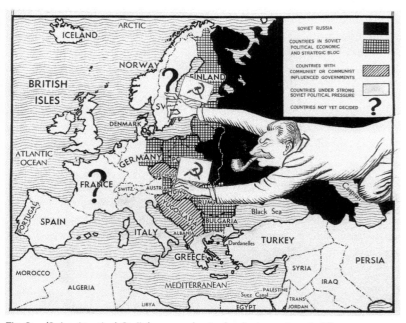

Fig. 3 *'Salami tactics': Stalin's game plan to dominate east central Europe*

Conflict with the United States and the capitalist West

The wartime summit conferences reflected the latent disagreements between the United States, Great Britain and the USSR. At Tehran in 1943, the Allies agreed to demand unconditional surrender from Germany, not because Britain and the US thought it a good idea (they did not) but to prevent any of them from making a separate peace with Hitler. There were ideological differences; and Stalin was very critical of his Western allies not opening a 'Second Front' in the European war, to relieve the pressure on the Red Army. The meeting between Stalin and Churchill in Moscow, late in 1944, was plagued by disagreements over the future of Poland. The **Yalta** conference in February 1945 was dominated by conflicting ideas about the post-war borders of Germany and Poland.

Warsaw Uprising

On 1 August 1944, as the advancing Red Army approached Warsaw, fighters in the AK (Home Army) launched an uprising to liberate the city from German occupation, and to support the nationalist Polish Underground State. But Soviet forces halted their advance east of the Vistula; they did nothing to assist the AK. Over 63 days, the uprising was crushed. Warsaw was razed to the ground. Later, it was claimed there were 'operational difficulties', but the motives behind the Red Army's inaction were essentially political.

Salami tactics

The idea of the 'salami-slice strategy' was named by the Hungarian communist leader, Miklos Rakosi, to explain the subverting 'bourgeois' parties to gain power from within by small incremental steps. Sometimes, this was quiet infiltration of trade unions, journalism and local government. Sometimes it was targeting individuals by harassment or violence; in 1948 the anti-Soviet foreign minister of Czechoslovakia died in a fall from a high window in Prague. The American historian Robert Tucker claimed salami tactics were part of Stalin's 'game plan' to push communism into the heart of Europe.

Put a large map of post-war Europe on your classroom wall and use threads to label the satellite states, and cards to explain what happened to each of these between 1945 and 1948.

Stalin and the Yalta conference

At the Yalta conference, arrangements were agreed for Germany to be placed under zones of occupation, but Stalin pushed hard for recognition of Soviet interests in Poland and new Polish-German borders which recognised Soviet gains in what had formerly been part of Poland. Stalin played on divisions between Roosevelt, who was more conciliatory, and Churchill. (It was clear at Yalta that Roosevelt was dying.)

ACTIVITY

Using this bullet point list of the developments between 1946 and 1949, create a flow diagram to show the stages by which the relationship between the USA and USSR evolved from alliance to Cold War enemies. As you read the following sections add some key information to illustrate these steps.

A CLOSER LOOK

Iron Curtain: Winston Churchill's speech at Fulton in 1946, warning of the extent of Soviet power and influence in east central Europe, used this term to give his warnings maximum dramatic impact.

KEY TERM

containment: the 'Truman Doctrine' of March 1947 asserted the need to contain (that is, halt and keep within limits) the spread of Soviet communist influence

The Potsdam conference in July/August 1945 ended with no final peace agreement. Differences that had been papered over, or just delayed, at Yalta became more urgent. By this time, it was clear how the USSR was asserting political control over the countries it had liberated. Stalin was also now the 'senior partner' of the three allies: Roosevelt had died in April and been replaced as US president by Harry Truman; Churchill had lost power after the Labour Party won a landslide victory in Britain's general election. Clement Attlee took over from Churchill midway through the conference.

The breakdown of East–West relations

Between 1946 and 1949, conflict between the Soviet bloc and the capitalist West hardened into Cold War confrontation. Attempts at diplomatic cooperation broke down in growing mutual suspicions and hostility, over a series of disagreements:

- Soviet expansionism and the USSR's demand for recognition of its right to have a safe 'buffer zone' against aggression in the future
- the Long Telegram: a report sent to Washington from Moscow by the American diplomat George Kennan in February 1946, urging the US to take action to contain the spread of communism in Europe (See Source 1, below)
- Winston Churchill's speech at Fulton, Missouri in March 1946 warning of the existence of an **Iron Curtain** dividing (See Source 2, page 209)
- the announcement of the Truman Doctrine in March 1947, committing the US to a policy of **containment**
- the Marshall Plan for US aid for European economic recovery; and the hostile Soviet response to the Plan
- the Berlin Blockade of 1948 to 1949, hardening the division of Germany
- the formation of the North Atlantic Treaty Organization (NATO) in 1949. The establishment of this Atlantic Alliance for the defence of Europe was seen by the USSR as a hostile act. By this time the Cold War was fully formed.

Stage 1 – the Long Telegram, and the Iron Curtain speech

The US fear of Soviet expansionism was exacerbated by a telegram sent to Washington from Moscow in February 1946, by the American diplomat George Kennan. Kennan was a long-serving American expert on Soviet affairs, who had been sent to Moscow after the war. It became known as the Long Telegram.

SOURCE 1

Adapted from Kennan's Long Telegram, February 1946:

At the bottom of the Kremlin's neurotic view of world affairs is traditional and instinctive insecurity. Soviet leaders are driven by necessities of their own past and present position to put forward a dogma that pictures the outside world as evil, hostile, and menacing, but as bearing within itself germs of creeping disease, and destined to be torn by internal convulsions until it is defeated by the rising power of socialism and gives way to a better world. This dogma provides justification for that increase of military and police power in the Russian state, and that isolation of Russia's population from the outside world, and that constant pressure to extend Russian police power, all of which are the natural urges of Russian rulers. But in the new guise of international Marxism, with its honeyed promises to a desperate and war-torn world, it is more dangerous and insidious than ever before.

The horror with which the capitalist West viewed what was happening in eastern Europe was made clear in a speech delivered by the British ex-Prime Minister, Winston Churchill at Fulton, Missouri in USA in March 1946, in which he claimed that an 'iron curtain' had descended across Europe. Churchill spoke of 'communist fifth columns' in western and southern Europe and advised 'strength' in dealing with USSR.

SOURCE 2

Adapted from an interview with Stalin in *Pravda* in March 1946, questioning Stalin about his response to Churchill's Iron Curtain speech, given at Fulton, Missouri a few days earlier:

Pravda: What do you think about Mr Churchill's most recent speech in the USA?
Stalin: I consider it a dangerous act, aimed at sowing discord between allied states.
Pravda: How do you rate that part of his speech attacking the democratic systems of the European states neighbouring us, and their good-neighbourly relations with the Soviet Union?
Stalin: It is a mismatch of slander, rudeness, and tactlessness. As a result of the German invasion, the Soviet Union lost about 7 million people; and many were driven into German slavery. Maybe in certain places they are willing to bury these colossal sacrifices in oblivion, sacrifices that ensured the liberation of Europe from Hitler's yoke. But is it really surprising that in wishing to safeguard itself in the future the Soviet Union tries to ensure there are governments in these countries with a loyal attitude to the Soviet Union? Communist influence has grown because during the dark days of fascist domination the communists were trustworthy and bold fighters against fascism, for the freedom of the peoples.

Stage 2 – Containment and the Marshall Plan

By early 1947, Western Europe was in crisis, with fears of complete economic collapse, and of political instability, especially in Italy and France, where communist parties were very strong, and in Greece, where there was a civil war. In March 1947, the Truman Doctrine asserted the new US policy of 'containment' and 'rolling back' of communism. In June 1947, the United States put forward the Marshall Plan: a massive injection of aid to rebuild Europe. The plan was supposedly a generous offer of assistance open to all European countries, East as well as West, but many historians believe the Marshall Plan was a political weapon, deliberately designed to extend American influence.

Stalin was convinced the Plan was fundamentally hostile to Soviet interests, part of a drive towards US economic and political dominance. He expressed particular fears that the US would rebuild the industrial economy of Western Germany, leading to a resurgence of German power. Soviet bloc countries were pressured to reject Marshall Aid. In February 1948, Kliment Gottwald, leader of the communists in Czechoslovakia, took full control of the government. The West regarded the events in Czechoslovakia as a 'communist coup' backed by the USSR. For Stalin and the Czech communists, it was 'Victorious February', the legitimate success of 'anti-fascist' politics. The timing of the coup in Czechoslovakia intensified splits between East and West over the Marshall Plan.

Adapted from a speech to the United Nations General Assembly in September 1947, in which Andrei Vyshinsky, Soviet deputy foreign minister, outlined his government's response to the Marshall Plan:

The so-called Truman Doctrine and the Marshall Plan are particularly glaring examples of the manner in which the principles of the United Nations are violated, and ignored. As the experience of the past few months has shown, the proclamation of this doctrine meant that the United States government has moved towards a direct renunciation of international collaboration and concerted action by the great powers, and towards attempts to impose its will on other independent states; while at the same time obviously sing the economic resources distributed as relief to needy nations as an instrument of political pressure. Moreover, this plan is an attempt to split Europe into two camps and, with the help of Britain and France, to complete the formation of a Bloc of several European countries hostile to the interests of the democratic countries of Eastern Europe and most particularly to the interests of the Soviet Union.

Evaluating primary sources

How would you summarise the tone and emphasis of Source 3?

The Four-Power administration of **Berlin** after the Red Army captured the city in 1945 is covered in Chapter 22, page 192.

Stage 3 – The Berlin blockade and hardening Cold War divisions

The communist take-over in Czechoslovakia set the context for the **Berlin** crisis of 1948. There was a clear separation between the Soviet Zone and the British-American-French zones in the West. But Berlin was an 'island' within the Soviet Zone; and Stalin had always seen Berlin as a single city where Soviet interests ought to be paramount. He was frustrated by the way Soviet control of Berlin had slipped since 1945; and was especially alarmed by the introduction of a separate currency in the Western zones in June 1948. The next day Stalin launched the Berlin blockade, cutting off all road and rail links between Berlin and the West.

Fig. 4 *Zones of occupation in Germany and the situation of Berlin during the blockade*

Stalin believed the blockade was a trump card. He calculated, rightly, that the Western powers were not willing to risk war. The economic squeeze on West Berlin would force the US into settling the Berlin question on Soviet terms. But Stalin's plan was defeated by the Berlin Airlift, coordinated by the US military governor, General Lucius Clay. A massive operation by Allied aircraft flew essential supplies into West Berlin throughout the winter of 1948–9. Clay had calculated, rightly, that Stalin would not risk war by shooting Allied planes out of the sky. The population of West Berlin resisted Soviet inducements and pressure. After 318 days, Stalin called off the blockade in May 1949.

The end of the Berlin blockade in 1949 confirmed the division of Germany, and of Berlin. This was the year that the Cold War became fully formed: NATO (North Atlantic Treaty Organization) was formed to defend Western Europe against Soviet aggression. The first successful test of the Soviet atomic bomb was announced. In China, the long civil war ended with the victory of the Chinese Communist Revolution. This caused shock and dismay in the United States and hardened anti-communist attitudes. Stalin met the Chinese leader, Mao Zedong, in Moscow to agree a treaty of alliance. Conflict between the USSR and its allies against the US and the capitalist West had become the established norm; not quite war, not quite peace. It remained that way until 1989.

Fig. 5   *Cold War chess, 1949: Stalin's pieces include the Eastern bloc and Berlin blockade; Truman's pieces include Airlift and Atlantic Alliance*

ACTIVITY

In groups discuss whether the Soviet Union's international position by 1949 was, or was not, what Stalin had wanted in 1945.

ACTIVITY

Evaluating primary sources

Look carefully at Figure 5. What message do you think the cartoonist was attempting to convey? Undertake some brief research to explain the names of the chess pieces; and to suggest names for other pieces that might have been on the chessboard.

PRACTICE QUESTION
(A LEVEL)

Evaluating primary sources

With reference to Sources 1, 2 and 3 and your understanding of the historical context, assess the value of these three sources to an historian studying the conflict between the Soviet Union, and the United States and the capitalist West, in 1946 and 1947.

STUDY TIP

In order to assess the value of the sources it is important that you examine the provenance as well as the content, tone and emphasis. You do not need to compare the sources but you should provide a thorough analysis of each in turn together with an overall conclusion to show how the three work together to help the historian understand the topic.

Stalin's death

By early 1953, Stalin was what historian Robert Service called 'an ailing despot'. He was increasingly unpredictable and menacing, seemingly ready to force through another wave of repression and terror. The backlash against the Doctors' plot was in full flow. Since the 1952 Party Congress, it had been clear that he was planning a purge of the 'old guard', with Molotov and Mikoyan especially vulnerable, but also mounting pressures against Beria. This atmosphere of fear was the context for the climactic political events arising from the circumstances of Stalin's death on 5 March.

The circumstances of Stalin's death

On the night of 28 February Stalin watched a film in his private cinema at the Kremlin, before going back to his dacha for a long drinking session with his inner circle, lasting until 4:00 am. Stalin never emerged from his room; eventually, he was found on the floor, unable to move or speak after a massive stroke. Stalin took a long time to die. The Party leaders all hurried to the dacha, but did not call a doctor (if they had, one of the ironies of history is that the best doctors in Moscow were in prison awaiting execution). Stalin finally passed away on 5 March.

Extension

Investigate the death and funeral of Stalin by reading the fascinating detailed accounts in Robert Service's biography, and in *Stalin: the Court of the Red Tsar* by Simion Sebag Montefiore. An excellent short film of Stalin's funeral, narrated by Kenneth Branagh, can be viewed on YouTube.

Given the nature of power politics in Stalin's Russia, the manner of his death inevitably led to conspiracy theories: the favourite was that Beria had organised the murder of Stalin by poison. Beria had a motive, as did all the others, if Stalin did not die then they probably would. Stalin almost certainly died of natural causes. He was 73, and had suffered strokes previously, the first in 1946. But his daughter Svetlana was probably right to say in 1992: 'that is what I call helping a man to die'.

The funeral provided the occasion for one last manifestation of the Stalin cult. His body was embalmed and placed in an open coffin to be viewed by hysterical crowds. There was an explosion of national grief, accompanied by grovelling eulogies from the ruling elite. Behind the funeral celebrations, however, political change was in the air.

Fig. 6   *The funeral of Stalin, Moscow 1953*

Write an obituary for Stalin, either for *Pravda* or for the *New York Times*.

The death of Stalin did not provide a neat ending to High Stalinism. Stalin had not nominated any successor; he had deliberately made it difficult for any potential contenders for the leadership. His death led to a tense power struggle from which **Nikita Khrushchev** was eventually to emerge as the new Soviet leader.

Nikita Sergeyevich Khrushchev (1899–1971) was from a peasant background in eastern Ukraine. He rose high in the Party in the 1930s; he supervised the construction of the Moscow Underground, and had a key role in the purges. He was a member of GKO during the war, with special responsibility for Ukraine. He returned to Moscow in 1949. After Stalin's death, Khrushchev won the power struggle against Malenkov and Beria; and dominated the USSR until 1964.

Stalin's legacy at home and abroad

Stalin's legacy was problematic – the production of consumer goods had been underfunded and agriculture was failing to keep pace with industrial development. There was also the issue of relations with the West and the violence and repression within the USSR. Change would be all the more difficult given the 'cult' which decreed that all Stalin had done was so perfect that it could not possibly need changing.

ACTIVITY

Look back at what you have learned about Stalinist Russia and complete the following chart to illustrate Stalin's legacy in 1953.

Stalinist USSR	Situation in 1953	Problems and issues
Political		
Economic (industry and agriculture)		
Social		
International		

A CLOSER LOOK

Stalin's legacy in Europe and the world

Abroad, Stalin's legacy included Cold War tensions, a dangerous nuclear arms race, and pressure for reform in the satellite states in the Soviet bloc. Communist Yugoslavia had already broken with Stalin in 1948; after the 1956 Secret Speech, unrest spread to East Germany, Poland, and Hungary, where reform of the communist system spilled over into violent revolution in the 1956 Budapest rising. Stalin's statue was symbolically demolished; the USSR had to impose massive military force to restore control.

Fig. 7 *Fallen idol: Stalin's statue destroyed and derided in Budapest, 1956*

It is difficult to make an overall assessment of Stalin's legacy. Stalin's own daughter, Svetlana Alliluyeva, said of him in 1992: 'Even Hitler did not kill his own people', though she may well have been influenced by her own stormy relationship with her father. Khrushchev, who was one of the contenders for power after Stalin's death and revealed Stalin's crimes in 1956, said: 'Like Peter the Great before him, Stalin fought barbarism with barbarism – but he was a great man'.

A CLOSER LOOK

Stalin's legacy at home: Khrushchev and the 'Secret Speech', 1956

Khrushchev gradually extended his control until the Party Congress of February 1956, when he was strong enough to openly attack Stalin's legacy in his '**Secret Speech**'; the label simply meant it was a closed session of the Congress, without foreign delegates or journalists. The speech was long and detailed in denouncing Stalin's great 'crimes and errors'. It shocked Party members accustomed to adulation of the Stalin myth; but it began attempts to 'de-Stalinise' the USSR in order to reform the communist system.

CROSS-REFERENCE

Revisit the '**Secret Speech**' in Chapter 23, page 200.

ACTIVITY

Analyse Khrushchev's verdict on Stalin and weigh the arguments for and against his view. You will need to consider carefully what Khrushchev meant by 'barbarism' – and what the criteria are to justify the description 'great man'.

Summary

- In 1945, the USSR emerged from the trials of war as a military-industrial superpower.
- By 1948, Stalin's USSR presided over an extensive Soviet bloc that dominated eastern and central Europe (with the exception of Yugoslavia, whose leader, Tito, broke with the USSR in 1948 to assert his own brand of Stalinism).
- Partly by design and partly by accident, this rise of the 'Soviet Empire' caused the division of Europe and the Cold War.
- Soviet Russia was massively strengthened but had to face problems of reconstruction, and new fears in the nuclear age.
- The death of Stalin in 1953 exposed the depth of these problems and fears: Stalin's legacy proved almost impossibly difficult for his successors to cope with.

STUDY TIP

To answer this question you will need to consider the meaning of a 'superpower'. As well as the USSR's superpower attributes, it is important to consider the strength of the Soviet state politically, economically and socially. It could be useful to look back to Chapter 23 to help you with your planning.

 PRACTICE QUESTION

'USSR was far from being a 'superpower' in 1953.' Assess the validity of this view.

Conclusion

Making sense of the dramatic upheavals in the history of Soviet Russia means getting to grips with complex concepts such as **Marxism**, communism and dictatorship, as well as trying to make sense of the ideologies, sometimes referred to as **Leninism** and **Stalinism** or else as hybrids such as **Marxist-Leninism**. This book has examined a period of history during which individuals, such as Lenin and Stalin, had a dramatic impact on the evolution of the Russian/Soviet State and also one where governmental change was not only influenced by, but also produced, profound economic and social changes for the ordinary people.

Revolution

In 1917, following the abdication of Tsar Nicholas II, a group of revolutionaries seized control of the Russian State. None of these revolutionaries, not even Lenin or Trotsky, actually 'caused' the revolution; it had started without them, but their Bolshevik Party highjacked it, and used the rhetoric of 'Marxist-Leninism' to establish a Soviet State. Their success was underpinned by ruthless power politics, but the new state was founded on the theoretical principles of revolutionary Marxism. Over time, these Marxist principles were moulded and changed by the pressure of events and by the ideas and actions of key personalities – particularly by Stalin after 1924 – but revolutionary idealism remained a potent force. The USSR was a state born of revolution and one in which the leadership believed in the ultimate goal of 'socialism': a society in which everyone lived and worked in harmony with the rest of the community. Both Lenin and Stalin were well aware that their goal lay in the future, but both claimed to be working in its interests.

Dictatorship

While Lenin laid the foundations of this new Soviet State, Stalin made it what it was by 1953. He established his own unquestioned authority within the USSR so that communism or Marxist-Leninism was equated with Stalinism. Stalinism had many diverse aspects: a bureaucratic Party structure, a highly-centralised government, a heavy reliance on propaganda and a cult of personality, a ubiquitous secret police maintaining a state of terror – and all these were dominated by Stalin's tight control over the power struggles of his inner circle. Stalinism could be reassuringly fixed and certain, but mostly it was very frightening and for those in Stalin's ruling elite, life was just as dangerous as it was for ordinary people.

Revolution, dictatorship and the Soviet people

Between 1917 and 1953, the peoples of the Soviet Union experienced epic upheavals and social transformation. Millions died in great famines, after the Civil War, in the 1930s, in 1946 to 1947. Millions had their lives turned upside down by forced collectivisation and state terror. In the Great Patriotic War, 20 million died. For millions more, the war meant dislocation, through German occupation, the mass mobilisation of industry, and forced deportations. In 1953, millions were still trapped in the prison labour camps of the Gulag. The propaganda and repression of a dictatorial system permeated society and made 'normal life' difficult or even impossible for many Soviet citizens.

But people did not only endure hardships, mass deaths, social dislocation and fear. Millions were inspired by the ideals of the revolution, with genuine belief in a brave new world of progress. Millions believed in Lenin, and Stalin;

KEY TERM

Marxism: Marx used the term 'communism' to describe his theories, but Lenin preferred to refer to 'Marxism' as a distinct economic, social and political philosophy and 'socialism' as his ultimate goal

Leninism: Lenin claimed to follow Marxist philosophy and believed that the revolution he helped to propel in 1917 would rapidly move forward to its 'socialist phase'; however, he had expected revolution elsewhere to help to achieve this and when it did not happen, he adopted a pragmatic approach – embracing policies like the NEP and the ban on factions which contradicted his socialist goals

Stalinism: a term coined by Stalin's critics to describe his undemocratic and even dictatorial rule; Stalinist policies and practices, such as 'socialism in one country' and the purges, directly contradicted Marxist philosophy; Stalin placed the national interests of USSR above the struggle for world revolution

Marxist-Leninism: a term invented by Stalin after Lenin's death to describe the official ideology of the USSR; increasingly, it referred to the political and economic policies that Stalin chose to adopt

Extension

To really understand Stalin's legacy, it may be helpful to do some brief research on his successors, and how 'de-Stalinisation' ended with the collapse of the USSR by 1991. It is also interesting to look at present-day Russia to see how traces of the Stalin legacy still persist there.

during and after the war they believed in victory, and in a better future. They believed in equality, and in the social achievements of Soviet communism: in education, culture, science and technology. Many believed that the upheavals and suffering they endured were stepping-stones to a progressive society that would overtake the capitalist West.

When Stalin died in 1953, the Soviet people looked back at the 'Soviet achievement' with pride as well as regrets. They looked forward with hope, but also had great uncertainty about the future. Many, both in the Party and amongst the people, knew there would have to be yet more change, and that High Stalinism could not go on as it was.

Fig. 1   *In Russia today, many people look back at Stalin and the USSR with pride and longing*

Glossary

A

appeasement: a term widely used in the 1930s to denote the policies of negotiation rather than military action of Western democracies in response to Hitler's attempts to revise the Treaty of Versailles

arch-conservative: averse to innovation and upholding traditional values

autocracy: rule by one person who had no limits to his power

B

blitzkrieg: 'lightening war' was the term used to define the rapid victories achieved by the German armies in conquering Poland and France in 1939–40

blockade: preventing goods from entering a country

buffer states: the satellite states of Eastern Europe which Stalin intended should provide security for the USSR's western borders

bureaucratic centralism: government controlled from the Centre; this includes the central appointment of district officers and other party officials (the bureaucracy)

bureaucracy: the state's administrative officials

C

Central Committee of the Bolshevik Party: from 1912 this leading group determined the Bolsheviks' broad policies

Cheka: secret police force established in 1917

coercion: persuading someone to do something by using force or threats

Cold War: the state of hostility that existed between the communist Soviet Union and its satellite states and the liberal/democratic and capitalist Western powers between 1945 and 1990

collective farming: farming in a 'collective', a single unit, usually consisting of a number of farms which would be worked by a community under the supervision of the State

collective security: a key principle of the post-war peace settlement, aiming to replace the dependence on military alliances between the great powers by joint measures by all members of the League of Nations to prevent acts of aggression

Comintern: the Communist International was the international socialist organisation founded to promote Marxism and spread 'proletarian revolution' from Russia to the world

command economy: the top-down approach based on Marxist theory that the state should control the 'commanding heights of the economy' to enforce socialism on business and eliminate capitalism

containment: the 'Truman Doctrine' of 1947 asserted the need to contain the spread of Soviet communist influence

constitution: the set of laws by which a country is governed

constitutional monarchy: a form of democratic government in which a monarch acts as the head of state within the boundaries of a constitution giving real power to a representative assembly

consumer goods: products such as clothing and furnishings, which are wanted by the people, rather than by other manufacturing industries

Cossacks: people of Ukraine and Southern Russia noted for their horsemanship and military skill and loyal to the Tsar

D

dictatorship: a form of government in which absolute power is exercised by a single person or small clique

divine right: a ruling monarch was appointed by God and was answerable to God alone for actions

F

faction: a group of dissenting voices within a larger group or political party

Five Year Plan: a five-year programme covering all aspects of development and transformation including industry, wealth and communication with the aim of improving the supplies of power, capital goods and agriculture

former people: the old noble and bourgeois elites (including the imperial military and the clergy) who lost their social status after the 1917 revolution

G

GDP: Gross Domestic Product is measured by adding together the output of all economic sectors to estimate total wealth over one year

Gosplan: the State general Planning Commission which from 1921 helped coordinate economic development and from 1925 drafted economic plans

Guomindang: right-wing nationalist movement in China led by Jiang Jieshi, it fought a long political battle with the Chinese communists from 1926 until it was defeated in 1949 by the communist revolution

gulag: acronym for the 'Main Camp Administration', this agency administered the Soviet forced labour camps from 1930 and 'gulag' came to be used to describe the camps themselves

H

heavy industries: industries making products such as iron, coal, oil and railways, which help to support other industries, such as armaments manufacture

I

inflation: an increase in prices and fall in the purchasing value of money due to more money being in circulation than there are goods to buy

K

Kadets: Constitutional Democratic Party

Kolkhoz: a collective farm, typically made of small individual farms together in a cooperative structure

kommunalka: a communal dwelling or housing bloc where most urban families lived, sharing a hallway, kitchen and bathroom with up to seven other families

Komosomol: the all-Leninist Union Young Communist League was the youth division of the Communist Party

Kronstadt naval base: the headquarters of the Russian Baltic Fleet

kulaks: Russian peasants who were wealthy enough to own a farm and hire labour

L

La Marseillaise: the French National Anthem; it came to symbolise support for 'Liberty, Equality and Fraternity'

Leninism: Lenin's version of Marxism which embraced policies like the NEP and the ban on factions which contradicted his socialist goals

Liberals: political groups who favoured moderate reform and constitutional monarchy, such groups included the Constitutional Democrats (Kadets), the Octobrists and the Progressives

M

market forces: influences such as demand and availability that determine prices in an economy which is not regulated by the government

Marxism: Marx used the term 'communism' to describe his theories, but Lenin preferred 'Marxism' to refer to the distinct economic, social and political philosophy

Marxist-Leninism: a term invented by Stalin after Lenin's death to describe the official ideology of the USSR, it increasingly referred to the political and economic policies that Stalin chose to adopt

N

nationalisation: taking businesses out of private hands and placing them under state control

Nepmen: speculative traders who bought up produce from the peasants to sell in the towns and consumer articles in the towns to sell in the peasant markets, they controlled an estimated 75 per cent of retail trade by 1923

NKVD: People's Commissariat of Internal Affairs was a law enforcement agency which was closely associated with the secret police and ran the Gulag forced labour camps

nomenklatura: Party members who were appointed to influential posts in government and industry

O

OGPU: Joint State Political Directorate was reorganised in 1926 as the secret police to succeed the Cheka

Okhrana: the Russian Empire's secret police force

Old Bolsheviks: the Old Party Guard – those who had been members of the Bolshevik Party before 1917

Orthodox Church: the Eastern Orthodox Church, with Moscow as its spiritual capital, had its own beliefs and rituals following an eleventh century split in the Christian Church

P

pan-Slavism: a belief that Slav races should be united

party democracy: allowing dissent and debates within the inner circle of the Bolshevik Party elite, rather than true democracy

Patriarch of the Orthodox Church: the head of the Russian Orthodox (Christian) Church

permanent revolution: the concept that continuing revolutionary progress within the USSR was dependent on a continuing process of revolution in other countries

pogrom: an organised massacre of a particular ethnic group

popular front: an anti-fascist movement which became prominent across Europe in the late 1930s and the official policy of the Comintern in 1935 to counter the rise of fascism and Nazism in Italy and Germany

power base: a secure position over which political leaders can exert their control

power vacuum: this occurs when there is no identifiable central power or authority

proletarianism: turning the mass of the population into urban workers

purge: literally a 'cleaning out of impurities', this term was used to describe forcible expulsions from the Communist Party but in the later 1930s it came to mean the removal of anyone deemed a political enemy

R

reactionary: backward-looking and opposed to change, particularly political and social reform

real wages: what can actually be bought with money wages, taking into account the varying price of goods

Red Guards: loyal, young and old volunteer soldiers mostly recruited from factory workers and given basic training

Red International of the Trade Unions: also known as 'Profintern' with its headquarters in Amsterdam, it was set up by the Comintern in 1921 as a communist rival to the Social Democratic International Federation of Trade Unions

reformist: supporting gradual reform rather than revolution

repudiation: the rejection of a proposal or idea

S

sackmen: peasants with sacks of goods to sell

satellite states: countries that retained their national identity but had pro-Soviet governments

Sharia: Sharia law is divine Islamic law and in Sharia courts, people are judged by that religious law

show trial: a propagandist trial, held in public with the intention of influencing popular opinion more than securing justice for the accused

Social Democrats: the All-Russian Social Democrat Labour Party was founded in 1898, was based on the theories of Karl Marx and was led mainly by educated intellectuals with the main support coming from the industrial working class

social fascism: the view that social democratic parties in Western Europe were helping fascism as they compromised with capitalism and prevented progress towards class revolution

Social Revolutionary Party: formed in 1901, it evolved from groups that had tried to organise and improve the position of the peasantry from the 1860s and had also tried to attract workers as industrialisation grew in the 1890s

'Socialism in One Country': the concept that efforts should be concentrated on building the socialist state in the USSR irrespective of what went on elsewhere in the world

socialist: supporting a political and economic theory of social organisation which believes that the means of production, distribution and exchange should be controlled by the whole community

socialist economy: one in which there is no private ownership and in which all members of society have a share in the State's resources

socialist man: a person who was publicly engaged and committed to the community

socialist realism: a style of realistic art that was developed in the Soviet Union and became a dominant style in various other socialist countries

soviet: an elected council

Sovkhoz: a state farm, larger than a *kolkhoz* and created on land confiscated from former large estates, it was organised for specialised large-scale production

Sovnarkom: the 'Soviet of People's Commissars' was a Bolshevik cabinet created in 1917 to run the country and was led by Lenin

speculation: in the peasant economy, this meant buying up grain and hoarding it while hoping for the price to rise

Stalinism: term used by Stalin's critics to describe his dictatorial rule which contradicted Marxist philosophy and placed the national interests of the USSR above the struggle for world revolution

state capitalism: a 'compromise' economy, which embraced some elements of socialism by imposing a degree of state control but retained elements of capitalism such as private markets

State Duma: the lower house of parliament in the Russian Empire, it met for the first time in 1906 and was dissolved in 1917

state terror: a means to control the population and remove opposition through control and fear

Stavka: the top-level military command of the USSR in the Great Patriotic War

T

totalitarianism: a political system that demands absolute obedience to the state and that every citizen is subject to central state authority

U

utopian: 'idealised perfection' from Sir Thomas More's *Utopia* (1516), which describes an imaginary island that is almost too perfect to exist

V

Veshenka: the 'Council of the National Economy' was responsible for state industry from 1917 to 1932

W

war communism: the political and economic system adopted by the Bolsheviks during the Civil War in order to keep the towns and Red Army provided with food and weapons

war credits: the raising of taxes and loans to finance war

Whites: the forces ranged against the Bolshevik 'reds', consisting of both right- and left-wing political groupings

wrecking: acts perceived as economic or industrial sabotage, such as failing to meet economic targets, lowering morale in the workplace or incompetence

Y

Yezhovshchina: the period 1936–40 when Nikolai Yezhov led the NKVD and there was a large number of purges

Z

zemstva: elected councils responsible for the local administration of provincial districts

Zhenotdel: the women's section of the Secretariat of the Central Committee of the Communist Party

Bibliography

Books for students

Corin, C. and Fiehn, T., *Communist Russia under Lenin and Stalin,* Hodder, 2002

Lee, S.J., *Russia and the USSR,* Routledge, 2005

Oxley, P., *Russia 1855–1991: From Tsars to Commissars,* Oxford University Press, 2001

Todd, A., *The Soviet Union and Eastern Europe 1924–2000,* Cambridge University Press, 2012

Waller, S., *Imperial Russia, Revolutions and the emergence of the Soviet State 1853–1924,* Cambridge University Press, 2012

Wood, A., *The Russian Revolution 2e,* Longman, 1986

Books for teachers and extension

Those indicated with an asterisk are particularly recommended for primary sources

Acton, E. and Stableford, T., *The Soviet Union: A Documentary History, Vol I, 1917–1939,* University of Exeter, 2005

Acton, E. and Stableford, T., *The Soviet Union: A Documentary History, Vol II, 1939–1991,* University of Exeter, 2007

Applebaum, A., *Gulag,* Penguin, 2003

Christian, D., *Imperial and Soviet Russia,* Palgrave Macmillan, 1986

Davies, R.W., *Soviet Economic Development from Lenin to Khrushchev,* Cambridge University Press, 1998

Figes, O., *A Peoples Tragedy: The Russian Revolution,1891–1924,* Pimlico, 1997

Figes, O., *Revolutionary Russia, 1891–1991,* Penguin, 2014

Fitzpatrick, S., *The Russian Revolution 3e,* Oxford University Press, 2008

Gill, G., *Stalinism,* Macmillan, 1998

Kochan, L., *The Making of Modern Russia,* Penguin 1962

Lewin, M., *Russian Peasants and Soviet Power: A Study of Collectivisation,* Norton, 1975

Lewis, J., and Whitehead, P., *Stalin: A Time for Judgement,* Thames TV, Mandarin, 1990

McCauley, M., *The Soviet Union 1917–1991 2e,* Longman, 1981

McCauley, M., *Stalin and Stalinism 3e,* Pearson–Longman, 2003

Nove, A., *An Economic History of the USSR, 1917–1991"* published in 1993,

Overy, R., *Russia's War,* Penguin, 2010

Sakwa, R., *The Rise and Fall of the Soviet Union 1917–1991,* Routledge, 1999

Service, R., *The Russian Revolution 1900–1927,* Macmillan, 1991

Smith, S.A., *The Russian Revolution: A very short introduction,* Oxford University Press, 2002

Biographies and first-hand accounts

Cohen, S., *Bukharin and the Bolshevik Revolution: A Political Biography 1888–1938,* Oxford University Press, 1980

Deutscher, I., *Stalin,* Penguin, 1970

Kennan, G., *Russia and the West under Lenin and Stalin,* Hutchinson, 1961

Montefiore, S.S., *Stalin: The Court of the Red Tsar,* Phoenix, 2003

Serge, V., *Memoirs of a Revolutionary,* Writers and Readers Publishing Co-operative, 1984

Service, R., *Trotsky,* Macmillan, 2009

Service, R., *Lenin: A Biography,* Pan Books, 2002

Service, R., *Stalin: A Biography,* Macmillan, 2004

Williams, B., *Lenin (Profiles in Power) 2e,* Longman, 2000

Visual sources and websites

King, D., *Russian Revolutionary Posters,* Tate Publishing, 2012

King, D., *Red Star over Russia (a Visual History of the Soviet Union),* Tate Publishing, 2010

King, D., *The Commissar Vanishes,* Tate Publishing, 2014

Moynahan, B., *Russian Century: A Photographic History,* Weidenfeld, 2000

Stalin: A Time for Judgement, Thames TV, 1990 (available on YouTube)
   I: Revolutionary 1917–1929
   II: Despot 1929–1941
   III: Generalissimo 1941–1953

World at War, Thames TV, 1969
   5: Barbarossa, June–December 1941
   9: Stalingrad 1942–1943
   11: Red Star, The Soviet Union 1941–1943

www.marxists.org.archive/lenin/index.html (material on Lenin and the revolution of 1917)

www.choices.edu/resources/detail.php?id=46 (simulation games)

Acknowledgements

The publisher would like to thank the following for permission to use their photographs:

Cover: Heritage Images/Getty Images; **xii:** Mary Evans Picture Library/Imagno; **xv(t):** Shutterstock; **xv(b):** Mary Evans; **p1:** Photos 12/Alamy; **p2:** Mary Evans/John Massey Stewart Collection; **p3:** Classic Image/Alamy; **p5:** Hulton Archive/Getty Images; **p6:** INTERFOTO/Alamy; **p9:** Associated Press/Press Association Images; **p11:** Alamy; **p17:** Chronicle/Alamy Stock Photo; **p20:** Hulton Archive/Getty Images; **p23:** Larry Burrows/The LIFE Picture Collection/Getty Images; **p26:** SPUTNIK/Alamy Stock Photo; **p27:** ALEXA/Mary Evans Picture Library; **p32:** The Print Collector/Alamy Stock Photo; **p34:** Corbis UK Ltd; **p36:** Universal History Archive; **p38:** Private Collection/Archives Charmet/Bridgeman Art Library; **p40:** Universal Images Group Editorial/Getty Images; **p43:** akg-images/RIA Nowosti; **p45:** Heritage Image Partnership Ltd/Alamy; **p46:** Associated Newspapers/Rex Features – Shutterstock; **p49:** Superstock Ltd; **p50:** Hulton Royals Collection/Getty Images; **p54:** Hulton Archive/Getty Images; **p57:** Universal Images Group Editorial/Getty Images; **p60:** Hulton Archive/Getty Images; **p58:** Rex Features; **p61:** Universal Images Group Editorial/Getty Images; **p68:** National Geographic Creative/Getty Images; **p72:** bridgemanimages.com/Bridgeman Art Library; **p73:** Hulton Archive/Getty Images; **p75:** Punch Cartoon Library; **p77:** GL Archive/Alamy; **p78:** Hulton Archive/Getty Images; **p80:** bridgemanart.com/Bridgeman Art Library; **p82:** Associated Press/Press Association Images; **p83t:** SPUTNIK/Alamy; **p83b:** Hulton Archive/Getty Images; **p84:** ullstein bild/Getty Images; **p85:** Hulton Archive/Getty Images; **p87:** akg-images/Alamy; **p89:** Hulton-Deutsch Collection/Corbis UK Ltd; **p91:** ullstein bild/Getty Images; **p95:** Heritage Image Partnership Ltd/Alamy; **p98:** SPUTNIK/Alamy; **p99:** Rex Features; **p102:** Bettmann/Corbis UK Ltd; **p103:** Rex Features; **p104:** Archive Photos/Getty Images; **p106:** ullstein bild/Getty Images; **p107:** ullstein bild/Getty Images; **p109:** World History Archive/Alamy Stock Photo; **p110:** Novosti 4098/TopFoto; **p113:** Hulton Archive/Getty Images; **p114:** Hulton Archive/Getty Images; **p117:** Hulton Fine Art Collection/Fine Art Images/Getty Images; **p119:** Hulton Archive/Getty Images; **p122:** Universal Images Group Editorial/Getty Images; **p124:** Heritage Image Partnership Ltd/Alamy; **p127:** Corbis UK Ltd; **p132:** Fine Art Images/Age Fotostock; **p134:** Terence Waeland/Alamy; **p135:** Bettmann/Corbis UK Ltd; **p137:** Photos 12/Alamy; **p139:** Corbis UK Ltd; **p141:** Universal Images Group Editorial/Getty Images; **p143:** Heritage Image Partnership Ltd/Alamy; **p145:** Universal Images Group Editorial/Getty Images; **p148t:** SPUTNIK/Alamy; **p148m:** AFP/Getty Images; **p148b:** Universal Images Group Editorial/Getty Images; **p149t:** PAL/TopFoto; **p149b:** Universal Images Group Editorial/Getty Images; **p156:** John Laver; **p158:** Heritage Image Partnership Ltd/Alamy Stock Photo; **p161:** Photoshot; **p164:** John Lander/Alamy; **p167:** bridgemanimages.com/Bridgeman Art Library; **p170:** Punch Cartoon Library; **p171:** PARIS PIERCE/Alamy; **p172:** Associated Newspapers Ltd/Solo Syndication/British Cartoon Archive; **p173:** world war history/Alamy; **p177:** Heritage Image Partnership Ltd/Alamy; **p179:** Hulton Archive/Getty Images; **p185:** SPUTNIK/Alamy; **p186:** Novosti/TopFoto; **p188:** nsf/Alamy; **p189:** Sovfoto/Universal Images Group/Rex Features – Shutterstock; **p190:** Prisma Bildagentur AG/Alamy; **p191:** Mark Redkin/TASS/Superstock Ltd; **p193:** Hulton Archive/Getty Images; **p197:** Universal Images Group Editorial/Getty Images; **p200:** Universal Images Group Editorial/Getty Images; **p202:** Universal Images Group Editorial/Getty Images; **p204:** Heritage Image Partnership Ltd/Alamy; **p205:** Universal Images Group Editorial/Getty Images; **p207:** Associated Newspapers Ltd/Solo Syndication/Supplied by Llyfrgell Genedlaethol Cymru/The National Library of Wales; **p211:** Associated Newspapers Ltd/Solo Syndication/Supplied by Llyfrgell Genedlaethol Cymru/The National Library of Wales; **p212:** SPUTNIK/Alamy; **p213:** Gamma-Keystone/Getty Images; **p216:** AFP/Getty Images.

Artwork by OKS and OUP.

We are grateful to the authors and publishers for use of extracts from their titles and in particular for the following:

Edward Acton & Tom Stableford: *Soviet Union: A Documentary History Volume 1: 1917-1940* Liverpool University Press (1 Dec 2005). Reprinted by permission. **N Allen & G Breitman (eds):** *Writings, 1936-37*, 2nd Edition: 1978, Pathfinder Press Inc. Reprinted by permission. **A Bone (Ed):** The Bolsheviks and the October Revolution, Minutes of the Central Committee of the Russian Social Democratic Labour Party (Bolsheviks) August 1917-February 1918, Pluto Books Ltd. Reprinted by permission. **Robert Paul Browder and Alexander Kerensky (eds):** *The Russian Provisional Government, 1917.* Documents Volume 1 (1961). Copyright © 1961 by the Board of Trustees of the Leland Stanford Jr. University, renewed 1989. All rights reserved. Reprinted by permission of the publisher, Stanford University Press, sup.org. **Warren H. Carroll:** *The Rise and Fall of the Communist Revolution,* 1995, Christendom Press. Reprinted by permission of Christendom Press. **Winston S. Churchill:** *The Second World War,* (Boston: Houghton Mifflin, 1948-1955). Reproduced with permission of Curtis Brown. London on behalf of the Estate of Winston S. Churchill. © The Estate of Winston S. Churchill.; **Winston S. Churchill:** extract from a private letter to Herbert Asquith, 1908. Reproduced with permission of Curtis Brown, London, on behalf of the Estate of Winston S. Churchill. © The Estate of Winston S. Churchill. **Stephen F Cohen:** *Bukharin and the Bolshevik Revolution: A Political Biography 1888-1938,* Oxford University Press 1980. Reprinted by permission of Professor Stephen F Cohen. **Milovan Djilas:** Excerpt from *Conversations with Stalin,* translated by Michael B. Petrovich. English translation copyright © 1962. Renewed 1990 by Houghton Mifflin Harcourt Publishing Company. Reprinted by permission of Houghton Mifflin Harcourt Publishing Company. All rights reserved. **Tony Downey:** *Oxford History for GCSE Russia and the USSR* (OUP 1996). Reprinted by permission of Oxford University Press. **O Figes, R Milner-Gulland and L A Hughes (editors):** Adapted from *The Russian Chronicles: A Thousand Years that Changed the World,* Thunder Bay Press (2001). Copyright © Salamander Books Limited, 2001. **Sidney Hook:** *Out of Step: An Unquiet Life in the 20th Century* published by HarperCollins; 1st edition (March 1987). Reprinted by permission of Professor Ernest Hook. **George Kennan:** *Russia and the West Under Lenin and Stalin,* published by Hutchinson 1961. Reproduced by permission of The Random House Group Ltd. **R H Bruce Lockhart:** *Memoirs of a British Agent* published by Pen and Sword Books in 2011. Text Copyright © R H Bruce Lockhart. Reprinted by permission of Pen and Sword Books and The Marsh Agency. **Michael Lynch:** *Stalin and Khrushchev - The USSR, 1924-64,* Hodder Education. Copyright © Michael Lynch. Reproduced by permission of Hodder Education. **Robert H McNeal:** *Resolutions and Decisions of the Communist party, Volume 3, The Stalin years 1929-1953.* University of Toronto Press. 1974. Reprinted with permission of the publisher. **A Nove:** *An Economic History of the USSR,* Penguin Harmondsworth 1982. Reprinted by permission of Penguin Random House, UK. **John Reed:** *10 Days that Shook the World,* Penguin 1966. **Thomas Riha (ed):** *Readings in Russian Civilization, Volume 3 Soviet Russia, 1917-Present* © 1964, 1969 by The University of Chicago. All rights reserved. University of Chicago Press. Reprinted by permission. **Richard Sakwa:** *The Rise and Fall of the Soviet Union 1917-1991,* Routledge 17/6/1999. Reprinted by permission of Taylor & Francis Books UK. **Robert Service:** *Stalin: A Biography,* Pan; Reprints edition 2010. Reprinted by permission of Macmillan Publishers Limited. **Rudolf Schlesinger:** *The Family in the USSR,* 1998. Routledge is an imprint of Taylor & Francis, an informa company. Reprinted by permission of Taylor and Francis Books UK. **John Simkin:** Harold Williams, *Daily Chronicle* (22nd April 1917) from http://spartacus-educational.com/RUSwilliamsH.htm. Reprinted by permission. **Joseph Stalin:** *Foundations of Leninism,* 1940 by Lawrence and Wishart. Reprinted by permission of Lawrence and Wishart. **Joseph Stalin:** Speech delivered at a Reception in the Kremlin to Higher Educational Workers, 17 May 1938 reported in Pravda 19/5/38 from https://www.marxists.org/reference/archive/stalin/works/1938/05/17.htm. Marxists Internet Archive. **Joseph Stalin:** Report to the Plenum of the Central Committee of the RKP (b), March 3, 1937 (parts 1-3 of 5) from https://www.marxists.org/reference/archive/stalin/works/1938/05/17.htm. Marxists Internet Archive. **Leon Trotsky:** *Writings of Leon Trotsky: (1936-37)* 2nd edition, edited by Naomi Allen and George Breitman. Copyright © 1970 and 1978 by Pathfinder Press, Inc. Reprinted by permission. **Sally Waller:** Extract from *AQA A Level History: Tsarist and Communist Russia 1855-1964* (OUP, 2015), reprinted by permission of Oxford University Press. **Yevgeny Yevtushenko:** *A Precocious Autobiography in Yevtushenko's Reader* translated by Andrew R. MacAndrew (E. P. Dutton, 1972).

We have made every effort to trace and contact all copyright holders before publication, but if notified of any errors or omissions, the publisher will be happy to rectify these at the earliest opportunity.

Index